# CINEMA, NATION, AND EMPIRE IN UZBEKISTAN, 1919–1937

# CINEMA, NATION, AND EMPIRE IN UZBEKISTAN, 1919–1937

Cloé Drieu

*Translated by Adrian Morfee*

Indiana University Press

This book is a publication of

Indiana University Press
Office of Scholarly Publishing
Herman B Wells Library 350
1320 East 10th Street
Bloomington, Indiana 47405 USA

iupress.indiana.edu

Originally Published as:
"Fictions nationales. Cinéma, empire et nation en Ouzbékistan (1919–1937)"
© Éditions Karthala – Paris, 2013

English Language translation:
© 2018 by Indiana University Press

All rights reserved

No part of this book may be reproduced or utilized in any form or by any means, electronic or mechanical, including photocopying and recording, or by any information storage and retrieval system, without permission in writing from the publisher. The paper used in this publication meets the minimum requirements of the American National Standard for Information Sciences—Permanence of Paper for Printed Library Materials, ANSI Z39.48-1992.

Manufactured in the United States of America

Library of Congress Cataloging-in-Publication Data

Names: Drieu, Cloé, author. | Morfee, Adrian, translator.
Title: Cinema, nation, and empire in Uzbekistan, 1919-1937 / Cloé Drieu ; translated by Adrian Morfee.
Other titles: Fictions nationales. English
Description: Bloomington, Indiana : Indiana University Press, [2018] | "Revised and expanded from the original French." | Includes bibliographical references and index.
Identifiers: LCCN 2018019384 (print) | LCCN 2018025311 (ebook) | ISBN 9780253037855 (e-book) | ISBN 9780253037831 (cl : alk. paper) | ISBN 9780253037848 (pb : alk. paper)
Subjects: LCSH: Motion pictures—Uzbekistan. | Communism and motion pictures—Uzbekistan. | Motion pictures—Social aspects—Uzbekistan. | Nationalism and communism—Uzbekistan.
Classification: LCC PN1993.5.U9 (ebook) | LCC PN1993.5.U9 D7513 2018 (print) | DDC 791.4309587—dc23
LC record available at https://lccn.loc.gov/2018019384

*To my daughter Ellie*

# Contents

Note on Transcriptions ... ix
Prologue ... xi
Acknowledgments ... xiii

Introduction ... 1

**Part 1: Decolonizing Central Asia: Film Structures and Representations (1919–27)**

Part 1 Introduction: Turkestan Prior to the Birth of the Soviet Union: Revolts and Colonial Revolution ... 25

1 Cultural Autonomy and the Nation (1919–24) ... 28

2 Revolutionary Exoticism and the Colonial Imaginary: Cinema and Entertainment (1924–27) ... 54

**Part 2: Cultural Revolution and Its Paradoxes: Nation, Modernity, and Empire (1927–31)**

Part 2 Introduction: Cinematographic Cultural Revolution ... 85

3 The National Cinematographic Sphere ... 89

4 Uzbek Film and the Shift toward Imperial Domination ... 123

**Part 3: The Paradoxes of the Nationalities Policy: Nationalism versus Internationalism (1931–37)**

Part 3 Introduction: Working as an Uzbek Artist under Stalin: Ambivalence, Resistance, and Nationalism ... 161

5 The Nationalist Cinematographic Imaginary: Subjugating Class to Nation ... 164

6 The Empire of the Proletariat: Subjugating Nation to Class ... 199

| | |
|---|---:|
| Conclusion | 228 |
| Appendix | 233 |
| Glossary | 239 |
| Notes | 243 |
| Sources and Selected Bibliography | 271 |
| Index | 289 |

# Note on Transcriptions

The sources used for this work are predominantly Russian but also include works in Turki (Uzbek), which used four different writing systems over the twentieth century: Arabic script until 1929 (with the reform in the mid-1920s advocating that long vowels be indicated), Latin script (1929-40), Cyrillic script until 1993, and since then, Latin script once again. Diacritics have not been used for the transliteration system for simplicity.

The following concordances have been used for Cyrillic alphabets (Russian and Uzbek):

Ғ, ғ — Gh, gh; Ж, ж — Zh, zh; Қ, қ — Q, q; Ў, ў — U, u; Х, х — Kh, kh; Ҳ, ҳ — H, h; Ц, ц — Ts, ts; Ч, ч — Ch, ch; Ш, ш — Sh, sh; Щ, щ — Shch, shch; ы — y; ъ — "; ь — '; Э, э — E, e; Ю, ю — Yu, yu; Я, я — Ya, ya.

The following have been used for the Latin alphabet (Uzbek 1927-40):

Ç, ç — Ch, ch; G', g' — Gh, gh; ŋ — ng; Ɵ, ө — U, u; Ş, ş — Sh, sh.

And these have been used for the Arabic alphabet (Uzbek until 1929):

ث — th; چ — ch; خ — kh; ذ — dh; ژ — zh; ش — sh; ض, ز — z; س, ص — s; ع— '; غ— gh; ق — q.

The most frequently used names are transcribed in their habitual form. The letter *j* is used for the *dj* sound—for instance, in Khojaev (Khodjaev), Jadid (djadid), and Andijan (Andidjan).

# Prologue

Public readings with magic lantern images were held at Tashkent gymnasium and then at the public library. Among the measures taken to enable indigenous men of learning to discover modern science, the most spectacular trials with electricity were held on several occasions in the gymnasium, producing a great impression on the Muslim scholars of Tashkent. Afterward brochures were produced and translated by the editors of the *Tuzemnaia Gazeta* and read out for the auditors. One of these readings in Samarkand met with particular success and was described by an eyewitness in the following terms:

> At eight in the evening on March 18, 1901, at the height of the Muslim festival of Kurban Bayramı, for the very first time, in the Shir Dor madrasa, a reading took place accompanied by obscure images, organized by the Samarkand Public Reading Circle.[1] And now, fifteen hours after this reading, I still cannot clearly picture what this evening was—I cannot speak calmly of what I witnessed for the first time in my life, for I am still under the influence of the enchanting nature of the evening in question. Yes, the strength and clarity of the images made this an essentially extraordinary event in our Russian life, and even more so in the monotonous lives of the natives of Samarkand. I am convinced that since the days of Tamerlane and Ulugh Beg, the madrasas of Registan have never seen such a large number of spectators within their walls as there were yesterday to be found in the Shir Dor madrasa.
> 
> The theater was formed by the large, square courtyard of the madrasa, paved with marble slabs and surrounded by two-story buildings with numerous balconies and arcades in the Moorish style, entirely covered with magnificent ceramic tiles dating from the days of Tamerlane, which have remained unaltered for centuries. The screen for the obscure images was lit by the powerful light of an acetylene lamp, recently received by the Public Reading Circle, and carefully positioned so that the images on the screen were visible from any point in the theater.
> 
> There was a reading, for the first time, of Tolstoy's work "What Men Live By" in a good translation into the Sart tongue.[2] The reading was given by the young mullah Mahmud. It was not easy for him that evening to win the well-deserved honors that normally go to the first reader. He read from 7:30 until 9:30, during which time he left his place to others about five times in order to recover his strength. He read so loud, as only a mullah with healthy lungs can do, calling with his voice that resounded like a bell summoning his countless faithful to prayer! And despite all that, the size of such an open-air theater; the acoustic conditions, which were ill-suited to a reading; and the almost unbearable hubbub of several thousand excited spectators were so disagreeable for the reader

that the powerful and expressive declamation pouring forth from his lips all but died on reaching the back rows of those present. The spectators were all on the parapets and balconies and in all probability could not properly hear the reader bawling out at the top of his lungs. A final reward, comprised of a miraculous spectacle of flying birds, was out of sight for those sitting lower down.

How many and numerous were the people? It can be worked out based on the surface area, which was about 850 square meters.[3] It was entirely filled by children (at the front) and adults standing or sitting behind them. It may be said without exaggeration that there were at least 4000 people there, and about 5,000 counting those on the balconies. As may be expected, most of the public were Muslims from the towns, indigenous Jews, Persians, Russians, and Armenians.

Admittance to the reading was free. . . . Before the reading began, V. Medinskii [the military governor general] congratulated the indigenous Mohammedans on this day of festival and suggested raising a cheer to the long life of the emperor and sovereign. He hoped the natives would appreciate the true worth of this public reading held for them and that they would be as attentive to the readings as they were currently being. These words from the leader of the province were welcomed with long and deafening "hurrahs" from the crowd of several thousand people. An hour before the reading began, the Zerabulavskii Battalion wind band . . . played on Registan Square and then in the theater itself. The band may not have been complete, but what an incredible and joyous spirit was awakened among this countless and beturbaned public by the powerful, enchanting, and divine sounds of our Russian music resonating within the ancestral walls of Shir Dor!

On leaving this gathering, General V. Medinskii expressed his thanks to the organizers of this public reading, who were members of the Circle . . . , for having successfully put on this first reading for natives, even though it had been difficult to set up this innovative undertaking. His Excellency also thanked the Shir Dor madrasa principal teacher (mudarris), Isa Khoja, a respectable and pleasant scholar, for the support he had lent the circle and for his administrative adroitness during the reading.

As natives, had they understand what mullah Mahmud had read to them? Had they understood what was being illustrated in so spectacular and lively a manner by the views of the Karelin workshops, based on paintings by Ge?[4] Had they understood "what men live by"? Judging by the sustained attention and interest with which the hundreds of natives sitting at the front had listened and watched, enraptured, I believe that they had understood and recognized what our great philosophical author was telling them with such simplicity and artistic skill.

However, the influence of the religious institutes (ishans), which were powerful and of long date, and the instruction received by natives in their schools (maktab and madrasa) were not propitious for the future development of our Sarts. Modern Muslim education does not prepare the natives or predispose them to seeking a closer understanding of a culture that is foreign to them (Ostroumov 1908, 200–205).[5]

# Acknowledgments

THIS BOOK IS based on research presented in November 2008 at the Institut National des Langues et Civilisations Orientales. It was supervised by Jean Radvanyi, without whose help it would never have been completed. It was initially published in French by Karthala in 2013. I wish to extend all my gratitude to Stéphane A. Dudoignon, who answered all my requests for help and whose many remarks and criticisms helped me develop my ideas. Special thanks go to Stéphane Vibert for his infallible replies, frequent insights, updates, and help putting ideas into perspective—all of great help in completing this work. I wish to thank the members of the examining panel for all their comments and criticisms that I have sought to incorporate: Alain Blum, whose support and observations have helped improve this work; Nathalie Clayer, thanks to whom this work was published in the Meydan/Karthala collection launched by the Centre d'études turques, ottomanes, balkaniques et centrasiatiques; last, and especially, François Georgeon for all his support. I also wish to express my gratitude to Martine Godet, head of the Iconothèque russe et soviétique at L'École des hautes études en sciences sociales for her friendship and continual encouragement. Adeed Khalid's numerous comments and remarks have also contributed much to this work, as has the kindly support of Marc Ferro. I wish to thank all of them here.

My research was made possible thanks to the financial support of the Institut Français d'Études sur l'Asie Centrale and the encouragement of its former director, Rémy Dor. I also thank Bayram Balci and all the team at the institute, including Kirill, Muhabat, and Umid, for their help with trips to Central Asia and my research. I also extend my warmest thanks to Ulugbek Mansurov for having answered my requests for bibliographical information so rapidly. This work would not have been possible without the cooperation of the directors of the Uzbekistan National State Archives and the director of the Art Academy; the reading room staff, Sarofat F. Muminzhanova and Marhamat S. Turakhojaeva; and all the archivists. The research was initially conceived as a comparative analysis of the cinema in Uzbekistan, Tajikistan, and Iran during the interwar period, but lack of time meant it finally focused solely on Uzbekistan. The work nevertheless benefited from several months spent researching in Teheran, partially financed by the Institut Français de Recherche en Iran.

Many historians have helped me develop my ideas, including Naim Karimov, Boris Golender, Shirinbek, and researchers at the Institut d'histoire. Many people have participated directly or indirectly in my research as it progressed and in the writing of this book, including the Ismailov family (Tursun Oi opa, Abdurakhim aka, Adolat, Bobur, Saodat), Dilbar Rashidova and Uchkun Nazarov, Olia and Margarita, Anaita Khudonazar (whom I met at the Cinema Museum engrossed by *Alisher Navo'i*), Ömer Akakça, Agnès Devictor, Xavier Bougarel, Jean-Claude Penrad, Gilles Dorronsoro, Jean During, Philippe Tarabella, Samuel Frydman, Hamid Khezri, and many other friends and researchers. I wish to thank all of them here. Last, I would like to thank my family, and especially my father for his support and encouragement.

CINEMA, NATION, AND EMPIRE IN
UZBEKISTAN, 1919-1937

# Introduction

WHILE MAGIC LANTERNS might well have been used in the imperial period for spectacular representations of Russian culture in the majestic setting of Registan Square, this work focuses on the magic lantern's direct descendant—cinema, and, more specifically, on the fiction films produced from the ashes of the defunct Russian Empire in Central Asia twenty or so years later. Nikolai Ostroumov's description, quoted in the prologue, suggests numerous parallels between the imperial period and the first phase of Stalinism in Central Asia: grandiloquent cultural events held in imposing architectural sites; the appropriation of places emblematic of the eminence of a bygone era, when spreading Russian culture—in particular, literature—generating a feeling of pride and a degree of condescension; the massive scale of the performance and the public targeted; the receptivity to and fascination even with images; the promotion of new techniques and the use of music to accompany the projection of images; the support needed from local elites; and, finally, the need to retranscribe cultural representations. One major point of difference between the two periods relates, however, to the policies of integration and modernization, as suggested in Nikolai Ostroumov's conclusion, in which he underlines that the public were ill-prepared for "seeking a closer understanding of a culture that is foreign to them." (Ostroumov 1908, 200). This idea provides one of the narrative threads running through this work: What rationales underlie this cultural rapprochement? How did these rationales transpire? And exactly what reactions, ranging from acceptance and adherence to tension and resistance, did they provoke?

Still, this work does not concentrate solely on cultures. The research presented here, by linking filmic representations to their context of production and reception, draws extensively on analysis of political, economic, and social practices, all of which were undergoing profound changes at that time. More generally, this work provides an interpretation of the nationalist phenomenon in the "imperial interlude" of the 1920s and 1930s in Central Asia, looking more specifically at Uzbekistan. At this time, two great, singular historical trajectories—in schematic terms, a European, Russian, and proletarian trajectory and an Uzbek and nationalist trajectory—were overlapping and sometimes weaving in and out in step with the succeeding phases of violence and peace. This interweaving brought about a lasting and symbolic refounding of common destinies and helps us understand how these two ideological matrices, both of which were indispensable to the coherence of a zone of such great diversity, coexisted and evolved over time via the interplay of local/national and global/ Soviet scales. Analysis of the autonomy or heteronomy of the political and sociocultural fields in the Soviet system brings out the opportunities for negotiation, compromise, and arrangement. And, ultimately, such an analysis illuminates the scope that existed for initiative, invention, imagination—or, more simply, political accommodation—as employed by the various political and cultural actors operating beyond the coercive measures and fundamental structural violence of the state, nation, and societies. Cinema provides a useful way to explore all these processes and apprehend their complexity.

This work originated in an earlier research project that led me to study Kazakh New Wave cinema. This phenomenon, which ran from the late 1980s to the 2000s, coincided with the transformations brought about by perestroika, for which it was a form of catharsis. The New Wave flouted all taboos, thereby marking the final twist in the Soviet ideological adventure. For the first time in the history of Soviet cinema, Kazakhstan found itself center stage, with its filmmakers acquiring genuine renown in the Soviet Union and being feted abroad. Rashid Nugmanov's *The Needle*, combining cinema and protest in the milieu of rock music, attracted thirteen million viewers in 1989 (Pruner 1992, 795; Zemlianukhin 1994, 174), while Darejan Omirbaev's films, deeply inspired by François Truffaut, Robert Bresson, and Andrei Tarkovsky, were screened at the Cannes Film Festival in the "Un Certain Regard" section, winning praise from Jean-Luc Godard. This New Wave—the label used by Kazakh filmmakers was a deliberate reference to the French movement—benefited from a set of circumstances that were favorable to cinematographic experimentation. The filmmakers could express themselves freely while profiting from what was still a relatively well-endowed production system. Banks and companies were willing to invest, believing easy money was to be made; they were convinced the film business would continue to be as lucrative as it had been during the Soviet period. However, the world of film faced new constraints during this phase of rapid liberalization—this time, they were economic rather than political. I was able to witness the effects of economic shortfalls firsthand when I spent several months on set for the entire shoot of Darejan Omirbaev's fourth film, *The Road* (2001), in a coproduction with France. This experience—during which I performed diverse roles as production assistant, translator, and set photographer—allowed me to see how the various spheres involved in film production (in this instance, an international production) interacted and fit together. It also enabled me to understand how Kazakh studios were organized and recognize the recurrent sources of discontent: managers who had trained in other backgrounds (often civil engineering); slow, malfunctioning authorities; the state of decay of the distribution network; the degradation of film theaters and the uses to which they were put (often being abandoned or serving as warehouses); the incoherence of producing films not destined for a local public; and certain filmmakers' dismay or forced professional conversion. The economic and ideological system of Soviet film production had disintegrated.

Kazakh cinema had provided me with an insight into the tail end of a cinematographic adventure. It led me to wonder how cinema in this region had gotten started and how the saga of the film industry in Central Asia as a whole had originated. The choice of place was soon made, for the first local experiments in cinematography were conducted on the territory of Soviet Uzbekistan, created in 1924. The first studio was set up for the khan of Khiva by Khudoibergan Devanov (1878–1940). Larger ones were founded in the early 1920s as proper business ventures to produce and distribute films, first in Tashkent (in the Turkestan Autonomous Soviet Socialist Republic), and then in Bukhara (in the Bukharan People's Soviet Republic). Uzbekistan, from 1924 onward, together with, to a lesser extent, Tajikistan, as of 1929, were the only two republics in Central Asia to generate an early national cinematographic elite: Suleyman Khojaev (1892–1937) and Nabi Ganiev (1904–54) in Uzbekistan, and Kamil Yarmatov (1903–78) in Tajikistan.[1] They all made their first, silent films between 1931 and 1936. Even though, as of 1928, other cities in Central Asia (such as Alma-Ata and Ashkhabad) had subsidiaries of Vostokkino, the suprastate film production structure (Chomentowski 2009), the first national Kirghiz, Turkmen, and Kazakh filmmakers only started working after the Second World War. And so, unlike the other Central Asian republics, present-day Uzbekistan is the only country to have had an early national cinematographic elite producing full-length fiction films during the crucial and troubled interwar period.

Having settled on the place, I next needed to define the period. Several particularly significant dates cropped up both in the political sphere and in the world of film, enabling me to determine my chronological framework. The earliest of the films studied was produced in 1924. This year marked the ethnic and territorial delimitation that gave birth to Soviet Uzbekistan as well as the beginning of a new phase in cinematography. It coincided with the beginning of filming for the first full-length fiction film ever made in Central Asia (*The Minaret of Death* by Viacheslav Viskovskii). The date closing the study is just as significant, for 1937 corresponds, first, to a major technical shift with the first talking film made in Uzbekistan (*The Oath* by Aleksandr Usol'stev-Garf), Uzbekistan being late in comparison with other Soviet cinemas here.[2] Second, 1937 was the year of Stalinist terror, with a massive wave of arrests, deportations, and executions. In Uzbekistan, the "1937 moment" marked the end of the revolutionary rationale.[3] The main national architects of Soviet power disappeared, along with most of the intellectual elite, in what was a symbolic death but also an initial act of deconstruction containing within itself the basis for a new edifice. And so, in the field of film, 1937 not only marks the disappearance of a form of national cinematographic expression, it also provides a vision of the symbiotic relationship between totalitarian power and representations while bearing witness to the edification of a new Soviet so-called national culture.

Establishing a correlation between primordial sociopolitical events and the production of a cinematographic fictional narrative requires a global approach irreducible to any one specific domain, such as aesthetics or institutional history, for instance—and my overall experience on Uzbek film shoots was no doubt influential here, too. My approach is fairly similar to that of Howard Becker in *Art Worlds* (1982), though I insist more than Becker does on the role and place to be accorded to the state as a crucial actor imposing the rules of the political and artistic games. Film could thus, in reference to Marcel Mauss, be described as a "total social fact," for "all kinds of institutions are given expression at one and the same time," thereby representing human society in miniature (2004, 147). Film involves a chain of agents ranging from the most important to the most insignificant: the central or national bodies commissioning the film, extras, indigenous and nonindigenous artists, administrative staff, and, last, the public. And so, when analyzed in the context of its production and reception, film provides an exemplary cross-section of a system. First, it provides a vertical cross-section revealing the balance of political power—via censorship or the choice of subjects, for instance—and cultural or economic power relations—via funding and centralization—between the center and the periphery. This vertical cross-section entails looking primarily at institutional and economic history. Second, a longitudinal cross-section provides information about the relations between artists, political discourse, and public reception. Given this study's short time frame of about fifteen years (1924–37), the vertical cross-section demonstrates the speed of change and provides precise information about the dynamics operating within the Soviet regime and the changes to its nature that were taking place. The longitudinal cross-section, placed within a longer time frame, sheds light on what was happening in political and cultural forms of nationalism. These two cross-sections, once correlated, provide two insights. First, they allow us to understand the logic at work within the Soviet empire, as a form of territorial expansion of the state and means of establishing direct and coercive control over Soviet subjects (exerted, in the case of cinema, via institutions and economics). Second, they reveal the hegemonic and ideological logic—as well as the tensions generated within it—operating as an informal means of persuasion and means of winning consent, and even as a tool of subjugation and indoctrination.

## Issues at Stake in Analyzing the Interwar Period: Totalitarianism, Empire, and Nationalism

The aim of this work is not to provide a history of cinema in Uzbekistan—even though it does fill a gap in the history of national cinemas in the Soviet Union and the early experimentation with film in Muslim countries.[4] Its purpose, rather, is to offer a cultural and sociopolitical history that brings out the breadth and depth of the radical, fundamental transformations affecting Uzbek society in the years following the First World War and the civil war with anti-Soviet *basmachi* movement to just before the Second World War.

## Historiographical Debates

The analysis put forward here draws first on what is known as the totalitarian school, concentrating on the notion of ideocracy, according to which the central and all-powerful state is legitimized by its ideology and exerts absolute control over an atomized society. Equally, it draws on what is known as the revisionist school, which recognizes social groups' capacity for agency, even though this may have been constrained to varying degrees by an internal rationale and the context of "first-phase Stalinism."[5] However, this book seeks to move beyond the binary nature of these debates, concentrating on the points where these two trajectories come together, examining their zones of autonomy and areas of negotiation. On the one hand is the state (and then the party-state) endeavoring to bring about the total political "domestication" and subjugation of society. On the other hand, is a diverse society retaining multiple mechanisms for defense, adaptation, and action. As agents of cohesion and means of its transmission and as thinking, acting, creative individuals endowed with a capacity to interpret and translate an ideological dogma that had not been entirely codified, filmmakers and the films they make have much to tell us about this interstitial zone between power and society. Films show us how the "cultural and social fabric of hegemony" (Bertrand 2008, 11) functions. They are a locus of power, revealing the local interactions through which domination is implemented, negotiated, and consolidated by a multifaceted ideology. This power, as this work explains, was not solely produced by the party and imposed from above; rather, it was a social and cultural co-production, albeit one that was manufactured on unequal and asymmetric terms.[6] This ideology, understood as both a conception of the world and a behavioral norm, took on various vernacular forms depending on the geographical area under consideration.

Inquiry about the Soviet Union during the Cold War has been conducted largely along the lines of debate between the totalitarian and revisionist schools, which has also extensively shaped the methodology. Similar debates have not dominated in the same way the history of Central Asia, for which they are less relevant. Indeed, in the wake of recent historiography about the peasant world and Central Asia, for example, there is no longer any doubt that social bodies and peripheries were endowed with a capacity for agency, resistance, and action and that they partially negotiated the forms taken by their own "submission." Nevertheless, during the brief and singular period between 1937 and 1941 in Uzbekistan, the concept of totalitarianism as a new form of power (see also Pomian 1995, 4–23) is an appropriate way to describe the nature of the Soviet regime. The interval following the extreme mass violence of the great Stalinist purges—which quite simply eliminated political and cultural elites enjoying what, within a dogmatic regime, amounted to a form of autonomous, dissenting thought—to the beginning of the Great Patriotic War was notable for several characteristics: the disappearance of all forms of public expression of dissent or protest; the culmination of the ideocracy and omnipotence of the state; the establishment of complete monopoly over public discourse, to be used exclusively to praise Russian and proletarian identity; and the emergence of a secular, sociopolitical religion, which did not just ask the people to assent to it but, in exchange for a promise of salvation, to place their faith in it and to believe. The frontier between state and civil society became blurred in this nondifferentiated political system. Although civil society did not wholly disappear, it seems to have been at least momentarily annihilated, having been reduced to univocality and no longer having its own means of expression. It was during this same period that the permanent state of exception, which, in Giorgio Agamben's opinion, acts as the basis for modern totalitarianism, took on a particularly acute form, leading to the victory of what he calls "legal civil war" (2003, 11), with the physical elimination in 1937–38 of political adversaries and of entire categories of citizens who could not be integrated within the political system.

The need to grasp the nature of the Soviet state irrespective of its legal and constitutional forms—the terminology of a "multinational federation" being of little use in understanding how the system actually functioned (see below)—has led to the concept of empire, currently much in vogue, being taken up in the literature to characterize a set of power practices. Over the past few decades, this concept has clearly struck a chord in relation to the history of Central Asia and the crucial question of the relationship between the center and the periphery. But it has been used in a context at least as ideologically marked as the previously mentioned polarization between totalitarianism and revisionism. Until the 1990s, the deprecatory connotations associated with the term *empire* meant that it was applied to the Soviet Union to denounce and delegitimize a form of domination. However, this did not always yield an accurate understanding of the multiple processes and mechanisms of submission and reaction at work within the periphery—in this instance, Central Asia.[7] Finally, the postulate of totalitarianism was reproduced in a new guise, with power being unilaterally imposed by a political center on a periphery now defined not solely in social but also in geographical terms, and where any reaction could only take the form of anti-Russian sentiment.[8] Once again, we encounter the binary paradigm of resistance/collaboration, which is of little use in understanding the history of Stalinism, for it fails to apply to most situations, shedding light only on a few relatively rare circumstances. This postulate has continued to run through the historiography produced in the wake of the independence of the Central

Asian republics and the nationalist reconstruction of history carried out by their academies of learning. As a result, the countries in question have partially elided the issue of initial involvement by their elites in Soviet construction during the interwar period and presented themselves primarily as victims, thereby continuing to project a notoriously anti-Russian stance most of the time.

Nevertheless, with the opening of the archives and resultant new analyses that have emerged over the past ten years looking at the Soviet nationalities policy and the history of Soviet Central Asia in the interwar period, the concept of empire has been considered in a different and more neutral manner, as is the case in this book.[9] Several historians specializing in the Soviet Union have put forward a definition of empire applied specifically to the Soviet case.[10] These definitions are used here, supplemented by that provided by Maurice Duverger (1980, 7–21), as well as a return to the original, broad meaning of *imperium*, a command held by a person with supreme absolute power. Thus, empire is defined, in its Soviet version, as a state possessing a vast, multinational territory with centralized administration and communication, where the personalized and socialized power destroys the preexisting authorities and seeks to unilaterally and hierarchically impose a system that, though universal in intent, is rooted in national differentiation between cultures. Hence, the aim of this book is not to understand how the empire ended but rather to apprehend how it was formed. To this end, I deconstruct the mechanisms by which the empire came to establish its political, institutional, and economic dominance over the Uzbek periphery during the key interwar period and how the empire established its symbolic and hegemonic dominance as well. It is therefore necessary to emphasize that this periphery was endowed with genuine agency and retained its autonomy and to remember that "subordination" can also procure advantages (such as resources).

As for the paradigm of colonialism that has sometimes been used, it is not readily applicable to Soviet Central Asia, as, indeed, several authors have already argued—notably, Slezkine (2000) and Khalid (2006a).[11] There are at least three main reasons for this. First, even if many similarities exist—particularly in the domain of economics and demographics (Vichnevski 1995)—the nature of the Soviet state and the extent of its interventionism and policies for integration and socioeconomic modernization that were uniformly implemented throughout Soviet territory are more suggestive of a comparison with the policies of a state such as Kemalist Turkey than with those pursued by the French or British governments regarding their colonies (Khalid 2006a; Edgar 2006). Second, all "Soviet subjects," irrespective of the republic they came from, enjoyed equal rights and were equal citizens of the same state, albeit of distinct nationality. The system was therefore not founded on radical racial alterity. Last, colonialism is underpinned by the supremacy of a people regarded as imperial and entrusted with a mission, and this is only partially analogous to the Soviet system, for proportionately the Russians were the main victims of their "own" system of domination.

Ultimately, though, what matters is not the term used to describe the Soviet Union but the description actually provided of a singular system of domination. And the concept of empire provides a useful account here of the dynamics driving the conquest of power over a newly Soviet space, making it possible to apprehend the whole process of subjugation of Central Asia over a relatively short time span. Equally, this concept of a system of state that generates difference helps reveal the internal, contradictory logics of hegemony at work and the process by which a Soviet unit was created through ethnic and national differentiation. This concept of empire enables us to bear in mind that several ideologies coexisted—including those borne aloft by nationalist movements in this instance—and in this it differs from the concept of totalitarianism (to return to it briefly), which is based solely on an integrated system that silences dissent and plural, contradictory ideas about the nature of the collective body. Totalitarianism and nationalism in the periphery are incompatible, and, over the long run, the facts show how persistent and vibrant the constructions of a shared heritage and imagined communities actually were (notably, in their cultural dimensions). These constructions were based on a process of heritagization, the capacity for resilience, and the force of inertia. So nationalism here acts as a prism through which to analyze what is at work in what Jean-François Bayard and Romain Bertrand (2006) have called the "hegemonic imperial transactions" being played out during the interwar period.

### Promoting the Nation to Reconstruct the Empire

If we wish to appreciate the multiple facets of these transactions and how they occurred—the *fait national*—including the Soviet nationalities policy and vernacular nationalism, then we need to consider the pre-Soviet context in Central Asia, assessed in the light of the First World War and the defeat of the Ottoman Empire. We also need to bear in mind that the terms of the armistice instigated a rapprochement between pan-Islamism and anticolonialism, thereby further radicalizing the Muslim world (Khalid 2005, 217–18). Against the backdrop of the intensifying nationalist yearnings and the disappearance of the Ottoman and Habsburg empires, there was a fascination with the October Revolution and new Bolshevik regime and their accompanying discourse of anticolonial struggle and national liberation, which responded to the desire nourished by many Central Asian intellectuals for modernization, progress, and full-fledged citizenship (Khalid 2007a, 137, 141), even if for some of them the euphoria proved to be short-lived (Chokay 2001, vii). National slogans exerted undeniable political attraction, and the Bolsheviks would appear not to have counted solely on force and coercion (Hirsch 2005, 5).

Confronted with the intensifying nationalist demands, the national question—largely neglected in the theories of the great figures of Russian and European Marxism—began to take on greater importance in Bolshevik revolutionary strategy. The issue was addressed in the light of how it had initially been conceived by Stalin, who, at Lenin's request, had summarized the theoretical debates about the nation that were dividing the European socialist movement. This summary, along with the resolutions of the Tenth Congress of the Russian Communist Party, acted as the basis for the nationalities policy. Stalin's summary was first published in 1913 in the periodical *Prosveshchenie* (Enlightenment), before coming out as a pamphlet titled *Marxism and the National Question*. In this pamphlet, the nation, as a historical phenomenon bound up with capitalism, is defined in a very restrictive manner as a "historically constituted, stable community of people, formed on the basis of a common language, territory, economic life, and psychological make-up manifested in a common culture."[12] Stalin further envisaged the course taken by human communities in terms of a historical evolution, starting from an organization based on the tribe (*plemia*), then moving to the people (*narod*), and next the nation (*natsia*), before a time when, finally, with the advent of socialism, "in a historic distant future," national communities would fuse. Meanwhile, national cultures and the state, having developed to an extreme form, were supposed to perish of their own accord. Stalin, who was Commissar of Nationalities from 1917 to 1924 and official spokesman on the national question, agreed with Lenin on the main aspects of the policy to be implemented, even though they disagreed in 1922 over the pace at which to pursue it and how exactly it should best be applied.

This policy and Stalin's concept of the nation were opposed to how reformist intellectuals (Jadids) in Central Asia thought about the community.[13] With the Russian conquest and the turn taken by oriental studies and ethnography in the wake of colonization, together with writings in Tatar and Ottoman, the Jadids came to reassess the reasons that the old Muslim leaders had been defeated and to think of their community along different lines. In nineteenth-century historiography about Central Asia, political legitimacy was inextricably intertwined with religious authority, providing a coherent explanation for the origin of the community. This was based on a genealogy in which Islam acted as the cement, stretching back to the prophet Japheth (the third son of Noah) and to Turk, the eldest of his nine sons, who was already a Muslim (Khalid 2004, 129–31). To this were added new ideas such as progress and nation, implying a shift in conceptions of the community and in how to go about writing its history, with dynasties, sacred lineages, and local communities being replaced by the idea of a community now imagined along ethnic lines (Khalid 2004, 132–33). The role played by Islam as the foundation of the community was thus diminished, with a disjunction progressively opening up prior to the October Revolution between Islam and ethnic identity—although this new historiography was far from being endorsed by all. Discourse about history became progressively more secular, and by the early twentieth century, the idea of the community or nation (*millat*) was a central feature in reformist Muslim thought, where the nation was defied in terms of a territory (Turkestan) and religion (Islam), both of which dated back to the empires of the great Muslim dynasties, but without a common language—whereas this was a key factor in Soviet national construction (Khalid 1998, 191–92).

The term *Uzbek* already appeared from time to time in Jadid literature, sometimes as the "Uzbek people" (*Ozbek eli*), used synonymously with "national" and interchangeably with the "people of Turkestan" (*Turkestan eli*) (Khalid 1998, 206). The term thus started to drift away from its traditional meaning, the earliest instances of which dated back to the fourteenth century (with such variants as *özbek*, *özbeg*, and *ozbak*), emerging at more or less the same time in two distinct regions. One region was that of one of the most powerful Tatar tribal chieftains of the Golden Horde, Ghiyath ad-Din Muhammad Uzbek Khan (1312–41), a descendant of Genghis Khan (1155–1227); the other region was that of a confederation of nomadic Turkish Mongol tribes in the north of present-day Kazakhstan (Allworth 1990, 31–33). Until the early eighteenth century, the term *Uzbek* continued to refer primarily to a tribal confederation of varying size, one of whose greatest figures was Abu'l-Khayr Khan (1412–68), a member of the Shaybanid dynasty and sometimes considered the father of the Uzbek nation (Barthold 2008, 135; Mac Chesney 2008, 132–33).

At the turn of the twentieth century, this term was still far from being generally accepted, despite subsequently acting as the basis for vernacular nationalism and the Soviet nationalities policy. The indigenous populations of Central Asia, "a complex mosaic of fragmented identities" in the words of Adeeb Khalid, together with their various languages, were designated using numerous, often synonymous, terms. In addition to *Uzbek*, there were *Chaghatay*, *Turk*, *Sart*, and *Tajik*, together with *Muslim*, which was employed not only in its religious meaning but as a cultural referent (Baldauf 1991, 82).[14] Different terms were used depending on whether it was a matter of self-definition or identity assignment. These identities were not immutable but varied over time, only becoming fixed in the wake of two major historical events. The first of these events was colonization, which meant the Russian authorities needed to count more exactly the populations they governed and improve their knowledge about them so as to better control them.[15] Colonization was accompanied by a first attempt to normalize usage of these terms, and in the sole imperial census of 1897, Russian officials classified the populations using anthropology and categories of race, nationality, and language (Khalid 1998, 196). The process of normalization then continued with the Soviet nationalities policy, based on the constitution of a state deprived of any true sovereignty and a territory and administration with their own specific, nonsovereign, national, and ethnonational categories, with two censuses being carried out: one in 1920 and one in 1926.[16]

The administrative delimitation of 1924 provided Uzbekistan with a semblance of political sovereignty. This was the second key event, marking a clean political break and stabilizing the usage of the ethnonym *Uzbek* in the region, which had at times had derogatory connotations because it designated illiterate and uncultured people. In the mid-1920s, this ethnonym replaced *Sart*, which was employed for Turkish-speaking urban populations without any tribal tradition and used both by assignation and for self-designation. *Sart*, which had figured as a language group in the 1897 census, was definitively replaced in the list of nationalities in the 1926 census by the less connoted term *Uzbek*. Akmal Ikramov (1898–1938), general secretary of the Uzbek Communist Party, when speaking at the second plenary session of the Central Committee, condemned the use of *Sart* as a "manifestation of Greater Russian imperialist chauvinism" and synonymous to "bourgeois," for it corresponded very broadly to the representatives of the middle classes and the indigenous administration. *Uzbek* carried the positive ideological connotation of "laboring masses" (Baldauf 1991, 80, 82) and so triumphed over other appellations. *Turk* inevitably evoked pan-Turkism, and *Chaghatay* suggested Turkestanism. *Sart* was, as observed, evocative of Greater Russian chauvinism and the former imperial policy, and *Muslim* was caught up with the idea of Islamism (Baldauf 1991, 89, 91).[17]

Although nationality (*natsional'nost'*) was theoretically determined by the respondent in the first Soviet censuses, it raised several problems at first, because the reference framework tended to be based on local, clan, and religious identities.[18] However, people rapidly came to think in national terms, and considerations of ethnic or national self-determination became increasingly practical and rational given the new institutions and rules governing the allocation of resources. Depending on the circumstances, the populations on occasions also concealed their origins by adopting a dominant ethnonym instead. These group identities finally became fixed in the late 1930s, when Soviet historical discourse naturalized them and their corresponding "ethnogenesis," thereby "objectively" demonstrating the existence of nations since times immemorial, and so putting the finishing touch to the process by which identities were staked out and circumscribed, in a way similar to that described by Jean-François Bayart (1996) writing about Africa.

Promoting national categories and, to an extent, encouraging vernacular nationalisms (which were theoretically temporary) acted, above all, as a means of consolidating Bolshevik authority, which was confronted by independence and separatist movements. Allocating a national territory, setting up a state and administration, and developing a national culture were ways to undermine nationalist yearnings, to which Lenin—followed by Stalin—initially attributed revolutionary qualities. The nationalism of the former oppressed minorities and guaranteeing their rights in the face of imperialism and "Greater Russian chauvinism" were indispensable for furthering the October conquest and embedding it in the peripheries. Lenin and Stalin understood the dangers of building a state that could be assimilated to an empire and felt it was essential that the state have the image of being anti-imperialist, multinational, and federalist. The right of peoples to self-determination became a slogan that provided the Bolsheviks with an opportunity to "break with the Russifying heritage of the imperial State," to position themselves as "propagandists for an international project to emancipate the people," "to remove the grounds of strife between nations, to take the edge off that strife, and reduce it to a minimum," and thereby win the trust of the formerly oppressed people.[19]

Supporting the emancipation of the peoples and encouraging nationalism was a way to rebuild the empire—notably, by asserting the right of nations to self-determination. This right was legally enshrined in the Declaration of the Rights of the Peoples of Russia on November 15, 1917, in the first Constitution of the Soviets of 1918, and in the 1924 and 1936 constitutions, not for the peoples to actually request it be applied but as a "legal artifice"—slogans pronounced as a matter of "form" and as a "sign of remorse," as Yuri Slezkine has observed—to incite the development of "free and deliberate" federal ties (1994, 419).[20] Lenin's remark (as reported by Stalin) is particularly eloquent here, with a "disunion for the union"[21] (*raz"edinenie dlia ob"edineniia*) being the prerequisite for safeguarding the territorial integrity of the empire of the Romanovs (Blitstein 2006a, 282). And indeed, by 1922, the Bolsheviks had recovered virtually all the territories of the old Russian Empire (Hirsch 2005, 66). Although the right to self-determination was affirmed, that certainly did not mean that autonomy and separation were necessarily advantageous, for the interests of the proletariat took precedence over those of the nation. Separatism was finally condemned, and the Bolshevik project sought purely and simply to reestablish a unified and centralized state via the recognition of national differences, organized by territory and institution. Bolshevik power was opposed to all forms of national cultural autonomy, and hence all truly federal forms of state building, even though pragmatic considerations meant federalism was enlisted to help a rapprochement between the proletarian classes of the various nations and thus instigate a phase of transition ("the dictatorship of the proletariat") on the road toward communism (Lirou 2009, 127–42). The appearance of federalism struck a chord with Turkestani intellectuals, who tended to think of their union with Russia mostly in terms of cultural autonomy and only rarely in terms of independence or separatism (Agzamkhojaev 2006, 98–127).

The Soviet nationalities policy thus provided the Bolshviks with a promising framework to consolidate or create the nations and cultures they claimed to hail from while promoting an essentialist idea of the nation based on a dominant ethnic group. In addition, it resulted in the progressive solidifying of a legal and institutional framework that made it possible to impose a unique, central vision, to the detriment of any local initiatives, and thereby reestablish a relationship based on subalternity. Between 1924 and 1937, this conceptual matrix—which the post-1991 newly independent states found it very difficult to rid themselves of—gave rise to what may be regarded as genuine nationalisms, in so far as national unity overlapped with political unity (Gellner [1983] 1997, 1). Contrary to the affirmation of Olivier Roy, the nation building was not something imposed solely from above (2007, 93–137), and the first Uzbek elites played a role in the constitution of a national culture and a collective imaginary. The national construction resulted from a constant interaction between central policy and practices in the peripheries. Whereas the nationalism of the interwar period may basically be described as political, that which arose after the Second World War tended rather to transpire within the cultural sphere and, as Bennigsen has suggested, may best be designated using the neologism "mirasism," derived from the Arabic word *miras*, meaning heritage or legacy (1986, 142–47). Be that as it may, the forms taken by political and cultural nationalism in the Soviet peripheries were symptomatic of the imperial and hegemonic transactions taking place.

## The *Fait Cinématographique* as Source and Object of Historical Study

Cinema, as a visual narrator of the Uzbek nation, provides a valuable chronicle of Soviet state building. It also provides an excellent way of inquiring how this new common destiny was initially conceived of and how the subjective elements it comprised evolved over the interwar period. Filmic production, in the broad meaning of the term, can throw light on the transitions taking place from the disappearance of the Russian Empire up to the Second World War, on the processes of decolonization affecting representations and institutions, and on the discursive and symbolic negotiations that resulted in the formation of a national identity. Cinema can thus show how the contradictions between an internationalist ideology and the upheavals occasioned by its transposition into national terms were finally resolved in 1937. The *fait cinématographique* will be explored chronologically, first, as representation and, second, as the structure within which that representation is both produced and received. The colonial type of representations in the first films—made between 1924 and 1928 and revealing the progressive hybridization of colonial discourse and class discourse—gave way to a representation that was national in kind, drawing initially on the discourse of social progress (1928–32) and then on that of nationalist progress (in the mid-1930s), before finally arriving at the totalitarian representations of 1937, when Uzbekistan was denied any possibility of cinematographic self-representation. As Marc Ferro has observed, "even when under surveillance, film bears witness"

(1993, 39). Perhaps we should say "especially when under surveillance." For film—as both source and object of historical study—allows us to understand the symbolic and political issues presupposed in its making and to at least partially apprehend the degree of autonomy enjoyed by the artist. Film as well gives us an idea of how the "people" reacted—above all, showing how difficult it was to unite extremely heterogeneous populations around common values.

## Cinema, Institutions, and Representations

If film has so much to tell us, it is, in the first place, because the early Bolsheviks accorded it so much attention, and it thus crystallizes numerous issues. Through the role assigned by the authorities of political emissary to the people, film was first and foremost an arena for political discourse as a place where two ideologies (one central and Soviet, the other local and national) could converge, interact, and find some common ground—especially when it was a matter of the modernizing aspects of the overall Soviet enterprise (such as the emancipation of women and secularization). Film also came to act as a place of resistance, crisis, and conflict over the course of the 1930s. It was deemed comprehensible to all, irrespective of the language they spoke, and so appeared to offer a solution to multilingualism and illiteracy. Furthermore, thanks to its "technical reproducibility"—the serial reproduction of a unique instance (Benjamin 2010)—it is, at least in theory, a far more useful cultural propaganda product in terms of its diffusion, standardization, and uniformity than theater is, for instance (Youngblood 1991b, 79–80). Multiple identical copies can be made and diffused in numerous places at the same time. Second, film was a key economic stake in various regards. Leo Trotsky saw it as a solution to bigotry and the church, to drunkenness and the tavern, and, like Stalin a bit later on, he hoped that the revenue generated by film would replace that of vodka in state revenue, and in the workers' outgoings, too.[22] The desire for extensive political reach combined with the desire for economic profitability as expressed on several occasions led to the ever greater expansion in the means of diffusion (known as *cinefication*).[23]

Film thus occupied an increasingly large place within the social sphere. It was at the center of a series of interactions, the impact of which was all the greater since the public was fairly easy to manipulate, being particularly receptive to images and not yet accustomed to the medium. They were immediately fascinated by the "living" and "moving pictures," and the projection apparatus introduced an element of technical modernity since it ran on electricity produced by a dynamo, sometimes acting as the veritable precursor to electrification in remote areas. As Pierre Sorlin (2008) has pointed out, in the early days of cinema, "it was the scarcity of images which endowed them with veracity." This is corroborated by the report of the itinerant Iskra cinema team working in the surroundings of Tashkent in late 1924 for the International Red Aid. The projectionists observed how malleable the public was and how they could play on the credulity of spectators, who accorded the team a quasi-magical aura. Films were supposed to produce social consensus, but analysis shows the power relationships that existed between several cultural, political, and social agents (Cardinal 1997, 20) who were involved in negotiating the various concurrent processes, including devising a cinematographic rhetoric that was satisfactory to the authorities; developing a cinematographic language such that the intended public could appropriate the discourse in a critical manner; and developing ever greater means of diffusion to reach as many people as possible and encourage the formation of mass culture and opinions.

The approach taken here in analyzing Uzbek filmic production accords broadly equal interest to all the full-length fiction films produced in Uzbekistan, even though some films are analyzed at greater length than others, often due to the availability of archival documents. This corpus includes, first, films that are relatively mediocre in aesthetic and narrative terms (and which could be dubbed "gray films"). These works, while far removed from the classics of the great Soviet filmmakers and their theoretical considerations about editing (albeit sometimes drawing inspiration from them), have the advantage of revealing various acts of political parapraxis that are of particular significance within a system in which ideological constraints were being applied with ever greater pressure. It includes, second, films made by the first national filmmakers—and indeed the only national filmmakers in Central Asia at the time. Hence, the production studied here provides direct access to a precious vernacular discourse at a time when alternative forums for expression were declining. The corpus of fourteen films comprises nearly all the full-length films produced between 1924 and 1937 within the territory of present-day Uzbekistan.[24]

The films selected for the corpus have been analyzed in their entirety and deconstructed according to a "tripartite semiological division," using an approach borrowed from musicology (Nattiez 1974, 61–75)—that is, decomposed and analyzed at the three levels constituent of the creative act. Narrative analysis (of the structure of the plot and the motifs used, together with borrowings and innovations) is combined with in-depth study of the context in which the films were produced and the dynamics of their reception. These three levels of analysis and the connections between them form what I call the *fait cinématographique*, which is dynamic in structure because it both reflects and induces a social and political reality. Analysis of each film starts by studying the context, then looks at the representations, and, finally, turns to reception.

The first step—examining the context of production—is a matter of economic and institutional history and so is based primarily on archival documents (see details below) that provide information about how the state was constituted, bringing to light the relationship between the center and the periphery and the interplay between autonomy and subordination. Film production—considered an industry as of 1928—was repeatedly reorganized, and study of these restructurings provides a clear picture of how central power was imposed on the Uzbek periphery, revealing the progressive decline of cultural autonomy, which had been acquired de facto over the course of the 1920s but was destined to disappear, as Stalin noted on several occasions (and originally back in 1913).[25] Study of the context thus provides information about how the Soviet state was formed. This information can be direct, when it is a matter of understanding who the tutelary authorities were and the new links of dependency between the various film bodies, or indirect, when it is a matter of the progressive disappearance of archival documents (especially from 1931 and then from 1934 onward), from which it is possible to deduce the institutional restructurings that caused certain documents to be concealed.

After this study of the context, filmic analysis brings out the sociopolitical imaginary conveyed by the films, thereby providing information about the symbolic elements constitutive of collective identities at a time when nationalist discourse was particularly prevalent. This book therefore draws on research into the links between literature and nation but shifts the focus away from novels and the press and toward cinematographic culture to examine how cinema and nation are linked (Hjort and Mackenzie 2000; Frodon 1998). It therefore accords a central place to the book by Benedict Anderson (1983) and his idea of an "imagined community"—a work that has had an immense impact on research into nationalism (Chivallon 2007). Although Anderson does not directly mention cinema, he refers to other means of expression, such as radio and television, and the role they play in the "awakening of the nation." Cinema is inherently revelatory of modernization and the acquisition of new technology, and it developed in the Soviet Union in step with the idea of the nation on which the Soviet political organization was based. It provided the phenomena of national identification with a new means of expression as well as a means of standardization and homogenization. And, in the Soviet case, looking at analysis of the films in conjunction with their political reception can reveal the tensions arising from different conceptions of national identity. In discussing these conceptions, use is made of James C. Scott's (1990) idea of a "public transcript" and a "hidden transcript," thus making it possible to assess the different levels of meaning and language. Filmic analysis also brings out the symbolic violence and domination stemming from the progressive withdrawal of any possibility of cinematographic self-representation and by the imposition of a central vision to the detriment of local and national transpositions and interpretations.

Finally, this book analyzes the political reception (including the censor reports and press reactions) and the social reception (conveyed by the Russian and Uzbek press), both of which throw light on the processes of identification and the extent to which filmic representation conformed (or otherwise) to political requirements. It was in the film theater that the encounter took place between the film, those commissioning the work, the politically committed artist, and the public. It was in the theater that the relationships between the authorities, the newly formed community, and the image on the screen crystallized. The viewers were meant to recognize themselves in the images on-screen, to identify with them, and ultimately take them as behavioral norms, even though this mirror can be an alienating one to varying degrees, as Christian Metz has observed ([1977] 2002, 10). Film does not solely reflect a social reality; it is not just a mirror reflecting society but also a social reality in itself, inciting the audience to act in accordance with the model embodied by the positive hero, particularly in the case of propaganda cinema.[26]

*A "Community to Be Imagined" in Cinema: Sources and Outline*

This book is based on diverse sources. With regard to the above-mentioned question of reception, the difficulty for the historian—especially one working on 1930s Uzbekistan—resides in assessing the reception in general and that of the general public in particular. The press (both accounts and reviews) and archival documents (reports by the Committee for Cinematography and the Repertoire Committee) are the only means of apprehending the social and political reception of these films. I have consulted many daily newspapers and weekly or monthly periodicals—mainly in Russian, although some in Uzbek—published either in Russia or in Uzbekistan. Even though there are sometimes only a few such articles, some provide a wealth of detailed information about reception because they acted as the mouthpiece for public opinion. It goes without saying that while there was still extensive debate in the press during the late 1920s, as the 1930s progressed, the press functioned less and less as a reflection or relay of public opinion. Yet until 1937, tensions still break through to the surface and may be detected in the form of either oppressive silence or acrimonious accusation.

In addition to consulting the press, I made use of archival documents, mainly those produced by entities regulating cinema and sometimes by those appointed to monitor and control it. These are held by the Central State Archives of the Republic of Uzbekistan, the Cinematographic, Photographic, and Phonographic Documents of the Central State Archives of the Republic of Uzbekistan, and the Archives of the Academy of Arts of Uzbekistan. I consulted the regional archives in Bukhara and the National Archives of Tajikistan (in Dushanbe), but have not used them because they were posterior to the period under study. The archives of the Uzbek Communist Party, those of the political police, and those of the Commissariat for Internal Affairs are not made available to foreign researchers, or to most local researchers. However, I was able to gather some information from them. When the archives were opened very briefly in the early 1990s, several historians consulted them and published articles about cinema without being able to expressly quote their sources. These archives were rapidly closed again, and during my field visit (in 2004–5), only seven researchers were authorized to work there. The historian Naim Karimov, who was in charge of the "Memory of the Martyrs" association (*Shahidlar khotirasi*)—the equivalent of the *Memorial* association—was kind enough to share information with me, as was Hamidulla Akbarov. Other documents about the political and social situation produced by the political police have been published in Russia (D'iakov 2001–2008). Even if this kind of source clearly raises the problem of how representative or otherwise the documents and information might be (often being revelatory of a paranoid expectation of disorder or drawn up in response to a political request), they nevertheless provide precious material (Vinogradov 2001). Last, and as a counterpoint, documents held in Russia were also consulted, namely those in the State Archive for Art and Literature of the Russian Federation, the Russian State Archive of Sociopolitical History, the State Archives of the Russian Federation, and the Film Archives of the Russian Federation (*Gosfilmofond*).

In addition to these archival sources and the written press, filmic sources were of course used, though it was not always easy to gain access to them. Because they were relatively rare in the 1930s, they are a particularly informative, precious, and rich vernacular source. Although it was not always possible to precisely authenticate the copies studied, it was nevertheless possible to arrive at some idea of their authenticity by consulting the official documents detailing the films' technical characteristics (*literaturnyi stsenarii*) published subsequently or lists of title cards, which were generally available in the studio archives (the Uzbek Archives) or in the Film Archives in Moscow. With this information, it was possible to conclude in nearly all cases that the film studied was as originally edited.

Oral sources were also used, though these were often very problematic since they related to the cultural and political elites, many of whom had perished in the 1937 purges. The few people who were still alive, and their children and grandchildren, were not always forthcoming, either because they did not want to talk or because they knew little about the lives of their fathers or grandfathers. For instance, I had the opportunity to meet one of the pioneers of Uzbek documentary cinema, Malik Kaiumov (190?–2010), the prospect of which filled me with great enthusiasm.[27] His biography suggested that this could be a key moment, enabling me to see into some of the arcane workings of the Stalinist system in Uzbekistan. Kaiumov had started out as an actor in the late 1920s, had been acquainted with the main filmmakers I was interested in, had been sent off as a war correspondent in the early 1940s, and had been working in documentary and news studios in the not-too-distant past. He had lived through (and survived) the Soviet period, had behind-the-scenes knowledge of its history, and had taken part in its cinematographic mystification. But the interview turned out to be something of a disappointment. I listened to his tale but did not pick up on the history, even though many details of his daily life were useful. This sort of interview is revelatory of the long-term impacts of Sovietization and the acceptance of the violent policies used to push through Soviet modernization. When I tried to get him to speak about the years 1936 to 1938 and the purges, he briefly mentioned the hardships (famines) but without mentioning the arrests, then quickly went back to the topic of Afghanistan: "Just look at the current situation of Afghan women!" thus implying that Soviet violence had been a necessary evil to avoid the "backwardness" of his neighbors on the other side of the Amu Darya and the Pandj.

A similar difficulty was encountered in discussing the details of these dramatic years with Dunon Ganiev, the son of the Uzbek filmmaker Nabi Ganiev, though for a different reason.[28] He knew little about the political opinions of his father, who by his silence had endeavored to protect both himself and his children. This difficulty arose again with Ali Khamraev, the son of the screenwriter and actor Ergash Khamraev.[29] Khamraev is one of the great Uzbek filmmakers of the "poetic realism" movement of the 1960s and 1970s and has worked in Moscow since the 1990s. Because he had left Uzbekistan, I expected him to tell his tale more readily. But having been born in 1937, he knew very little about his father's life; E. Khamraev had died in 1941, shortly after the beginning of the Second World War.[30] As for Suleyman Khojaev, another Uzbek filmmaker who died young, his son Hamid Suleymanov—a renowned philologist—had died several years earlier, and his grandson, Rustam Suleymanov, did not respond to my request.

\* \* \*

This book charts the unfolding of the drama of the Stalinist system, proceeding chronologically and examining the sociohistorical process of national construction and deconstruction between 1924 and 1937, precisely resituating the establishment of a new structure of domination in the wake of the collapse of the Russian Empire. It is divided into three sections, corresponding to the three significant phases of the interwar period in Soviet Uzbekistan.

Part 1, "Decolonizing Central Asia: Film Structures and Representations (1919–27)," opens with an institutional history of the early film production structures that emerged at the end of the civil war in Central Asia and that enjoyed true national cultural autonomy as a result of the ethnoterritorial delimitation of 1924 (chap. 1). Although the country ran its own cultural policy, was in charge of selecting the main themes of the films, and oversaw their censorship, it still labored under the legacy of the former film production system and encountered economic difficulties along with widespread shortages and a lack of qualified indigenous staff (directors, technicians, and writers). These structural difficulties prevented the region from making the most of its new cultural autonomy. By using nonindigenous filmmakers who had trained at the time of the Russian Empire, the movies produced by Uzbekistan's studios conveyed representations that failed to correspond to the new political and social reality they were meant to express. These full-length films were intended solely for audiences in the large Russian cities, and the representations they conveyed were very similar to those of the colonial films produced in the major European empires (chap. 2). Some of these colonial clichés discredited and stigmatized native peoples; though the films soon started to offer a sort of discursive hybridization admixing colonial themes with Soviet (i.e., Russian and proletarian) ones, these were not clearly formalized at this stage. Thus, the cultural autonomy of the cinematographic institutions was not fully projected onto the screen during this phase.

Nevertheless, colonial influence over representations declined more rapidly in the Soviet Union than in other empires in a process that coincided with the beginning of the Cultural Revolution, which is at the heart of the analysis in Part 2, "Cultural Revolution and Its Paradoxes: Nation, Modernity, and Empire (1927–31)." This period saw the emergence of a truly national cinematographic realm (chap. 3), giving rise to a different kind of film directly targeting local audiences. *The Jackals of Ravat* by Kazimir Gertel' (1927) was the first film to be regarded as national because it embodied cultural autonomy both in how it was made (Uzbek decision making in the production and postproduction processes) and in what it depicted (native actors, native heroes, and a local plot). In the process, it sketched out a new, modern Soviet Uzbek community at a time when the public was starting to identify with the cinematographic image. Other full-length feature films lent their support to the modernization and social progress policy (addressing such themes as women's emancipation and the secularization of societies). However, criticism of these films by the censors indicates that the central authority now had new channels for interfering in Uzbek political life. The appropriation of cinema as a national product was short-lived; in 1931, a new framework of domination was set up. Control was exerted in three ways: economically, via the institutional centralization of the national film production structures; politically and ideologically, with purges in the studios and film organizations; and materially, with the expansion of broadcasting facilities, equipment, and networks. With these transformations, the Soviet Union became a truly imperial system (chap. 4). National, political, and social tensions were exacerbated by central policies promoting national positive discrimination—collectivization, sedentarization, and dekulakization—initiating unprecedented socioeconomic changes.

It is precisely in this context that the national filmmakers made their first films. The third and final part of the book, "The Paradoxes of the Nationalities

Policy: Nationalism versus Internationalism (1931–37)," starts by analyzing the works of the first generation of filmmakers, Nabi Ganiev and Suleyman Khojaev. Although they might appear to have used opposing filmic languages, their work in fact conveyed a shared national and nationalist imagination and one that integrated class discourse, only now placed in the service of national liberation (chap. 5). After these initial films, Suleyman Khojaev and Nabi Ganiev were rapidly silenced, just as silent movies began to talk and spread the word of totalitarianism. The process of nation building in Soviet Uzbekistan was dealt its final blow in 1937, a year marking the disappearance of the majority of the Uzbek national political and intellectual elites and the making of the first talking film ever produced in Uzbekistan (chap. 6). *The Oath*, by Aleksandr Usol'tsev-Garf (1937), who was invited by the Uzbek film studios because of the new dearth of homegrown filmmakers, conveyed a message of salvation wholly at odds with reality, just as Stalinist violence and terror was reaching its peak. It was the first in a series of films that successfully inferred and embodied central expectations, praising not just the greatness of the Russian people but the supremacy of class over nation. Embodying the slogan dear to Stalin, "national in form, socialist in content," *The Oath* is a celebration of the fiction of nation. But behind this surface appearance, the film was in fact a denial of national expression, with a mere envelope comprised of local actors, settings, and elements of folklore. Nation was divorced from culture, and from then on, Soviet domination through centralized state structures was coupled with a single ideology. The formation of a hegemonic empire excluding any form of accommodation and negotiation was complete, and it lasted at least until the outbreak of the Great Patriotic War.

# Part I
# Decolonizing Central Asia: Film Structures and Representations (1919–27)

# Part 1 Introduction

## Turkestan Prior to the Birth of the Soviet Union: Revolts and Colonial Revolution

TURKESTAN HAD BEEN a military province of the empire of the tsars since 1867.[1] Like many other colonial provinces, its fate underwent a fundamental shift in the second half of the 1910s—a period that, despite coinciding with a short-lived period of national liberation, was particularly violent and lethal for Turkestan's population.[2] The First World War and the resulting 1916 revolts sparked by the imperial decree to requisition the labor of Muslims in Turkestan—which were violently quashed by the Imperial Army—along with the attendant economic crisis all did lasting damage to the region, triggering general destabilization. Marco Buttino estimates that the indigenous rural population of Turkestan dropped by 30 percent between 1915 and 1920, amounting to nearly half a million people (1990, 65). The rural economy was devastated by the years of civil war and aggravated by famine, disease (malaria, typhus, rabies, and cholera), difficult weather conditions, and the suspension of railway communications that cut off cereal deliveries to Turkestan. Galloping inflation meant that it became increasingly expensive to produce cereals, which had already been hit by the promotion of cotton growing.

The economic crisis caused acute tension between the indigenous population and the Russian settlers who had arrived since the taking of Tashkent in 1865. Conflicts flared up over land disputes and over access to water and food supplies. The 1917 revolutions, which in Turkestan amounted to a "colonial revolution," to use the title of the work by Giorgi Safarov ([1921] 1985), led to the introduction of dictatorial Russian power.[3] This power was, for the most part, wielded by former settlers, who shut the Muslim population out from political life, thus putting an end to the cooperation that had existed between the Russians and influential segments of the indigenous population. "Paradoxically, in Turkestan, it was not the Bolshevik party which set up Soviet power, but Soviet power and the need to confirm the power of the Soviets [which] created a Bolshevik party," Safarov observes (110). The following years, in his opinion, were a time of "Russian-style anarchy" (*russkaia svobodka*)—a period of famine, pillage, exactions by Red Army guards against local traditions (*byt*), summary justice, the confiscation and requisition of livestock, arbitrary searches, and so on (127). The Red Army soldiers involved in removing former leaders from office (in Bukhara and Khiva) and establishing new governments were the same as those behind the quashing of the first independentist stirrings of the short-lived Provisional Autonomous Government of Turkestan, based in Kokand (also known as the Kokand Autonomy, which ran from November 1917 to February 1918), leading to further loss of human life and incipient disillusionment with local Bolshevik power (Agzamkhojaev 2006, 231).

The end of the Kokand Autonomy is generally viewed as marking the starting point for Basmachi anti-Soviet resistance, an insurrectional movement without any real political unity that wished to retain the traditional order.[4] The history of Russian colonization until the outburst of violence in the 1916 revolts had, however, been punctuated by episodes of armed resistance by various movements. The distance that had grown between Tashkent and the Bolshevik leaders now gradually shrank. Though the Russian Soviet elites in Turkestan initially became increasingly resentful of central power and sought to manage Turkestan's territory in autonomous fashion, the situation changed when the Commissariat of Nationalities sent a delegation headed by Petr Kobozev to reassert central authority (Sahadeo 2007, 209–11). In April 1918, the Soviet regional leaders declared the founding of the Turkestan Autonomous Soviet Socialist Republic (TASSR), which nevertheless remained part of the Russian Soviet Federative Socialist Republic—referred to as the Russian Soviet Federation in this work—and set up a Central Executive Committee of Turkestan, chaired by Kobozev. The advantages provided by central power (in terms of funds, grain delivery, and the promise of industrialization) meant that ties with Moscow were never completely broken off. Indeed, Kobozev managed to involve the local elites to a greater extent in the functioning of the TASSR.

The role played by the Red Army and the military authorities (and especially Mikhail Frunze) was crucial in establishing Soviet power in Central Asia, convincing the local population to participate, and winning the backing of members of the indigenous communist elite who were granted influential positions (Haugen 2003, 21).[5] Difficulty in accessing some sources makes it difficult to establish the background of certain high-placed individuals in the state apparatus, but it seems clear that the local communist elite were appointed primarily to regulatory bodies involved solely in positive government action. Those in charge of coercion, such as the political police (the GPU, the OGPU, and then the NKVD) were run by men appointed by Moscow.[6] The Turkestan Bureau (replaced on May 19, 1922, by the Central Asian Bureau), as the plenipotentiary representative of the Central Committee of the All-Russian (subsequently All-Union) Communist Party, was behind a number of actions that strengthened the local grip of the Bolshevik authorities. This Bureau disappeared on October 2, 1934, once central authority had been firmly established (Keller 2003).

But in the wake of the February Revolution, Russians who had acceded to local positions were not prepared to recognize the indigenous elite as their full equals: "We must not forget our status as conquerors, and we need to occupy positions within the Republic that are fitting to our importance," they declared.[7] Bolshevik discourse and policies were imbued with anti-imperialism—especially their pronouncements on agrarian reform (Pianciola 2008)—and for the indigenous elites involved in establishing new regimes they were a source of satisfaction (albeit wholly relative) after several years of political frustration (S. Becker 2004). The Bolshevik nationalities policy, which ostensibly encouraged national movements so as to win over Eastern populations to the revolutionary cause, thus had a positive image. The Russian Soviet Federation, which presented itself as an anti-imperialist power, was perceived as an ally. But local Russians, including communists, were viewed unfavorably (Khalid 2001, 151).

\* \* \*

The political, economic, social, and symbolic issues affecting first Turkestan and then Uzbekistan after the end of the civil war are viewed in this book through the prism of film activity in the broad sense of the term, embracing both institutions and representations. The institutional history of the early film organizations brings into focus the initial stages of Soviet state building and the fashioning of the relationships of dependency and autonomy taking root between 1920 and 1925, a key period during which national cultural autonomy was won (chap. 1). Yet despite the assertion of sovereignty in the cultural field, amounting to the decolonization of the way institutions functioned, the first films—produced by filmmakers from outside Central Asia—still bore testimony to Russia's former imperial hegemony. Those films are marked by colonial stereotypes comparable to the social imaginaries conveyed by cinema in the great European empires, even though Soviet political codes were timidly being taken up (chap. 2). Decolonizing social imaginaries would take longer.

# 1 Cultural Autonomy and the Nation (1919–24)

THE HOPES HELD out by cinema in the mid-1920s as an object of technical and social modernity are perfectly symbolized by the studio logo that appeared on posters for films produced or distributed by the Uzbek film organization (fig. 1.1). It is not possible to ascertain who created this logo, but it appears to have been designed by someone from the region given that the image reads from right to left, like Arabic script that was in use at that time. This drawing presents two Muslims. The one at the top, shown against a background of a five-pointed star, is presented in a "modern" manner, wearing a military-style cap (*topi*) and holding out to his compatriot, depicted manacled and with a turban, a spool of film that serves as a rope that releases the man from the dazzling divine light. This light emanates from a crescent moon, almost forming a perfect circle, thus reinforcing the idea of imprisonment and repetition, whereas the five points reach inexorably outward in all directions. The vertical composition of the image, a classic feature of Soviet iconography, creates an opposition between heaven and hell while reversing the terms; religion and creed are generally said to free man, yet here they imprison him. The nature of this opposition is corroborated by the fact that the man at the top shows his eyes and is prepared for confrontation and conflict, with his gaze associating him with fighting spirit and dynamism, unlike the man beneath, who does not even show his face. Yet while the image appears very clear-cut, there are two elements that disturb any univocal interpretation: first, the lower figure is apparently as easy to blind by film as by light; and, second, to produce any image whatsoever, the film projection needs a source of light, here found at the intersection between the Soviet star and the Muslim crescent moon.

The institutional path leading to this presumed liberation by film was to be a long and tortuous one. Indeed, the Soviet authorities in Central Asia inherited from the colonial period a legacy of disorganized and largely noncentralized film activity, though there was a network of film theaters, a collection of films, and a certain experience and audience. As in the Maghreb, colonization provided fertile ground for cinema to spread because it created powerful circulation networks, such as railways. European districts were built that became outlets for initial screenings, such as in Tashkent, and perhaps also delimiting a geographical space deemed comparatively secure by entrepreneurs working in fairs (Fomin 2004, 14–19; Akbarov 2005, 9; Corriou 2012).

Figure 1.1. Uzbekkino logo.

The situation in colonial Central Asia did not differ markedly from that in North Africa, the Ottoman Empire, and Iran, and the first experiments with cinema were comparable to spectacles in fairs and street performances that were organized to celebrate popular and religious festivals. Indeed, for vernacular societies, cinema was very much an extension of this tradition (Günther 2008; Drieu 2012). And then, as elsewhere in the world, cinema started to become sedentary. In 1908, the first coffeehouse screenings were held by private entrepreneurs (first in Tashkent and then in Samarkand, Bukhara, and Andijan). In 1910 and 1911, the Khiva winter and summer cinemas (figs. 1.2 and 1.3) were built in Tashkent by Prince Nikolai Konstantinovich, a cousin of Emperor Nicholas II (Akhrorov 1971, 5).[1] In tandem with the operation of agents from the Pathé and Gaumont film companies, such as Félix Mesguich, local elites started appropriating the new invention of cinema and enlisting it to serve power. Khudoibergan Devonov (1878–1940) made films showing Khan Esfandiar of Khiva and his region.[2]

In Central Asia and elsewhere, cinema soon became caught up in the field of politics, for notables and the authorities sought to exploit the fixed or moving image to undergird their power and entrench their legitimacy. What sets Central Asia apart, however, is the Bolshevik project to politicize film images and production to an extreme degree in the period after the civil war.

### The Complex Territorial and Institutional Bases of Film Production and Distribution in Turkestan

The founding of the Turkestan Autonomous Soviet Socialist Republic (TASSR) in April 1918, at the Fifth Congress of Turkestan Soviets, saw the setting up of the first film institutions against the chaotic backdrop of the civil war. But

Figure 1.2. Khiva winter cinema (1911). By kind permission of Boris Golender.

Figure 1.3. Khiva summer cinema (1912). By kind permission of Boris Golender.

attempts to structure a viable film production system for Turkestan as a whole were hindered by the introduction of the New Economic Policy (NEP), which generated a tension between using cinema for political ends and using it for commercial profit. Moreover, the TASSR was a territorial entity in the Russian Soviet Federation (RSFSR) and so in a position of dependency and administrative and legislative subordination. Last, the lack of interest displayed by the early film studios for a place such as Turkestan—which was not only peripheral but Muslim to boot—meant that no films were made especially for local audiences. Nevertheless, this was the context in which the Russo-Bukharan Cinematographic Company was formed and made the first fiction film ever produced in Central Asia, *The Minaret of Death*.

## Film Activity amid the Chaos of the Civil War

The first Cinematographic Department, tasked with running all photographic and cinematographic activities and implementing scientific education, political education, and agitprop activities, was set up on January 13, 1920, by a decree issued by the People's Commissariat for Education (*Narkompros*) of the Turkestan Autonomous Soviet Socialist Republic during the final stages of the civil war.[3] The formation of this department flowed directly from the founding decree setting out the Bolsheviks' political objectives for cinema, issued on August 27, 1919, by the Russian Soviet Federation's Council of People's Commissars (*Sovnarkom*), which was chaired by Lenin at the time (Lebedev 1939; Schmulevitch 1997). This decree to nationalize film activity (in the economic sense of the word)—taken up and adopted as it stood by the Turkestan authorities—set out to place all photographic and cinematographic trade, industry, and material under the oversight of the People's Commissariat for Education.[4] Despite the primordial political will to bring cinema under state control, it took the entire 1920s to subordinate all film activity in Soviet Turkestan, and indeed elsewhere in Russia, because the introduction of the New Economic Policy ran counter to its effective implementation (Listov 1991).

The tasks facing the new Cinematographic Department were enormous, even leaving aside the issues of film production, supply, and distribution, which were the responsibility of other economic commissariats. The Cinematographic Department had to start by drawing up an inventory before regularizing, centralizing, and relaunching film activity, which was in great disarray because the region was not yet pacified due to the activities of the Basmachi movement. No new films had arrived in Turkestan since the beginning of the civil war. Baku, one of the major towns for supplying films, was occupied by the Whites, and military operations at Samara on the Aral Sea meant Turkestan was cut off from the town of Orenburg, the next major source of film supplies. The region made do with limited reserves, made up of the collections from the former private rental bureaus that had been in part requisitioned by the Cinematographic Department.[5] The work of assembling the inventory of this collection was hampered by military organizations refusing to recognize the nationalization decree of August 1919 and the decree implementing it in Turkestan. The military organizations continued to requisition the best film equipment and facilities for their own use and refused to communicate information about the films and equipment in their possession—which they rarely returned to their owners.

Although the Cinematographic Department acquired some of the films held by private rental bureaus and imposed a tax that brought in some funds, by April 1928, it had only 180 film programs, plus an additional 60 or so programs owned by film theaters.[6] The situation became critical when the Cinematographic Department faced bankruptcy due to the absence of any new films, leading it to try to exchange programs with rental bureaus in Baku, Samara, and even Moscow.[7] Any outright purchase of films was tricky, because those selling films and film equipment demanded payment in cash, something that the Turkestan Council of People's Commissars refused to contemplate due to inadequate financial resources.[8] Looking for a solution, the Cinematographic Department floated the idea of buying films on the open market and using equipment smuggled from Finland.[9] The possibility of buying films from the Russian Soviet Federation's Cinematographic Department was also considered even though it was not in a stronger position.

The condition of the films was another problem; they had been worn by countless screenings. Their ideological content did not correspond to new political requirements, and some of them were even deemed "harmful" for the population, a recurrent reproach during the 1920s and early 1930s.[10]

In late 1920, across Turkestan as a whole, there were sixty or so buildings that could be used for screening films, though many of them were not used for this purpose or were inoperative (see table 1 in appendix). Cinemas were closing one after the other, and even when their equipment worked, they had to share their premises with theater troupes.[11] Some projection equipment was housed in places such as railway meeting rooms or stations (as was the case in Kokand and Samarkand) and were primarily for the European population (as in Charjui). The projection equipment often belonged to the education authorities and sometimes to the Red Army, being attached to garrisons (as in Samarkand, Katta-Kurgan, and Bukhara), or they were owned by political organizations such as the Communist Muslim Organization in Skobelev (present-day Fergana). But the film equipment was dilapidated due to incorrect use and lack of maintenance and repairs. In addition, the electricity supply for theaters, cinemas, services, and concert rooms was limited by decree.[12]

The countryside and indigenous parts of towns were less well equipped than the modern European areas that had previously been colonial districts.[13] In late

1920, there were only ten or so mobile screening units (*peredvizhki*) traveling around the countryside and through the indigenous districts in towns. In many cases, film theaters were found only in new towns (such as Namangan and Kyzyl-Kya), and the indigenous areas had no film theaters at all. In Andijan and Osh, for instance, it was not possible to open a film theater because the old town was being "terrorized" by Basmachis.[14] The town of Kokand had two cinemas in the old town and three in the new town. Tashkent—the capital of the Turkestan Republic—had seven film theaters, two of which were in the old town. The largest cinemas in the capital were controlled by the Cinematographic Department. Film theaters in the indigenous districts of towns were often seasonal, operating only during the summer and in the open air.

In addition to these film theaters and mobile screening units, agitprop trains (*agitpoezd*) toured the former Russian Empire as of 1918. These trains were a solution to the emergency situation, especially during the civil war, and made it possible to hold free screenings of short and medium-length *agitki*, or propaganda films. The Russian Soviet Federation's Central Executive Committee had eight of these trains in all, replicating in reduced form the organization of Soviet propaganda and its modernization policy. The first of these trains (called Lenin) left Moscow station on August 13, 1918, for Kazan. The train was composed of four goods wagons carrying political publications, travelers, and a single instructor who prioritized Red Army detachments based in Kazan (Mezhenina 1962, 9–10).

These agitprop trains also included the Red East (*Krasnyi vostok*)—run by Safarov—set up on January 11, 1919, to operate in the Central Asian territories (fig. 1.4). It was kitted out in late December 1919, and came into service on January 23, 1920, just when the Cinematographic Department was founded. It left Moscow carrying more than 150 people, of whom there were about 20 Red Army soldiers, about 30 people in the political unit, a projectionist, a pianist, and a single woman in charge of emancipation issues. Screenings were held in a specially equipped wagon with a mobile projector that could be used to visit villages and camps lying at some remove from the stations. Talks about communism and the role of the party were just one of the agitprop methods used by the team; it also employed more coercive methods and surveillance tactics (Mezhenina 1962, 14, 17, 19, 35; Argenbright 2011).[15] The Red East was not only a channel for distributing propaganda, it also provided Bolshevik leaders with the means to establish order and assert local control over how the Soviets wielded power. It served as a complaints bureau (for receiving letters and declarations), which were then studied by a representative of the People's Commissariat for State Control and, if necessary, presented to the local judicial authorities (Mezhenina 1962, 24–25). Detecting the presence of "anti-Soviet elements" was one of the prerogatives of the team on the Red East, which ran until mid-1921.

Figure 1.4. The Red East train at Katta-Kurgan station (January–July 1920), UzRKSOKh 0-102061.

*A Timid Return to Film Activity under the New Economic Policy*

The New Economic Policy, adopted at the Tenth Congress of the All-Russian Communist Party in March 1921, marked a period of transition between Leninism and Stalinism, between "war communism" (with forced requisitions) and economic liberalism, in a region that—by the end of the First World War, the February and October Revolutions, and the Russian Civil War—had been bled totally dry. The NEP displays the tension that existed between the ideological objectives assigned to cinema and the commercial reality at a time when economic activities were being restructured on basis of the private sector. The only way to restore and develop the economy was to draw on internal resources, because soliciting foreign finance was not an option (Rosenberg 1991, 3, 7). Cinema, rather than being viewed as a means for political education, was initially perceived as a lucrative activity in need of entertaining films meeting audience demands.

The Turkestan Autonomous Soviet Socialist Republic officially approved the NEP at the Sixth Congress of the Communist Party of Turkestan in August 1921 and then at the Tenth Congress of the Soviets in September 1921 (Alimova 2000, 435). The NEP was applied to film activity, making it possible for private individuals to operate cinemas in exchange for a rent proportional to their operating revenue.[16] Cinemas were rented out in Tashkent, as indeed they were in many other towns across Russia. In November 1921, the Khiva cinema belonging to the Tashkent Department for Political Education was rented out to private operators.[17] The contract fixed the rent at 40 percent of income, counting on an average of two and a half screenings per day, with daily sales of 1,450 entries, amounting to 580 spectators per screening (bearing in mind that the Khiva cinema had 700 places). It is difficult to ascertain whether these large figures reflected actual attendance. Operating a cinema was profitable, as was film distribution and rental. Rental bureaus had to be officially recorded, and their activities were taxed by the state, which was perceived as a hindrance to their development.[18]

The economic recovery in Turkestan brought about by the NEP led to film activity becoming autonomous and splitting away from other performance arts (such as circus and opera) and especially from theater. Cinema and film income were now plowed back into film activity.[19] The Cinematographic Department, which was renamed Turkkino in December 1922, was an association of the existing studios, photo workshops, and film theaters in the TASSR (with the exception of those belonging to the Red Army and Navy), and it held a monopoly over distribution.[20] Film activity was both a tool for political education and a source of revenue; and it was dominated by this dual objective, and it was difficult to balance the two sides of the equation. The Soviet authorities were confronted with a dilemma they were not yet in a position to resolve: how to profit from film activity while also using it for ideological purposes and as a cultural product to which workers and the "laboring masses" were entitled.

The operation of cinemas by private individuals and the granting of operating permits to rental bureaus implied setting up a specific policy to control these activities, the films that were distributed, and the issuing of film licenses.[21] Itinerant distribution was also regulated, with it becoming obligatory to return any films borrowed.[22] But in practice the means for exerting this control were lacking; nor was there any permanent projection room for editing and reediting films. An acute shortage of films available for hire led to a shortage of sixty-nine cinema programs in June 1922, plus many programs were unusable due to excess wear and tear.[23] The film collection was always in a dire situation, and two-thirds of the films that Turkkino owned were screened on between just three and seven occasions.

The first attempts at film production occurred in May 1922, with a project to make a film called *Biket Batyr* based on a script written by the Turkologist ethnographer Abubekr Divaev (1855 or 1856–1933). Responsibility for making the film went to the head of Turkkino, but the project was never carried out. In addition to material and financial difficulties, there were not enough actors among the local population.[24] It was, however, still possible to make comparatively cheap films, as was the case for two films made with the help of the Commissariat for Supply, *Children Teaching Their Elders* (*Deti uchat starikov*) and *Agitator Domovoi*.

But Turkkino was in no position to compete with the productions from the Russian studios or with the many war films made in Germany and sold cheaply.

Neither the pre-1917 film rental bureaus and producers nor the film bodies in the Russian Soviet Federation displayed any interest in Muslim populations, viewed as an uninteresting and unprofitable target audience.[25] This led to the notion of local production—setting up a studio to train the first local film producers and actors and making films for local audiences. A plan was drawn up in June 1922 for organizing the film studios, with courses being taught for cinema (including directing, editing, scriptwriting technique, and shooting) and theater and the performance arts in general (acting, pantomime, rhythm, acrobatics, dancing, and fencing). Theoretically this eight-month training course, with four and a half hours of lessons per day, was to train 300 students (225 Muslims and 75 Russians), but the project never got off the ground.[26]

### Turkestan: A Periphery Subordinated to Moscow (1922–24)

The shift to the New Economic Policy and the geographical and political setup of the TASSR as part of the Russian Soviet Federation made it impossible for cinema to be economically and culturally independent. Quite the contrary, because until the administrative and territorial delimitation of 1924, the TASSR was in a position of complete subordination to the central cinema authorities, preventing the republic from establishing any viable film production system. To function independently, the system would have needed to work as a closed circuit, with locally generated operating and distribution revenues being invested back into film production. But such a system was not yet able to emerge, and its advent was delayed even further when a new Moscow-based film authority was set up to manage film activity across the entire Soviet Union, the State Committee for Cinematography (Goskino). Goskino was established in December 1922 and held the legal monopoly over distribution for the entire territory of the Russian Federation.[27] It was the only body legally authorized to import films from abroad and was theoretically established to encourage the development of production studios (Kenez 1992, 41).

But Goskino found itself in an ambiguous position, for it was both an actor in and regulator of film activity. Goskino had no authority outside the territory of the Russian Federation, and it encountered stiff competition from many other dynamic and powerful film organizations, such as Sevzapkino (which was directly involved in setting up the first film studios in Bukhara 1924; see below), Kino-sever, Kino-Moskva, the Rus' corporation, Mezhrabpom (the latter two merging in 1923 to form Mezhrabpom-Rus'), Proletkino (which produced *The Muslim Woman* in Central Asia in 1925), and, finally, the Ukrainian studios VUFKU (Laurent 2000, 31; Gak 1962, 132–33). These studios produced news reports and fiction films that they distributed themselves. Goskino sought to assert its legal monopoly over distribution by establishing contractual relationships, sometimes taking as much as 50 percent of its rivals' income.[28] But it struggled to secure its monopoly, and private distributors continued to operate, paying Goskino for its authorization.

Distribution and cinema operation formed the heart of Goskino's commercial concerns to the detriment of production efforts. In six months, its revenue was composed primarily of operation (56 percent) and distribution (34 percent), with production accounting for the remaining 10 percent.[29] The profits from distribution and operation came almost exclusively from foreign-produced films. Various competing organizations sought to set up operations in the regions, with the competition being particularly fierce in large towns. But Goskino did not have the coercive means that would have enabled it to oblige these organizations to respect its regulations. Although Goskino exerted stronger control in the large towns, the situation in the regions allowed numerous private film distributors to continue to operate, even though they were supposedly banned from doing so.

The setting up of Goskino and subsequent attempts to regulate film activity had repercussions in the Turkestan Republic. One such repercussion was that Turkkino, which held the legal monopoly over distribution across the country, was now legally obliged to relinquish it, even though it had generated most of its revenue. The head of Turkkino found himself in a complex situation and could not refuse to sign the contract transferring the distribution monopoly. There was little competition in Turkestan, and Goskino was in a position to render commercial activity unprofitable by introducing expensive licensing fees, for instance.[30] Nor could Turkkino buy films abroad without the prior agreement of Goskino.[31] The head of Turkkino therefore acquiesced, ceding the monopoly for distribution across the entire territory of the TASSR. In exchange, Turkkino hoped it would get Goskino to include in its production plan films that would meet the needs of the local Muslim populations.[32] Two contracts were signed with these terms: As compensation for ceding the monopoly over distribution, Turkkino was to receive 8 percent of operating profits made in Turkestan on Goskino-produced films and 10 percent for films for which Goskino held the distribution rights.[33] Goskino also undertook, on paper at least, to provide agitprop films and educational films to be screened for free.

But there was no mention of producing films for the local population, even though this was an essential point for the heads of political education in Turkestan. In the end, Goskino was able to profit from its monopoly without fulfilling its obligations, and in 1924 the *Proletkino* newspaper reported that 99 percent of the films produced in the Soviet Union were not shown on the screens of Central Asia.[34] In addition to the difficulty in acquiring new films, Turkkino no longer had the legal means to tax the distribution of films belonging to other producers or distributors, because these rights had been ceded to Goskino.[35]

In the light of this situation, the head of the agitprop section of the Communist Party of Turkestan decided to allow the Proletkino studios to open a subsidiary in Tashkent. This decision was a direct echo of the situation in Russia, where the agitprop section of the Central Committee of the All-Russian

Communist Party, dissatisfied with Goskino's policy and inertia, had decided to found Proletkino to produce "proletarian films." Proletkino operated from February 1923 to September 1928, producing a dozen films in all. Theoretically these films were more appropriate for the working masses (Tsikounas 1992, 26). New hopes emerged in Turkestan. Despite inadequate means, several local organizations (such as the Union of Metal Workers and workers' organizations) became shareholders in the Proletkino subsidiary,[36] hoping to receive and distribute Proletkino films in exchange for this funding. But one year after this capital had been raised, no films had been purchased.[37] The shareholders called for their money back and demanded that the Proletkino plenipotentiary provide them with some explanation; they were unsuccessful in both endeavors.

*The Short-Lived Russo-Bukharan Film Company Bukhkino (1924)*

Although the attempt to establish a full range of film activity (distribution, operation, and production) in Turkestan ended in failure, this was not the case in the Bukharan People's Soviet Republic.[38] The relationship between the Turkestan Republic and the Bukharan Republic was affected by the complex nature of the legislative regimes, and especially by the varying relationships between the Russian Soviet Federation and the Soviet republics. The Bukharan Republic was relatively autonomous and, like the Khorezm People's Soviet Republic, was not part of the Russian Federation. Consequently, these two Central Asian republics were not subject to decisions taken by Goskino, nor even to legislation passed in the Turkestan Republic.

The differences in the way film activity was regulated from one territorial entity to another were viewed as an obstacle to establishing a monopoly over distribution across the whole of Central Asia. Indeed, the territory of the TASSR was split in two by the People's Republics of Khorezm and Bukhara (see map 1.1). The absence of an agreement between the republics led to speculative activity that flouted censorship rules and distribution regulations.[39] First, films sent directly to the territory of Bukhara were not subject to the tax levied by the Turkestan government. Second, the Bukharan state could not be put on trial for any acts viewed as illegal. Turkkino therefore approached the Republic of Bukhara's Commissariat for Education to seek an agreement on supplying films, which would not only allow for closer ideological control of the films transiting via the various republics but bring in additional money. But the Bukharan education authorities refused point-blank.

The heterogeneity of the legislative systems was a boon to production. The government of the Republic of Bukhara called on Russian film organizations to set up its own film production unit in February 1924 (Abul'khanov 1962, 56). This initiative was carried out after a visit by the Bukharan plenipotentiary representative, a certain Yusuf-Zade, to the Sevzapkino Studios in Leningrad (Bratoliubov

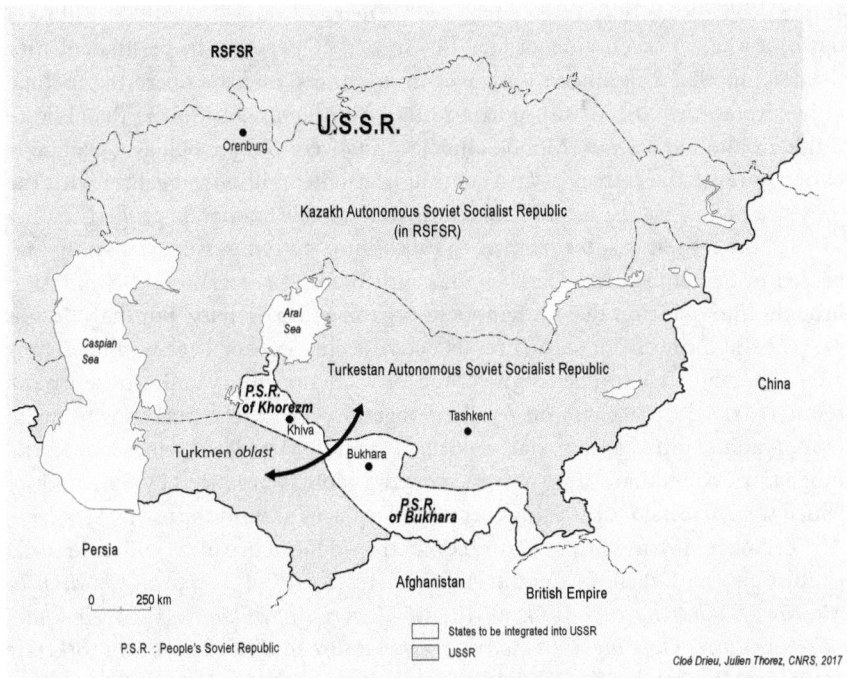

Map 1.1. "Central Asia at the Eve of National-Territorial Delimitation." *Source:* Julien Thorez, 2011, "Les nouvelles frontières de l'Asie centrale: États, nations et régions en recomposition," Cybergeo, https://cybergeo.revues.org/23707. Translation: Cloé Drieu.

1976, 99). The Russo-Bukharan Cinematographic Company (*Bukharo-russkoe kinotovarishchestvo*), or Bukhkino, was founded in Moscow on April 12, 1924, when a contract was signed by the head of Sevzapkino and the plenipotentiary of the Republic of Bukhara. The shareholders in this new company were Sevzapkino (45 percent), which contributed films, equipment, and film stock, and the Bukharan Commissariats for Education and for Trade and Industry, which provided capital and constituted the majority shareholders (with the remaining 55 percent).[40]

Bukhkino operated throughout the territory of the Republic of Bukhara but already looked ahead to the demarcation of national territories of late 1924, because its objective was "to create national Uzbek film activity" by producing films (fictions, news reports, agitprop films, and works of popular science), centralizing film theaters and other places to screen films, developing distribution networks, and establishing a profitable economic basis.[41] Logically, production was to be financed by distribution revenue, with a first set of films being sent by Sevzapkino. But this system was only viable if it was based on a satisfactory distribution and film theater network, as was the case in Russia and Ukraine.

In 1924 there were only three permanent cinemas in the Republic of Bukhara out of a total of seven cinema facilities in all.[42] Operating in permanent film theaters implied a significant turnover in programs, and the operating income only covered the cost of transporting films from Leningrad to the Republic of Bukhara and back again. Mobile cinema units were not particularly profitable either, because the transport and communication conditions, together with the presence of Basmachis, meant these units were unable to operate properly.

All the legal measures relating to Bukhkino's activities were drawn up and passed in September and October 1924, just before the territorial delimitation brought into question these attempts to organize film activity. But that did not prevent Bukhkino from launching its activities in late April 1924, immediately after the contract had been signed. Ten or so fiction films and a dozen news reports arrived in Bukhara on April 20, together with a first film crew to make ethnographic films and social reports. For the May Day celebrations, the inhabitants of Bukhara were able to see news reports produced by Sevzapkino, which were screened for free in several public places around the town.[43]

Between May and July 1924, the company produced five films with title cards in Russian and Uzbek: *In Central Asia* (*Po srednei Azii*), *Bukharan Children in Moscow* (*Bukhdompros v Moskve*), *The 5th Congress of Bukhara* (*V-i Vsebukharskii Kurultai*), *Opening Ceremony for the Railroad* (*Torzhestvennoe otkrytie Vostochno-Bukharskoi Zh. D.*), and *Bukhara on the Path to Cultural Renaissance* (*Bukhara po puti kul'turnogo vozrozhdeniia*). Fictions were also on the agenda, and the Commissariat for Education accepted plans for two feature-length films—*The Minaret of Death* and *Gul Saryk*—on reading the scripts (Bratoliubov 1976, 102). In October, the director Viskovskii arrived in Bukhara with a team of four people—transporting films with title cards in Uzbek, film, equipment, and material—to shoot *The Minaret of Death*, a "grandiose historical film" set in the seventeenth and eighteenth centuries (see chap. 2). Because the company was short of funding, certain shareholders, institutions, and leading political figures provided support in kind. Fayzulla Khojaev (1896–1938)—a major figure in the political history of Soviet Uzbekistan—allowed Bukhkino to use part of his house, which lay near the fortress in the old town.[44] The Bukharan government and the Commissariat for Trade agreed to provide traditional dress, saddles, and the many old weapons needed to shoot the films, and especially for *The Minaret of Death*, which required many accessories (costumes, weapons, and horses) and a very large number of extras for certain scenes (Bratoliubov 1976, 103–4).

### The Awakening of Soviet Uzbekistan (1924): Nation, Cinema, and Cultural Autonomy

Bukhkino operated for only ten months (from April to November 1924), but study of the early studios and of the reorganization of film activity provides a clear picture of how the territorial reconfigurations and redefinition of state prerogatives impacted the constitution of Central Asian national identities—and Uzbek identity in particular. The territorial delimitation of October 1924 resulted in national cultural autonomy in the domain of film. And the first national and independent film studios in the Soviet Federation appeared with the birth of Soviet Uzbekistan.

## Territorial Delimitation: National Demarcation for Soviet Unification

For the populations of Central Asia, the national question—which had been put on hold in 1921 before being rekindled at the Twelfth Congress of the All-Russian Communist Party in April 1923—took on full meaning and significance with the administrative and territorial delimitation of 1924. There has been lively historiographical debate about the nature and objectives of this Soviet political undertaking and about the extent to which Central Asian political figures were actively involved or passively submitted. Although the territorial reconfigurations genuinely radicalized the nationalization of Central Asian identities, homogenizing them into different categories, this process nevertheless issued directly from a change that was already taking place—at least in Uzbekistan—during the brief political experimentation of the Bukharan People's Soviet Republic (Khalid 2010).

### Preliminary Observations about the Historiography and Origins of the 1924 Territorial Delimitation

The 1924 territorial and administrative delimitation (and later that of 1936 for the Kazakh and Kyrgyz Soviet Socialist Republics) took place against the larger backdrop of territorial reconfigurations being carried out throughout the Soviet sphere (Martin 2001a, 31). It was a fundamental element in establishing modern nation-states in Central Asia and in the territorialization and ethnicization of national identities (Roy 1997, 11). The most complete study available is that by Arne Haugen, who rejects the ideas of "divide and rule," the "omnipotent regime," and the "people as victims." This vision of the situation, which had predominated until recently, viewed the delimitation as a new lever of domination instigated by the central authorities.[45] For Haugen, this way of viewing the delimitation results from teleological reasoning, concealing the fact that "cooperation and consensus" were still possible in the early 1920s (2003, 18, 29). The delimitation thus needs to be placed within the context of the NEP and the resulting transformations in both the economic field and the cultural and intellectual life of the Soviet republics.

In addition to these complex debates and the difficulties in apprehending the exact nature of the political intentions behind the delimitation, there is the colonial issue explored by Francine Hirsch, for whom the delimitation and the creation of nations provide a new model of colonization governed by three principles: a national (or ethnographic) principle, with the territory being organized to contain an ethnic majority and act as the foundation stone for nation building; an economic principle, enabling resources to be shared fairly among various territories; and a principle corresponding to the need to "maintain administrative order," invoked by the Soviet regime without necessarily providing any further explanation (Hirsch 2000, 202, 211). The delimitation thus generated a dual process of assimilation: First, various peoples were assimilated into national categories, tending toward their homogenization within a determined national sphere; second, these categories were assimilated in turn within the Soviet state. This way of viewing the process is related to a form of imperialism and conquest that uses political discourse about nationalities as a key instrument for subordinating and unifying people within a larger Soviet entity.

Clearly, Central Asian political leaders were able to influence Soviet policy, had their own specific political goals (which coincided on occasions with the overall line pursued by central policy), and played a decisive political role in creating Soviet Central Asia. It was equally clearly their intention to retain or win control over a vast territory corresponding to the former Russian Empire. This was expressed by Stalin in a letter to Lenin in September 1922, in which he reiterated that the peripheries had to rapidly and undeniably submit to the center.[46] This will to rule was built on the divisions brought about by creating national units that fragmented existing solidarities, which were sometimes perceived as a potential threat. These divisions crushed any pan-Turkist or pan-Islamist stirrings, with Islam being perceived as something to combat when promoting nationalities (Cadiot 2007, 131; Laruelle 2008, 201). Central power acted as the arbiter between national forces, playing on fluctuating states of union and disunion. The territorial delimitation enabled the central authorities to establish relationships of dependency and legislative and administrative subordination, which, in the long run, expanded to cover the economic, political, and cultural spheres in their entirety. Local initiatives sustained the subordination of the periphery. The first communist elites in Central Asia drew upon the emergent nationalist ideologies—contrary to the view put forward by Roy, for whom the creation of nations in Central Asia was not driven by any preexisting indigenous form of nationalism, and who denies vernacular social and political groups any capacity for action and thought (Roy 1997, 8, 11, 15).

It is difficult to ascertain exactly how the initial ideas about reconfiguring the territory of Central Asia into national units originated. It had been a latent issue for at least several years when it was brought up in early 1920 by Turar Ryskulov (1894–1938) at the Fifth Territorial Congress of the Communist Party of Turkestan and at the Third Conference of the Muslim Bureau (*Musbiuro*).[47] Ryskulov suggested creating a supranational state based on the unity of the peoples in the region, with a communist Turkestan acting as a "revolutionary magnet" to attract other oppressed Asian peoples and "overcome local differences within a larger Turkic identity" (Carlisle 1994, 104, 107). This first suggestion to reconfigure the territory was rejected by the Turkestan Commission (sent in late 1919 to establish Soviet power in Turkestan), with Mikhail Frunze in particular arguing that the issue needed to be dismissed since Soviet power and party organizations there were weak (Eisener 1994, 110; Carlisle 1994, 107). The question was put on hold before being brought up again in May 1920 by Ryskulov, who headed a delegation to Moscow to meet Lenin. The proposition was rejected once again.

Although Ryskulov seemed to have failed, the same cannot be said of the Bukharan elites. Fayzulla Khojaev had long cherished the idea of delimitation, for which a concrete plan started to emerge in the early 1920s (Haugen 2003, 18). It is hard to identify exactly who was behind this plan, because it resulted from a series of interactions between central leaders and local representatives of Soviet power in Turkestan. Nevertheless, the Twelfth Congress of the Soviets of Turkestan in February 1924 emphasized the need to move ahead to a more concrete phase of action. Delimitation became an issue in its own right.[48] The Turkestani elites tabled it at the Thirteenth Congress of the All-Russian Communist Party, which was visiting Turkestan, and subsequently the Central Committee of the Communist Party assumed a substantial role. Stalin, in a report about Turkestan affairs, confirmed "the need to move to working on and resolving the issue of delimiting the Central Asian republics."[49] The Central Asian Bureau—the intermediary of the Central Committee and the representative of Soviet authority across the Central Asian territory—played a key role in interpreting and presenting the situation in Central Asia. Moscow's omnipotence has, however, been brought into question by a recent focus on local actors involved in this delimitation process (Haugen 2003, 6, 76). The situation in Central Asia in the early 1920s (in the republics of Turkestan, Khorezm, and Bukhara) was characterized by the comparatively limited influence of the All-Russian Communist Party and Soviet authorities.

Government rhetoric presented delimitation as a voluntary union corresponding to the needs and expectations of the people themselves (Eisener 1994, 113). Stalin, in a 1925 speech to students at the Communist University of the Toilers of the East, praised the implementation of the Bolshevik territorial delimitation plan, asserting that it corresponded to the aspirations of the local populations.

> The time has now come when it has become possible for these scattered pieces to be *reunited in* independent states, so that the toiling masses of Uzbekistan and of Turkmenistan may be brought closer to the organs of power and linked solidly with them. The delimitation of Turkestan is, above all, the *reunion* of these scattered parts of these countries in independent states. That the states

later expressed the wish to join the Soviet Union as equal members of it merely shows that the Bolsheviks have found the key to the deep-rooted aspirations of the masses of the people of the East, and that the Soviet Union is a voluntary union of the toiling masses of different nationalities, the only one in the world. (Stalin 1925)

Speeches about nationality exerted a genuine power of attraction—of fascination even—over formerly colonized peoples, and they need to be placed within the European context of the collapse of empires (Khalid 2007a). Although some local leaders (Bolshevik or otherwise) put up resistance against the territorial delimitation project, the project encountered no monolithic opposition from the moment that there was no attack against Islam and local traditions (Carlisle 1994, 115), despite the existence of local conflicts and territorial claims pertaining to very specific frontier zones (Khamraeva 2006). Certain Soviet government dignitaries, such as the chairman of the Central Asian Economic Council, Nikolai Paskutskii, felt that the national demarcation bore the mark of "Greater Russian imperialism" (Carlisle 1994, 115). Others, such as Georgi Chicherin (1872–1936), the Commissar for Foreign Affairs for the RSFSR and then for the Soviet Union between 1918 and 1930, warned of the risk of exacerbating local interethnic conflict and of vehement protest from bordering parts of the Muslim world should the state of Bukhara disappear. All this occurred against the backdrop of Basmachi resistance and Russian/British rivalry in the "Great Game" playing out between them (Karasar 2002).

## A NATION AWAKES

The territorial delimitation resulted in Uzbekistan emerging as a strong central economic power. The Uzbek bourgeoisie viewed the delimitation as creating a vast territory, giving rise to great commercial opportunities, especially for the cotton-growing regions.[50] Fayzulla Khojaev initially refused—at a plenum of the Central Asian Bureau (in late January 1923)—that the Republic of Bukhara be politically or administratively united with the Republic of Turkestan, since the latter was part of the RSFSR.[51] But the territorial delimitation and creation of the Soviet republics, no longer as an integral part of the RSFSR, marked a concrete step toward comparative independence. Fayzulla Khojaev lent his official support to the project despite stating that the disappearance of "Bukhara the Venerable" might well upset the urban population, middle-class merchants, and peasants.[52] He felt that the creation of new states, which until 1929 included Tajikistan as an autonomous region within the Uzbek Soviet Socialist Republic, was a just return to the status quo ante and a solution to put an end the tsarist colonial policy, said to have been rooted in "divide and rule."

Looking at the new map of Central Asia, we are convinced that there is no other way to improve our economic situation. On this map there is no longer any distinction between Tajiks from the mountainous zones around Samarkand and Tajiks from the east of Bukhara. Everybody knows that we drink the water of the River Zeravshan and that we use it to irrigate our fields, and it is only when the Uzbeks of Bukhara and of Samarkand are united that there is no longer any tension over the water. The question of water—an essential question for Central Asia—resolves itself. What will happen if we destroy our old, artificially created frontiers and settle our accounts? Would it be worse if the two and a half million Bukharan Uzbeks were to unite with the Uzbeks of Turkestan to form an Uzbek Soviet Socialist Republic with a population of five to six million? . . . We would become the effective masters of a country drawn in a just and rational manner, of national republics by which we would automatically become members of the powerful Union of Soviet Socialist Republics. This event will be of grandiose significance for history. A new era is starting in the East. New republics, voluntarily supporting each other and uniting their forces, shall lead the peoples of the East on the road of liberation and rebirth to a glorious end. . . . . The East is turning the most important and most significant page in its history. (Khojaev 1970)

Uzbekistan was set up as a result of Bukharan reformists' influence and lobbying (see map 1.2). Thus, the newly founded Uzbekistan, with its capital in Samarkand, was viewed and presented by these elites as a new and more powerful extension of the Bukharan state (Carlisle 1994, 105).[53] When the people of Bukhara viewed this delimitation as renouncing their state independence, the government conducted a promotional campaign that presented things differently. Fayzulla Khojaev countered those who protested, saying: "We have said that we will not be 'united to,' but that the USSR is adjoining regions to us that had been taken away by the government of the tsars. Then, we said that we needed to unite in agreement with a certain part of the population and found an Uzbek Republic, since we were Uzbeks."[54] How valid was this official discourse? Khalid notes that after the 1926 publication of Fayzulla Khojaev's pamphlet *For a History of the Revolution in Bukhara*, there was a period of "hegemony of official doctrine over how Central Asian history was written" (2004, 140). Upon publication, Fayzulla Khojaev's version of the history of the Bukharan revolution was sharply criticized for assimilating "Jadidism" and "Bolshevism." It was, in fact, a corrected version, dating from 1932, that was included in his complete works when these were published in Tashkent in 1970 (Fedtke 1998, 492). After 1926, Soviet historiography progressively denied the role played by indigenous politicians in building the Soviet republics, instead constructing a past based primarily on the action of communist elites in Moscow. Nevertheless, Carlisle points out that "Fayzulla Khojaev did in fact fulfill the objectives that for centuries the Emirs of Bukhara had failed to realize; with Russian support he now

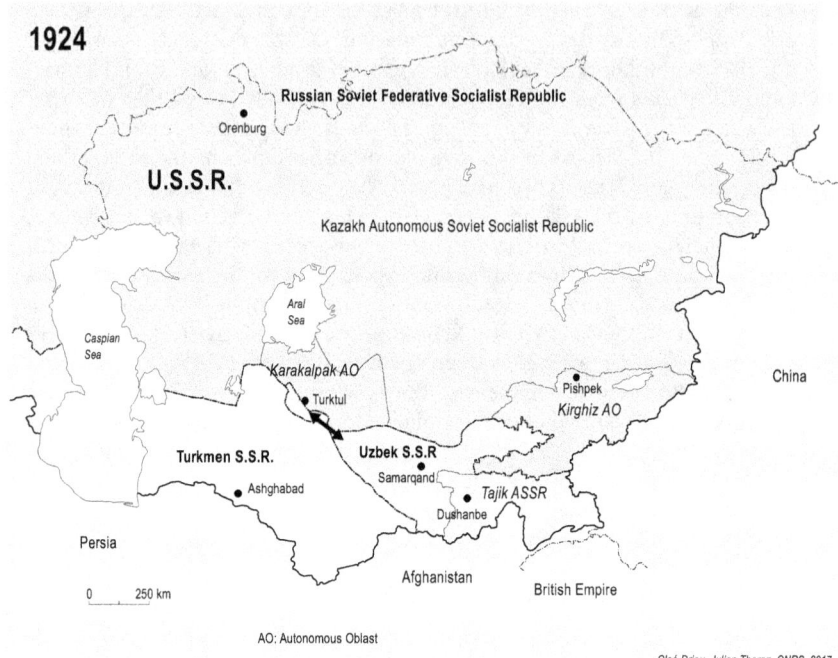

Map 1.2. Central Asia after the National-Territorial Delimitation of 1924. *Source*: Julien Thorez, 2011, "Les nouvelles frontières de l'Asie centrale: États, nations et régions en recomposition," Cybergeo, https://cybergeo.revues.org/23707. Translation: Cloé Drieu.

presided over the absorption of territories which had previously belonged to the Khanates of Kokand and of Khiva; he built a political entity reminiscent of the earliest periods" (1994, 111). And indeed, when speaking about the new state and the populations it comprised, Fayzulla Khojaev used two words to reunite two entities and insist on the inclusive nature of the territory: *millat*, designating the urban Muslim community, corresponding to Uzbeks without any tribal tradition (either Chaghatays or Sarts), and *qawm*, designating a tribal community dating back to the earliest tribes (Turks) (Baldauf 1991, 92).

While the plan for delimitation was undeniably a victory for the Bukharan elites, it was also a victory for the new Uzbek identity. This notion had been gestating within the Bukharan Peoples' Soviet Republic, with the idea emerging in the political realm in terms of a comparatively sedentary Turkestan identity. The plan was also a victory against the Kirghiz (Kazakh) elites, who were in favor of creating a Central Asian Federation, arguing that this would preserve a vast and economically united territory.[55] They were opposed to "cutting up a unique living organism," which would have problematic consequences, especially for the Kirghiz, Kazakhs, and Turkmens, who saw themselves allocated states that were

Figure 1.5. Fayzulla Khojaev (*front*) and the frontier delimitation commission. UzRKSOKh 4-4282.

not particularly viable.⁵⁶ The role to be played by Tashkent—a multiethnic capital and economic, cultural, and administrative center—was also a problem. In the end, the only ones to "unanimously support" the Central Asian Bureau's plan to delimit the territory in accordance with a national principle were the Uzbeks of Turkestan and of Bukhara. As part of the territorial delimitation, a study was carried out of the Tajik population and its distribution across the territory, with an eye to creating an autonomous Tajikistan region. But pro-Tajik positions were largely informal and unvoiced at the time of the delimitation, although they subsequently emerged rapidly (Fedtke 2007). Resentment against the Uzbeks bubbled up in the following years due to their "chauvinistic attitudes" toward Tajiks living outside the autonomous region (Fedtke 2007; Bergne 2007, 45–47, 102).

## The First Film Studios: National Autonomy and Federal Independence

The territorial delimitation reveals the important role of local populations and Central Asian communists in appropriating national categories (Haugen 2003, 117). It also marks the birth of an Uzbek state and an Uzbek nation that acquired autonomy and territory. Acceding to the status of "Soviet Socialist Republic" brought a new degree of independence, even if it was not full independence. The creation of these "independent" republics implied their de jure integration within the Union of Soviet Socialist Republics, resulting in their increasing dependence on the center.⁵⁷ Although in practical terms the Soviet nationalities policy initially amounted to national emancipation, it is clear—in fact, since Stalin's

1913 *Marxism and the National Question*—that the cultural national autonomy conceded was only transitory. On a more pragmatic (and cinematographic) level, the territorial delimitation and the setting up of a national state film body were perceived as a real step forward, primarily because the body in question had financial autonomy and enjoyed decision-making power at both the national and federal level.

THE PRIMACY OF NATIONAL INTERESTS

The territorial delimitation led to the restructuring and merging of the only two film organizations in the territory of the Uzbek Republic, Bukhkino and Turkkino, resulting in some rivalry. Bukhkino, the former Russo-Bukharan Film Company, hoped to become a Russo-Uzbek company and operate across the Uzbek Soviet Socialist Republic as a whole. This position was lent legitimacy by Fayzulla Khojaev's support of the initiative when he had been chairman of the Bukharan Council of People's Commissars. He was now chairman of the Revolutionary Committee of the Uzbek Soviet Socialist Republic and, as legal successor, was meant to enact former obligations he had contracted.[58] Fayzulla Khojaev had agreed in principle, stipulating, however, that the definitive decision would rest with the Uzbek Commissariat for Education. To this end, Sevzapkino management sought an agreement between the governments of the new administrative entities that had just been created (the Kazakh Autonomous Region, the Tajikistan Autonomous Republic, and the Turkmen Soviet Socialist Republic), which had agreed to become shareholders, hoping to establish a supranational body (with a production unit based in Tashkent) to produce appropriate films for their populations.[59]

This project was studied and accepted by the Central Asian Bureau and Komintern, but Bukhkino's track record for film production was patchy. The only fiction film it had made, *The Minaret of Death*, had been a commercial success (see chap. 2), but it was a propaganda failure due to lack of experience and a failure to understand the objectives of the former Bukharan government.[60] Sevzapkino management sought to conduct an apologia of its work in order to benefit from the new geopolitical situation and obtain the distribution and production monopoly for the Uzbek territory. This endeavor pitted Sevzapkino against Turkkino, which it denounced for having ceded its monopoly over distribution to Goskino. Turkkino, too, hoped to emerge victorious from this restructuring and warned the Uzbek education authorities against plans to restructure Bukhkino by turning it into a corporation. A new Russo-Uzbek company, dominated by Sevzapkino, would be largely independent, so it would be difficult to convince it to comply with the Uzbek authorities' ideological and economic obligations. Furthermore, collaborating with the Russian-based Sevzapkino organization might deprive film activity of any profits, which could be reinvested elsewhere. Last, ceding the monopoly over film production to a Russo-Uzbek entity would prevent other film companies from shooting on Uzbek territory.[61] It was thus suggested that an Uzbek state film company be set up, answerable to the head of the education authorities and with a monopoly over distribution. This proposition was accepted, and Turkkino was reorganized as Uzbekkino.[62]

Consequently, all the film companies operating on Uzbek territory now became part of Uzbekkino, which had exclusive rights over film production and distribution.[63] Sevzapkino, the Commissariat for External Trade, and the education authorities continued to quarrel, with tensions crystallizing around the liquidation of Bukhkino.[64] These quarrels finally died down when film activities in the Russian Soviet Federation were reorganized with Goskino being turned in Sovkino, which definitively asserted its monopoly across the entire territory of the federation. Sevzapkino's field of action was cut back to production, and even this was limited to the northwestern territories of the Federation (Bratoliubov 1976 106).

Uzbekkino's statutes were modified in light of these reorganizations and were definitively approved on August 1, 1925. Uzbekkino was no longer a corporation but a state enterprise financed by public and local funding.[65] Despite a plan to move to Samarkand—the new Uzbek capital—the company remained in Tashkent and managed to raise initial capital of 63,000 rubles, derived solely from distribution.[66] For the time being, the new entity operated only in distribution; a production unit had not yet been formed.

THE QUESTION OF JOINING VOSTOKKINO, THE FILM STUDIO
CONGLOMERATE FOR NATIONAL MINORITIES

All these restructurings bear witness to Uzbek national cultural autonomy—something that was confirmed when Uzbekkino refused to join Vostokkino, a group of production organizations from several republics and autonomous administrative entities, such as Kazakhstan, Bashkir, Tatar Autonomous Soviet Socialist Republic, Dagestan Autonomous Soviet Socialist Republic, and the Crimean Soviet Socialist Republic (Chomentowski 2009). Vostokkino had been set up in Moscow at the initiative of the Scientific Association for Oriental Studies, chaired by Mikhail Vel'tman (1871–1927), a member of the Commissariat of Nationalities from 1921 to 1923 and rector of the Moscow Institute of Oriental Studies as of 1921. Vostokkino's purpose was to produce films for publics in the Soviet East. The first suggestion to join was made in October–November 1924 and was turned down by the Commissariat for Education.[67] At the time, Uzbekkino was benefiting from an event that had accidentally boosted its independence: The latest contract between Sovkino and Turkkino to cede the distribution monopoly, signed in Moscow in December 1924, had not been recorded.[68] It thus exerted this monopoly once again, which was bringing in significant distribution revenues.[69]

The profits on this arrangement enabled Uzbekkino to accumulate 300,000 rubles in capital, with distribution covering not only the territory of Uzbekistan but that of Turkmenistan and Kazakhstan. According to its head, Uzbekkino was starting to control the network of film theaters. It had also managed to make some popular science films and regularly released newsreels. Studios were thus created, with a carpentry workshop, a technical workshop, the opening of a newsreel department equipped with a photo lab, and a studio to train film professionals (directors, camera operators, actors, and mechanics).

Anatoli Lunacharsky (1875–1933), the Commissar for Education since 1917, suggested again that Uzbekkino join Vostokkino. Vel'tman supported the participation of all the Soviet eastern regions in the project, stating that "the Soviet East, whose economic growth only started after the October Revolution, is too poor for each region of the USSR to set up its own production unit" (1927, 24). These propositions were turned down for a number of reasons: first, because Uzbekkino had enough initial capital to make a feature-length fiction film; second, because the material means at its disposal were proportionally greater than those of Vostokkino, which operated across a large geographical swath of regions, with divergent themes corresponding to its multiple audiences; and, finally, Vostokkino did not have a monopoly over distribution and so had to raise the capital required to produce films. Thus, Vostokkino's films needed to be commercially successful, which made for an urban public and skewed its activity away from its initial political objectives. The head of Uzbekkino concluded: "If Uzbekkino became a shareholder in Vostokkino, we would be obliged to shut down and put an end to the film organization we have successfully created, and which, with the territorial delimitation, is a pioneer in Central Asia. We must therefore categorically refuse to take any shares in Vostokkino."[70] But the question of joining Vostokkino remained open, and the head of Uzbekkino suggested observing how it functioned with an eye to perhaps joining Vostokkino in the future. The *Pravda Vostoka* greeted this refusal with an article titled "Uzbekkino Retains Its Autonomy," concluding with the words of the head of the Uzbek film organization: "We will thus be able to develop film production in Uzbekistan, which will produce the useful films that are eagerly awaited in the East."[71]

THE STAR OF THE EAST: THE FIRST UZBEK FILM STUDIOS

Launching film production was a relatively complex operation given the shortage of film managers, a phenomenon affecting the entire Soviet Union. Uzbekistan had to rely on professionals from neighboring republics who were already very busy, which necessitated squeezing film shoots and postproduction into a short time frame.[72] Uzbekkino sought to attract local intellectuals by sponsoring scriptwriting competitions—an initiative that was greeted with limited enthusiasm.[73]

Figure 1.6. The front of the Sheykhantaur madrasa (ca. 1930). UzRKSOKh 0-77376.

The lack of involvement of intellectuals was a recurrent problem, as was the lack of equipment and material; for the Soviet Union was not yet self-sufficient, and the studios had to import what they needed from abroad. Uzbekistan did not have the right to import from abroad, so it had to purchase equipment and film via the intermediary of a third-party Soviet republic that did have such a right in exchange for a hefty commission. Thus, the price of any film Uzbekkino purchased was double what it would have been if the film were bought directly from Berlin.[74]

Despite all this, the Star of the East (*Sharq Iulduzi*) workshops, photo laboratory, and cinema studios started operating in the buildings of the Ishankul madrasa in the Sheykhantaur neighborhood between the Tashkent old town and new town, which they took over in February 1925 (figs. 1.6 and 1.7).[75] They had to work alongside the former mullahs and students who were still there and who, according to Malik Kaiumov, viewed them with suspicion.[76] Management of the buildings was taken away from the directorate for pious foundations (*waqf*) and officially handed over to Uzbekkino.[77] The new Kino-fabrika, with its film studios, technical workshops, and photo laboratory, was equipped partly with material purchased in Baku and imported from the United States.[78]

Working conditions were very basic. It was hard to get the water that was needed for working in the laboratory and developing film. The electricity supply

Figure 1.7. The surrounding neighborhood (1930). UzRKSOKh 0-84877.

was not any better, with the laboratory being operational only between midnight and six in the morning, when the tramways were not running. The negatives were not stable, forcing the filmmakers and editors to produce duplicates of even poorer quality.[79] Lighting was makeshift, with Jupiter spotlights and studio projectors that were in poor condition. The wide variation in temperature also caused several problems. The buildings were not heated in winter, and the high summer temperatures made it difficult to develop and conserve film. The dry heat produced a fine dust that found its way into all the equipment and into the cameras. Film deformed due to the heat, and the light brought out particularly marked contrasts (of white clothing and outdoor scenes), making it difficult to focus and necessitating filters that compromised the quality of the image.[80]

Despite the many challenges, the establishment of a film organization with its own studios was viewed locally as a real step toward modernization. The idea was first raised by one of the founders of Muslim reformism in Central Asia, Mahmudhoja Behbudi, when discussing how theater, like the press, presented society with a mirror image of its faults, enabling it to improve.[81] A few months later, Mirmuhsin, a reformist intellectual from Tashkent, described the film theater as a place for edification (*dar al ibrat*).[82] Although these opinions were put forward before the First World War, it was not until 1924 that the region had a film studio, something other developed countries had been familiar with for several years. Film fascinated people by including audiences within a larger reality and, as a counterpart presenting this reality to them, acting as a window to the world: "Cinema is called the 'great mute' [*buiuk tilsiz*]. Cinema is indeed great. For anyone who can see can understand its language. The scale of cinema is great. In a film you can see twenty or thirty different places. Cinema can invade our life and thoughts. Thus no one can deny the greatness of cinema."[83]

Uzbekistan now had "unheard of and unbelievable things,"[84] in the words of an anonymous reader of *Yer Yuzi*, the first illustrated cultural daily in Central Asia. The reader invited people to welcome and take pride in this new film activity in Uzbekistan. Not only could cinema produce films about the population and life in the country, there was no doubt that the other peoples of Russia and Western Europe would watch Uzbek film productions with interest: "As things stand, the specificities of Uzbekistan are not revealed to the world. This can be compensated for by film production. Film is a very important thing for simply representing and giving life a soul. Thus, thanks to film, the 'mysteries' of the East and those of Uzbekistan will be able to reveal all their truth."[85]

# 2 Revolutionary Exoticism and the Colonial Imaginary

## *Cinema and Entertainment (1924–27)*

WHAT MYSTERIES AND truths did the films produced between 1924 and 1928 reveal about the East? These films were set in prerevolutionary colonial—and sometimes medieval—Turkestan, and they were all made by nonindigenous filmmakers invited by local institutions to come with their film crews. The creation of a national Uzbek studio in charge of film production shows that the ruling elites thought that cinema needed to serve the government. Uzbekistan—which inherited the structures of the now-defunct Bukhkino and Turkkino—had significant control levers due to its newly acquired cultural autonomy. But a key element was still lacking: filmmakers from vernacular societies.

Thus, the films made during this initial period relay the vision that filmmakers from Russia had of Central Asia, inspired by the oriental films that were fashionable at the time. Their films, analyzed as discourse embodying a social imaginary that was a relic of a former imperial hegemony, had much in common with films produced in European empires and the United States, such as George Melford's *The Sheik* (1921) and Raoul Walsh's *The Thief of Bagdad* (1924). Many aspects of these films issue from orientalism as denounced by Edward Said, and they are similar to earlier literature and art exploring oriental themes, such as Vasili Vereshchagin's (1842–1904) paintings, for instance (de Meaux 2010, 61, 367–72; Schimmelpenninck van der Oye 2009). This observation holds true in two of the three meanings Said attributed to orientalism, being both a "style of thought based on the ontological and epistemological distinction between 'the Orient' and (most of the time) 'the Occident'" and "a Western style for dominating, restructuring, and having authority over the Orient" (Said 1979, 2–3). The Orient/Occident (Russia) dichotomy, which was very marked in both the Russian Empire and the Soviet Union, provided a justification for conquest and for a new sort of civilizing mission (Khalid 2000a, 697). While the frontiers of this imaginary geography were somewhat flexible regarding the zone of intersection between Orient and Occident, they were far less so regarding Central Asia. Orientalism as a cultural and political fact transpires in the cultural hegemony to be found in the films discussed here.

Each empire had its own Orient, its own colonies, natives, and intrepid horsemen, its own sandy deserts and caravans, its own odalisques, harems, and dancers. From the earliest days in the United States and Europe, filmmakers explored the distant and the foreign—Thomas A. Edison's *Ella Lola* depicts Sioux dances and belly dancers, while the Egypt of the pharaohs is the backdrop for Georges Méliès's *The Terrible Turkish Executioner* (1904) and *The Monster* (1903). A bit later, the Drankov studios in Russia released *Stenka Razin* (1908). Other films from the prerevolutionary period depict Jewish and Rom populations, but it was not until a few years later that the peoples of the Soviet Orient (Central Asia and Caucasia) appeared on-screen (Chomentowski 2009, 110–18; Stites 1992, 13–14).

European film production during the period 1900–1940 needs to be set within the context of colonial expansion. Film made people aware of the scale of the empire and resonated with public opinion by diffusing images of an elsewhere that enthused audiences; the resultant social imaginary provides a privileged way of apprehending societies' reactions to territorial expansion (Ferro 2003, 22). Film provided a way for the social imaginary to appropriate a vast territory, bringing back a trove of moving images that looked fully real. Cinema and photography were the media for this geographical expansion, but they were also its mediators, and as of the earliest days, camera operators traveled the world to bring back striking new images (Castro 2008). Official discourse in the Soviet Union might have been resolutely anti-imperialist, yet these films conveyed an imaginary realm of conquest, comparable to films made in other European centers of power. The filmmakers and production organizations operated according to the same principles as those prevalent at the end of the Russian Empire, being motivated by commercial gain. Film was a profitable form of entertainment, and producers were more attentive to public taste and meeting demand than they were to assuming the role of political educator that the party wished to see them adopt and that certain filmmakers fulfilled voluntarily. Film still held out against politics, despite an early hybridized form combining a declining colonial imaginary with emergent Bolshevik discourse.

The five films explored in this chapter can be divided into two types: "oriental fantasy" films depicting heroic adventures set in an unreal Orient, drawing many of their stereotypes from European and Hollywood oriental films as described by John Eisele (2002, 70); and "realist colonial" films that discredited and stigmatized indigenous populations and their way of life. In this second category, the depictions of natives, the relationship between the center (Russia) and peripheries (colonies), and people's relationship to the territory are largely comparable to French colonial cinema (Benali 1998). That cinema was a relatively unified genre based on a narrative structure opposing modern, developed mainland France to a "primitive" Orient (Slavin 1997, 24; O'Brien 1997). However, despite this exotic colonial vein, there were some timid showings of political discourse. The films sketched out the official codes of representation, even though these were not yet full-fledged. Filmmakers sought to prefigure the causes of an imminent indigenous revolution, though without much conviction or particular persuasiveness.

## Soviet Exoticism and the Orient as Fantasy

The first feature-length fiction films made in Central Asia, *The Minaret of Death* by Viacheslav Viskovskii (Bukhkino, 1925) and *The Muslim Woman* by Dmitri Bassalygo (Proletkino, 1925), exemplify the Soviet oriental fantasy film. These Soviet "Easterns," while meant to promote the new ideology to the populations in the Soviet East, were beyond the control of the political authorities, who did not yet have the means to ensure the films' ideological quality. In practice, oriental films (*vostochnaia kartina*) were entertainments, primarily targeted at publics in large towns and cities, as confirmed by the fact that they were often released in Russia several months before being released in Uzbekistan (see table 2 in appendix). These oriental films referred to a Soviet East which, pace Smith (1997), was not limited to the Muslim realms of Caucasia and Central Asia and the shamanic, Buddhist, and animist sphere of Siberia and the Far East (thereby excluding Christian peoples). In fact, the Soviet East included republics that were not part of the Slavic world. Georgia and Armenia fell somewhere between the two categories; when they were associated with the Soviet East, they figured among oriental republics at a "superior stage of nation-building" (Martin 2001, 127, Stalin 1925).

### *Film Experimentation in the Hollywood of the East*

In the mid-1920s, the filmmakers working in Central Asia were mandated by their studios (Viskovskii by Sevzapkino and Bukhkino), approached by party organizations (Bassalygo and Proletkino by the Central Asian Bureau), or were later invited by Uzbekkino, the newly created Uzbek organization in charge of film production and distribution. In addition to being attracted by the high likelihood of financial gain, the filmmakers were motivated by the possibilities for experimentation when filming outside in favorable conditions. Filmmakers were attracted to Uzbekistan—and to Baku, which was meant to become the "Hollywood of the East" (Smith 1997, 652)—by the natural and climatic conditions, which were sometimes compared to those in California. Shooting a film in this region, which, according to technicians sent there, had nearly three hundred days of sunshine per year, made it possible to avoid working on set in a studio, which was expensive and required a lot of electricity.[1] Uzbekistan's continental climate offered a "stark alternative to the overcast skies" of northern Russia, while the wealth of nature, varied landscapes, and populations with "typical and characteristic" faces were a serious and particularly "cinegenic" advantage.[2]

Film expeditions were presented as epic journeys bringing to light how sincere and naïve the local populations were. Crew members were exposed to dangers, such as the crew on *The Muslim Woman*, for instance, who were heroic in working in places where the mountains and caves "were 'crawling' with what was left of the defeated bands of Basmachis . . . ready to pounce on them at a moment's notice."[3]

However, this sort of description was not specific to Central Asian populations, and some film expeditions were greeted "with sticks and stones in certain European regions of the USSR."[4] Mesguich, when working in Russia twenty or so years earlier (in 1898), had on several occasions encountered unpleasant circumstances while filming at the Nizhny-Novgorod fair. He describes the "fanaticism" of the spectators and how these "primitive" people found it impossible to understand the mechanism of cinema; to their minds, it could only be explained by "the operation of a supernatural power," and the audience left making the sign of the cross (Mesguich 1933, 21–22). Shooting a film could be a challenging adventure for the crew when confronted with such backwardness. It was also a civilizing mission. The film expeditions for *The Muslim Woman*, for instance, were devised as a way to modernize the region and left "profound traces in the monotonous life of the population," bringing new ideas and new rhythms, breaking the way of life and traditions dating back a thousand years or more.[5]

This discovery of new places was accompanied by an explicit desire for realism that the directors and actors saw as a way of pushing the boundaries of what they had been trained to do. On the shoots for *The Eyes of Andozia* (*Klokochushchii Vostok*, or *Glaza Andozii*) and *The Muslim Woman*—half of which was shot outdoors, a feat of technical prowess for the period—the director, Bassalygo, sought to achieve perfect mimeticism between the Russian actors and "real Uzbeks" by avoiding the use of sets and spotlights.[6] The actors in *The Muslim Woman*, which used solely local extras, only had a dozen days to prepare for the shoot. The actor O. Tretiakova inquired about the customs of women and learned how to dance, while the actor G. Levkoev soaked up the ambience of the town in order to play the main character, Umar.

And yet, despite the praise for these films' authenticity and typicality and the realism the film crews strove for, the image they gave of the East was significantly derealized by the Russian studios' poor-quality reconstitution of Bukharan interiors and by the fairy-tale life of the harem. The veracity of the external scenes was thus undermined by the picturesque, fantastic scenes that were shot indoors. The Orient as represented in these films is "transposed and delocalized"—a characteristic they have in common with colonial films (Benali 1998, 33). This was expressed by Bassalygo about *The Eyes of Andoziia*, a film with an anticolonial theme, when he observed that he chose Turkestan because it was an "archetypal Orient" (*uslovnyi vostok*) (quoted in Vel'tman 1927, 5), justifying his choice on the grounds that he could not go to India or some other colony. Turkestan could have acted as a good example—having been a Russian colonial military province, though Bassalygo was not aware of this—but it instead became "Andoziia, the flourishing colony of one of the great European powers" (quoted in Vel'tman 1927, 5). Bassalygo shows a territory, people, and setting that enabled him to figure a different reality, thereby stripping them of their colonial past and the imperial domination they had undergone. The Orient becomes an imaginary territory, and the film conveys no clear awareness of its frontiers or of its belonging to the Soviet sphere. This is a characteristic feature of 1920s cinema, in which space seems limitless, vast, and unknown—in contrast to the conception of space in films from the 1930s, which reveal a precise awareness of frontiers to be defended against the threat from without or the enemy within (Widdis 2003a).

The representation of Central Asia is thus ultimately disconnected from its own specific social, human, and historical reality, and instead hitched to a foreign colonial reality through the interplay of cinematographic influences. In *The Minaret of Death*, the Basmachis look just like Arabian horseman dressed in white with their turbans and sabers; the harems are populated with dancers; and Oleg Frelikh, the film's main actor, is virtually a replica of Rudolph Valentino in *The Sheik*.

People working on the average production (that is, leaving aside great works of cinematography) rarely showed any great originality, borrowing from foreign films produced by European companies that had been competing with the Americans since 1923. These foreign films, which were distributed in the Soviet Union until the late 1920s (Tsikounas 1992, 89) and probably beyond, were a great success with European, American, and Soviet audiences. Ernst Lubitsch's *Sumurun* (Germany, 1920), Joe May's *The Mystery of Bombay* (Germany, 1921), and Walsh's *The Thief of Baghdad* (United States, 1924) were just some of the films to be shown on Soviet screens, and the audiences' preference went to such foreign actors as Douglas Fairbanks, Mary Pickford, Harold Lloyd, and Charlie Chaplin (Kenez 1992, 72; Leyda 1976, 238).

The oriental film was in vogue and an object of fierce competition between studios in the United States and in Europe, particularly in Germany.[7] Soviet filmmakers were inspired by the fantastic Orient of foreign films, which acted as the theater for incredible and historically incoherent adventures. They arrived in the Orient from Moscow and Leningrad "full of kindliness and curiosity" and still under the influence of countless variants of the "Arabian nights" (Kaiumov 1982, 13). The audiences had been prepared by orientalist novels and by short clips produced by operators traveling around the world looking for fresh new images (Slavin 1997, 24). Oriental films went on to provide a means of linking narration and image to a geographical sphere with which the audiences of the Soviet Union were progressively becoming familiar.

### The Minaret of Death: *The First Soviet Oriental Film—Revolutionary Conflagration and Love at First Sight*

*The Minaret of Death*, the first oriental film to be made in the Soviet Union, was the work of Viacheslav Viskovskii (1881–1933), who had started his career in 1915 by writing screen adaptations of popular novels and classical plays for various film organizations. In 1917, he started making melodramas and historical films before migrating to the United States in 1920. On returning several years later, he was hired by the Sevzapkino studios for *The Minaret of Death*, his third film, and then by Sovkino in 1928 to make *The Mullah's Third Wife*, about the policy to emancipate Tatars in Kazan.[8]

Filming on *The Minaret of Death* started in October 1924 in Bukhara and was completed in February 1925 in specially built pavilions in Leningrad. It was promoted in the press,[9] and the head of the Russo-Bukharan studios was very enthusiastic about the first shots, with images exceeding "all expectations" and the scene of the emir's downfall and the taking of the fortress involving between three thousand and five thousand Central Asian extras: "The realism of the assault is stupendous. The peasants from the surrounding villages (within forty to sixty kilometers) who were filmed that day were so fully in their role that they climbed the fortress walls and crossed the ramparts and intake channels with cries and an inimitable naturalness and savagery, to the point where we were scared when viewing the rushes."[10]

About ten thousand people were involved in the film, and agitation work was carried out with the local extras,[11] for staging recent history made it possible to "reawaken in the eyes of those present the horror of the Emirate that the people had recently experienced."[12]

---

*The Minaret of Death* (Rus. *Minaret Smerty*, Uzb. *Azhal Minareti*) by Viacheslav Viskovskii (Bukhkino, 1925)

Jemal (N. Vendelin), a beautiful young woman from Khiva, and her servant Safo (Baranova) want to go to Bukhara, but they are captured by Basmachi bandit on the way there (I. Jalilov). The two women manage to escape and meet the courageous *jigit* Sadyq (O. Frelikh), who falls in love with Jemal—a feeling she reciprocates. Jemal and Safo head back to Khiva, but on the way they are once again taken prisoner, this time by the emir of Bukhara (A. Bogdanovskii), who is pillaging the town. The emir's court holds a great celebration in honor of their victory over the people of Khiva and organizes a *bozkashi* with Jemal as the trophy. Sadyq wins, but the emir's son, Shahrukh (I. Talanov), is jealous of this victory and the trophy that is eluding him. He kidnaps Jemal from Sadyq and offers her a place of choice in his harem. The emir wishes to punish Shahrukh and "send him to Allah's paradise," but the emir is stabbed by his son and dies. Shahrukh accuses Jemal of the murder and throws her in prison. He becomes the new emir and is even more tyrannical than his father. Sadyq incites the oppressed peasants to revolt, and they enter the fortress and free the prisoners. Finally, it is Shahrukh who perishes, thrown from the top of the minaret, where Sadyq passionately embraces Jemal.

The film is inspired by a legend in which one of the emir of Bukhara's wives, having committed adultery, is to be put to death by being thrown from the top of the Kalân minaret, but she is saved by her many layers of clothing, which break her fall. The film includes many scenes of the harem and palace, interspersed with entertaining interludes typical of the "cinema of attractions," with fire-breathers, contortionists, dances with snakes, and "traditional" dance forms that are wholly inauthentic but part of the field of popular entertainment that dominated films of the first two decades of the twentieth century (Studlar 1995). The film does not strictly speaking convey a colonial imaginary in that it does not discredit the native world. But several title cards and expressions reveal a degree of naiveté and lack of knowledge of local history, with the Basmachis being designated as the bad guys, for instance, and a reference to the "bandit Ataman," which applies a Cossack title (Ataman) to Central Asian Basmachis (bandits) while depicting them with stereotypes of Arabian warriors on horseback.

The representations are exotic, presenting unusual landscapes, settings, and people that are removed from reality. Seventeenth-century Bukhara is shown as a prerevolutionary place and used as a pretext for a love story that in fact constitutes the hero's sole "revolutionary" motivation. The love intrigue is thus, as the critics noted with irony, the "driving force behind class struggle," and it is only at the end of *The Minaret of Death* that the political and social domination the people undergo at the hands of the emir is evoked, leading them to rise up against the emir's son. Love for a woman as a motivation for overthrowing the oppressor was one of the major motifs of cinema of the period (Vel'tman 1927, 9).

### Exoticizing Rewritings: The Example of The Muslim Woman

While *The Minaret of Death*, though produced by Bukharan studios, was wholly conceived by filmmakers and a scriptwriter who were not from the region, this was not the case of *The Muslim Woman*. This film provides a different example of how Central Asian reality was exoticized. The film was commissioned from Proletkino by the Women's Division of the Central Asian Bureau. In November 1924, the two institutions signed a contract in Tashkent setting out the obligations and financial contribution of each party. Out of a total budget of 27,000 rubles, the Women's Division was to provide 10,000 rubles, Proletkino 8,000 rubles, and the Revolutionary Committee 9,000 rubles.[13] The film was to be distributed by Proletkino, and the Women's Division would receive 50 percent of the distribution income once Proletkino had recouped its costs. The script for *The Muslim Woman*—the original title of which was *Karim's Daughter*—was jointly written in 1924 in Tashkent by Anatoly Mayer and Serafima Liubimova, who had been head of the Women's Division for many years. Unfortunately, only three of the seven parts of the original script have been found in the RGASPI archives.[14] The script is for a film about the "modern life of women in the East" and their emancipation, emphasizing the work done by women's clubs.

The original script emphasizes the social situation, and the conflicting pulls exerted by a traditional society on the one hand and the emerging political model on the other hand are presented through two main characters: Ali Khojaev, a Bolshevik devoted to his cause, and Zeynab, Karim's daughter, who is to be married against her will. The surviving parts of the script emphasize the work conducted by the women's club, illustrated by Zeynab being freed from her physical and psychological imprisonment. The script presents the broader social and political context (the Basmachi rebellion and the domination of landowners over seasonal workers), and the reality portrayed by the film is relatively complex. Yet some scenes come across as clichéd, although it is difficult to ascertain how they would have been perceived in the context of the period. Such is the case, for instance, with the description of the "clean and comfortable" club with "posters, diagrams, and drawings on the walls," while "a choir of Uzbek women accompanied by a piano perform the *Internationale* in their mother tongue."[15] Women in the background listen to a young Uzbek woman reading aloud from *Yangi Yol*, the first women's newspaper (Ernazarov and Akbarov 1977, 33–34). Men also go to the women's club, as Zeynab discovers when she arrives with Turkmen women sold for the *kalym* and Uzbek women beaten by their husbands.

The director, Dmitri Bassalygo (1886–1969), who had started his career during the imperial period, did not retain much of the original script suggested by the Women's Division.[16] The film crew arrived in Tashkent in February 1925 and set up quarters in the old town of Bukhara, where they worked with a woman in charge of the women's emancipation policy. Bassalygo considered the initial script to be poor, and he used it as a rough draft that underwent numerous alterations, including a title change.[17] He acknowledged that he had talked with women who attended the women's clubs but did not draw on this experience even though it had been informative. Despite Bassalygo's acknowledgment, the Moscow newspaper *Vecherniaia Moskva*, in its July 2, 1925, issue, promoted the film on the basis of its authenticity, referring to how it had been inspired by accounts provided by people working in the Women's Division.

Unfortunately, the film has not been conserved in Uzbekistan or Russia, though a copy might exist in Europe or Latin America, where it was sold extensively. Thus, although it is difficult to discuss the film, the available documents clearly show how the original script was substantively reworked.[18] The seasonal worker Karim has become a gardener named Sheykhuly, and his daughter Zeynab is now named Saodat. The Bolshevik Ali Khojaev is replaced by the seasonal worker Umar, whom Saodat (Zeynab) falls in love with, and, in return, Saodat's "eyes light up with happiness when she hears his songs of love." The Basmachis of the original script are now the men of the wealthy Ahmet Bai, who notices Saodat and convinces her father to agree to their marriage. There follow a series of kidnappings and chases until Saodat leaves to study in Moscow.

> *The Muslim Woman* (Rus. *Musul'manka*, Uzb. *Musulman qyzy*)
> by Dmitri Bassalygo (Proletkino, 1925)
>
> The rich landowner Ahmet Bai (N. Beliaev) forcibly gives his daughter Guliar in marriage to an old man named Nurul Bai (B. Burov). During the wedding, Ahmet Bai notices a young woman, Saodat (O. Tret'iakova), the daughter of a gardener named Sheykhuly (N. Firsov). Ahmet Bai negotiates with Sheykhuly to arrange his marriage with Saodat, who is in love with the seasonal worker Umar (G. Levkoev) and suspects nothing. Saodat dreams of emancipation and attends the women's club until the day when one of her friends tells her of her imminent marriage to Ahmet Bai. Saodat is overcome by sadness and tries to refuse the marriage. Her father beats her and shuts her away. She manages to escape but unfortunately encounters Ahmet Bai. The wedding is fixed for the next day. Umar disguises himself as a woman and helps Saodat to flee. She takes refuge in the women's club, where she becomes interested in science and even becomes the club's delegate. However, Ahmet Bai asks Urbashi and his Basmachis to kidnap her. They take her to a ruined village. Urbashi in turn is won over by Saodat's courage and beauty and chases away Ahmet Bai. Saodat resists him, and Umar arrives just in time to save her. A few days later Saodat goes to study in Moscow.

The motivations of those who commissioned the script clearly differed from those involved in producing the film. The objective of the Women's Division of the Central Asian Bureau was to make a social and educational film for a female Muslim population, illustrating the tensions running through society. Emphasis was thus placed on the work of the Women's Division and its role in the emancipation policy. Bassalygo, for his part, was motivated by commercial gain and changed the story to include numerous twists and turns that were not part of the initial idea. Proletkino produced the film (and distributed it) within the context of the New Economic Policy, with profitability being a key component. The advertising inserts published in the September 1995 *ARK* journal emphasize the oriental exoticism and promote the film by noting that, for the first time on-screen, there were "luxurious views of Bukhara, Tashkent, and Samarkand," together with "many interesting and striking moments" as well as picturesque sketches of the oriental way of life (social life, harems, and the customs of Muslim society). The initial project for a "protest film" (Liubimova 1928a, 33) gave way to an adventure film wagering on exoticism.

## Public Satisfaction and Political Disappointment with the First Oriental Films

"How beautiful it is!" one spectator cried on seeing the opening images of *The Minaret of Death*. Then laughter broke out in the room when an old man went by on his donkey. A "long loud laugh" also welcomed the title card, "It is thanks to you, Allah, that they left me my khalat on which I can pray to you." These are the words of the poor man who has exchanged his camels for the horses that Jemal and Safo have stolen from the Qorbashi in order to escape. The action then returns to the streets of the old town: "What a beautiful film! It's very beautiful!" Then the emir of Bukhara comes back from pillaging Khiva and is surrounded by his subjects in stately dress: "Interesting! It's wonderfully well made!" The observations that members of the Association of Cinema Workers wrote down at a screening of *The Minaret of Death* at the Fantomas Cinema in Moscow on January 15, 1926, are not particularly numerous.[19] The audience was composed primarily of women, most of whom were workers or assistants. On leaving, they praised the film, but without any particular enthusiasm. The women had enjoyed it more than the men. While it was being screened, someone had said it was beautiful, and the general impression was that it was "good but lacking in depth." Some people were skeptical, however, and wondered, "What was the link with the minaret?"

Despite this lukewarm reception, *The Minaret of Death* was a success in the Soviet Union (Abul'khanov 1962, 64). It was screened on February 10, 1925, in Tashkent for members of the government, then was released publicly to great success, including in the old town.[20] A report by the Workers' and Peasants' Inspectorate observes that, while the local population did not watch foreign and Russian films, attendance increased by 40 percent when *The Minaret of Death* was released.[21] Like other oriental films such as *The Muslim Woman*, it was on the program for several months, which is indicative of its success.[22] The Women's Division acquired twenty copies translated into Uzbek.[23] Kaiumov remembers having greatly enjoyed watching these two films on the screens of the old town of Tashkent when she was only twelve or so: "I found the legend of *The Minaret of Death* in Bukhara amazingly entertaining. . . . It had everything—escapes, chases, harems, and lastly the minaret of death from which is thrown not the beautiful heroine but the handsome Shahrukh, the cruel son of the Emir" (Kaiumov 1982, 13).

Whereas the film was appreciated by the general public, certain intellectuals, such as the writer Abdulla Qodiry (1894–1938), found the representations somewhat laughable.[24]

> Thus far the scenes and images of our daily life conveyed in films about the life of the Uzbeks and the customs of the Central Asian peoples in general

have clearly been fictions. This situation is not specific to cinema. In the literature, journals, and European and Central Asian newspapers currently being published, there are lots of "horrors" in the extracts about us, and similar legends and inventions in the films. Naturally, an Uzbek cannot but laugh when confronted with these representations. And in reply to this slight, he jokes a while with his friends and those with a good sense of humor about this "artistic discovery."[25]

Some politicians, such as Turar Ryskulov, claimed that this sort of production met with "abject political failure" in the national republics and that the Uzbeks viewed them with "disgust"—to such an extent that some audience members left the film theater (quoted in Ol'khov 1929, 96).[26] Certain oriental films produced in the Soviet Union were viewed in the 1960s as the result of "European colonizing pretentions," and Bassalygo was accused of having based his US work on American experience in producing colonial films (Abul'khanov 1962, 66, 68). The Uzbek press reacted favorably to *The Muslim Woman*; the wedding scene and the scene when Saodat is bought were regarded as "noteworthy" and "of great interest": "*The Muslim Woman* is one hundred times closer to us, not least because its action takes place in the Soviet Uzbekistan of today and concerns one of the most vital issues in our customs—the emancipation of Uzbek women. The great success of the film lies in its provision of a sufficiently true portrayal of the living conditions in which women live not only in Uzbekistan but throughout the East."[27]

The commercial success of *The Minaret of Death* was not limited to the Soviet Union, and it was widely distributed abroad. On November 15, 1927, it was sold to fourteen countries, including Germany, Austria, Romania, Yugoslavia, and numerous Latin American countries (including Venezuela, Colombia, Ecuador, Bolivia, Peru, Chile, and Argentina).[28] France and the United Kingdom did not purchase the film. A year later it had been sold to twenty-nine countries.[29] It was fifth in the 1928 ranking of Soviet films by foreign sales, just behind Vsevolod Pudovkin's *Mother* (sold in thirty countries) and ahead of Protazonov's *Aelita* (twenty-eight countries) and Sergei Eisenstein's *Battleship Potemkin* (twenty-seven countries), although this last film topped the chart of foreign sales revenues.

The difference in the opinion of the public and that of political leaders was flagrant. The specialized press might appreciate or criticize films, praising *The Thief of Bagdad* for its special effects, for instance, while the critics relaying political opinion in Tashkent and Russia denounced the "exotic orientalism" and the influence this sort of film exerted over the public, studios, and directors.[30] The cinematic representations generated by exotic adventure tales, Bassalygo's "archetypal Orient," and the absence of any clear political message prevented the audience from identifying with the characters in the film, even though propaganda films need to be based on such a process. As Vel'tman observed regarding *The Eyes of Andozia*, "It is not surprising that a worker or peasant from the East is unable to find this Andoziia on the map—for it is the unfounded fruit of an author's fantasy" (1927, 5). The political authorities insisted on using cinema to educate people and to represent the grandeur of the Soviet Union, its peoples, and their diverse traditions, with all the rigor of an ethnographic exploration of the wealth of the Soviet human multitude.[31] This is also what Kaiumov suggests in recognizing that the Orient of *The Minaret of Death* is off the scale in its exoticism, writing that it would have been better to observe the exotic "not in the harems and palaces of the khans, but outside, in the people, and their customs, languages, way of life, and traditions" (1982, 13). Bukhkino's involvement in producing *The Minaret of Death* ought to have guaranteed the realism of the film.[32]

The director of *The Minaret of Death* was unanimously criticized for his incapacity to use "the rich ethnographic material of Bukhara." Instead of conveying "the true Orient," "it is an endless ballet with an unconvincing and highly improbable happy ending," in which "the ethnography is undermined and eclipsed by the poor and personal plot." The Orient becomes the "pretext for a tawdry passing libidinous romance" in a film described as "Turkish delight."[33] "The harem and odalisque triumph on the screen in all their honeyed chic."[34] The critic for the Moscow newspaper *Trud*, writing in its December 12, 1925, issue, wondered what the point was of spending money on an expedition to Bukhara with such a script. Even the author who had put forward the idea behind the film was surprised by the results: "My God! That doesn't look like Bukhara at all."[35] When the film was screened for members of the Association of Cinema Workers, the scriptwriter defended himself, declaring that nothing had remained of his script. Blame was attributed primarily to the director.

Political criticism focused on the importance to be attributed to "Soviet construction" and the presence of official bodies to account for political and social progress. For these critics, cinema should generate cultural and economic awareness of prior colonial oppression.[36] But there were not enough scenes showing the struggle of the people against the former authorities, while the love plot and string of kidnappings diluted the meaning of those that did exist. *The Minaret of Death* failed in terms of both political education and the ethnographic expectations placed on it. Being a "banal, flat, and exotic bourgeois film," it "had no social meaning" and was an instance of "pre-revolutionary boulevard cinematography," "an expensive and large-scale flop . . . for a public of NEPmen."[37] The film's director, Viskovskii, went through a critical phase, and it was even said that he had committed suicide.[38]

The spontaneous and uncontrolled production of oriental films, together with the representation they conveyed of the Orient, was considered as a hindrance to their export (with countries such as Turkey, Russia, and China being key targets).[39] The fear was expressed that *The Muslim Woman* might offend the peoples of the East, but Kemalist Turkey showed interest in the film.[40] The formation of the Russian-Bukharan Cinematographic Company ought to have met the need for an export channel to neighboring countries such as Persia, Turkey, Afghanistan, and even India.[41] For Vel'tman and other critics, the problems stemmed from the dearth of scriptwriters.[42] The poor quality of scripts with the Orient as their main theme was part of a more general problem of mediocre scripts during a period of crisis (Rubailo 1976, 23). In 1924, 85 percent of the scripts submitted to the Russian Committee for Cinematography (Goskino) were turned down on the grounds that they were useless, lacking in ideological content, or aesthetically poor (Vel'tman 1927, 4). The situation was much the same the two following years. The causes put forward for the subpar scripts are the lack of managers from local cultures, the general impoverishment of literature, and the scarcity of ethnographic documents for scriptwriters to use.[43]

## Colonialism Meets Sovietism: Hybridizing Discourses of Domination

Discussions about the chronic crisis affecting scripts and criticism of early oriental films both converged on the idea that the Soviet films representing the Orient had to become both more realistic and adopt a clear political angle. But this enjoinder to adopt realism led to a clear devaluation of formerly indigenous populations—an outcome that is evident in the three films that will now be analyzed: *From Under the Vaults of the Mosque*, made by Kazimir Gertel' in 1927 about the aborted emergence of a revolution in Central Asia; *The Leper* (1928) by Oleg Frelikh; and, to a lesser extent, *The Second Wife* (1927) by Mikhail Doronin. The latter two films deal with the reclusion of women and the impossibility of setting them free. The unity of representation in these three films derives from the fact that they treat the same historical period and often involved the same scriptwriters (Sobberey, Seifullina), directors, and actors (Messerer, Chechelashvili).

### Sovietized Muslims and the Impossibility of Portraying a Soviet Subject On-Screen

Early films produced by Uzbekkino were similar in genre to colonial films. Both convey stereotypes about the indigenous populations and places where they live. Although *colonial cinema* in the broad meaning of the term refers to films shot in the colonies (Dallet 2003, 943), it is used here in a more restrictive sense to refer to films produced by the great imperial powers—France being taken as the point of reference here—that portray the peoples in the colonies and, most significantly, convey stigmatizing discourses about indigenous populations as a whole (Memmi 1985; Benali 1998; Dallet 2003, 950–51). An archetypal example of this is *Pépé le Moko* by Jean Duvivier (France, 1937), starring Jean Gabin, which was a runaway success (Boulanger 1975, 129–31). This film associates the native milieu to idleness and lies, a world "crawling" with men and women like ants in an ants' nest, populating the humid and labyrinthine Kasbah with its "dark, stinking depths" and "dripping porches," as the voice-over comments about the documentary images shot in situ (O'Brien 1997). The negative characters in this film are played by indigenous actors, not the ones from the mainland. Instead, actors from the mainland portray only virtuous characters.

COLONIAL SUBJECT—SOVIET SUBJECT

The similarities between these early Uzbek films and colonial films transpire clearly in the way colonial populations are represented: Either the "native" remains himself and is "part of the decor," in which case he is backward, dangerous, and unsavory; or else he wants to become civilized, in which case he is a sham. This aggressive character awakens fear and suspicion, is generally dehumanized or de-individualized by a number of processes, and is characterized by his bestiality or "typical idleness" (Memmi 1985, 99). Natives are also presented on occasion as "good savages" or "true Asians," who are gullible and backward and embody the immobilism stretching back through the centuries to the Middle Ages, as reflected in the place where they live. The native environment is a territory with no history, "an immobile decor in which the native, filmed like an animal, moves about mysteriously, and which the colonizer cautiously discovers" (Dallet 2003, 940). All these characteristics justify the civilizing mission conducted by a few "virtuous men of action" (Memmi 1985, 99).

The Uzbekistan portrayed in these three films is characterized by its countryside; its villages of dried mud; its landscapes; its customs, which "have remained unchanged since time immemorial"; and its peasants and indolent merchants, prostrate from the stifling heat—"the bazaar beneath the blazing sun" (*The Second Wife*). Only the Uzbekistan of villages and the old towns is portrayed in the film. The atmosphere is always peaceful: "Life flowed silently on in the peaceful villages," "one day replaced another . . . and the suffering of the *dekhkan* [peasant] sufficed each one" (*From Under the Vaults of the Mosque*). These title cards are accompanied by shots of the villages, where the immobilism is often accentuated by the presence of surrounding mountains, further hemming the place in. Like the carefree *bais* drinking tea under the shade of the coffeehouse mulberry bushes, "The old town slumbered tranquilly in the shimmering heat of the sun and the dust" (*The Leper*). Something similar transpires in the film *Turksib* (1929), by Viktor Turin, in which the steppe, the desert, and the heat are equated to stagnation and death (Honarphisheh 2004, 191). The old town, with its desolate, silent streets, is devoid of people. A driverless *arba* passes slowly along an alley (*The Leper*). It is a dirty and diminished world that seems to repeat itself indefinitely: "by dusty paths, narrow alleys, and from village to village" (*From Under the Vaults of the Mosque*).

> *From Under the Vaults of the Mosque* (Rus. *Iz-Pod svodov mecheti*)
> by Kazimir Gertel' (Uzbekkino, 1927)
>
> The action takes place in Turkestan at the end of the imperial period. Oberuchev (L. Lazarev), a cotton manufacturer from St. Petersburg, goes to Moscow to sign a delivery contract with the army before going back to Turkestan, his "homeland." Together with his assistant Yastrebetskii (A. Poliakov), Oberuchev exploits the local population with the connivance of the local *bais*. An old man, Pir Nazar (A. Khojaev), is one of his victims and has to sell his belongings to pay off his debts. His adoptive son Umar (K. Yarmatov), who is studying in a Koranic school, progressively turns away from his religious teaching under the influence of a revolutionary worker, Mikhail. The 1916 revolts are starting to flare up in Central Asia. Umar decides to take part and leaves for Jizzakh. Mikhail tries to find Umar and to guide the insurgents. To pass unnoticed and get to the place of the confrontations, Mikhail dons traditional dress and asks Umar's sister, Gul Assal (O. Spirova), to go with him. But Gul Assal and Mikhail are taken prisoner by a regiment of the Imperial Army (commanded by Oberuchev). Umar arrives in time to rescue Mikhail, who was about to be shot, and saves Gul Assal, who is almost raped by Oberuchev.

*From Under the Vaults of the Mosque* was Kazimir Gertel's (1889–1938) second feature-length film. Gertel started working in Belarus, and it would appear that he did not make many films.[44] The setting in this film is a peaceful exterior dominated by craft industry, as opposed to the European sphere characterized by modernity, progress, and rational and efficient production in a world where machines triumph (as illustrated by shots of factories and turbines against those showing manual work). Pir Nazar's family spend most of their time in the inner courtyard of their house, which is also a farmyard, thereby reinforcing the human/animal association. In opposition to this, Oberuchev, his wife, and Yastrebetskii are shown in the grand villa belonging to the industrialist or on the factory premises. Whenever they venture beyond these clearly demarcated boundaries, they leave behind a safe, closed space and enter a dangerous outside world. This climate of insecurity is magnified by nighttime attack scenes, for the native world is dangerous, as in colonial films, and "full of ambushes" (Dallet 2003, 943).

These characters are not the only victims. The viewer is also placed in a position of danger on several occasions by the use of subjective camera work—a technique that takes the camera as a subject in the action or expresses the point of view of one of the characters in such a way that the viewer shares the

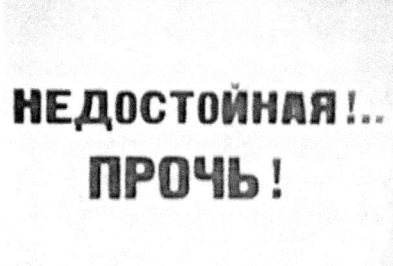

Figure 2.1, a-b. Umar repudiates Gul Asal when he sees her dressed in European fashion: "Unworthy daughter! Get back!" *From Under the Vaults of the Mosque*. Screen stills.

character's visual field, thereby accentuating the process of identification. Umar and his father, Pir Nazar, seem to directly attack the public, who are placed in the position of victim, when they throw themselves at, attack, or push away a character embodied by the camera itself (fig. 2.1).

Aggressiveness, hatred, and the desire for revenge are often the only motives governing Umar, excluding any desire for social justice from his revolutionary path. He is an unpleasant character. There are hints of an incestuous relationship; Umar has an ambiguous relationship somewhere between family love and sexual love with his sister Gul Assal, who is repudiated twice, coming across as both an unworthy sister and an unfaithful woman—an interpretation that some critics mistakenly reached.[45]

There are several elements in a similar vein characterizing the "native masses," who are de-individualized and hostile to Russian authority. Umar manages to escape the police by disappearing into a crowd of men who have gathered to watch a tightrope display. This "mass" closes in behind Umar like a door swinging shut, allowing no one through—a representation that differs from Eisenstein's crowd images, where the collective is a single, heroicized living body. This de-individualization also transpires in the fact that some male characters have no first name and thus no identity. The dehumanization is sometimes reinforced by parallel editing associating men to animals. When the decree ordaining the conscription of Muslim populations for work away from the front line is read out (which sparked the 1916 revolts that are briefly shown in the film), a shot showing a first wave of unrest cuts across to one showing two dogs fighting. As at the end of *The Leper* (see box below), lepers come out of their lair looking like wounded animals or insects, crawling, biting, and bringing death and disease in their wake (fig. 2.2).

Figure 2.2, a-c. Lepers leave their lairs and crawl toward Tilla Oi. *The Leper.*

INCORPORATING EARLY SOVIET CODES

Although there are several points of resemblance between colonial films and early Uzbek films (particularly *From Under the Vaults of the Mosque*), there are also divergent factors that reveal the hybridization between colonial-type discourse and a not yet fully formulated Soviet (proletarian Russian) discourse. Equally, unlike in colonial films, local actors were not used solely as extras but also assigned secondary roles—Kamil Yarmatov (1904–78) played the role of Umar in *From Under the Vaults of the Mosque*, for instance. Female characters were still performed by Russian women actors, though. Furthermore, and this is the key point, "European supremacy" was not exacerbated, as was the case in other films about native populations made at this time.[46]

These films portray the progression away from the status of colonial subject toward full-fledged Soviet subjecthood, where the negative stereotypes associated with the former justify political action and conquest (Bhabha 1997, 127). But while the image of the "native" is especially demeaning, that of the Russian "civilizing agent" is not entirely positive either. The action in *From Under the Vaults of the Mosque* and in *The Leper*, which takes place just before the October Revolution, does not openly articulate any Western (Russian) superiority. Since the historical period is that of empire, the main characters are imperial officers or from the upper ranks of the industrial and commercial bourgeoisie, and so most ill-suited to idealization. They are therefore represented in a relatively neutral, understated way and are not heroized. No doubt this makes them positive characters in comparison with the particularly stigmatized indigenous population.

In this scheme of things, European supremacy is logically embodied by the worker of Russian origin, Mikhail, who calls on the people to assert their revolutionary commitment; he is the sort of positive hero who was beginning to emerge at the time. But this new stereotype is not readily transferred to the situation in Central Asia. Although there is a nascent attempt to portray the imminent revolution in Central Asia, the revolutionary commitment of the former colonial subjects comes across as somewhat incongruous. In *From Under the Vaults of the Mosque*, Umar, before meeting the revolutionary worker Mikhail, was already starting to question the religious instruction he received at the madrasa, doubting his faith in light of the injustice experienced by his adoptive family when his father's belongings are confiscated due to scheming Russian industrialists and *bais*. Umar's "revolutionary commitment" takes on a different scale after a chance encounter with Mikhail, whom he was trying to rob. Umar understands the error of his ways, releases Mikhail, and they subsequently discuss politics in a *choikhona*, although there are no title cards transcribing their discussion. On returning to the madrasa, Umar's doubts increase further: "Mikhail spoke true—it's hard to believe in Allah." And so, as noted by the report of the State Repertoire Committee (Glavrepertkom), Umar becomes revolutionary by chance and, as the censors sarcastically observed, abandons "banditry to embrace socialism."[47]

Press reviews noted that Umar's role was unconvincing, pointing out that the "sort of worker" he embodied was not credible—and rightly so, since he is a Koranic student who does not work. He is "an organizer and agitator who profits from money obtained by theft."[48] His character is more akin to a bandit or performing acrobat than to a genuine revolutionary. But how was film to represent a laborer or native worker? Although it was relatively easy to establish the archetypal Central Asian peasant—an old man with a white beard working the soil is not fundamentally different from that of a peasant in Russia or elsewhere—filmmakers had more difficulty portraying the figure of the laborer or worker.

Filmmakers and scriptwriters needed to reorganize a complex historical imaginary at the zone of overlap between the Russian Empire and the October Revolution by combining, in the case of Central Asia, anticolonial struggles with class struggle, thus assimilating colonial oppression to bourgeois domination. Filmmakers needed to situate the films within a rhetoric based on central archetypes within Soviet cinema (such as the revolutionary Russian worker). This approach functions relatively well for the character of Mikhail, who is convincing in his role as the person who rebels in his factory. Nevertheless, a problem remains: How was the narrative to establish a link between colonial domination and the Russian proletarian revolution? The 1916 revolts in Central Asia provided a point where these two historical trajectories met and then needed to converge toward a single goal. This attempt to create a link founding a new common Soviet destiny prefigures the volte-face in 1930s historiography about the Russian Empire and the 1916 revolts. Thus, on several occasions, the worker Mikhail finds himself relaying revolutionary ideas and acting as a leader for the 1916 anticolonial revolts, which he would like to head. The disparate and mixed narrative elements and the attendant difficulty of giving this complex historical situation a clear political orientation result in the film not being able to deliver a clear and coherent message, as pointed out by the reviews.

The State Repertoire Committee was surprised that Mikhail was the only person capable of commanding the revolts and felt that it was a weakness that Mikhail appeared to know the place better than anyone else. In addition, Umar and Mikhail, whom the censors expected to display genuine "proletarian solidarity," do not act together but rather "wholly separately."[49] The committee went on to point out that Umar's sole explicit motivation for becoming involved in the revolts is expressed in the interjection, "My people are groaning [with suffering]!" His involvement in the emergent protest is not properly motivated. *From Under the Vaults of the Mosque* was a first attempt at using the 1916 revolts (a theme discussed in detail in chap. 5 in relation to Suleyman Khojaev's *Before Dawn*), but the press reviews accused the film of not doing enough to show how the anticolonial movement originated. The revolts "occur unexpectedly" at the end of the film, the viewer is unable to understand what caused them and how they developed over time, and Umar makes a poor insurgent. In short, there is nothing exemplary or authentic about his path to revolution.[50]

In parallel to this attempt to take the political subordination of the former colonial subjects of the tsarist empire and ground it in the Russian proletariat as embodied by the worker Mikhail, *From Under the Vaults of the Mosque* also portrays the territorial organization based on the dependency on Russia. This relationship is enshrined in the railway, which is centered on Moscow and St. Petersburg, the places of departure for rich, healthy men. In *From Under the Vaults of the Mosque*, Oberuchev travels by train from Russia to Turkestan to expand his cotton business there, while the sick and wounded returning from the front arrive by the wagonload. Geographical subjection is primarily assimilated to repressive action, and the intrusion of imperial power to restore order in the native sphere passes via the railway, which transports the punitive expedition against the insurgents—for instance, "The punitive regiment advanced, slowly but surely." The railway also provided the means for waging "war against the primitive peoples" and established itself as an agent of conquest and "pacification" (Honarphisheh 2004, 190; Payne 2001b, 41). *The Earth Is Thirsty*, produced a few years later in Turkmenistan for Vostokkino by Iulii Raizman, took the traumas associated with the railway as a symbol of the repression of the 1916 revolts and inverted the symbolism. When the train arrives, the Turkmen population shut themselves inside their homes, fearing a wave of violence, but the train disgorges singing Komsomol members who have arrived to build a canal. The railway, and the great canals linking the dispersed territories (Salys 2009, 208–9), are thus represented as a means of establishing the unity of the territory (unlike the abstract image of unity conveyed by *The Minaret of Death*), organized around a center based in Russia.

## *The Position of Women: Lifetime Imprisonment*

While far from perfect and denounced for their exoticism, populism, and the incongruous portrayal of the revolutionary venture, these early films started to articulate codes of representation require by the authorities and attempted to establish a line of political descent linking the Russian revolutionaries to the formerly colonized peoples. Although the representations the films convey of imperial and native society are negative, the racial hierarchy is nevertheless maintained. The most fiercely stigmatized characters are those from the native bourgeoisie, shown in ascendancy over Russian colonial society. Analysis of the depiction of women—at the bottom of the social hierarchy and victims of both male indigenous society and imperial domination—and, more specifically, the portrayal of mixed couples highlights the stereotypes regarding the nature of the sociocultural relationships holding between the center and the periphery. This narrative motif is a key dramatic component around which the plot tends to be played out, as is particularly the case in Oleg Frelikh's *The Leper*.

### Pre-Algerianist French Literature as a Source of Inspiration

Oleg Frelikh (1887–1953) had already come to the attention of critics in his role as Sadyq in *The Minaret of Death*, and shortly afterward he became a director. *The Leper* was the first film he made in Uzbekistan, before *Sar Pige* in 1927 (Chuvashkino), *The Covered Wagon* (1928), *The Ishan's Fiancée* (in Central Asia in 1931), and *Zelim Khan* (1929) in Caucasia (Vostokkino).

> **The Leper** (Rus. *Prokazhennaia*) by Oleg Frelikh
> (Uzbekkino, 1928)
>
> Tilla Oi (R. Messerer) lives with her father, Ahmet Bai (M. Guliamov), the intendant to Colonel Karonin (V. Liubushkin), the military governor of Turkestan. The rich merchant Said Vali (G. Chechelashvili) takes Tilla Oi as his wife. One day, thinking it will please her husband, Tilla Oi dresses in European clothes; in doing so, she loses all his esteem. Her life becomes unbearable, she is beaten and mistreated, and she writes a message on her head scarf asking the colonel's wife to help her. Unfortunately, the message is intercepted by Igor (A. Fait), the colonel's son, who sees this as an opportunity to conquer the young woman. Tilla Oi and Igor meet on several occasions, and Tilla Oi's husband finally realizes she is adulterous. She is tried by a traditional religious court, and her father is obliged to leave his job. The entire family leaves, but Tilla Oi's bad reputation follows them, and she is obliged to leave the family home forever. She wanders for several days and arrives in a ruined village inhabited by lepers. She is scared and runs away, but she encounters some young *jigit*s who beat her to death thinking that she is contagious.

    This film, like *The Muslim Woman*, is an example of a script being rewritten. This time the basic plot is taken from literature and draws on European colonial imagery that was particularly modern for the period. *The Leper* is adapted from the pre-Algerianist novel *Kamir, roman d'une femme arabe* (1926) by Ferdinand Duchène (1868–1956). The fact that the authors of the film were so quick to take up the novel is illustrative of the deep links between the European and Soviet markets, the exchanges that were becoming established, and the public enthusiasm for this sort of literature. The book was published in France in 1926, and within the space of two years, the book had been translated and adapted as a script, filming had been carried out, and all the postproduction work had been completed.

    Although not much research has been conducted on popular culture—unlike elite culture—portraying the Orient (de Meaux 2010; Schimmelpenninck van der Oye 2010), borrowings would appear to have been relatively frequent. Michael Smith notes that many film heroes imitate characters in colonial short stories written in British India (spies, maharajas, lovers, and murderers) and that the imagery of European superiority and native backwardness is omnipresent (1997, 671). The poetry and prose of Rudyard Kipling (1865–1936), which was published in Russia in the early 1890s, was starting to be extensively translated by the early 1920s and regularly appeared in literary journals of the period

(Hodgson 1998). These writings had a large popular readership and, though officially criticized for their imperialistic nature, displayed extensive areas of overlap with Soviet ideology—such as their praise of progress and technology as personified by engineers and other "men of action," an admiration for the military virtue of camaraderie, and feeding a taste for exotic adventures in a "hostile environment." Despite the anticolonial political rhetoric, the Soviet taboo on the idea of empire did not exacerbate the formation of popular cultural stereotypes, which were only rarely brought into question by any critical stance toward this sensitive issue. For instance, Kipling's most critical texts about the British Empire in India were excluded from the Soviet edition, as were those condemning certain imperial crimes (Hodgson 1998, 1067–68). The public took up the imperial idea and imaginary in more subtle fashion, but the taboo over this term obliterated any critical reflection about the structures of domination reproduced in different format by the Soviet ideology.

This was precisely the case with the film adaptation of Duchène's novel. The interpretation of society provided by the French author is radically different from that put forward by the Soviet filmmaker. In the novel, Kamir (Tilla Oi in the film, the daughter of the intendant of the colonel in Turkestan) is the daughter of a naturalized citizen, and she attends a French school where she is taught by Jean (Igor, the son of the colonel in *The Leper*), who becomes her lover. She is torn between her modern French education (as wished by her father) and a more traditional education (as wished by her mother, who was "brought up as a true Muslim") (Duchène 1926, 17). Kamir is confronted with a dual existence that becomes difficult to maintain once she is married against her wishes to Mohammed (the rich merchant Said Vali in the film). Although Mohammed comes across as naturalized, this is only a facade and he remains attached to Islam and to tradition. When Kamir dresses in European clothes for her wedding night, her husband is convinced of her disloyalty and attacks her with a knife. He supposes she is in a relationship with Jean, a suspicion that finally becomes true. Mohammed repudiates his young wife, who embarks on a life of vagrancy and degeneration until she manages to find Jean, but she dies in his arms.

Duchène's novel depicts the life of a young Arab woman during the colonial period and shows how the emancipation of this "forever sacrificed" figure is in fact impossible (Benammar Benmansour 2000, 44), since she is neither French nor Arab. Kamir is presented as the victim of men, who are attached to Muslim traditions and do not want to see the condition of women evolve—with the exception of the character of her father, who rises up against these customs. He regrets, for instance, that his daughter has to wear the veil from the age of thirteen and that she finds herself "imprisoned" on getting married. Social relationships are presented in all their complexity and portrayed precisely by the author. Kamir's life cannot go anywhere, because her father, while wishing to have an emancipated daughter, cannot accept to marry her to a Christian and expects her to conform to and become fully part of society (Duchène 1926, 11–12). The male characters in the novel are negative, being attached to tradition despite their pro-French appearances. The naturalization of the native population is depicted as a utopian ideal, and the sincerity of the Gallicized elite is brought into question (Benammar Benmansour 2000, 50).

### The Impossibility of Assimilation and Conjugal Boundaries

What does the film retain of the original story? Although certain scenes are kept, the modernity of Kamir and her father—the key point—has disappeared. Critics were ironic about the failed "indigenization" of the French novelist and the fact that the adaptation did not reflect Uzbek traditions.[51] The character of Tilla Oi (played by the actor Rakhil' Messerer)[52] is a highly sexualized object of desire, a dancer or prostitute with a slyly coquettish animality, imbued with colonial stereotypes that are not found in the novel. On several occasions, she dances at receptions given by the colonel, which are a place of gambling (with cards, money, and alcohol), debauchery, and seduction. She is also animalized as an object of desire, and the viewer first sees her behaving in a suggestively feline manner (reinforced by the immature and infantile nature of her character), jumping down from a branch where she has been playing, to advance stealthily on all fours. As a gentle and magnificent animal, she becomes relatively easy prey. On reading the message she has written on her head scarf, Igor (her future lover) refers to her as *utichka* (duckling) and dances with joy at the prospect of his coming conquest—which takes place during a hunting party, thereby reinforcing the image of hunter and prey.

Last, Tilla Oi symbolically becomes an insect bearing danger and death, a threatening scorpion whose adultery is a mortal blow to both her father and herself. This is the meaning of the scene in which a scorpion stings the father on the neck as he is talking with his daughter's in-laws. The shot of the father crying out with pain is crosscut with one of his daughter crying out as her husband, Said Vali, violently grabs her wrist. Tilla Oi is both the person who is stung (the parallel between the scorpion sting and her husband's hand grasping her wrist) and the person who wounds her father. It is after this scene that she writes a message on her head scarf asking for help, which is intercepted by her future lover. As a symbolic sting, this act obliges her father to leave his job. The association between the woman and the animal was noted by the critic of *Sovetskii Ekran*, who in 1927 remarked with irony on the preponderant role played by animals in films produced in Uzbekistan.[53]

The key scene in *The Leper*, in which Tilla Oi dresses in European clothes, is carried over in its entirety from Duchène's novel (1926, 112). She thinks that she will please her husband, wearing a muslin dress that reveals her arms with

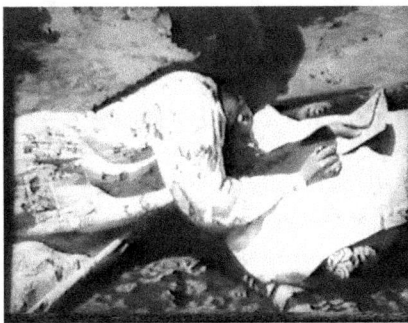

Figure 2.3, a-c. Tilla Oi asks for help on her head scarf: "I am humiliated and beaten!" A joyous Igor receives the message. *The Leper*. Screen stills.

jewelry and a hairstyle that complete her modern appearance. But Tilla Oi's husband considers her new look a blow to his dignity and a form of prostitution: "What is that disguise? . . . A cabaret virgin or my wife? Have you forgotten you are a Muslim?" Modern styles of dress ushered in by the removal of the veil could have been presented as presaging social modernization—the campaign to emancipate women (*hujum*) had started in 1926, two years before this film was released (see chap. 3). But the film is fully shut off from the social and political context in Uzbekistan, despite the fact that there was a consultant present on the shoot. Tilla Oi, who takes advantage of the presence of the colonel's valet to speak of her despair and the rough treatment she receives, consigns her misfortune to her head scarf: "I am humiliated and beaten!" Since the actual (not intended) recipient of this message is Igor, the effect of removing her veil and calling for help is what leads to her downfall, for it is assimilated to an invitation to adultery (fig. 2.3).

The theme of the Europeanization of clothing is also present in *From Under the Vaults of the Mosque*, which, in exploring the theme of a mixed union, evokes a form of cultural assimilation symbolized by clothing. The representatives of the Russian authorities suddenly appear and lay waste to the places where the indigenous population live (Pir Nazar's house), whereas the Russians live in places that are almost entirely shut off from the natives. If natives are to be fully accepted there, they need to go beyond the "savage" state, to use the term Oberuchev employs when he sees Gul Assal for the first time: "She is afraid, a real savage!" She is only accepted when she starts wearing European clothes, which fascinate her. Echoing the Europeanization of Gul Assal, Oberuchev becomes oriental in hoping to take the young woman as his second wife. The "Russian native" couple, as in colonial films, is doomed to failure (Benali 1998, 47, 272). It was not until the late 1930s, with *Assal'* by Mikhail Egorov and Boris Kazachkov, that Uzbek cinema presented the formation of mixed couples on-screen, although the Stalinist conservatism of the period meant they had to be evoked in relatively platonic terms (Drieu 2015; Salys 2009, 327–33).

THE ONLY ALTERNATIVES: TRADITION OR DEATH

*The Leper* (like *From Under the Vaults of the Mosque*) portrays a situation in which there is no hope for the woman. She is entirely subjected to the local indigenous bourgeoisie (the *bais*), who dominate both the native peasantry and the imperial world. Colonel Karonin and his son Igor are obliged to borrow money from Said Vali, who has inherited his wealth from his father. The colonel and Igor become Said Vali's debtors on two occasions, even though their social and administrative status ought to ensure their financial preeminence. Furthermore, this local bourgeoisie is able to thrive and corrupt the Russian administration. When Tilla Oi is about to be judged, the wronged husband pays the Russian administration not to interfere so she can be tried by a traditional Muslim court—which he also pays, even though the situation is already in his favor. This incoherence was remarked on by the critic writing for the journal *Kino*: "Why do the violent husband and wealthy father have to corrupt the religious dignitaries and the Russian colonel in order to have the young woman, who has already fallen, condemned?"[54] *Pravda Vostoka* also remarked on this incoherence in its issue of July 26, 1927: "The adultery is discovered, the guilty woman chased away from her home, and her husband hurries off to bribe the district chief. For what reason? The scriptwriter alone knows."

The truly dominant class is made up of wealthy natives who are implicitly responsible for the corruption and backwardness of colonial Turkestan and who block any emancipating acculturation that might improve the condition of indigenous women. They are victims of these two worlds, and their emancipation and salvation are thus impossible. There are only two possible outcomes: death or a return to traditional life. "There is no movement. Everything is stagnating!" remarked the *Trud* critic in his review of *The Second Wife*, a particularly accurate interpretation of women's confinement.[55]

> *The Second Wife* (Rus. *Vtoraia Zhena*, Uzb. *Ikichi khanum*)
> by Mikhail Doronin (Uzbekkino, 1927)
>
> Adolat (R. Messerer) lives happily with her mother and father, leading a joyous life alongside her best friend, Qumri, who is later happily married to Umar. But this happiness comes to an end the day she is given in marriage as a second wife to the wealthy merchant Taji Bai (G. Chechelashvili), whose first wife Khadija (M. Grineva) is infertile. After this marriage, Adolat gives birth to a daughter, Saodat (Zh. Voynova). The first wife decides to take revenge and manages to persuade Taji Bai that Adolat is lazy and careless. One day when Taji Bai is away from home, his brother Sadyqbay (M. Doronin), who likes young boys (*bacha*), takes advantage of Taji Bai's absence to steal money to buy a ring for a young adolescent who has taken his fancy. Sadyqbay encounters Adolat when carrying out this theft and tries to abuse her. The husband discovers the theft and wrongly accuses Adolat, who flees to her parents. Taji Bai brings her back and confines her. The weather is turning cold, and Adolat is provided with a stove to keep warm. The room catches fire and Adolat dies from asphyxiation.

The title cards used in this film insist on the idea of confinement: "Behind the windowless walls of the *ichkari* where no sound penetrates, they [the women] know nothing other than housework, children, and 'love,'" or they are shut away behind "their stifling *chachvon*." Their life is like "the wearisome grinding of a large wheel along a grey and dusty path." Adolat's reclusion is such that on being wrongly accused of adultery, she is shut away in a room without light, like an animal's lair. Death seems the only possible salvation. Tilla Oi (*The Leper*) dies after being beaten, while Adolat (*The Second Wife*) dies from asphyxiation after her martyrdom. The press reviews considered *The Second Wife* "fully satisfactory," "close to the spectator," and "interesting to watch" and emphasized that the film provided a successful representation of women's confinement.[56] Certain members of the Uzbek government also approved of the film, and one commission reckoned it was "truthful" and emphasized "its satisfactory artistic merits."[57] For the commissar for education (Mu'min Khojaev), the film proved that the Uzbek studios were progressively finding the right approach, giving "grounds for hope."[58] To the commissar, *The Second Wife* had no propaganda elements, but the film nevertheless presented a faithful vision of the East thanks to its simple, accurate, and precise representation of Uzbek women "enclosed and cloistered behind four walls."

Although the account that the film provides is realistic, it does not offer any concrete answer or a pathway toward liberation or modernization, despite

Figure 2.4. R. Messerer (second row, far right), Nabi Ganiev, the future Uzbek filmmaker, who played the role of Umar and was customs consultant for the shoot; the man wearing a turban is G. Chechelashvili, who played many roles in films produced in Uzbekistan, *The Second Wife*. Source: AI (file *The Second Wife*).

a few scenes that portray the new Soviet life of the modern, happy Uzbek couple of Qumri and Umar. The critics regretted that no link was established between this couple and the reclusive life of traditional women. The two realms—Adolat's traditional enclosed world and Qumri's liberated Soviet one—coexist without ever coming into contact, despite having a common origin in the childhood friendship uniting the two young women. This is one of the major criticisms of the film: "The film provides very expressive details about ancient traditions entirely subordinated to custom..., but does not offer the public any convincing propaganda about the particular characteristics of Soviet construction that liberates women from domestic tyranny, leading them towards a full and creative life."[59]

### Toward a Decolonization of Images

"But when are our Orientophiles [*vostochniki*] going to come out from behind the vaults of triteness?" the press inquired.[60] The films discussed in this chapter were denounced for their lack of "social and political meaning." *The Leper* "managed with difficulty to be the worst film produced by Uzbekkino," combining "superficiality in the approach adopted to the Orient by the director Frelikh with Duchène's exoticism adapted without any talent by Seifullina [the scriptwriter]."

The film contains scenes that do nothing to advance the plot, presents a "fake and false" Orient inhabited by the actor Messerer, "a princess in a *paranji*," and makes superficial decorative use of Uzbek traditions.[61] The film is a work of "dull grey banality" and sheds no "new light" on its theme, while the transfer of a foreign fable to Soviet reality is unconvincing.[62] Critics denounced the films for being "petit bourgeois" because they targeted a comparatively wealthy, foreign, or Soviet audience.[63] The descriptions of cultural traditions (*byt*) and customs and the title cards were "superficial," "random," and "dictated by a rapacious and predatory appetite," whereas it would have been simple to provide "ethnographically useful" shots of native villages.[64] The censors and critics feared that Soviet political discourse would be discredited among the populations for whom the films were made.[65] In addition to the filmmakers and scriptwriters, Uzbekkino was blamed for the poor quality of the films, because it reproduced mistakes that had been regularly denounced. The State Repertoire Committee of the Russian Soviet Federation warned Uzbekkino against its policy for selecting scripts and films, and "in friendly manner" brought these deviances to the attention of Uzbekkino and the national Repertoire Committee.[66]

In fact, the films making up this first group were not directly intended to modernize the Soviet East. Although not yet devised as a way to relay the forthcoming Cultural Revolution, they did provide observations about a recent historical period and establish a link between the historical destinies of Russia and Central Asia. They might not have prefigured the coming upheaval that would affect Central Asian societies, but they did play a timid role in integrating Central Asia into the Soviet Union and making people aware of just how vast this new territory was. Although the films failed to fulfill their political and social purposes, they sketched out an emergent Soviet imaginary. They functioned as an intermediary realm of acculturation, enabling audiences to become acquainted with the indigenous realm. In addition to the images and narration, the title cards used a fair number of vernacular words which, while generating a feeling of strangeness and exoticism, also brought that realm closer.

Although film was meant to be of use to the East, film, in fact, made use of the East (Kotiev 1931, 69). The mistakes in films such as *The Minaret of Death* and *The Muslim Woman* had been denounced. The critics had hoped the mistakes would act as a lesson, and they demanded more realism. But this sought-for realism, together with the recurrent historical inconsistencies, exacerbated the relationship of domination, perpetuating the colonial discourse that, in order to justify the conquest and civilizing mission, stigmatized the indigenous population and its way of life. As a result, the discourse was hybrid, combining colonial stereotypes with a rhetoric of Bolshevik hegemony—although the latter was not portrayed as openly as it would be in the late 1930s. This hybridization and the conditions in which it was produced served to entrench racial hierarchization while inverting the habitual terms, since the class discourse of these films presented the native bourgeoisie as dominating Russian military and colonial society (*The Leper*). A new form of (Russian and proletarian) imperialism may already be detected, timidly embodied by the figure of the Russian worker invested with the mission of transmitting his revolutionary knowledge. The idea of the "advanced, progressive West" and the "backward, primitive Orient" of traditional colonial discourse was starting to be articulated in new terms, along political as opposed to racial lines (Hodgson 1998, 1070).

Certain representations in 1920s Soviet cinema of the Orient and its conquered populations converge chronologically with those produced in European colonial empires. But the paths taken by the two rapidly diverged. At the beginning of the 1930s, Soviet cinema went through a process in which images were symbolically decolonized—the exotic and orientalist expression "oriental films" disappeared, and as of 1928–29, the press was referring instead to "national films." By point of comparison, this process only started in France in the late 1940s (Dallet 2003, 941; Boulanger 1975, 159, 223). In the Soviet case, this process thus took place fifteen or so years earlier—just before the official beginning of the Cultural Revolution in 1928, which brought other forms of domination, shaping all film production, along with new elements fashioning the Russian proletarian hegemony. Soviet Uzbekistan, which since 1924 had exerted mastery over cultural policy for what had become its national territory, was now in a position to draw on these early experiences and the criticisms they had attracted as it sought to place cinema at the service of political and social progress.

# Part II
# Cultural Revolution and Its Paradoxes: Nation, Modernity, and Empire (1927–31)

# Part 2 Introduction
## *Cinematographic Cultural Revolution*

From 1917 onward, the Bolsheviks launched numerous initiatives to instruct the population, and many independent, autonomous projects sprang up spontaneously under the New Economic Policy without yet amounting to a systematic policy (David-Fox 1999). While the expression "cultural revolution" appears in Lenin's final texts (1922–23), it only came into regular use after being employed by A. Krinitskii, head of the Central Committee's Agitation and Propaganda Department, at a conference on cultural issues held in Moscow from May 30 to June 3, 1928 (Fitzpatrick 1978, 10). Behind its modernizing appearance, the Cultural Revolution was in fact essentially a radical change, and the film productions of the late 1920s differ clearly in theme and function from earlier films. The Cultural Revolution was fashioned by the tensions and conflicts that existed under the New Economic Policy, with a tendency to reduce the cultural specificities of the many varied Soviet populations (Kurbanbaev 1930, 72) by taking urban, atheistic, proletarian Russia as the norm. But this revolution also sought to counter the emerging nationalisms and thwart the elites that had formerly held power (Martin 2001a, 175). The period of the Cultural Revolution—which also corresponds to the first Five Year Plan, industrialization, and the rationalization of economic activity—shows the fundamental shift from the Soviet system characterizing the 1920s to that of the 1930s.

The Cultural Revolution—as a mass policy of unprecedented scale and violence implemented more or less homogenously across the Soviet sphere—radicalized the debate about the modernization of traditional societies that had first arisen during the imperial period. It led to two major transformations in Central Asia: the emancipation of women and the secularization of Muslim societies. However, these phenomena were not solely attributable to the Soviet authorities, but also in part to the work of reformist Muslim intellectuals (Jadids). The period of the Cultural Revolution may thus be considered a "locus of convergence" between central ideology and certain reformist political ideals, with a proportion of the henceforth Uzbek cultural elite seeing the Communist Party as offering a political opportunity to legitimize their thought—in particular, with regard to the issue of women (Khalid 2007b, 65; Kamp 2006, 3).

The Uzbek elites took up this new sphere of political speech and national expression while drawing on the "positive discrimination" officially conceded by the central authorities and reaffirmed in 1923 under the so-called indigenization policy (*korenizatsiia*). But contrary to appearances, this positive discrimination—which was intended to promote national cadres in the state apparatus—was thought of as a strategy to counter the emerging nationalisms, and thus marked the first blow against existing elites. In fact, the indigenization policy did not seek to bring about the nationalization of cadres, being primarily a matter of forming a new cultural elite within which each "national" would be educated as an "internationalist" (Kurbanbaev 1930, 75) and act in the light of class interests. The many modernizing visions were progressively whittled down, starting with the removal of the old national elites when the Bolsheviks launched their first press campaign in 1926 against the reformist legacy, Greater Russian chauvinism, and local chauvinisms—including Jadidism. This was followed by a campaign to purge the party that was launched at the Tenth Congress of the All-Union Communist Party in 1921 (Fedtke 1998, 483, 487). The period of the Cultural Revolution was thus also a "locus of divergence," with the central party seeking to topple the cultural authorities inherited from the ancien régime and set up a new proletarian intelligentsia in their place (Fitzpatrick 1978, 8).

The Cultural Revolution, as viewed through the prism of the national question, was based on a major ambiguity. It sought to both topple the former elites—labeled "bourgeois nationalists" and "former elite" (*byvshie liudi*) in the authorities' rhetoric—and encourage the development of national cultures by indigenizing personnel and promoting national languages and particularities (Martin 2001a, 26). The old cultural heritage was partially denigrated and its elites condemned, yet at the same time traditions started to be collected (with a tendency toward folklorization), constituting another way of valorizing and pinning down the traditional heritage on which Soviet cultural productions were based. In the long run—not until 1937 for film production in Uzbekistan—the new culture had to be "national in form, proletarian in content," to use the expression consecrated by Stalin and that is meaningful for all Soviet peoples.

* * *

Cinema reflected the Cultural Revolution in many ways, bringing out the fundamental shift that occurred in the late 1920s and acting as a sphere of tension between the central authorities and local national power. How did the cinematographic representations produced by the Uzbek studios appropriate the national sphere? Chapter 3 explores the production of the first film to be deemed Uzbek before examining the role allotted to cinema in social modernization policies (the emancipation of women and secularization). Chapter 4 seeks to understand the shift toward empire. How did the institutions lose control over

Uzbek cinema, which became subject to a process of economic and ideological centralization? What were the reactions to this (acceptance, resignation, or resistance), and what were the consequences? And how did this control ultimately transpire at the lowest geographical and hierarchical echelons in a typical everyday film screening?

# 3 The National Cinematographic Sphere

THE FILMS EXAMINED in this chapter date from 1927–28 until 1931–32, with the first Five Year Plan, and they address the major modernization issues affecting Uzbek society. It is hard to set a fixed starting point for this series of films that distinguishes them from those studied earlier. Films such as *The Jackals of Ravat* by Kazimir Gertel' (1927) and Mikhail Averbakh's *Chachvon* (1928) came out after *The Minaret of Death* (1925), *The Muslim Woman* (1925), and *The Second Wife* (1927), but they were being screened in cinemas just a few months earlier than *From Beneath the Vaults of the Mosque* (1928) and *The Leper* (1928). Yet the films discussed in this chapter stand out for having different themes. They turn away from the prerevolutionary period and examine the early years of Soviet power in Central Asia. Furthermore, the function of these films is more openly propagandist. They no longer sought to entertain the major Russian cities but instead were made for the Uzbek population among whom they sought to awaken community feeling (*The Jackals of Ravat*) or trigger social change, such as the emancipation of women (*Chachvon*) and the secularization of society (*The Ishan's Fiancée*).

## *The Jackals of Ravat*: Projecting an Image of the Nation

The issue of national film production was tackled during the May 1928 party conference on cinema, which had a decisive influence on subsequent Soviet film policy. The existence of many national film organizations was perceived as something positive, though the authorities felt that the results were unconvincing in ideological terms (Krinitskii 1929a, 29). The debate was taken a step further with the conference of the Central Committee in May–June 1928, addressing the issues of agitation, propaganda, and cultural construction. Several political decision makers warned against the nationalistic "imperialistic and chauvinistic tendencies" that were appearing in Ukraine and Belarus—which by idealizing ancient history negated the directing role played by the proletariat in developing national culture (Rubailo 1976, 66). The first national films failed to live up to the objectives put forth by the party, a failure that was pinned on "cultural weakness" (*slabost' kul'tury*), corresponding to the weakness of their "political culture," and on a dearth of artistic cadres within national organizations.

The dividing line between a national film and a nationalistic film is very fine, but *The Jackals of Ravat* by Kazimir Gertel' (which came out in 1927) manages to remain within the limits of the politically acceptable. It is considered to be the first film considered as Uzbek and offers committed politicized discourse rooted in the new reality of Central Asia. The national character of this film, which criticizes the Basmachi movement, was fashioned by four criteria: the participation of the local elite in the production process (as technicians and actors), the financing and overall economics of the film (production, distribution rights, and censorship), and the symbolic elements of its public reception and the representations it conveys. The nationality of the filmmaker is not a determining factor in its own right.

*The National Imaginary*

*The Jackals of Ravat* was designed for a local audience who needed to be able to identify with the customs and scenes being represented, which were "close, current, and troubling."[1] This full-length film differs from oriental films and their "ideological meanderings," and it "boost[ed] the morale" of the critics.[2] Though not made by an Uzbek filmmaker, this film is nevertheless an example of national appropriation of film. For the first time, the main roles were played by Uzbek actors. Suleyman Khojaev, the future Uzbek filmmaker, was involved as an actor, a "consultant ethnographer," assistant director, and translator. Shooting started in the summer of 1926.

---

*The Jackals of Ravat* (*Shakaly Ravata*)
by Kazimir Gertel' (Uzbekkino, 1927)

Jalil (R. Akhmedov), a peasant from the village of Ravat, is in love with Karamat (K. Pimenova), the daughter of his neighbor Yusuf (A. Khojaev). Yusuf owes money to the *bai* Abdu Nabi (Kh. Jalilov), and to pay off his debts has to agree to give him his daughter's hand in marriage (as a third wife). This saddens Jalil, who decides to join the Basmachis, the allies of *bai* Abdu Nabi, for he sees a way to exact his revenge. Karamat is unhappy with her new husband, and Sadyq (Suleyman Khojaev), Jalil's best friend, regularly comes to visit her. Sadyq talks to Karamat about how the Soviet authorities could provide protection. They meet regularly, and Abdu Nabi suspects his wife of adultery. He beats her violently before she flees. Alerted by Sadyq, the Red Army guards hasten to help Karamat and take her to the infirmary, where she learns how to read while convalescing. Abdu Nabi asks Basmachi chieftain Akram Khan (R. Pirmukhamedov) and his men to kidnap Karamat. The Red Army soldiers and Sadyq fight them but are taken prisoner. Sadyq manages to escape thanks to Jalil, who has infiltrated their ranks. In parallel

> to this storyline, a mutiny is brewing. The poor peasants realize they will obtain nothing by remaining with the Basmachis, so they rise up in revolt and, together with Jalil and Sadyq, manage to free Karamat. A military plane arrives to provide backup, and Sadyq informs them that the Red Guards are still being held prisoner by the Basmachis, who are finally defeated. As a reward for his bravery, Sadyq takes Karamat's hand and places it in Jalil's. The village of Ravat is liberated from the Basmachis, and the Red Army guards depart.

The film seeks to portray daily life, with title cards using vernacular language and insisting on traditional life. The audience is shown several ethnographic sequences, such as cooking near an earthenware oven, children playing jacks, an old woman spinning wool, the sound of a *karnai* announcing the wedding, and a woman burning *isirik* (wild rue, a plant with antiseptic and magical properties) to ward off the evil eye. The realistic nature of the representations was a key element in its reception, and the film—a joint work by Russians and Uzbeks—was warmly received by critics. It was screened in Tashkent on January 10, 1927, before an audience of four hundred people, and judged to be satisfactory and apt in its depiction of daily life (*byt*).[3] The film was due for commercial release in March, triggering extensive debate in the national press—*Qizil Uzbekiston*, *Komsomolets Vostoka*, and *Pravda Vostoka*—with a dialogue being struck up between critics and open letters from audience members. The initiative behind this public debate came from *Pravda Vostoka*, which called on "workers, representatives of the Uzbek intelligentsia, and those taking part in the struggle against the Basmachis to give their opinions" about the realism (or otherwise) of the representations that the film conveyed.[4] This was the first time this question had been raised in such pressing form.

Opinions were many and varied, once again showing that a range of views could be expressed just prior to the turning point of the 1930s. The film's detractors accused it of being dependent on a "banal" plot, similar to that found in oriental films (*The Minaret of Death*, *The Muslim Woman*), in which the love story is the driver of social and political progress, the emancipation of women, and liberation from class domination. The Red Army liberates the village of Ravat from the Basmachis to return Karamat to Jalil.[5] Moreover, although the realism of certain scenes was recognized, their "illustrative" function was decried. The acting of Russian-born Pimenova, who played Karamat, was also a target for criticism.[6] The most critical voices argued that, even though the film was not very satisfactory, it could be used as "propaganda for the Soviet Orient."[7]

But many thought that the film spoke to the local population, who watched it with pleasure, recognizing the archetypal *bai* in the character of Abdu Nabi and seeing episodes of their daily life played out on-screen.[8] For Abdulla Qodiri, the great Uzbek literary figure of the first third of the twentieth century, and for Said Ziia, both the film and its title affected the people:

> When people started talking about the Uzbekkino production *The Jackals of Ravat*, coming out on-screen, I very much wanted to go and see it but I had doubts . . . Because the experience of the previous years had more than once turned out to be right. So I went to see *The Jackals of Ravat* with doubt and anxiety. But I did not regret it. . . . I saw the dishonest *bai*, the poor peasant, Karamat-bibi, the *domla-imam*, Saqyq, Jalil, luxurious ceremonies, the poor landless peasant who, lacking class consciousness, is abused by the Basmachis and joins the ranks of the jackals. . . . And I don't know what the impression of most Europeans was when this film was screened or what they understood, but every Uzbek was delighted and appreciated this screening.[9]

Kamil Yarmatov, who was involved in making the film, remembers that it met with "magical success" in the country and was widely distributed: "For almost the first time the Uzbek spectator could see himself on screen while seeing modern life" (Yarmatov 1987, 74–76). The Muscovite critic writing in *Sovetskii Ekran* praised the film for being the best Uzbekkino production for the wealth and exactness of the Uzbek landscapes and their marked and "spicy" contrasts.[10]

> There is no trace of Oriental sentimentalism. In *The Jackals of Ravat* there is the sun of Uzbekistan, its mountains, its forests, its rivers, and villages. Everything is there, cotton fields and rice paddies of lifeless sand, tumbling mountain torrents, peaks crowned in eternal glaciers, the narrow lanes of Uzbek villages . . . Uzbek daily life as it is. Many instances of daily life are captured unadorned. The red line running through the film is the life of the Uzbeks enslaved by the *adat* and *chachvon*, together with the struggle against the Basmachis who have clearly tormented Uzbekistan for many years.[11]

*The Jackals of Ravat* was considered to be the first Uzbek film (*uzbekning tungghach kartinkasi*), and one that stood out from what had gone before.[12] This national character confirms that processes of identification, be they national or not, are far from being natural—as pointed out by Hobsbawm (1990) in another context and as shown by the films studied earlier. But the coming process of Soviet nationalization tended toward the reification of national specificities and, in the long run, their folklorization. Jay Leyda gives an illuminating example relating to *Storm over Asia*, a film by Pudovkin (1893–1953), the famous filmmaker and pupil of Lev Kuleshov. The lead actor (Valeri Inkijinov) was of Buryat-Mongol origin but had been educated in Russian manner and had to "re-mongolize" himself by learning to ride bareback and downplaying his Western bearing by mastering and concealing emotions, smiles, and so on (Leyda 1976, 287).

*The Jackals of Ravat* is part of this same process. Though a silent film, its soundtrack (and, consequently, its language) nationalized it by deploying a large-scale musical accompaniment. The Soviet composer and ethnomusicologist Viktor Uspenskii (1879–1949) was asked to write the musical score, and he made recordings in Tashkent of a singer (*hafiz*) named Shah Rakhim Shah Umarov and collected songs to preserve the "tradition".[13]

> For the musical illustration of *The Jackals of Ravat* we used . . . old Uzbek songs that suited the atmosphere and rhythm of its episodes. . . . Working on these motifs entailed an unusual and very interesting approach to harmonies to ensure their specific melodic and rhythmic particularities did not disappear. The orchestration sought to bring together the various elements and included a small orchestral ensemble in order to produce the desired sonority and effects. . . . Uzbekkino's conclusive beginnings suggest that when they come to make other films, they will draw on all the possibilities of the ethnographical and musical treasures of Central Asia, which have hitherto unfortunately attracted little attention. This is an important situation, for the particularities of popular song are changing under the effect of various causes. It is being sullied by external elements, and song is being bastardized and progressively disappearing. And the older men, the singers of the people, are dying and taking this heritage of the past with them, a treasure of the greatest value representing the musical creation of the people.[14]

But it would be wrong to suggest that this reification of traditional cultures was solely the fruit of Soviet policy. While for Uspenskii the work of Uzbekkino as embodied in this film was to record disappearing traditions for posterity, this tendency had already emerged in the early 1920s at the initiative of Bukharan intellectuals such as Abdurauf Fitrat (1886–1938), who at the time was the Bukharan People's Soviet Republic's minister for public instruction.[15] At Fitrat's request, Uspenskii had recorded the six modes of the classical repertoire of *shasmaqâm* using the Western system of musical notation to transcribe the music (though he did not set down the texts sung in Tajik).[16] This research was published in Moscow in 1924 without its author being informed of the fact (Aminjonov 2006, 161). At the same time, Fitrat also published a work about Uzbek music (Fitrat 1993 [reprint]). This tendency to collect folklore was not specific to Uzbekistan; it was found in Kazakhstan (Rouland 2005) at the same time, and indeed throughout the Soviet Union, with the development of local ethnography (*kraevedenie*) and other types of expedition, including cinematographic ones (Widdis 2003b, 97–119). While film helped capture costumes and traditions on the verge of disappearance and so define national particularities or initiate social change, it also started to partake in a process of national particularization. It initially served to provide an attributive definition of Uzbek identity, which, after the Second World War, became increasingly based on differentiation from Tajik identity (Drieu 2005).

## Images of Power: The Red Army as a Means of Liberation

Compared with earlier Uzbekkino productions, the film displays few changes in the way space and the environment are represented. The title cards insist on how immobile the region is and on the medieval nature of life there: "The land of iron Timur the Lame is harsh and tough," "For dozens of centuries the snow has not thawed atop the peaks leaning against the sky," "Any adventurous travelers to these torrid deserts are stifled to death by the burning sands," "and for hundreds of years the village of Ravat has continued to stand." But the film breaks with the colonial rhetoric in its representation of men and women, who are transformed from unconvincing, if threatening, revolutionary natives into revolutionaries trained by the Red Army seeking to spread the benefits of the new Soviet order.

For the first time, the heroes are Uzbeks and are played by local actors (except Karamat, who is played by a Russian actor). Sadyq (Suleyman Khojaev) embraces the Bolshevik cause and relays its ideas, praising the strength of this new power. He takes up the defense of Karamat, who is being mistreated by her husband, and encourages her to emancipate herself with the support of the Red Guards, said to be "loyal friends." Sadyq then joins the ranks of the Red Army and becomes a "brother" to Karamat, which arouses the indignation of the entire village (for she has deserted the conjugal home and taken refuge with the Bolsheviks). The Red Army soldiers are protective once again when Karamat's father tries to get his daughter back. But their response—"We will not give the girl back. She is going to live and will find her way by herself"—enables her to be born as an individual. Last, the Red Army is the initial driver of literacy, since it is from a soldier that Karamat receives her first lessons.

The soldiers of the Red Army symbolize Soviet power, order, instruction, and emancipation and offer protection from internal threats such as the Basmachis and the *bai*s, who oppress the common peasants. But the Red Army and its soldiers—most of whom are Russian—are, above all, a means of liberation, and once they have completed their mission, they leave the place for good. On two occasions, the Red Guards protect the Ravat villagers. First, they repel the Basmachis before calling out to the finally liberated inhabitants, "Now you are masters in your own home!" On the second occasion, the title card insists that the Red Army departs: "The Red Army rid the surrounding area of Basmachis and bade farewell to the village of Ravat." The film closes on tanks and farewells: "The Basmachis pillaged us. Our land has become sterile. And now you have brought us back to life," one of the villagers proclaims. His wife continues, "You have brought help and protection to us women. Let the world now look us in the eyes!"

This local conception of Soviet power was rejected by the State Repertoire Committee of Soviet Russia, whose decisions were at this stage only advisory. On watching the film on two occasions, a month apart, the only aspect of the film to be applauded by the committee were the scenes portraying daily life and women, which they found "fairly successful." Their criticisms were focused on three points. First, the Basmachi movement was not depicted as an anti-Soviet movement, and the struggle supposedly conducted against it was insufficiently portrayed. Furthermore, the title cards needed to be more explicit about it and mention that "Soviet power got the better of it."[17] Second, the representation of the Red Army was "not satisfactory," because, first, it worked to liberate a woman (Karamat) and, second, there was only a single Uzbek in its ranks, yet many in the ranks of the Basmachis. This point was emphasized by the Uzbek *Komsomolets Vostoka* newspaper, which felt that the great problem with the film was the failure to develop the Basmachi theme and examine the reasons behind the movement's emergence and collapse.[18] The *Pravda Vostoka* also noted that the true nature of the movement was not portrayed.[19]

The final and most significant criticism leveled against film by the committee was that the central Soviet institutions (symbolized by the Red Army) were largely absent from the film. The committee insisted that those institutions should instead be depicted as the lasting referents of order and social progress, triggering the involvement of the local population.[20] The committee concluded that the film could not be authorized as it stood and that certain points needed reworking before screening it again in the presence of representatives of the Red Army Political Directorate and Uzbek political authorities. But the opinion of the committee was not taken into account, and in a new version of the film, the same "errors" were found in the way the Basmachis and the Red Army were represented.[21] The title card mentioning Tamerlane ("The land of iron Timur the Lame is harsh and tough"), who had become an undesirable figure over the course of the 1930s, had disappeared, but the degrading shots of Red Army soldiers taken prisoner by the Basmachis were still present. The caption "Red Army soldiers dozed in the inaccessible hideout of the Basmachis" had also disappeared, and without it, the shot suggested that they were dead rather than asleep.

Overall, two conceptions of Uzbek nation building may be detected in the debates and criticisms sparked by the film. In one, Soviet power is a means of liberation—a national vision, conveyed by the filmic discourse, that prevailed in the short term. In the other, Soviet power as symbolized by the Red Army is the lasting referent for order—a central vision conveyed by the Repertoire Committee, which came to dominate over the years.

Yet in many ways the Bolshevik rhetoric struck home. A study of the film's reception shows another form of identification pertaining to the assimilation of the forms of stigmatization deployed in Bolshevik discourse and their transposition to reality. When the film was screened for three days in July 1937 in Andijan—a significant pocket of Basmachi resistance—it played to a full house each time. As a journalist reported, the feeling of suspicion and distrust of the enemy (Basmachis)—compared to jackals, "scavengers circling around the villages" and always ready to attack and pillage with the complicity of the *bais*—was successfully communicated. During a discussion with the journalist, one spectator suddenly realized that "jackals" existed not in Ravat, but in his own village. He started listing them, targeting two people in particular (Kadyrov and Tajibaev) who worked in a procurement center. The characters in the film became examples of loyalty to be followed in reality. "Kadyrov and Tajibaev, with their wallets in their pocket, pilfer money. . . . They are like jackals, on the alert, adapting, observing, and then snatching bloody chunks of life. Let them carry on! In the heart of the villages the new inspector is maturing, not Gogol's Khlestakov, but the masses who will sweep away . . . the Kadyrovs, the Musaevs, and other bandits."[22]

## Cinema and the Policy to Emancipate Women: Central Propaganda and Local Reception

*The Jackals of Ravat* was a pro-Soviet national film that was accepted by the public and rejected by the central authorities. Another feature film that enables us to address the issue of the presentation of women is quite the opposite: in line with central ideology but rejected by the local public and parts of the Muscovite film industry. *Chachvon* (*Chadra* in Russian) by Mikhail Averbakh (1904–80) shows the first indirect implication of central party policy in Uzbek film production through the involvement of the Association of Cinema Workers.[23] It also illustrates the difficulty in creating a common sphere of communication.

Under the influence of Bolshevik discourse (Pis'mennyi 1928, 11), the issue of the emancipation of women had become a matter of acute importance for the Central Asian Soviet republics. It had first been raised by reformist intellectual elites under the Russian Empire who criticized polygamy, denounced the violence perpetrated against women, and asserted that women had to be educated; in these claims, they were influenced by the debates that had taken place in the Ottoman Empire and among Tatar intellectual circles (Khalid 1998, 222–23). The historiography on this issue reveals two opposing tendencies. For some historians, the policy to emancipate women may be traced back to the Jadids' reformist discourse and was a response to the aspiration of a section of the female population who were appropriating the new resources at their disposal in order to pursue their goals (Kamp 2006, 3–18, 32–52; Khalid 1998, 222–28). For other historians, it was a new "colonial practice" that sparked violent resistance (Northrop 2004). An analysis of *Chachvon* shows how these two contradictory approaches could nevertheless converge. Emancipation is something the local women in the film are hoping for, but it does not meet their expectations, and it is rejected within a context of extreme violence that was characteristic of the first "offensive" in the policy to emancipate women (*hujum*). In this specific film, it is the "language" and the means of communication used by the filmmaker—rather than the policy itself—that convey the discrepancy between the views of the center and those of the periphery.

## Cinema at the Service of the Emancipation of Women, or How to Imperceptibly Plant the Seeds of Rebellion

In autumn 1926, party organizations in Central Asia felt that it was henceforth necessary to go literally on the attack (*hujum*), and they launched a violent struggle against the subjugation of women—a policy that had been only marginal in the early 1920s (Liubimova 1928b, 20; Northrop 2004, 80).[24] At first this emancipation movement consisted in drafting legislation favorable to women, with the abolition of practices such as bride money (*kalim*), polygamy, marriage of underage girls, and bride-snatching. By 1919, degrees and laws were in place, but they were not applied. As of 1926–27, the Soviet leaders in Central Asia started to oppose the *chachvon* (a horsehair veil to hide a woman's eyes) and the *paranji* (a full-length body veil), which they considered to be a symbol of religious subjugation; they were not necessarily in agreement with the women who chose to remove their veils (Kamp 2001a, 7).[25] They also viewed the veil as an "obstacle to work," depriving the country of a sizable source of labor by preventing two million women from working in the factories or in the fields during the cotton harvest (Liubimova 1928b, 22).

The first resolutions were passed at the Third Inter-regional Summit of emancipation activists for women in Central Asia in October 1920, with the Communist Party wanting to organize collective unveiling events as "rituals symbolizing the break with Muslim tradition" (Kamp 2001b, 22) (fig. 3.1). The first such event was held to mark International Women's Day on March 8, 1927. Officially nearly ninety thousand Uzbeks removed their veils over the following months (Liubimova 1928b, 24), but this figure then slumped abruptly. The "attack" (*nastuplenie/hujum*) gave way to "retreat" (*otstuplenie*). The emancipation policy encountered stiff resistance due to a lack of psychological and educational preparation. But the setbacks only resulted in the policy being toughened up. Those who failed to present themselves for the collective unveiling were fined, pressure was exerted on people in their place of work (where they ran the risk of being fired), and threats were made to which the population responded whenever a woman removed her veil, with rumors of apocalypse (the end of the world or an earthquake) (Kamp 2001a, 8; Liubimova 1928b, 24–25).[26] Many women were assassinated, and those who had removed the veil started wearing it again (Kamp 2001a, 2; Liubimova 1928b, 25; Northrop 2004, 183–86). While the decision to remove the veil had been a personal decision prior to 1927—sometimes motivated by reading *The Arabian Nights* (Kamp 2006, 123–31)—the act of emancipation

Figure 3.1. "Let's put an end to the paranji!" Photo: Max Penson (1935). UzRKSOKh/0-147633.

underwent a shift in meaning now that the party was massively involved. From signifying a desire for social and national progress, unveiling became a marker of women's adherence to communist policies and to the Soviet authorities, who were perceived as an external colonizing force. The act of unveiling thus became inauthentic, and the wearing of the veil swapped connotations to become a national symbol (Kamp 2006, 123–34; Edgar 2006, 272).

As of the mid-1920s, cinema participated in the emancipation policy by triggering a "feeling of protest against religious laws and customs" and inciting "a desire to combat ancient customs" (Liubimova 1928a, 33), as reported by two projectionists with the Iskra itinerant film crew—V. Aleksandrov and Ia. Kalimullin—who traveled the area around Tashkent in late 1924 working for International Red Aid.[27] The first question posed by the emancipation work of cinema was to figure out how to draw women into darkened rooms, given that most of them were unable to attend a public event alongside men. The invaluable report left by the head of Iskra, Aleksandrov, shows just how imaginative and skillful the agitators were. The first stage of their task was to drum up interest among the female audience they were targeting. Aleksandrov recommends starting by holding a screening for a predominantly male audience and announcing at the end a "special free screening" exclusively reserved for women and children, carefully pointing out to those present that adolescents and men would not be admitted.[28]

*The National Cinematographic Sphere* | 99

Figure 3.2. Mobile equipment of the Iskra crew, late 1924, in the region of Tashkent. UzRMDA 34/1/2559, 15–16.

A "more discreet phase of agitation" then followed, with influential men being approached to "firmly" direct their wives or sisters to attend the special screening. These free screenings attracted less than twenty or so women for several dozens of children under the age of ten or twelve (both boys and girls)[29] (fig. 3.2).

Then, since "women are very shy and distrustful," this specific public was "approached" using "attractive programs" (*primanki*) made up of about ten short popular science documentaries, films about the landscape (*vidovaia fil'ma*), or tales for young audiences. This type of film of "straightforward novelty," intended primarily to entertain and without any truly ideological content, enabled women to attend and become accustomed to cinema:

> Drawing on our own experience, we launch the first film without expecting there to be a large audience, 10 to 15 people are enough. On hearing the laughter and enthusiastic exclamations, the public who have stayed outside, hesitating at the idea of entering a dark and mysterious room, are unable to put up any longer with the inner struggle between their curiosity and their timidity, and they ask to be let in. That is what we needed! The film comes to an end after fifteen or twenty minutes and the ice has been broken, fear and doubt have been dispelled, and the female spectators are now accustomed. We henceforth inspire blind trust, as does our entertainment. We then announce a short break and invite the spectators to run and fetch their female friends,

sisters, and mothers who might still be hesitating. The kids set about this task with joy. We promise we will wait. And very quickly those who had run off come back with new spectators. Gradually the room fills up.[30]

For the first few cinematographic agitation events in the villages, and on the basis of his own experience, Aleksandrov recommends offering solely entertaining films for a female audience, leaving aside more politicized films. "After which, being more strongly accustomed to cinema and being taken with a passion for it, it will become normal practice, and we may courageously and successfully use it to work with women. In this way the cinema is irreplaceable since it makes it possible—without any noisy struggle or friction, and under the guise of a wholly innocent entertainment—to bring together an ever larger mass of women and plant and imperceptibly inculcate emancipatory ideas, in highly effective forms. This new and difficult business demanded political finesse."[31]

There may follow an opportunity to work with a delegate from the women's club, who will use the occasion to do some "light preparatory agitation." But it is essential "that nobody realizes that the cinema is an ambush being laid by the women's club! Otherwise the husbands, fathers, and brothers will forbid the women from going to the cinema!" and "In the villages cinema takes over the *ichkari* [women's lodging], and catches reclusive women in its nets, progressively contaminating them with a feeling of rebellion against their subjugation, and giving a taste for social life. The delegates of the Women's Division, schoolteachers, and other comrades all jump on Iskra in their search of even temporary support and help."[32] Women were admitted free of charge to encourage them to attend. This was the case in the old town of Tashkent from late September 1926. On occasions there were more women than men.[33]

While this type of agitation was probably unique, the film theater, along with the locations and studios where the films were shot, symbolized a new, modern, public space where women were free to remove their veils and sit alongside men. This aspect is emphasized in a scene in *The Jackals of Ravat*. After a speech by feminist activists, a screening is held in which men and women come together in the same place. Cinema emancipates those in front of and behind the camera. When the film was being shot, about one hundred Uzbek women agreed to remove their veils in front of the lens, even though one of them subsequently regretted this and asked the team to "give them back their image."[34] The Soviet press of the period mentions women removing their veils during and after screenings. The *Yer Yuzi* journalist indicates that women removed their veils at an open-air screening of *The Jackals of Ravat* in March 1928. The screening that day was accompanied by an agitator (*tashviqotchi*) introducing the film and attracted many spectators despite the biting cold. Some woman started to remove their *paranji* during the screening, and others then followed their example. The journalist states that the speech by the orator finally convinced the last remaining women wearing veils to follow suit.[35] The Armenian director Amo Bek-Nazarov (1892–1965) also recounts how he saw a woman remove her veil during a screening and leave the film theater uncovered (Smith 1997, 662).[36]

*Propaganda and Subjectivity in* Chachvon

As a film made for the tenth anniversary of the October Revolution, *Chachvon* in particular was used for the emancipation campaign. It was completed just in time and was distributed widely in Uzbekistan.[37] The Uzbek studios initially thought of asking Pudovkin to make it, before approaching Yevgeni Ivanov-Barkov (1892–1965), Pavel Petrov-Bytov (1895–1960), and even Dmitri Bassalygo.[38] It is not known why they all turned down this offer, but the film was finally made by Mikhail Averbakh, a "young director without any practical experience" (*kino-molodniak*) and a member of the Association of Cinema Workers.[39] He visited Uzbekistan with a film crew in September and October 1927. *Chachvon* had to comply precisely with ideological requirements given that the director was a member of the Association of Cinema Workers, which had been set up in Moscow in 1924 on the initiative of members of the film industry (Kuleshov, Eisenstein, and Pudovkin) and literary figures in order to subordinate cinema to communist culture. In a declaration published on February 26 in the *Kino-gazeta*, all filmmakers sharing this point of view were called on to join the movement to meet the "demands of the dictatorship of the proletariat." This was the context within which the Association of Cinema Workers sent a letter to the head of Uzbekkino offering the services of its young directors, with the inviting body to pay their remuneration.[40] Averbakh was appointed and, on arriving, found a first scene written by two Uzbek press writers, which he deemed unsatisfactory. He rewrote the scene "in a hurry, in four days."[41]

Unlike *From Under the Vaults of the Mosque* and *The Leper*, which represented women as animals, or *The Second Wife*, showing them as martyrs, *Chachvon* insists on women as full of initiative and endowed with masculine traits (sometimes to the point of caricature) and emphasizes their ability to win their freedom thanks to Soviet power. The veil, a negative and subjugating object, is turned into a driving force in their emancipation. It is a shroud that, once lifted, reveals life. The woman who removes her veil is frequently associated with the camera itself, enabling the filmmaker to make extensive use of subjective camera shots to directly address the audience members, include them in the film's plot, and incite them to action. Although these techniques had been deployed in films before (*From Under the Vaults of the Mosque* and *The Leper*), *Chachvon* used them extensively.

> *Chachvon* (Rus. *Chadra* or *Chachvan*, Uzb. *Chochvon*)
> by Mikhail Averbakh (Uzbekkino, 1928)
>
> Gulbibi Haidarova (S. Askarova), a feminist activist, and Suleyman (Suleyman Khojaev), an electrical engineer, return to the country after having studied in Moscow to put the education they have received into practice. Gulbibi works at the women's club and comes to the assistance of poor Lola (Pavlova-Marozova). After losing her husband, Lola was given in marriage by her mother to the rich *bai* Haidar (G. Chechelashvili), becoming his third wife. She has been dreaming of emancipation when she hears the speech of another delegate at the women's club, Halima Niazmatova (Kh. Fish). The *bai*'s first two wives also happen to be present, and they tell their husband of Lola's desire for emancipation. Haidar decides to exorcize his wife of the "red devil" and calls on a traditional healer (*azaimkhon*) to do so. The exorcism takes place with several dervishes, and the *azaimkhon* tries to chase the evil spirit by whipping Lola. Halima witnesses this scene and alerts Gulbibi and Suleyman, who arrive with the militia. Lola is taken far away from her husband and, after convalescing, leaves to study in Moscow. When she returns to Uzbekistan, the emancipation campaign (*hujum*) is in full swing. But to take his revenge Lola's former husband asks men to abduct her while she is resting at the women's club. Halima notices her disappearance and alerts Gulbibi and Suleyman. With the help of the militia, they pursue Haidar's men and save Lola once again. Life returns to normal. Suleyman goes back to work at the waterworks, Halima starts working as an intern in the cinema studios while the *hujum* carries on. Women march with banners proclaiming "Long live the liberated Orient, long live liberated women," while Haidar looks on disapprovingly from behind the bars of his prison.

From the very beginning of this film, two worlds collide. National modernity is embodied by Suleyman and Gulbibi, who form a united, egalitarian, and companionable couple and are vectors for change. The imminent radical transformation is signaled by the flashes of lightning accompanying their return home by train and the whistling of the locomotive bringing them back from Moscow, where they have studied: "Several hundred kilometers away" (as the title card indicates) lies Tashkent (the second scene of the film). It is a poor, sad world, where a woman is baking (Lola's mother), covered by her *paranji* and *chachvon*. All she encounters are the shadows of camels and a few men who stop to give her a crust of bread. The point where these two worlds converge is the central railway station. It is at this precise moment that the viewer is invited into the plot.

The interior of the station concourse is vast, with a series of great pillars, and a tidal wave of men advance toward the camera with frequent looks-to-camera (subjective) shots, while a left-to-right traveling shot seems to be looking for Suleyman and Gulbibi.

The longest use of subjective camera shots is in the key scene where Halima describes the recent International Youth Day, praising the Soviet policy to emancipate women. She is facing Lola, her mother, and Haidar's two other wives. With a long look-to-camera shot and parallel edits, Halima talks about the speeches given by determined, directive women activists like Gulbibi and explains what she has seen—virtually military gymnastic exercises (*fizkultura*) by Komsomol women in sports outfits and striped jerseys and military training exercises (gas masks, rifle firing) in accordance with leitmotifs of Stalinist propaganda of the period, especially the recurrent idea of a "threat of war" in the late 1920s (Werth 2007, 105). The day was rounded off by a supreme recompense: the screening of *The Jackals of Ravat*. Halima is beaming with happiness, her eyes fixed on the camera, and launches into a long educational tirade (the shot lasts seven seconds) forestalling any potential questions from the characters or spectators. There are two opposing camps: the women who are emancipated or who wish to be so (Halima and Lola) and those who are against it. The aggressive, skeptical looks of the latter are met with Halima's cordiality, calm, and enthusiasm. And the enjoinders denying the possibility of removing the veil—"May a Muslim woman show herself without a veil!" "Your face will be eaten up by anthrax,"[42] and "People will call you a prostitute"—are met by Halima's response, and the final word: "It's not true, in our club many Uzbek women do not wear a veil, their face has not been attacked by anthrax, and nobody dares call them prostitutes," "Gulbibi is a beautiful and intelligent woman. I have listened to her, and everybody respects her!" (fig. 3.3).

Lola is the only one to be convinced, and she asks for Halima's help to meet Gulbibi in secret. Halima thinks with lowered head, then looks up at the camera (the spectator) and nods in agreement. This time the look-to-camera shot seeks to establish a direct relationship with the woman viewer, inciting her to do the same thing. Lola meets Gulbibi, who explains to her—once again with a look-to-camera shot and a flashback—how she managed to escape her condition as a subjugated woman and to go away to study. At other moments, subjective shots seek to awaken feelings of compassion and pity. Lola is in tears as she is preparing for her wedding and has to leave her mother, and she turns toward the camera with a look of extreme sorrow that is intended to move the viewer. Although the film does not wholly do away with the parallel between women and animals, the purpose of the comparison takes on a more political and protestatory tenor. The wedding scene opens with a shot of an animal being disemboweled with a knife. "The entrails of a sheep once again" (title card). In

Figure 3.3, a-f. Halima narrates the events at the International Youth Day. *Chachvon*. Screen stills.

the next shot, the camera is backing away from Lola's face, and the viewer has the impression of emerging from her soul, like the viscera that have just been removed from the sheep.

Lola is fairly complex compared with the other women characters, who are attracted by sex and scheming (Haidar's two wives), are masculinized (Gulbibi, the women's club activist), or are dynamic, such as Halima. Lola's position, her state of ascetic poverty, her forced marriage, her poor treatment at the hands of her husband, her repeated abduction, and her journey to Moscow all portray her as a martyr who manages to rise above her ordeals. This kind of Way of the Cross is symbolized by a shot presenting her in front of a traditional embroidery, transforming her into an icon and setting up a correlation between emancipation and Christianity (fig. 3.4).

The women's sphere is one of action and liberation, playing on feelings of pity and compassion via direct discourse in an exhortative process intended to encourage the audience to act—a characteristic that is typical of propaganda. These exhortations addressed to the female public are countered by another sort of "emotional communication"—this time taking the form of an accusation targeting the male public and intended to awaken feelings of guilt over having acted wrongly. The sort of behavior to be stigmatized is embodied by Haidar. The viewer first meets this character sitting beneath the mulberries at a teahouse. He takes a bowl of tea, which appears to come straight from the camera lens, placing the viewer in the position of Haidar's companion holding out the bowl, and thus his confidant. Haidar explains that he wishes to have a new wife (Lola) because he is "tired"—as he says—of his two other wives. Haidar becomes aggressive and directs his ire toward the viewer. When Lola arrives in her house for the first time after her wedding, Haidar drags her forcibly toward the bed. He tries to cover her eyes, but in fact covers the camera lens in a subjective shot involving the viewer and placing the audience in the position of the victim. When he invites the healer for the exorcism scene (*kuchirik*) to chase out the "red devil" inhabiting Lola's mind, numerous accusatory look-to-camera shots denounce this practice and are intended to awaken a feeling of guilt among those who might act in a similar manner.

## Stereotypes and Symbols as Viewed from Tashkent

Did *Chachvon* meet the expectations of its women viewers? How did the public perceive its symbols and associations of ideas? While the official cultural magazine *Yer Yuzi* felt the film offered a fair account of the harsh life of cloistered Uzbek women, others, such as *Pravda Vostoka*, noted numerous inconsistencies and included accounts of how women audience members reacted to the film.[43] The article in *Pravda Vostoka* starts by describing the everyday practical difficulties encountered by the emancipation campaign, referring to articles in regional newspapers (*Iangi Farghona, Azad Bukhoro*) and in the national press (*Qizil Uzbekiston*). In one case, a local public instruction official accepted his wife's removal of her veil at a collective event, but once the event was over, he hurried off to buy her a new *paranji*. In another case, a husband refused to show his wife to his family without her veil for fear

Figure 3.4, a-b. Lola as a martyr and an exemplary woman. *Chachvon*. Screen still.

of creating a precedent. And in a third case, a madman (*divona*) in the old town of Bukhara approached indigenous women not wearing a veil and scared them, following them in the streets and shouting at them.⁴⁴ The journalist depicts these daily obstacles without mentioning more violent exactions (such as rape and murder) and insists that women expected the film to provide behavioral models to move beyond such situations. Hence the film, "which seemingly ought to have been perfectly intelligible to local Uzbek women, struck them as uninteresting." It only provided an "approximate" reflection of their concerns, intermixing "chases with endless discussions," or showing Halima working in women's clubs on caricatures and "blackening the walls" all around town. There is no reference to her educational work or place of work. The public are said to regret that the most important stages in the emancipation campaign were not evoked in the film. How was it prepared? What concrete measures were taken? Who was opposed to it? What did the representatives of the Muslim "clergy" do?

In addition, the public perceived several scenes as particularly "fantastical," such as the exorcism rite, or as disconnected from their reality and personal experience. Audiences could not understand how Gulbibi manages to flee after being imprisoned. And when, at Halima's suggestion, she puts on a *paranji* to secretly enter Lola's house, this disguise appears to be devoid of meaning to the two women when they are supposed to have been oppressed by such clothing. Other scenes are comical, such as those of Komsomol members studying their newspaper beneath the watchful portraits of Lenin and Marx. The film is thus "lame and offensive": "*Chachvon* is a shameless and pretentious lie, like the veil itself. It hides our life and customs from everyone's view, as the *chachvon* hides a woman's face from the light. . . . Because of the script and director of *Chachvon*, the film is transformed into an offence to the liberation of women, turning it into a subject of derision."⁴⁵

All these opinions bring out the incompatibility between two registers—that of the symbols and allegory employed by the filmmaker and that of the straightforward discourse the Uzbek audience members expect. By taking Lola as the symbol of the archetypal woman becoming aware of her subjugation, dreaming of emancipation, and managing to free herself, the filmmaker presents his film as a universal example. Lola embodies all women. But this message went wholly unperceived: "One gets the impression that for the tenth anniversary of October only a single woman threw out her *paranji*, and that no steps were taken along the road of liberation."⁴⁶ While the process of identification is plausible on a technical level, thanks to the subjective shots, it ultimately fails to work due to the inconsistencies and what local audiences viewed as unrealistic details.

The press reaction to *Chachvon* highlights the gap that could exist between the work of a filmmaker fashioned by intellectual, aesthetic, and ideological debates about cinema and the Uzbek public, who had not yet assimilated the complexity of filmic language and who, especially, did not have the same cultural referents; in other words, certain images failed to convey anything to them. While the filmmaker was seeking a propaganda art form to be placed at the service of the political sphere, the public wanted an "agitation film" (*agitka*) where all that matters is the content and where the formal and artistic aspects are thus secondary. This incomprehension was not due to some East/West opposition; rather, it was indicative of the gap between urban intellectual culture and rural culture, in Uzbekistan or elsewhere. Marc Ferro observes that Eisenstein's *Strike* was acclaimed in Petrograd but provoked strange reactions in the countryside. He argues that the allegory of the tsar as butcher (with crosscut footage of animals being slaughtered) was incomprehensible to peasants, for whom there was nothing criminal in killing an animal ([1977] 1993, 200). Under these circumstances, how was the public to react to the shot of a disemboweled sheep and the close-up on Lola's imploring face?

In addition, *Chachvon* presents a very Russian-centric vision of Soviet territory. Whereas the Uzbek critics and the women they spoke for wanted to know how to set off for Moscow to emancipate themselves, the filmmaker privileges Gulbibi and Suleyman's return as conduits for Soviet modernity—not their departure. Thus, on returning after their travels, which are part pilgrimage and part initiatory voyage, the resultant transformation has turned them into strangers. Shirbek's article emphasizes how strange they are; instead of going to live in their home, Gulbibi and Suleyman stay at the House of the Soviets, which was reserved for prestigious guests. And the price of this accommodation would appear to be incoherent: "How can they pay for such expensive lodging where it costs 3 or 4 *sum* per night, given that their monthly salary as government-funded students is no more than 75 *sum*?"[47]

The *Komsomolets Vostoka* offers the following summary of the debate and expresses the wish that the film be banned:

> The main characteristics of this film are its idiotic and unrealistic subject in an adventurous style, a monstrous alteration of the character and customs of the Uzbeks, and weak and clumsy acting! . . . But where is the veil? Where is the fearful heroism of the Oriental woman? Where are the causes which make a woman want to remove her *chachvon*? Is it not pretentious to explain the desire for emancipation in terms of hatred for a husband? . . . *Chachvon* is a lie from beginning to end. What with the customs altered to the point of implausibility, the unrefined handling of the subject, and the quality of the acting, which is beneath all criticism, we deplore that the request made by social circles to ban the release of this Uzbekkino masterpiece should have been deemed impossible. It is still not too late, for pity's sake![48]

*Chachvon* was poorly received by the local Uzbek population, as it was in Moscow, though there the criticism was less virulent. The film attracted criticism for its unrealistic nature after a public screening in Moscow held by the Association of Cinema Workers on November 26, 1926. Members of the film industry and the press regretted how inaccurate its representations were and how hazy the knowledge of the society depicted was. Averbakh defended himself, referring to the complexity of the film shoot and lack of time.[49] He mentioned the difficulties he had encountered in getting people to understand him, working in relative isolation and unable to apprehend the social reality of Uzbekistan in the late 1920s: "It was incredibly hard for me to work there. I could not explain what I wanted to the Uzbeks. You need to realize that when I wanted to direct and construct a complex artistic composition I was unable to explain it to the Uzbeks as they did not understand me. . . . It is very hard to work when you arrive in the village and people do not understand anything other than the words "tea" and "bread." . . . So how can you talk about a film?"[50]

But these explanations failed to satisfy members of the filmmaking profession. In the resolutions taken after the screening, it was judged that Averbakh had good technical knowledge and so managed to create "good moments" but that the overall result was unsatisfactory due to the weakness of the script and the lack of immersion in Uzbek customs. "Comrade filmmaker! You have wholly failed to study living conditions in Uzbekistan. . . . The filmmaker and scriptwriter have only glanced at Uzbekistan, even though they were working for the Uzbek government. . . . The people have not studied national particularities enough. When you make this sort of film, you need to invite national [consultants] who know local customs. . . . That way the film is more successful."[51]

But unlike the film professionals, the guardians of ideology—the members of the State Repertoire Committee of Soviet Russia—were satisfied, though they did reproach the film for being like the agitation films of 1919–20.[52] The Repertoire Committee gave its consent to distribution throughout the Russian Federation (for all film theaters), and even for export abroad. Equally, the Uzbekkino representative in Moscow, speaking on behalf of the studio's executives and displaying no awareness of the virulent press criticism detailed above, deemed that Averbakh had carried out his task to the full: "I would like to say . . . that this young filmmaker has no reason to blush, for we will give more films to such directors. [APPLAUSE] . . . The film was made at the request of the government especially for our population of wild Uzbeks who people Uzbekistan. They liked the film. It worked well there. The film talks about Uzbeks—though perhaps it does not speak to you. You say the film is primitive, but we are dealing with a people who are not civilized. The film was not made for Moscow but for Uzbeks." [LAUGHTER, APPLAUSE].[53]

In all these debates, the only person to present the national point of view was a Tatar:

> I may not be a direct representative of the "wild people," as the Uzbekkino representative put it, but still, I am close to them, for I am Tatar.... We have been shown here a public screening of a film about Uzbek life—but where are the representatives of the Uzbek people? Even though these people are "wild," since the October Revolution there has been a Political Education Institute, Uzbek representation, writers, film artists. In my opinion the great error of the ODSK Central Committee is that it has not invited their representatives. They no doubt see this people as a "wild" and uncultured people![54]

One final important point needs to be made about the discussions of the film, which reflects an essential characteristic of the emerging propaganda, which sought to not only represent but "figure" and anticipate future society. This brought about a transition from "objective realism" (calls for ethnographic-style representation guaranteeing the authenticity of future films, unlike those made previously) toward "subjective realism," the precursor of Socialist Realism. While blaming the credulity of people who "believe what they see on the photos of Women's Clubs sent to Moscow," Averbakh reproduced the same sort of defect by creating a positive representation of women's clubs. He denounced the fact that nobody had remarked that they had been brave enough to show a women's club, pioneers, and Komsomol members:

> In the [first] scenario there were burials and weddings . . . whatever you want, everything that has already been criticized. I removed the funerals [to put in] clubs, and suppressed the weddings. [LAUGHTER] . . . It is more important to show a Soviet club than funerals that don't add anything . . . but simply provide the ethnographic context. . . . The clubs in the old towns are frightening, and we shot in the new part of town. And then our club was different from the others, as the floors were swept and it was a lot cleaner. Other Women's Clubs were so dirty we didn't even try to enter them. They told me it was because they were poor and didn't have any cleaning women. If you show Women's Clubs, you have to do it in a way that makes people want to go there. I think it's better to show the "good" side than the "bad" side.[55]

All these criticisms lead to the question of whether a "modern language" (cinema) is in fact predisposed to translating a modernization policy. *Chachvon* and its reception show how complex it can be to assimilate diegetic and ideological discourse (the message, the signified) at the same time as the codes of the new language (the form, the signifier). Prior to the arrival of cinema in Turkestan, intellectuals had encountered similar difficulties in founding modern theater in Central Asia, which they wanted to distance from the long tradition of popular theater, such as masquerade (*masqarabozlik*), on which they nevertheless drew for comic and satirical scenes (Khalid 1998, 13). For a modern conduit such as cinema (or theater) to serve a modernization policy, the language of images and editing needed to be acquired and pan-Soviet common cultural codes needed to be established to make them intelligible to all. Yet one might consider, along with Nariman Narimanov, that cinema and images were an essential channel of communication given that, "in the Orient people are not used to thinking in logical reasoning but in images" (quoted in Smith 1997, 646).

## Cinema and Antireligious Policy: Secularization, Entertainment, and Economic Rationale

In parallel to this propaganda to emancipate women, there was a virulent antireligious policy in the 1920s and 1930s (Keller 2001b; Khalid 2007b) combined with a destructive militant atheist activism in Central Asia targeting the Muslims—predominantly Hanafi Sunnis—the second largest religion in the Soviet Union after Christianity. This continued until the middle of the Second World War, when the Spiritual Directorate of the Muslims of Central Asia and Kazakhstan was set up in 1943.[56] Antireligious policy was one aspect of the Soviet authorities' plan to radically transform society and human conscience, and they focused particular attention on it from the early 1920s onward. Religion was viewed by the Bolshevik leaders as subjugation and "spiritual rot-gut" (*dukhovnaia sivukha*), and hence one of the principal obstacles to the total revolution to liberate the working masses (Yaroslavskii 1928, 31–33). The Bolshevik authorities replaced religious beliefs and ideas with new, secular values to transform ways of thinking. Media such as theater, radio, and film were mobilized along with other art forms to "plant anti-religious consciousness within the peasant and working masses." "'We need to get the support of our artists of the word, chisel, paintbrush, stage, photo, cinema, and music,' observed one of the principal architects of the Soviet and religious policy" (Yaroslavskii 1929, 7). Antireligious cinema in Uzbekistan really started to be used as part of this grand project in 1930–31.

### Antireligious Action and the Adaptation of Religious Discourse

Starting with the civil war, bloody exactions were made against religious dignitaries in Turkestan and Russia (Husband 1998, 79). At this time religious courts were shut down, pious foundations (*waqf*) were requisitioned, and mosques were destroyed, but new government measures rapidly attenuated and even countered the initial violence. The courts were reopened for want of an adequate judicial system to replace them and, in some regions, functioned in parallel with the Soviet courts until 1927 (Keller 1992, 29–32; Khalid 2007b, 61; Sartori 2010). The decree on the separation of church and state, passed on January 23, 1918, by the Bolshevik government in Russia (and on which Patriarch Tikhon laid an anathema) had no real impact in Turkestan (Husband 1998, 78; Keller 2001b, 50). In late 1919, the Central Executive Committee of Turkestan decided that Friday would be set aside for prayer, and in the mid-1920s some of the pious foundations were handed back to the mosques and madrasas. A proposal for an antireligious campaign was presented to the Turkestan Communist Party in 1923, but it was turned down by the Central Asian members. A few initiatives were launched in the old town of Tashkent in 1923 but were met with stiff resistance from the local population and party cadres.

The secularization policy in Turkestan and then in Uzbekistan tended to be conducted via local initiatives stemming from the party or the Red Army. In the 1920s, the policy was characterized by the variable, contradictory, disorganized, or generalized nature of the measures used (Keller 2001b, 63). This policy primarily targeted the Orthodox faith but also affected Islam, initially focusing on religious institutions (*maktabs* and madrasas) and their representatives, clergy, and property, before hardening in 1925 with the founding of the Atheist Union—also known as the Union of the Godless (*bezbozhnikov* in Russian, *khudosizlar* in Uzbek)—who were behind the first campaigns.[57] Yemelian Yaroslavskii (1878–1943), the main engineer of Soviet antireligious policy and supporter of a moderate line, thought that the way to combat religion was to use cautious yet persevering propaganda so as not to upset the religious feelings of believers.[58] However, this moderate tendency was not always observed in practice, and violent methods were employed, mainly by activists carrying out the policy rather than those in charge of it. Antireligious propaganda was not really systematized during the 1920s, but it intensified with the policy for the emancipation of women in 1927, and especially with the forced collectivization of agriculture and the "dekulakization" (the extermination of supposedly well-off peasants as a class), amounting to a violent assault against religion in the countryside and against believers themselves (Ohayon 2006, 63; Husband 1998, 79–80). This resulted in arrests, deportations, and prison sentences.

The pace of propaganda accelerated in 1928, but the Bolshevik authorities believed the pressure could be stepped up even more.[59] In practice it was hampered in Uzbekistan by inadequate means, and the members of the Union of the Godless complained that they had unqualified personnel who were unable to plan actions. In late 1928, they had no idea of the size of their union, its hierarchy, or the number of members; did not know what initiatives were being undertaken in the country; and admitted they were unable to apprehend the situation or benefit effectively from the great Soviet celebrations. They also deplored the lack of support from the press and from professional, political, and social organizations in the country.[60] Furthermore, there was no written material. Drawing up antireligious propaganda in the Muslim regions ran into a shortage of publications—including in the pages of the antireligious newspaper *Bezbozhnik*. In this it differed from the Orthodox religion, which was better documented (Uspenskii 1927).[61] The only exception was *Islam*, a work by Fillipov

(1926)—and the sole reference up until 1927—of which two thousand copies had been printed and which was deemed adequate for the work of the Union of the Goddesss. What was lacking was "the Marxist book about the Muslim religion," and propaganda was conducted using methods employed against the Orthodox religion or using knowledge about Islam dating from the imperial period that the Russian communists felt to be insufficient and superficial (Uspenskii 1927, 30; Lukachevskii 1930, 114; Keller 1992, 35).

As of the late 1920s, a small amount of antireligious material was drawn up by local writers and thinkers. One of these works, *From Illusion to Truth* (*Khaialdan haqiqatga*), written by Mannan Ramiz (Abdullaev) (1898–1939), adheres to the moderate line advocated by Yaroslavskii and is adapted to local conditions.[62] Antireligious propaganda needs to be done gently and without using any force, the key tool being "scientific and materialist teaching" (quoted in Keller 1992, 40). Others such as Mir Said Sultan-Galiev (1892?–1940) felt that humor was more effective than violent attacks against religious dignitaries or the Koran (Sultan-Galiev 1921, 50).[63] Still, while Bolshevism and Muslim cultural reformism were incompatible on questions of religious substance (Khalid 2007b, 69), certain stigmatizations to be found in the press and literature prior to the October Revolution—such as anticlericalism and the denunciation of superstition (*khurofat*)—provided points of convergence in practice.[64]

The implementation of the antireligious policy caused the population and religious dignitaries to adopt strategies to resist and avoid it, ranging from the use of physical and moral violence (murder, intimidation, reprisals, threats of apocalypse) to more subtle accommodations and less fierce reactions (civil disobedience, petitions, and protest marches by women). Religious discourse was also marked by recently devised discursive inflections—something for which the atheist activists were, to their great regret, even less well prepared (Lukachevskii 1930, 114; Keller 1992, 38). The new preachings and sermons absorbed the ambient social and political discourse and integrated new vocabulary, identifying certain religious issues with communist principles, and above all displaying a remarkable adaptability.[65]

For instance, the Baptist brothers now preached that "Jesus Christ was of proletarian origin" and that he was "a great socialist, a communist, a spiritual father and precursor of the Communist Party." The Buddhist representative Khashbo-Agvon Dorjaev (1854–1938) announced to the Buddhist Congress in 1927 that the teachings of Buddha, Marx, and Lenin were largely the same thing, with the only "slight difference" being that the communists did not recognize reincarnation:[66]

> I say to you that between communists and the disciples of the pure teaching of Buddha, there is for the moment only a slight difference. The communists do not recognize the future migration of souls, but do recognize the transformation of nature from a materialist point of view, as taught by the great sage

Karl Marx and his disciple and great reformer of socialism V. I. Lenin. We, the true disciples of the teaching of Buddha, who teaches that the soul migrates, take as proof what has happened before our eyes these past eleven years, when what was once below has found itself raised up high. (quoted in Lukachevskii 1930, 113)

And Lukachevskii went on to regret that "Buddha is the spiritual father of the entire Komintern" (114).

The Muslim reformists, for their part, referred to the "proletarian tendencies" of the Koran. "And for reformers, the 'supreme judge' Allah with his faithful servant Mohammed follow . . . 'the proletarian line,'" Lukachevskii carried on indignantly. The Muslim "clergy" no longer approached peasants with an "old and fossilized dogmatism" (Arsharuni, quoted in Keller 1992, 38), but toned down their discourse for women, allowed Komsomol meetings to be held in mosques, and even sometimes played the "Internationale" after speeches described as reactionary by toadies of the Soviet authorities.[67] The "red mullahs," covered by Bolshevik sympathizers, continued to preach and spread out even beyond their areas of origin. The presence of Tatar mullahs "at the very heart of the Bolshevik Revolution" (here referring to Moscow and its surrounding area) was denounced. They openly went to factories and local agricultural councils for workers of Tatar origin to collect funds to build mosques. "And the Dombass, the proletarian base in Ukraine, is the preferred place of dozens of travelling mullahs who arrive from the four corners of the Tatarstan republic" (Said-Galiev 1929, 63). Whereas even the most backward peasants went back home as genuine atheists after serving in the Red Army, the Tatars followed the opposite path, toward "religious regression," according to Lukachevskii.

Islam was perceived by those in charge of propaganda as a more complex religion than Christianity or Judaism as well as proportionately better represented.[68] It provided a basis for political and social organization because it regulated all aspects of a believer's life while leaving room for reform (Said-Galiev 1929, 65). Thus, by reinterpreting the Koran, it became possible to recognize that women were the equal of men, leading to increased female attendance at mosques. In this way, "reformed" Islam was used to help build socialism: "In identifying with our party's program, Islam, alongside communism and Mohammed, finds itself to be the political friend of Karl Marx," Said-Galiev observed, once again with regret.

### Antireligious Propaganda in Cinema: Entertainment Plus Denunciation

Films denouncing Islam played on several different registers that were on occasion contradictory, thwarting the antireligious objective as initially defined. In seeking to present scenes that were both authentic and spectacular, they accorded religious personnel an important place in film, along with public existence on the screen and in the film theater. With their fondness of Sufi ritual ceremonies, *dhikr* scenes, and collective spiritual ecstasy, films attacked Islam through "peripheral" practices that were not unanimously recognized by most Muslims in Central Asia. And when the propaganda to emancipate women combined with the fight against religion, the main purposes were primarily economic rationality and potential productivity gains.

### Dervishes, Ishans, and Mullahs in the Limelight

As noted by atheist activists, the sometimes violent nature of antireligious propaganda led Muslim and Christian brotherhoods—described by the authorities as "sects" (*sekt, sektanstvo*)—to step up their activities. They had greater influence in the countryside due to the direct and indirect economic support they provided for women and young people by forming "youth circles" and "women's orders" (*sestrichestvo*).[69] Women were targeted by Muslim dignitaries who were quick to oppose the practice of reclusion and encourage women's involvement in society.[70] It was probably the increase in religious brotherhoods and their expanding influence that caused these phenomena to be of particular interest to cinema. Antireligious cinematographic propaganda exploited the spectacular potential of religious ceremonies, especially as of the 1930s (Drieu 2010a). Productions appeared to be attacking the Muharram ceremonies of Shi'ite Islam in A. Sharifzade's *Bismillah* (Azerbaijan, 1925) and *Shakhsei-Vakhsei* (Roskino, 1927), the practice of pilgrimage in G. Tasin's *The Guest from Mecca* (1930), and the *yazidis* and Ismailis in M. Verner and D. Vasiliev's *The Living God* (Tajikistan, 1931).[71] The *ishans* (the heads of religious brotherhoods), viewed by the authorities as "the most reactionary part of the clergy," were a privileged target in Uzbekistan. Yet while antireligious films denounced the exactions carried out by mullahs, dervishes, and *ishans*, they nevertheless accorded them a privileged role.

The use of local extras was a way of increasing a film's authenticity while satisfying the curiosity of audiences and the authorities, for whom cinema was a way of promoting knowledge about the Soviet peoples. This endowed film with considerable documentary and ethnographic value. The use of local figures was motivated by the savings it offered; it cost less to pay an extra than a professional actor. The realism of the images and scenes—especially those portraying religious ceremonies—was something Pudovkin actively sought in *Storm over Asia* (1929), in which a Buddhist ceremony was filmed after the Great Lama of Buryat-Mongolia intervened to overcome the reticence of the monks (Leyda 1976, 188). Equally, *Bismillah* (1925), by Abbas Mirza Sharifzade (1893–1937), portrays moments of the Muharram in Azerbaijan, when Shi'ites commemorate the martyrdom of Hussein at Kerbala, also known as Shakhsei-Vakhsei (Shah

Hussein, Ya Hussein).⁷² The shots of the procession in the village triggered disapproval among the faithful, which explains the use of fairly distant long shots, since the filmmaker and his camera operator were afraid of being targeted (Smith 1997, 658).

In *Chachvon*, for instance, real dervishes took part in the filming of the exorcism scene:

> We needed to shoot the scene with dervishes. . . . Amongst the people filmed for this scene we also found real dervishes, who initially refused to put on their sacred attributes since their rules stipulate they must bathe first before putting them on. We had to give them money and wait for them to return. During filming the dervishes were so caught up in their role that when we turned off the projectors and called out that shooting had finished they did not notice but continued with their "holy action," which consisted in convulsive movements, cries, wild groans, and possessed dances. It went on for another two hours until we heard the voice of the mullah calling the faithful to prayer, since the studios were next to the mosque. Our "actors" first refused to do the shoot, saying they absolutely had to pray and that they could not carry on with this story with the *shaitan* [devil]. . . . We called together these real dervishes and offered to double the proposed remuneration for the shoot. After a short discussion a representative told us they agreed to do so. Money was stronger than the Koran and their faith. So we filmed until nine in the morning. And once again the dervishes had to go to the baths (this time irrespective of their law), for they had caught lice from their "holy" costumes.⁷³

An *ishan* was also used to film Sabinskii's *Last Bek* (1930), a film about Enver Pasha (1881–1922) of which there are no existent copies.⁷⁴ "We looked for an old man with a suitable appearance for the role of the *ishan*. When I asked him, as we were filming tests, if he had already seen a real *ishan*, so as to perform the role as accurately as possible, the 'actor' looked down, embarrassed, and timidly mumbled 'I am an ishan myself.'"⁷⁵ The same article explains that the team also used a mullah and the muezzin from the mosque in a sequence involving about a hundred people depicting a public trial and Muslim judge:

> It was interesting to observe the way the mullah "acted." When he noticed the lens turning towards him he buried his face in his hands. His lips moved incessantly as he mumbled something (he was asking Allah for forgiveness or else cursing us). But the "holy Father" got mixed up. He hid his face during rehearsals and by a stroke of fortune remained calm during the shoot itself. At the end of each shot he ran to the *aryk* and did his ablutions. And he was frightened when he realized we had tricked him. What calmed him down was when we said as a joke that the film would not be shown in the Uzbekistan but only in Moscow.

DENOUNCING ISLAM THROUGH SUFI PRACTICES

The spectacular potential of the religious ceremonies of the Sufi brotherhoods is put to use in *The Ishan's Fiancée*, Oleg Frelikh's third and final film, which served the antireligious campaign in the early 1930s, both in Central Asia and in Soviet republics elsewhere. Some of the film was shot at the Shah-i zenda necropolis in Samarkand (Gaidovskii 1930, 18). The action starts at the beginning of the century and progresses to the 1920s and the early days of collectivization.

> *The Ishan's Fiancée* (Rus. *Doch' sviatogo*, Uzb. *Avliia Qizi*)
> by Oleg Frelikh (Uzbekkino, 1930)
>
> Shots of a mosque in ruins. Men and the women go on pilgrimage to the *ishan* Abdu Nabi (Suleyman Khojaev). One of them is Tursun (R. Turakhojaev), accompanied by his wife Hakima (Z. Shakirova), who is sterile. While Hakima is waiting with her husband, her *chachvon* unfortunately falls to the ground, and the *ishan*, having noticed her face, calls on his disciples to bring her in to him. After being raped, she gives birth to a girl, Oiniso (L. Jalilova). The years pass and Oiniso becomes a beautiful young woman. One day, when Oiniso is near the river, the *ishan* notices her and decides to ask her father for her hand in marriage. Hakima tries to oppose this union by going to the *ishan*, but her determination gives way to fear when she notices the Koran to which the holy man points her with a glance. The only way she can see out of the situation is for her daughter to go and join the Komsomol, and she organizes her escape. Tursun notices that Oiniso has disappeared and goes off to look for her, but without success. He asks the *ishan* for advice, who suggests washing away in blood the affront done by his wife. When night comes, Tursun decides to kill Hakima. But she wakes up and flees through the narrow streets, alerting her neighbors, who prevent Tursun from following her. She admits to them that she was raped. Men set off in pursuit of the *ishan* for him to be charged, while Tursun remains sitting motionless and dumbstruck on the ground. Morning approaches and the muezzin starts his call to prayer: "God is great," "There is no god but God." Tursun sees once again the scene described by Hakima and deduces that religion is nothing but "LIES."

Islam (in fact in this film it is the *naqshbandiyya jahri* brotherhood, a minority within the *naqshbandiyya* order), the influence of religious dignitaries, and the devotion of the faithful are described as dusty ancestral practices from another period, like the shots of the ruined mosques and minarets with which the film opens. Significant title cards are inserted between the shots: "In the old towns," "Amidst the dusty mosques," and "There is no god but God." The imposing and austere vaults of the mosques, shown in traveling shots moving downward from the top, also conceal "dusty prayers" and strange "festivities." The *ishan* takes a Koran, lifts it toward his face, and recites a formula while swaying. It is the beginning of a *dhikr*.[76]

A crowd of "sick people," "destitute people," and "sterile women" (title cards) flock to this holy place in the hope of finding a solution to their afflictions. The crowd is largely dehumanized by distant long shots, showing women in *paranji* and then a stream of sick men hobbling along. The women hardly show their faces and are filmed from behind, huddled over as they walk up the steps leading them to the gigantic Koran lectern that they hope will cure them. At first, the men's faces are not shown, and "people pray" in a state of immobility, "wait[ing] resignedly" for "the miracle." The appearance of the *ishan*, Abdu Nabi, puts an end to this waiting and causes a stir among the men and women, who come up to him, touch him, and pass their hands over his face to benefit from his powers. A woman picks up the dust from beneath the feet of the holy man and strokes the cheeks of a child. Another woman shows the *ishan* her baby's mouth in the hope that he might spit in it to cure him. Tursun and Hakima are among the pilgrims. Tursun is unhappy not to have children and accompanies the procession of the faithful, expecting Ishan Abdu Nabi to deliver the long-awaited miracle.

After Abdu Nabi has spotted Hakima and asked his disciples to bring her to a room, he locks the door behind him and advances toward her. The threat is signified by the "spectral" shadow of the *ishan* advancing toward Hakima. The rape scene is not portrayed but invoked through numerous shots showing the faithful performing the *dhikr* crosscut with close-ups of faces in ever faster and particularly suggestive succession. The practice of the *dhikr* and spiritual ecstasy are contrasted with that of the sexual act. Oinisso is born of this rape, and for Tursun she is the hoped-for "miracle." But this is not the end to the "sexual decadence" of the *ishan*, which comes to take the form of incest since he hopes to wed his own daughter without knowing it. Islam, here reduced to mystical practice, is associated with sexual aggression. The image of religious dignitaries as rapists would appear to be quite common, appearing notably in the film *Bismillah*, as referred to above.

When Hakima wants to oppose the marriage between the *ishan* and her daughter, he tells her cynically, and triumphantly, "Was it not God who gave you your child?" "Do you not believe in the miracle?"

## From Religious Subjugation to Economic Servitude

From the early 1930s onward, there are fewer press sources about the reception of films, and almost no reviews were published in the newspapers examined for the

Figure 3.5, a-f. The rape of Hakima by the *ishan*, Abdu Nabi. *The Ishan's Fiancée*. Screen stills.

period between late 1930 to late 1932. Press photographs, Stakhanovite exploits, and cotton production graphs took up more space, however. In the archives, a report from the person in charge of the Uzbekkino subsidiary in Khorezm asked his superiors to send him more films of this sort, "with subjects that are accessible to the local population," indicating that *The Ishan's Fiancée* was well received among the public. It is unlikely that viewers established a direct link between spiritual ecstasy and the sexual act, as clearly signified by the editing. The local population had difficulty understanding parallel editing and fade-outs, because these techniques broke the flow or sequence of the action more than they established any potentially significant link (Bunegin 1933). However, the rape and sexual violence are clear even without this editing technique. It is also worth noting—as explored in more detail in chapter 4—that the perception of the film was largely dependent on the oral "pitch" accompanying it and on the tenor of the commentary.

*The Ishan's Fiancée* was distributed not only in Uzbekistan but in other Soviet republics as well. Evidence of this wider distribution is provided by the exposé published in the antireligious propaganda newspaper *Bezbozhnik*, which accompanied the film and was used as material by the orators in charge of explaining it before or after the screening. This text gives the film a mark of three out of five, saying little about the antireligious message properly speaking, which is dealt with in a short introduction mentioning "the cultural backwardness of the masses in a state of religious captivity," "the cabalized situation of women who don't have the courage to remove their veil," and the need to "break the shackles of religious prejudice" in order to build a new life (Kefala 1931, 92–94).

In fact, the antireligious tenor of the exposé is inversely related to the place accorded in the film to Islam and its representations. The text emphasizes industrialization and the collectivization of agriculture in Uzbekistan, backed up with extensive indicators about the evolution of the economic situation in the country and its place within the Soviet Union. The film quite clearly insists on these aspects. The *bai*s, the allies of the mullahs and *ishan*s, are stigmatized as "class enemies" and opposed to economic and agricultural change. They also make anti-Russian comments and criticize the policy of planting cotton instead of rice. The building of the kolkhozes offers a way of presenting the representatives of the various peoples of the Soviet Union as heroes by extolling "the friendship between the peoples," thus countering through this multinational support the perception of agricultural policy as being purely foreign and Russian. The national question is subject to internationalist work. Close-ups of faces of various Soviet nationalities interspersed with title cards present a unanimous vision: "All . . . " " . . . the republics of the Union" " . . . are for . . . " "the kolhozes." "Young Tajikistan . . . " "and the distant regions of the North," to which are added the Turkmen, the Caucasian peoples, and so on.

To a large extent, the antireligious propaganda is based on promoting the construction of the kolkhozes and the industrialization of the country. The female characters play an essential role here. In Grigori Cherniak's film *Her Right*, a woman symbolizes the fusion (*smychka*) between the town and country and the transfer of industrial methods of production to agriculture (*otkhodnichestvo*). The film deals with how women from the East are involved in building socialism, thereby validating their emancipation once and for all. *Her Right* was deemed "suitable for a mass audience," even though the psychological transformation of the heroine was not shown clearly enough by its author (*Ee pravo* 1932, 3).

---

*Her Right* (Rus. *Ee pravo*) by Cherniak (Uzbekkino, 1930)

The cotton harvest is drawing to a close, women are busy in the fields, and men are loading produce and looking after the machinery. Taji (I. Volodko), covered in a *paranji*, wants to go and work in the factory with Komsomol members, but her husband, Qasym Iusupov (R. Akhmedov), refuses. When winter comes, another wave of departures of workers for the Komsomol is organized. Taji manages to join the group, jumps on the train, and though Qasym runs after, he only manages to catch hold of her *paranji*. At the factory Taji becomes a member of a "shock brigade" and distinguishes herself over her male counterparts in a scene of socialist emulation. She is victorious and speaks in praise of the work methods in the factory that need to be transposed to the kolkhozes. The factory shock brigade returns to the fields to apply these new methods to agriculture. To help the kolkhoz workers understand, a film is made and screened about Taji's brigade. Qasym then recognizes his wife on-screen. He gets up, takes out a knife, and symbolically slits her throat (slitting the white sheet used as a screen). The image stops, and men get up to immobilize Qasym. Once Qasym has calmed down, the film starts again and Taji continues making her speech with her throat cut. Qasym recognizes his wife's heroism and heads off to the factory, where he is reunited with her.

---

Women (and first and foremost Taji) are central as an economic resource, supplementary labor, and "substitute proletariat" (Massel 1947) symbolizing movement and change. As Michael Smith observes, oriental women offered cinema considerable potential for propaganda and entertainment (1997, 660). In *Her Right*, Taji strengthens the links between town and country and between factory and kolkhoz. And through a *mise en abîme* she becomes the cinematographic hero of her own story, and of the unstoppable Cultural Revolution as signified by the screen on which the film is shown. The face of the young woman freezes on the screen after Qasym slashes it with a knife, forcing the projectionists to stop turning the handle of their apparatus. Men get up to quell Qasym, while the people in the room ask for the screening to continue. Taji continues her speech with her throat cut: "Socialist work will emancipate all the female workers of the Soviet Orient from traditional and religious slavery, as it has me" (fig. 3.6).

Taji carries on and attacks Islam and the *bais*: "Thousands of women are still subject to *sharia*, still subject to the power of the *bais*." Then the men reason with

Figure 3.6, a-c. Qasym recognizes his wife on-screen and cuts her throat without being able to silence her. *Her Right*. Screen stills.

Qasym: "You ought to be proud to have a wife who is a shock worker." Qasym drops his knife, and Taji completes her apologia, eulogizing the role of women, "The war duty of all workers is to get 1,600,000 women involved in the industry." Qasym's act proves how backward he is and shows "that the kolkhoz workers are still insufficiently educated politically." He is overcome at the thought that everyone at the kolkhoz might see his wife with her face unveiled "another one thousand times," at each new screening. The filmmaker personifies the Cultural Revolution and its inevitable nature: "Nothing and nobody will be able to halt the powerful movement of the Cultural Revolution," as the communist orator says after the screening of the film. And so women swap their traditional clothing for workers' overalls.

# 4 Uzbek Film and the Shift toward Imperial Domination

> If we don't try now to adapt the form of the relationship between the center and the peripheries to a state of de facto interdependence, by virtue of which the peripheries must in general submit incontestably to the center..., then it will be incomparably more difficult in a year's time to defend the de facto unity of the Soviet republics.
>
> Stalin, letter to Lenin, September 22, 1922

This assertion, coming shortly before the creation of the Soviet Union—and, consequently, of the Uzbek Soviet Socialist Republic (1924)—reveals how certain Bolsheviks, and Stalin in particular, conceived of the relationship between central power and regional or national powers as being fundamentally unilateral in nature. Yet despite the Bolsheviks' doctrinal rejection of federalism and cultural autonomy, in the wake of the October Revolution, they were the first to seek to adapt these principles to the Soviet case, for both pragmatic and strategic reasons (Lirou 2009, 109–42). Although the Soviet Union was not a truly federal system from the point of view of constitutional law (144–70), the way it actually operated closely resembled such a system. Initially, the center interfered little in cultural policy, according each nation a considerable degree of autonomy regarding objectives and how it ran its policy. But as of the end of the New Economic Policy and the resultant process of centralization, there was a change in how the Soviet state was organized, reflecting the way Stalin conceived of the relationship between center and periphery, and the genuine unification of the Soviet republics into "a single economic whole."[1] To apprehend this shift and its various characteristics, I will use the concept of empire as defined by Maurice Duverger, which may be summarized as a vast multinational space with centrally organized territory, administration, and communications, where power is personalized and sacralized, forming a system that is universal in vocation and that destroys preexisting authorities (1980, 7–21).

Although it would be misleading to suggest that the Soviet empire had been fully constituted by this stage—a single ideology had not yet been fully imposed—it is nevertheless possible to apprehend its structure being put in place. The analysis conducted in this chapter of film production and distribution, concentrating as it does economic and institutional factors (centralization), political issues (purges), and material questions (the means of distribution), sheds particular light on the shift toward empire, with the progressive disappearance of national and territorial spheres of competence and the setting up of a hierarchy that would underpin central hegemony at least until the Second World War. The process by which the film industry became centralized and politically unified was launched by the first Five-Year Plan (1928-32) and the founding of Soiuzkino, a unified central committee operating across the Russian Soviet Federation, which emerged over time as the sole regulatory body for cinema in the Soviet sphere for economic issues (the allocation of resources) and ideological ones too (determining the themes of the films made).

How did this economic and political hegemony come to assert itself from the end of the New Economic Policy (in 1928)? How was the process of centralization perceived locally? What consequences did it have on the way work was organized on a daily basis? What gaps opened up between decisions and their application? While centralization corresponded to objectives formulated early on, and in fact to the hegemonic desire to dominate the peripheries by setting up an integrated economic system—that is, one that was not viable at a national scale due to the interplay of interdependence and subordination—it also struck local actors as a rational solution to their financial difficulties. The process explored here reveals how subordination was both imposed and accepted; it also accounts for the local actors' incomprehension of the initial political purposes and of the fundamental transformations that were afoot. This misunderstanding about the conception of the state—economic and centralized for some, interventionist and regulatory for others—generated substantial tension and an increasing number of contradictions. Three levers were used to subordinate the Uzbek periphery: an economic lever (centralization and the allocation of financial resources), which played a major role; a political lever (with ideological unification and purges); and a material lever (with the expansion of projection facilities) making it possible to exert sway across the territory and extend the communications network.

## Economic Centralization and Political Purges Assert Sway over Film Industry Structures

The ideological quality of films produced in Uzbekistan came in for criticism from the earliest days of film production in the country. From 1928 onward, the film industry's economic management and profitability were criticized, and the Council of People's Commissars, the Workers' and Peasants' Inspectorate (RKI), and the Uzbek Finance Commissariat commissioned several audits, thanks to which we can assess the four years of activity and understand the situation at the moment when the Stalinist Great Turn (*velikii perelom*) took place.[2]

## Uzbek Film Management Judged a Failure

It is not easy to draw up a commercial and financial assessment of film activity prior to economic centralization, because results can only be compared accurately from 1933, when accounting data and the frequency with which they were collected were homogenized. But it is still possible to determine the major trends affecting Uzbek film activity, which was assessed on several occasions from 1927 onward. The conclusions of a first report drawn up by the RKI for the period 1925–26 are relatively positive, recognizing that Uzbekkino had managed to conduct its activity without drawing on state subsidies. It had set up national production that had won over a significant market share and generated growing interest in oriental films.[3] Furthermore, ticket prices for the films made by Uzbekkino and distributed locally (in cinemas and clubs) were among the lowest in any of the republics. The financial statement for 1925–26 showed a profit thanks to the sale of films to other Soviet republics, especially to Russia (and Sovkino).[4] It is interesting to note that Uzbekistan no longer owned its first national film—*The Jackals of Ravat*—prefiguring in eloquent manner what Soviet nation building held in store (see table 3 in appendix).[5] But the sale of films and distribution revenue did not fully cover production costs, even though they did generate cash flow at least until 1934.[6]

Thus, until 1928, there was a systematic overshoot on the budget for fiction films (a frequent occurrence in film production in general), with costs often doubling by the time the film was made (see table 4 in appendix).[7] These overshoots were attributed to management errors and to inaccurate estimates for logistics and postproduction costs (for the laboratory, editing workshop, and so on) that were drawn up by Uzbekkino management.[8] In addition, shooting sometimes took a long time, with delays (in building sets) and fruitless, distant expeditions.[9] Furthermore, the filmmakers sought to exploit the poorly controlled situation while also finding it hard to assess the cost of working in the natural and climactic conditions of Central Asia; mastering the light in the region was not easy, resulting in a great deal of money being spent on film stock.[10] The assessment reports thus accuse the filmmakers and camera operators of being self-serving (*rvachestvo*) and of accumulating several jobs on any given film.[11] This sort of criticism was leveled against both national and invited personnel. The future director Nabi Ganiev, who at the time worked on newsreels, was criticized for presenting budgets and synopses in Uzbek while asking for additional payment for translating the title cards.[12]

The ideological quality of the Uzbek scripts was also singled out by the RKI, which was symptomatic of a more general situation. The fiction films were considered to be failures that falsified cultural traditions, conveying unacceptable ideology conjoined with superficial exoticism.[13] The scriptwriters working for the Uzbek studios came in for particular criticism, especially V. Sobberey

(*The Jackals of Ravat* and *From Under the Vaults of the Mosque*), who was accused of plagiarism, and Lola Khan Seifullina (*The Leper, The Covered Wagon*, and the agitprop film *How to Vote in the Soviets*), an acquaintance of the writer Chulpan.[14] According to the writers of the report, Uzbekkino's work required strong "ideological realignment," starting with the establishment of a script section worthy of the name. On March 31, 1928, only fifteen of the eighty-seven scripts in Uzbekkino's possession had been read by the department concerned, which reviewed two or three scripts at each weekly meeting. Other scripts, such as that for *Chachvon* (1928), were accepted without taking the opinions of the party and of literary or social organizations into account. Sometimes shooting started before a script had been accepted. These problems in how Uzbekkino operated and the way it worked with the literary authorities were endemic.[15]

The causes for the administrative dysfunctions, which were fairly standard, were highlighted in the report (Blum and Mespoulet 2003, 71–72). The reasons were multiple: poor management (*bezkhoziaistvennost'*), planning, and method; pernicious attitude (*golovotiapstvo*); lack of proper planning (*bezplannovost'*); and absentee management, without any authority and incapable of assessing financial potential, thus forcing it to borrow money.[16] Articles in the central press published these criticisms and called for an "exemplary trial" against the "saboteurs" of the Uzbek film industry, a call repeated by the Moscow newspaper *Vecherniaia Moskva*.[17]

All these difficulties encountered by Uzbekkino led to the activities of the studios being put on hold (*konservatsiia*) from January 19 to April 28, 1929, during which time staff found themselves without employment, with negative consequences.[18] This period of unemployment hindered the process of increasing the number of indigenous studio managers, most of whom were Uzbek and now obliged to look for another job.[19] The situation in the studios was the opposite of that in other administrations, for which the indigenization policy came into effect in 1928 (Martin 2001a, 138). The new management appointed after this period of inactivity was inexperienced.[20] Since no additional funding was forthcoming, the studios had only fifteen people to complete films, produce newsreels, and work in the laboratory. Without external financing, it was not possible to return to full activity—a situation that had been complicated by the intervening project to move Uzbekistan's capital to Samarkand.[21] At the time, it took about eighteen months for a film to start generating a profit, and with no production and hence no revenue in the pipeline, Uzbekkino was unable to relaunch its activity.

## Soiuzkino and Control over Film Institutions: Economic Unity, Resistance, and Resignation

The problems affecting Uzbekkino were reproduced across Soviet cinema. A general audit was drawn up during the first party conference on film, which took place March 15–21, 1928, in Moscow. It was attended by the press, various government representatives, and all the representatives of the Soviet film industry—with the exception of Uzbekkino, even though its head, Umar Mukimov, had received the go-ahead to attend from Fayzulla Khojaev.[22] Those attending the conference deplored the fact that potential profitability was undercut by poor organization and planning and by the underdeveloped network of film theaters (Krinitskii 1929b, 442; Kosior 1928, 6; Kosior 1929, 11; Krylov 1928, 3, 34–36; Shvedchikov 1929, 238). For the local institutional actors and central authorities, the solution was to align operations on a pan-federal scale in order to rationalize production, establish a larger distribution network, and control the ideological messages. Certain filmmakers, such as Eisenstein, agreed (Rubailo 1976, 32–33). This forthcoming centralization met two needs: first, managing the national film organizations operating across the Soviet world that generated profits from the distribution and sale of films and, second, getting the party more involved in filmmaking to obtain ideological results (Taylor 1979, 102–23). But ultimately it made filmmaking on a national scale unviable, and the case of Uzbekistan provides lessons that can probably be transposed to other national studios.

The political and economic aspects were intimately linked, and after several restructurings they came together in the Soviet supranational film organization Soiuzkino, founded on February 13, 1930 (Kepley 1996, 42). The organization centralized all Soviet film production, distribution, and operating organizations under the Supreme Economic Council and enjoyed oversight of the equipment and spare parts manufacturers.[23] Soiuzkino, headed by Boris Shumiatskii, provided unified commercial and financial management, leaving ideological management to the national republics' Commissariats for Education.[24] Soiuzkino thus headed all the film organizations, conducted planning at the federal level, regulated production activities, and made decisions about investment (building studios, for example), expanding the network of film theaters, film promotion, management training, and the development and approval of themes for films.[25] In addition to imposing a daily output for shoots (twelve per day), Soiuzkino provided the film stock, equipment, and foreign-produced films.[26] It was during the period 1930–33 that the Soviet Union became self-sufficient in film stock.[27] Last, Soiuzkino was henceforth the only organization allowed to enter into bilateral contacts, preventing Uzbekkino from directly exporting its films abroad.[28] The national republics lost virtually all their autonomy and their specific spheres of authority.

The Uzbek authorities were not opposed to the principle of centralization and accepted certain forms of delegating authority, but their attitude was nevertheless part of a federal conception of the Soviet state, for they believed they could retain some degree of representativity and room for maneuver. They felt that setting up a central unified body was a "rational and necessary step," though a complex one.[29] Hence the decision-making centers of the Uzbek Soviet Socialist Republic (the Agitprop Directorate of the Central Committee of the

Uzbek Communist Party, the Supreme Economic Council, and the Council of the People's Commissars) emphasized how important it was for the country to be able to defend its interests to conserve its national prerogatives.[30] The Uzbek authorities hoped in particular to obtain a right of veto on the Soiuzkino management board and to retain autonomy across their territory for pursuing specific national interests.[31] Consequently, Uzbekkino agreed to become part of Soiuzkino only on the condition that it retain its independence as a national body for planning and ideological management.[32]

But, in fact, room for maneuver was limited. These restructurings came at a stage when Uzbekkino no longer had any real market presence. It was emerging from the period when its activity had been frozen and was encountering difficulties in starting up again.[33] In addition, the Moscow representations of national film boards were closing down one after the other, making any form of negotiation increasingly difficult.[34] Now that Soiuzkino had been founded, it was the one opening offices in the national republics as part of a more general trend of administrative devolution, which undercut cultural autonomy and acted to the detriment of a more federal system.[35]

Although the principle of centralization was not questioned, the means and methods used were denounced by Uzbek political and cultural actors.[36] The decree issued by the Uzbek Soviet Socialist Republic Council of People's Commissars on February 28, 1931, completed the process of economic centralization in the film industry—an indicator of the Great Turn and of the reversal in the relationship between the center and the periphery.[37] The Uzbek film industry was now run by Soiuzkino and the Supreme Soviet of the National Economy. All these institutional and administrative transformations were taken a step further with the second Five-Year Plan, which definitively introduced an integrated economic system (which was thus not viable on a national scale), setting up the State Directorate for the Film and Photo Industry to replace Soiuzkino (Soviet Union Sovnarkom decree of February 11, 1933). This decision was validated in Uzbekistan in May 1933, and the Uzbekistan Directorate for the Film Industry was created.[38] It comprised two distinct entities: Uzbekfilm, in charge of producing films, and Uzbekkino, which managed, planned, and regulated distribution and the operation and building of new film theaters. These two bodies were thus no longer run by a national Uzbek higher authority but instead answered in parallel to the Soviet Union State Directorate. This split between production and distribution meant the film industry was henceforth no longer viable. Financing production in a national film economy system relies on reinvesting revenue from distribution and operation in production. This was how Uzbekkino had hitherto gotten by, despite its problems in managing and organizing work.

## Exerting Control over Film Discourse: Political Purges for Ideological Unity

The establishment of Soiuzkino was accompanied by political purges intended to reinforce the ideological nature of the films. This is not the place for a detailed discussion of the desire of Bolshevik leaders to make cinema subservient to political demands. But it is worth briefly pointing out that these positions had existed for quite some time; Lenin first became interested in film in 1907 when staying in Finland. These ideas were behind the nationalization of film activity as of August 1919 and were reiterated throughout the 1920s (Lebedev 1939, 13, 32, 39, 41, 45). For his part, Trotsky saw cinema as a way of keeping workers out of the churches and taverns (Trotsky 1923, 2).

Despite this history, establishing political control over film was a neither a simple nor rapid process. The 1928 film conference marked a new stage in the party's policy to combat the "ideological deviance" of film cadres who had started work during the tsarist period and who were reckoned to still account for 20 percent of the total (Rubailo 1976, 6, 9; Kosior 1928, 5). One aspect of establishing political control was the importance attached to developing "script" sections and having quantitative plans for producing films on given themes, while centralizing censorship was another. The primary concern here is the practice of political purges and cleansing. When viewed on the national scale, this was also a way to neutralize the indigenization policy by establishing control over the national staff so as to ensure their apparent political subordination.

### Why Purge Film Organizations?

Purges (*chistki*) were used by the Soviet authorities to replace non-Stalinist political elites and promote local cadres who were younger and "politically and ideologically more malleable and obedient" (Werth 2007, 270). The three main waves of political purges (1928–30, 1932–33, and 1937–38) occurred in parallel to the economic centralization described in the previous section and to the affirmation of the aesthetic norm of Socialist Realism (in 1932 for literature and in 1934 for cinema), which is analyzed in chapter 6. Party cells, working on the basis of assessments drawn up by the Workers' and Peasants' Inspectorate, were in charge of controlling management and staff by setting up verification commissions. Soiuzkino was probably more affected than other organizations by the purges of the 1930s, each time strengthening the role of the party, yet apparently the Uzbek film organization was not subjected to these practices in the same manner, the party cell being virtually nonexistent there at first. The head of Uzbekkino, who had taken up his position on November 15, 1930, deplored that the cell "has not listened once to an organization report," that it played no role in managing or supporting the application of a thematic line, and finally admitted that the cell only existed in very theoretical fashion.[39]

Available reports about the purges relate to Uzbekkino's work organization and staff and were produced by the RKI. A first verification was carried out in March 1931, extending into April.[40] The commission set up on this occasion conducted agitprop work via slogans and posters displayed in the studios and thirteen film theaters. The press played little part in the process and only published three articles about the subject. The members of the commission openly admitted they were not the best qualified for the job, lacking the skills needed to assess film activity.[41] Moreover, members on any given commission could find themselves subjected to a verification process. This was what happened to the filmmaker Nabi Ganiev, for instance, who took part in an ongoing script assessment while being subject to verification himself.[42]

The commission's report mentions that various local party cells (in the studios, film theaters, and Uzbekkino) were "hard at work," as were the administrative staff who presented the required documents and reports on time—unlike management, who displayed greater resistance.[43] The report notes that the participation of studio employees and workers was more "one-off," with communist activists and specialists being dynamic and happy to collaborate, unlike most of the poorly qualified staff and workers who were more recalcitrant and only showed any real motivation at the end of the operation. Among staff of national origin, only those belonging to party cells and professional collective organizations took part. Workers of national origin were the most reticent, and the commission recognized that it had not managed to "shake them up" (*raskatat'*) despite its efforts.

The verification conclusions pinpoint the usual malfunctions and only pronounce an opinion about work organization, regretting that they had not been able to "single out any notorious elements" (*yarkii element*). According to the members of the commission, those who were truly responsible for the malfunctions had already been removed by the political police, and they regretted having to target people playing a secondary role.[44] Several aspects of the verification conclusions came in for criticism, with fresh insistence on the existence of family networks, which the political police used as a basis for repression throughout the Soviet Union (Blum and Shapoval 2012). The film organizations were reckoned to be too voluminous overall, with some departments having only one person working in them, and several problems were highlighted: the lack of planning, the "de-responsibilization of workers," and unclear power relationships between management, studios, and the Uzbek authorities. "The protectionist, family nature" of appointments was thought to hinder self-criticism, with family conflicts erupting and undermining the proper conduct of work. The report also mentions that, as a result of its work, nine people had been arrested by the political police, leading to a disequilibrium in the workshops.

During the 1931 purges, it was primarily accountancy staff who were targeted.[45] Out of the 188 people working for Uzbekkino, only nine were troubled; they were considered "socially foreign elements" and were accused of "bureaucracy," "incompetence at work," and an "asocial frame of mind."[46] The sanctions meted out included bans from working (for a period of two to three years) or being fired or reprimanded. There was an appeal process against the decision to fire someone, and the director Suleyman Khojaev had the verification commission's decision to fire him overturned on the grounds that it was unfounded.[47] Most of the staff targeted by inspections in fact either kept their jobs or were appointed to new positions with less responsibility.

PERSONAL ENMITY: NABI GANIEV AND HIS DIRECTORS OF PHOTOGRAPHY

The verification report also indicates that there were national tensions between personnel from outside the Uzbek Soviet Socialist Republic (Russians who had trained during the tsarist period) and recently promoted national staff. This was the case with the relationship between Nabi Ganiev and his directors of photography. The letters, accounts, and typed transcripts drawn up in the presence of the person being questioned and other members of the studios are largely undated and unsigned, and they were produced during meetings of the 1930–31 RKI purge of Uzbekkino. It has not been possible to triangulate the information they contain with other administrative sources, but analysis of Nabi Ganiev's films (in chap. 5) would appear to confirm these elements.

Ganiev was first targeted in late 1930 because of his social origins, being the son of a meat wholesaler viewed as a *bai*. At the time, this word had drifted from its traditional meaning and now meant "bourgeois." The verification procedure involved a neighborhood (*mahalla*) commission of forty-three people, some of whom were members of the party or Komsomol, to debate whether the accusation that Ganiev was the "son of a *bai*" was justified, as confirmed by the report this commission drew up on October 16, 1930.[48] The report also emphasized that Ganiev had been expelled from the Workers' University and the Komsomol. His father was denounced for having criticized Soviet power and expressed his nostalgia for the imperial period, for which he was accused of "anti-Soviet agitation."

Ganiev was deemed to be a "socially foreign element" and targeted for personal differences with two directors of photography with whom he had worked: E. Velichko (*Upsurge*) and Fridrikh Verigo-Dorovskii (*The Last Bek* and the agitprop films *Araby* and *The American from Baghdad*). Ganiev's observations in his correspondence and under questioning are particularly eloquent, providing clear descriptions of the working relationships that existed between native and nonnative personnel and the resultant national tensions. The first dispute, between Ganiev and Velichko, was over camera lenses (apparently Velichko had used a 35mm instead of a 28mm as requested by Ganiev).

Velichko lodged a complaint with Uzbekkino management about Ganiev's attitude, which he deemed to be "chauvinist," and asked to be released from his position on the shoot. Velichko reports that Ganiev reputedly said: "We will get by, for as long as we don't have our own people with us," implying that he only tolerated Russian technicians because of their skills, but that they would no longer be welcome on Uzbek territory once people had learned what they could from them.[49] The system of national preference promoted by the indigenization policy meant that there were frequent tensions in the world of work (with fights, strikes, and refusals by qualified Russian personnel to teach national personnel), and this transpired both in public declarations and in private correspondence (Martin 2001a, 149–52; Payne 2001a). Ganiev was questioned by the commission and denied, with a certain degree of insolence on occasions, that he had expressed any wariness vis-à-vis the Europeans and that he had raised the issue of his director of photography's nationality. In fact, he turned the accusation of nationalism back against his accusers, attacking his camera operators for being "foreign by class," since they hailed from the old tsarist generation, something that could be criticized openly.[50] He thus asserted that the incoming specialists were only useful for as long as he could learn from them, adding that it was necessary to "resist firmly and cleverly," drawing on their knowledge with the sole purpose of preparing "proletarian cadres."

A similar scandal opposed Ganiev to the director of photography Verigo-Dorovskii (figs. 4.1 and 4.2). During the same session of questioning, Ganiev stated that "Verigo-Dorovskii's attitude toward Uzbek customs was revolting," and Ganiev accused Verigo-Dorovskii of "vulgarity" and "chauvinism" because of his disdainful and violent behavior toward Uzbek personnel. Ganiev accused Verigo-Dorovskii of having refused to teach what he knew and of attacking national traditions by his use of swear words. When it had been suggested that Verigo-Dorovskii might eat the national dish (*plov*), he had answered that he would not eat that "shit."[51] Verigo-Dorovskii, too, was considered a "socially foreign element" since he was of "noble descent" with bourgeois origins, having previously owned a film laboratory and held shares in the studios.[52] These accusations led to his being barred from working in the national republics for five years. In a letter sent to the purge commission, Verigo-Dorovskii stated that he felt this sanction to be "particularly cruel" for it amounted to "his physical and moral death" as a citizen and specialist. In response to the accusation that he had struck a young Uzbek during a film shoot, he said he had only "bumped" into him.[53] Verigo-Dorovskii admitted that he had "an impulsive temperament," but nevertheless asserted that he had two assistants of national origin, reproaching other camera operators for having only European assistants. He also took pride in having accepted a drop in salary, before finally confessing that he had carried out a "nitpicking [attack] imbued with personal enmity" toward Ganiev (figs. 4.1 and 4.2).

Figure 4.1. Nabi Ganiev in Moscow, 1923. AI K (F) A17 no. 34.

Consequently, Ganiev was accused of "impoliteness" and "bad behavior" toward certain people he worked with, a lack of "discernment in organizing the work of the film crew" leading to increased costs, and, last, "not having sufficiently shown the class struggle relating to the cotton issue" in his films.[54] He was viewed as "disagreeable in his working relationships" by those in charge of the Uzbekkino party cell, and a "severe reprimand" was meted out, even though

Figure 4.2. Fridrikh Verigo-Dorovskii. AI, no reference.

he was viewed as "indispensable" provided he was managed by someone stronger than him.[55] The purge commission asked the studio party cell to place him under surveillance while authorizing him to continue work.[56] No information has been found about the implementation of this surveillance. It is highly probable that the sanctions against Ganiev were relaxed in part due to personnel shortages and a lack of competent management. Nevertheless, it is clear from his questioning by the commission that he now knew how to "speak Bolshevik," indicating a form of political domestication (though not genuine submission), which was definitively established by the 1930s. The purpose of these verification practices (together with the political "taming" process) was not solely to criminalize daily behavior (Werth and Blum 2010, 9); they also provided a way for the authorities to control the effects of the indigenization policy and partially neutralize it (Lirou 2009, 194).

The 1930–31 purges and the various verifications were judged to be "insufficient" by the official Uzbek press in 1934, having failed to produce the expected results.[57] The Council of the People's Commissars asked the RKI to verify the social and national composition of film management, with a view to carrying out a new wave of political cleansing.[58] It is impossible to ascertain from the available archive documents what verification procedures were employed in 1934 and how the process unfolded in Uzbekkino. However, it was not the "control commissions" that verified how institutions functioned but rather "brigades"—a term that highlights the increasing militarization of the political vocabulary of the period. The Workers' and Peasants' Inspectorate disappeared and was replaced by a Peoples' Control Commission, placed directly under the orders of the Soviet Union Council of People's Commissars.[59] This marked a new stage in the stripping away of Soviet Uzbekistan's national and territorial attributes and prerogatives, and a new step toward the concentration of administrative power.

The information available about the 1934 purges makes it possible to draw up an overall assessment of the four preceding years, but without much detail. The only real difference is the increasing tension. Staff were still underqualified; the equipment used by mobile units was still poor, as were conditions for conserving and transporting films; and staff were still being reprimanded and fired.[60] There were no profound changes, and the film industry remained the least organized sector of Uzbek industry—and the one with the most catching up to do. It was not really profitable, was in need of major investment, and continued to suffer from a shortage of directors, scriptwriters, actors, and directors of photography with a basic grasp of Socialist Realism.[61] The financial situation had already been very bad in 1932, when the Uzbek Sovnarkom had proposed to lay off 35 percent of the staff and to borrow money, but it had worsened in the meantime.[62]

DAILY LIFE IN THE STUDIOS: THE FILM SHOOT FOR *GHARM*

In addition to the increasing political tensions and difficulties in adapting to the new management conditions under Soiuzkino, operating on a pan-Soviet scale, the production of films was hit by numerous complications and shortages in 1931. There were not enough accessories, costumes, and props, with reference to numerous thefts, particularly of weapons.⁶³ Shortage of film stock hampered the preparation of title cards in vernacular languages, and poor technical knowledge resulted in a significant amount of waste.⁶⁴ Furthermore, the laboratories were set up in workshops that were too small, ill-suited, and insufficiently equipped, making it possible to work on only two or three films at a time.⁶⁵ The water and electricity supply were intermittent. In winter it was not possible to ensure a stable temperature in the dilapidated buildings of the old madrasa, and leaking roofs led to high levels of humidity that caused lenses to work loose and the metallic parts of the equipment to rust. This affected all the work carried out by the laboratory. The film lost its sensitivity and became fogged, and the poor conditions for developing it resulted in dull gray images.⁶⁶ The film also broke easily, meaning that the film collection aged more rapidly and the screenings dropped in quality. Many unreleased films remained in the reserves, amounting to much lost capital. This situation became worse because it was now Soiuzkino that supplied Uzbekistan with films, without taking into account the specific needs of the populations. The already shaky financial situation became worse, and the organization sank further into debt.⁶⁷

The film shoot for *Gharm* provides a concrete example of the difficulties encountered. The audits mentioned above refer to its malfunctions.⁶⁸ Despite the humorous aspects in the descriptions of these daily setbacks, revealing the subaltern stakeholders' incomprehension of the genuine political intentions of the Soviet authorities (Blum and Mespoulet 2003, 130), the shoot ended in tragedy. The whole series of complications started with those related to staffing. Although the director, the director's assistant, and the director of photography (who was replaced once) remained on the shoot, there was a string of twelve administrators.⁶⁹ The film was about the "events in Gharm" that took place in late April 1929, in the province of Karategin, with some filming to be carried out in Tajikistan. For the Soviet authorities, these events marked the victory of the Red Army over Fuzail Maqsum's Basmachi thanks to the air force (Ritter 1990) and were worthy of being shown as cinema. The film, depicting the "heroic struggle against the Basmachi," needed to describe "Tajik customs" while also insisting on the nefarious role played by the British.⁷⁰

Work on the film got off to a bad start. On arriving in Tashkent, the director, from Moscow, did not find any script in the studios.⁷¹ Between the moment when the contract had been signed and the director's arrival in Uzbekistan, the management had changed, and the script, written by El' Registan, had been misplaced.⁷² It therefore needed rewriting, and the director initially considered Nina Agzhanova, who had written the script for *Battleship Potemkin*. But the director had to work with El' Registan to produce a detailed synopsis within one week, because the film had to be finished before November 7, 1930, to commemorate the anniversary of the October Revolution. It was written in time but only accepted a month later by the Uzbekkino artistic board. The writers had one month to write the script for the film, which they completed on April 10.[73] There was still no budget at this date, the actors had not been appointed, the costumes were not ready, the film equipment was lacking, unfortunately nobody was able to inform the director about "Tajik customs," and the "management did not provide any solution to these problems, despite El' Registan knocking every day on all the Uzbekkino office doors and exhausting everybody."[74]

Given the lack of national cadres, the director headed back to Moscow in late April to assemble a film crew. But the technicians in Moscow and Leningrad were party members and already occupied. He therefore had to wait until the head of Uzbekkino arrived, for his plenipotentiary in Moscow refused to take any responsibility. After postponing filming twice, the head of Uzbekkino arrived on May 9, which prevented inter alia the director from shooting the May 1 events that he needed for the film. On returning to Tashkent, the director was told that there were still staff shortages and, notably, no administrator. The team finally acquired two administrators—one invited from Moscow and the other appointed in Tashkent.

Budgetary problems followed. One of the administrators suggested an estimated budget of 300,000 rubles, whereas senior management suggested only 120,000 rubles. The director estimated the cost of the film at 180,000 to 220,000 rubles. The cost of the shoot could be brought down with the help of the commander of the regiments of the Central Asian Military Department, who "enthusiastically" agreed to provide the artillery, cavalry, and airplanes free of charge. But Uzbekkino did not get back to him in time, and the regiments were sent on maneuvers without it having been possible to film them. Accounting disputes interrupted filming for about three weeks, until a small group went out scouting in Tajikistan, in the region of Khorog (at 2,200 meters above sea level in Upper Badakhshan), where the local authorities agreed to take part "as much as they could." But a bad surprise awaited the director on returning to Stalinabad.[75] The Council of the People's Commissars, the Central Committee of the Tajik Communist Party, and the political police declared that the script was unacceptable because, "from an ideological, political, and historical point of view, it was not faithful to events in Gharm."[76] The script needed to be revised; otherwise the authorities would not lend their support. An additional week was lost before a new script was accepted. The team sent a telegram from Stalinabad to Tashkent asking the rest of the technicians to come and join them. Ten days went by. In fact, the telegram never reached its destination. Rather than risking losing another ten days, since there was no guarantee that a second telegram would get through, the crew opted for the locality of Karatag. Filming started, but the assistants had to relay one another, because for the director was in hospital, having been struck down by malaria. Then it was the turn of the Karatag authorities to refuse to lend their support (by providing extras, material, and animals).

The stay in Tajikistan was a failure. By September 10, over 50,000 rubles had been spent (mainly on transport) but only 4 percent of the film had been made.[77] Uzbekkino management then designated the village of Brich-Mulla in Uzbekistan to finish filming. But there was already another crew working there, and Klado (*The American from Baghdad*) was quick to affirm his monopoly over this village a hundred or so kilometers from Tashkent; thus, the place became the scene for open conflict between the two film crews.[78] Filming continued in an "atmosphere of swearing, threats, and fights" among *Gharm* team members and against a backdrop of a "total lack of discipline." To this were added difficulties arising from the population's categorical refusal to take part in the filming, the lack of involvement by the local authorities, and unfavorable meteorological conditions (only twenty-nine days in all were spent filming). Despite this fraught situation, team members continued to be paid their costs, even though they did not have any effective work to perform due to accountancy problems and the "marinading budget" (*marinovka so smetoi*).[79] In early December, the leading actor and the administrator were fired, even though work was far from complete.

The affair was brought before the Supreme Court of the Uzbek Soviet Socialist Republic, which ruled on the case of the Uzbekkino "saboteurs." The head of the artistic and production departments and the former director of the Tajik studios were "sentenced to the highest measure of social protection"—that is, they were to be shot since the acts of sabotage were "proven."[80] The sentence of the artistic director was finally commuted to eight years' imprisonment due to his "war service" during the civil war. The director Vasil'chikov, who had been invited by the studios, was sentenced to at least ten years in prison, but he did not serve the full sentence (Miller 2010, 80). The decorator, Chelli, who had worked on most of the films produced by the Uzbek studios, was sentenced to several years' imprisonment. The director Klado only received a public reprimand. The case also investigated the involvement of the former management of Uzbekkino as well as the deputy chairman of the Tajikistan Supreme Economic Council.

## Conquering Space: Distribution Branching Out across the Country

The economic and political changes analyzed above that subjected film production and distribution to central decision-making authorities via top-down structural transformations were backed up by measures to extend the geographical hierarchy of power across the entire Soviet territory. At the lowest levels, this was based, first, on *cinefication* (*kinefikatsiia*)—the creation of an ever larger distribution network of permanent theaters and mobile units to reach as many spectators as possible both in the towns and in the countryside. Thanks to this infrastructure, the ideological messages were able to reach the most distant regions of the Soviet

Union, quite literally bringing light (the screening equipment used dynamos and arrived before the electrification of some localities) as well as conveying knowledge and promoting new rights through film.[81] The authorities thus appropriated the idea of social, technical, and cultural modernity as embodied by the cinema. They also sought to master the subjective elements of film reception by paying attention to the visual and audio environment in which films were screened. Though silent, film was not mute (in theory at least), because musical and oral accompaniments fulfilled several functions. These accompaniments acted to control the emptiness and silence and so avoid any misunderstandings, any alteration of the film's message, and any counterdiscourse while also including the audiences within a greater Soviet reality. Unlike the mechanisms of political and economic subordination that were implemented fairly easily—though with a certain degree of violence—by purges and centralization, all did not go smoothly with the expansion of the means for distribution and controlling reception.

## A Territory of Itinerant and Permanent Cinema

In 1924 there was no ideologically correct national film production, but this did not prevent political education being carried out with current affairs films and newsreels. Though rare, this work could, on occasion, bear fruit. The Uzbek archives house two accounts by itinerant projectionists describing their work in Uzbek villages in the 1920s. The first account, already mentioned in chapter 3, details the work of the Iskra team that traveled around the region of Tashkent in 1924.[82] This team, working on behalf of International Red Aid, consisted of three people, two of whom spoke local languages: the head, Aleksandrov, and Kalimullin, who was of Tatar origin. Iskra was the first mobile film unit in Uzbekistan to concentrate solely on political education, and it answered to the Central Committee of the Uzbek Communist Party. A second account, dating from a bit earlier, was written by a projectionist working for the Uzbekbrliash Consumer Society.[83] What changes took place over the course of the 1920s and 1930s in the way mobile and permanent units operated? How did the equipment actually function? How did the units work? What films did they use? And, in parallel to these questions, how did the projection network (of both permanent film theaters and mobile units) expand?

### THE AURA OF THE PROJECTIONIST: ITINERANT CINEMA IN THE COUNTRYSIDE (1924–28)

Although most of the itinerant projection equipment used in Uzbekistan was manufactured by GOZ, Iskra used a Gaumont projector (bought in Paris) that stood on a wooden leg. It had a bicycle saddle on which the projectionist sat and a dynamo producing twelve volts and four to five amperes. It weighed about seventy-five kilograms in all, which included the slide projection apparatus, the

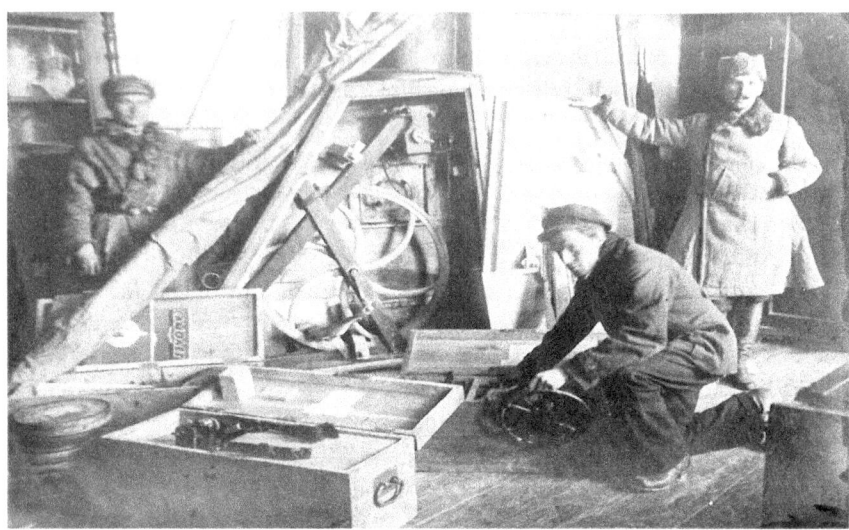

Figure 4.3. Iskra photo, late 1924, in the region of Tashkent. AI K (F) A18 no. 34.

spools and reels, the films, the lantern (which could be dismantled), spare bulbs, kerosene lamps, spare electrical equipment, assembly instruments, agitprop literature (*agit-literatura*), four posters, insignia, and other supplies (accounts books, tickets, paint and brushes, paper, and so on).[84] The team had not been able to obtain posters and documentation in the "Muslim tongue," as they called it, something it regretted as prejudicial to the quality of its work (fig. 4.3).[85]

The Iskra equipment was purchased in May 1924, and the first tour started on August 1, lasting until late December. From May to July, preparations concentrated on building specially designed protective cases to transport the material and protect it when the team was traveling along particularly bad roads. A first tour took place to the east of Tashkent between November 4 and December 4, when the team covered ninety kilometers and visited five villages, holding fourteen screenings in all. The second tour was to the north of the town, covering a total of a hundred kilometers. Although Iskra stopped for only a day or two in the Russian towns, the team stayed for three or four days in native villages.

Iskra's work plan was determined in advance, starting with the identification of the main villages and the principal settlement in the district under consideration.[86] Then other places were selected with the local authorities, enabling the team to branch out and visit smaller places. On arriving in a locality, Iskra spent about two and a half hours choosing the right spot for the screening, assisted by representatives from the local authorities. Working in the countryside did not require the same sort of preparation as in the larger villages with more infrastructure (schools, hospitals, hostels, workers' clubs, and women's clubs). A warehouse, a former caravanserai, a place of worship (a mosque, church, or synagogue), or a large room sufficed, for the two men and equipment were technically flexible enough to adapt to any sort of building. A wall or white cloth was used as a screen, and the spectators sat on the ground.[87] The only factor for deciding how large a place to use was the expected number of spectators. Open-air screenings were privileged, weather permitting. Those interested in film gathered in the evening in the caravanserai or red teahouse (*choikhona*), where it was forbidden to play cards or consume alcohol or opium (*anasha*). The somewhat unusual experience is described here by various observers:[88]

> In July 1923 we found ourselves by chance at the opening of a red *choikhona* in Tashkent, on the edge of the old town. The highlight of the evening was a film screening. The room, or rather the garden, since it took place in the open air, was packed with Uzbek and Kyrgyz (Kazakh) *komsomols*, who cheered enthusiastically. It was strange in the 50° heat to see the icy winter of northerly Russia and its *izbas* on the screen. . . . Uzbeks and Kyrgyz (Kazakhs) stared wide-eyed at the screen, saluting the appearance of Vladimir Il'ich with great cries of "Lelin! Lelin!" (Lenin! Lenin!). (Vainshtok and Yakobzon 1926, 62)

But the choice of a place to screen the film was sometimes more complicated given the reticence of the inhabitants, religious personnel, and owners of land and livestock.[89] Once the place had been selected, the news generally spread quickly throughout the village—"they've brought films!"—and then Iskra started drumming up interest:

> The Komsomols, the young people attending, and even the adults lent a hand. A contingent rapidly formed of six people to act as a "living billboard," composed of street urchins and adolescents, carrying a banner slung between two poles. Their job was to go around the hamlets near or further away from the village, show the posters, and announce to the population that the cinema had arrived. "They're showing a film!" Large posters and red flags were hung on the front of the building. In fact our role was to create a festive atmosphere so as to stimulate extensive interest, making it easier to attract spectators. The local authorities also took steps to inform the population and attract the public, and there were even cases in which the authorities were very zealous, using a militia to round up the population. But then after seeing the film, the citizens who had been brought never complained about the executive committee treating them in this manner. In general the news spread through the town like wildfire, and come evening there was not a single villager who did not know a film was being shown.[90]

Unlike the newspaper readers in the factories who sought to attract the workers' attention during their brief lunch break, and who were often obliged to position themselves in the smoking room, the "cinema propagandist" was genuinely popular, reinforcing his authority.[91]

> On arriving in a place with the cinematograph, the propagandist acquires—from the very first screenings—a popularity that would have been hard to obtain without cinema. Thanks to the entertaining films, and on perceiving the perfection of the technique, its novelty, and so on, the mobile cinema unit and its personnel are surrounded in the eyes of the rural population with a slight aura of superiority and respect, cinema becoming instantly popular with the population. And if the cinematograph acquires this popularity easily and rapidly, then it is also transmitted to the propagandist, the head of the team, and all those working for the itinerant cinema.[92]

But their work was not without risk:

> Interesting things can occur when the mobile cinema unit first arrives in the villages. This was the case when the cinema came for the first time to the village of Yangibozor. There were a lot of people. The light coming from the machine projected strange images onto the white cloth, which surprised people. Suddenly a horse appeared on the screen and ran towards spectators. The people in the front rows started to rush towards the back. Chaos reigned. The projectionist was almost trampled. After that we managed to calm the spectators down with difficulty. Now the inhabitants of Yangibozor are well acquainted with cinema and welcome it with great joy each time.[93]

It could sometimes be hard to get the public to leave once the screening was over. The audience members would gather around the mechanic and ask him to stay another day; on occasion, audience members would even refuse to let him leave and would take him hostage.[94]

### The Ideal Film for an Ideal Screening (1920s)

Supplying films was more difficult in the countryside than in the towns. The best films were requisitioned by the urban film theaters, and itinerant projectionists had to make do with what was left. In late 1924, there were few "good films" in Turkkino's catalog.[95] Supply was a thorny problem for Iskra, but given that distribution was not yet fully centralized, it could turn to various institutions. For the end of Iskra's late 1924 tour, Turkkino provided films such as *The Tale of Father Pankrat*, antireligious propaganda comedies by N. Preobrazhenskii (1918), and *The Fourth Komintern Congress*, while the Political Directorate of the Red Army provided a fiction film, Ivan Perestiani's *The Red Devils* (Georgia, 1923). Iskra had these films for less than two weeks, which limited its scope for action. In general, popular science works and newsreels were shown, while a feature-length fiction film was a rare treat.

Iskra took two or three additional films on each tour in case there were extra screenings. The head of the team described the ideal film for showing in the countryside as follows:

> A modern film with strict ideological content, a simple, clear storyline, a host of lively moments, good acting, and close to daily life. The best solution would be an American visual effects film about Russian revolutionary activity. . . . Livelier and overflowing with life and action. . . . The key thing is action! The working masses watch such films with particular interest and they are also well suited to a young public. The films need to be realistic and historically accurate. Any erotic element at the heart of the plot is to be banned completely, but if it is justified in terms of veracity then it must be shown in the most moderate form, with a slight touch of artistic zest, and portrayed as a normal, healthy sentiment in a working atmosphere.[96]

Comic films were particularly successful with the public, but to Iskra's regret never reached the villages for they were distributed initially to the network of commercial film theaters in urban areas, which paid a good price for them, before then going to the film clubs. The head of Iskra railed against Turkkino's commercial policy, as a consequence of which mobile units were the least well served. In 1926, film distribution was "beneath the critical level"; although equipment was available and operational, their activity was paralyzed due to a lack of films.[97]

For popular science films, the narrative element was essential:

> Films with a specifically scientific content (land distribution, or agricultural and technical propaganda) are boring for a rural audience if shorn of any narrative element, and such programs will not attract a full house. They can only be shown as an adjunct to the main film. Thus when a popular science film is good, it needs to be presented as a lecture. There have been cases, in the resort of Chimgan, for the sick, and for employees and the population from neighboring villages, when Iskra has shown an excellent film with a strictly scientific content, *High-Yield Cereal Farming*, produced in 1924, with explanations by Professor A. Blagoveshchenskii. The wonderfully successful complementarity between the lecturer (a well-designed film and an expert) meant that the rural audience watched three large parts (of seven hundred meters each) with sustained interest. The holding of such cine-lectures no doubt needs to be pursued in its own right in order to bring knowledge to the people.[98]

The head of Iskra points out that it was important that these films be made as a narrative—with a plot, dramatic development, and an ending—to make an entertaining film: "It is hard to appreciate how very helpful such films are for the propagandists, and the extent to which they facilitate the role of the organizer, and how enormously helpful this is."[99]

In just three or four days of work in the countryside, the Iskra team observed the clear influence the cinematograph had on social life in the village.

After showing *The Red Devils*, for instance, the children who had seen it started imitating the heroes and tried to set up a camp of pioneers. Of course, it all depended on the film's content. One case of suicide was reported after a film was shown in Irkutsk, and a letter from two Komsomol members describes their ideal based on what they had seen on-screen: "They wanted to go in the air, fly in airplanes, drive cars, know how to fence, shoot, swim, dance the foxtrot, smoke, and wear suits like those they had seen in American films" (Ol'khov 1929, 50).

Iskra was exempt from paying tax and had independent financial accounts. It relied on selling tickets to accumulate the working capital it needed (to buy equipment, pay the wages of the projectionist and porters, buy fodder, and pay for the upkeep of the horses and for repairs) without drawing on the slender political education budget. Ticket prices were decided in consultation with the local authorities; in late 1924, prices ranged from five kopecks (the price of a tea or loaf of bread) to thirty kopecks. Seasonal workers, the poor, and those with no fixed abode attended free of charge. Peasants were often unable to pay cash and thought of the price of a ticket in terms of equivalence, offering to pay in wheat. Iskra refused such offers to avoid having to transport these goods. A twenty- to thirty-kopek ticket was the equivalent of eight kilos of wheat, which was relatively expensive for a population whose annual agricultural resources amounted to three thousand to four thousand kilos on average. However, "5 to 10 kopecks for a rare entertainment such as cinema is a comparatively cheap expenditure in comparison to tobacco, etc., not to mention beer or home-made alcohol, and thus within everyone's means."[100]

The average audience was of 150 to 250 (paying or free) spectators per screening, but could be as high as 3,000. The open-air screening Iskra held on July 14, 1924, in Brich-Mullah (1,680 inhabitants) was typical of their work. Two Soviet films were shown: *Workers of the World, Unite* (two reels, four hundred meters) with episodes about the life of Karl Marx and the "great French Revolution," and *The Fourth Komintern Congress* (one reel, three hundred meters). Tickets were priced five, ten, or twenty kopecks. No screening was held specifically for women, and the public was composed primarily of peasants. For the two screenings taken together, total attendance was 1,257 (257 paying spectators, and 1,000 free admissions). The head of Iskra provided some explanations to accompany the films. The public reacted especially strongly on seeing Karl Marx on-screen (applause), and was clearly most enthusiastic when Lenin appeared (everybody applauded).

Other examples of screenings are provided by the projectionist who worked for Uzbekbrliash. His itinerary was longer than that of the Iskra team, and in addition to the area around Tashkent, he toured the regions of Samarkand, Kokand, Andijan, the Middle Zeravshan Valley (in Bukhara), and the Qashqadaryo Valley. A successful screening in the countryside could attract up to 1,500 people, and 3,000 in more urbanized areas. At these screenings, the proportion of native women could be up to 16 percent, though it tended to be less than 5 percent (see table 5 in appendix).[101]

But such large screenings were rare overall due to a lack of mobile equipment. Between May 1927 and May 1928, only three units were working in the area around Tashkent. Nevertheless, the projectionists held 226 screenings in nearly eighty different villages, showing mainly Soviet films, including Uzbek works (thirteen), and six foreign films. These screenings drew 27,970 spectators in all (averaging just over 120 spectators per screening), of whom 9,570 paid for their ticket at a cost of between ten and twenty kopecks (with women being admitted free).[102]

REGIONAL DISTRIBUTION: THE EXAMPLES OF KHOREZM AND TAJIKISTAN

The work conducted by Iskra would appear to have been exemplary, in terms of both the quality of the accompaniment and the films shown, most of which were Soviet productions at a time when the Uzbek market was dominated by foreign films. In 1928, Uzbekkino's distribution policy came in for sharp criticism in a report by the Workers' and Peasants' Inspectorate, which pinpointed the priority given to profitability to the detriment of politically educating the local public. Most of the films it distributed were "foreign to proletarian ideology," especially American visual effects films, which brought in substantial revenues.[103] Uzbekkino bought a series of films (thirty-three in all, ten of which were in several episodes) that was in poor condition and intended to distribute them on the screens in "old towns for the local population"—a plan the RKI deemed "inadmissible."

Equally, the head of Uzbekkino's subsidiary in Khorezm denounced the lack of interest shown by the head office and accused it of only supplying old films, in poor condition, and with "dubious ideological content."[104] He requested films with subjects that would be accessible to the local population, such as *The Ishan's Fiancée* and *The Last Bek*.[105] The distance from Tashkent, Uzbekkino's careless packaging of films, and the state of transport infrastructure meant that there were frequent interruptions in supply. "Communication conditions are atrocious. Automobile communication has not operated for the past two months. There are not many automobiles and those there are do not accept to take merchandise. Boat transport does not function regularly and is not very promising, for the film equipment taken on board at Charjui on May 4 for Urgench has not yet arrived [on June 20. . . . It is somewhere en route."[106]

The worsening economic situation (with poor living conditions, collectivization, and dekulakization) meant that many Europeans departed despite the system of resident permits, leading to a drop in attendance and diminishing operating revenues. The situation had become critical by the summer of 1931. Khorezm sent sixty films back to Tashkent but received only eighteen in return, and the subsidiary was reduced to showing the same old films so as not to interrupt its screenings. Films were sometimes supplied by "good neighbors," such as Turkmenistan (which sent sixteen films), who also sent a projectionist at seeding time. But the situation as officially described by a visiting member of the Commissariat for Education differed markedly from the reality on the ground. The head of the Uzbekkino subsidiary explained: "What he was most interested in was the statistics, distribution revenue, and supply conditions. Of course I was unable to answer these questions but, regarding supply, I told him that everything worked wonderfully and that Khorezm received two hundred and forty films per year."[107]

Uzbekkino's work in Tajikistan also came in for criticism, on the grounds that there was no attempt to implement the *cinefication* of the region, that the films were ideologically "unbearable," that the films produced paid insufficient attention to the specificity of the country, and films were distributed with title cards in Uzbek.[108] This led to a decision by the Tajik education authorities to set up their own film base, build permanent film theaters, and acquire fifteen or so mobile units for the autonomous republic as a whole. But the films were still hired from Uzbekkino. In 1929, out of the ninety-five films distributed in Tajikistan, the majority (73 percent) were either banned or "shown with severe caveats."[109] And even when the films were satisfactory, they were old, and most of them had already been seen. In 1933, 50 percent of the films distributed in Tajikistan did not have a screening certificate, and for the period 1932–33, only 35 percent were translated into Tajik (including newsreels). In all, 93 percent of the films distributed in Tajikistan did not have title cards in Tajik.[110]

THE PROPORTION OF SOVIET FILMS AND EVOLUTIONS
IN SCREENING EQUIPMENT

From 1928 onward, and as part of a general trend in the Soviet Union, the proportion of Soviet films (53 percent) owned by Uzbekkino caught up with that of foreign films (47 percent). Subsequently Soviet-produced films dominated (with 93 percent in late 1933 and 95 percent by 1935; see table 6 in appendix). This reversal in the ratio of Soviet to foreign films, which is indicative of the growing isolation of the Soviet market, was accompanied by an expansion of the means for distributing films to rural and urban populations, which consolidated the communications network. At the beginning of the first Five-Year Plan (in 1928), Uzbekkino supplied films to about one hundred sets of screening apparatus in Uzbekistan as a whole (counting both permanent and itinerant units). It owned sixteen commercial film theaters (with eighteen belonging to other organizations), fifty-two commercial workers' clubs, eleven closed clubs, and twenty-two mobile units.[111] Within four years, the number of screens had almost doubled (standing at 255 by 1931) and was theoretically meant to reach 5,402 by the end of the second Five-Year Plan (in 1937) (see table 7 in appendix).[112]

But despite the increased number of film programs Uzbekkino owned in actual terms, the average film per theater dropped from 4.73 in 1927–28 to 0.26 in 1934.[113] Uzbekkino was obliged to use its old films given the lack of recent production. In 1934, for instance, new copies of old Uzbek films were made, with fifteen copies of *The Jackals of Ravat*, fifteen of *The Covered Wagon*, nine of *The Second Wife*, and eight of *The Ishan's Fiancée*.[114]

Although production was unable to keep pace, the network continued to grow, albeit often with difficulty. In rural areas, the preferred means was to develop the number of mobile units, but there was insufficient funding and the number of units was far from meeting the demand from political, social, and economic organizations, nor even from the population. In 1924, equipment was scarce, with Turkkino having only two sets of apparatus (one for workers' clubs and the other for Red Army clubs) (Goldobin 1924, 61). To this needs to be added private equipment owned by various organizations (the Red Army Political Directorate, workers' unions, and regional authorities). In 1929, the *cinefication* of rural zones was declared a priority, and Uzbekkino henceforth had to allocate 20 percent of its profits to the village *cinefication* fund.[115] In accordance with its plan for 1929–30, it ordered about a hundred mobile units and about twenty permanent sets of equipment from the manufacturer GOZ and the Ukrainian studios (VUFKU), which turned this order down.[116] The number of mobile units was lower than targeted (in 1933, twenty-five mobile units were operating in the district of Kokand instead of the forty that had been planned).[117] But the situation was improving in the countryside, because Uzbekkino had changed its supply policy and now endeavored to distribute three copies of each fiction film, making it possible to distribute simultaneously to commercial cinemas, clubs, and mobile units. This situation stabilized around 1933, even though in 1934 one-third of the mobile units (96 out of 282) were out of order.[118]

Regarding permanent facilities, it was the new districts in Uzbek towns that were the best equipped. The available figures indicate that attendance was high in these film theaters. The cultural supplement *Sem' Dnei* announced that the three cinemas on "cinema avenue" in Tashkent drew thirty thousand people over the course of five evenings.[119] But the few places where films were screened in the old town of Tashkent were described as "primitive," and there was no permanent film theater. Uzbekkino stated that building new film theaters was not part of its remit, but recognized its failings in supplying foreign films to the population in the old town (and in the new town, too, for that matter) due to the lack of Soviet films. It also recognized it had fallen short in installing "reading corners" in its screening premises.[120] In 1932, the operation targets set out in the plan were exceeded (at 240 percent of the target), but so were expenses (at 250 percent of the target).[121] This placed Uzbekkino in a tight financial position, meaning it was unable to invest in or build new cinemas. In 1933, urban film theater attendance stood at 2,724,600 spectators for a total of 9,800 screenings (representing 278 spectators per screening).[122]

The shift to talking cinema and the resulting need to reequip or build film theaters threw up further obstacles for expanding the projection network.[123] By the end of the second Five-Year Plan (1933–37), each district in Uzbekistan was to have its own film theater equipped for sound (with industrial and economic centers and the more populated zones being prioritized), enabling the population to go to the cinema at least once per week (sixty times per year in towns and fifty times in the countryside).[124] The reequipment and building works started in late 1932. The Khiva film theater in Tashkent was the first cinema in Uzbekistan to be equipped for sound. Work began in November 1931 but was hampered by a shortage of building material (wood and iron) even though the sound equipment was available and had been in storage since November in a warehouse.[125] The sound equipment was fully installed by May 1932, but there was a problem operating it since the chairman of the Council of People's Commissars had only given Uzbekkino spoken authorization to obtain enough electricity to run it, and the theater had to pay a fine for the illegal use of electrical energy.[126]

By late 1933, out of a total of 371 sets of screening apparatus, only twelve were equipped for sound instead of the fifty-five that had been planned.[127] A first change came in 1934, when permanent film theaters equipped for sound started to be built, as was the case in Kokand.[128] In Tashkent, one film theater was rebuilt to replace the former Iskra cinema, which was in poor condition, and four other theaters were to be reequipped. In 1934, there were 25 film theaters equipped for sound in Central Asia as a whole.[129] In Uzbekistan, the towns of Samarkand, Termez, Ferghana, and Kokand had two film theaters each, and there was one film theater equipped for sound in the towns of Bukhara, Namangan, Andijan, and Kagan. As for sound-equipped mobile units, there were only twenty-nine of them in 1937, a very small number (see table 8 in appendix).[130] By way of comparison, only 54 percent of projectors had sound capability in all of the Soviet Union by the end of 1938, with the European parts and urban areas being better equipped (Miller 2010, 23–24).

*The Film Theater: Visual and Audio Accompaniment to the "Human Passions Projected On-Screen"*

"Why are our films generally considered by the press to be silent?" Dmitri Shostakovich wondered.[131] For a screening held in the village by an itinerant projectionist and one in a permanent film theater followed, theoretically, exactly the same course. There were numerous recommendations about oral, musical, and visual accompaniment published by the Soviet authorities in specific booklets. This was not a matter of occupying the geographical space via *cinefication* but of controlling as much as possible the subjective reception of the film by exerting a firm grasp over the film's extradiegetic environment.

## The Power of Speech in Silent Film

The sheer number of publications reveals the desire to closely control screenings and to establish as univocal a discourse as possible. Oral accompaniment was a means of "total" control, filling the space and silence and reducing any form of resistance or counterdiscourse. It was thus a fundamental factor in the public reception of a film. Its effectiveness depended of course on the use of vernacular languages, especially when there were high levels of illiteracy (Bunegin 1933, 14).

The function of oral commentary had evolved since the early days of cinema and the private operators of the imperial period whose commentary had been rooted in showmanship (Günther 1994). This lasted until the beginning of the Soviet period, as proven by the performances given by Qurban Charbaev in the 1920s, a film lecturer from old Tashkent who was famous for his oratorical skills. His "performance lecturing" met with great success for films such as *The Adventures of Tarzan* (United States, 1921) by Hill and Sidney, to such an extent that the public probably came more to hear the orator perform in person than to see the film. His performances left an indelible mark on the memory of Malik Kaiumov: "No masterpiece of cinema to have received a prize in a festival since has impressed me as much as this silent illusion projected onto a white sheet, accompanied by the delightful commentaries of the master of this unique establishment, Qurban Charbaev. . . . When he started to recount each episode of the film in his typical fashion, the spectators were grateful. He was certainly a remarkable storyteller who gave free rein to his imagination, for each tale was in itself a piece of cinema. I am no longer sure which was the most interesting of the two" (Kaiumov 1982, 13).

At the time, there was also a more politicized form of oral commentary. The account provided by the Iskra projectionists emphasizes that an unaccompanied screening could not fulfill the political agitprop purposes assigned to it. The key figure was the film lecturer, who had several functions (Lacasse 2000).[132] Given the shortage of films, oral accompaniment made it possible to reuse "ideologically poor" films, and sometimes to diametrically alter their original function. For instance, in 1928, it was suggested that American religious films could be used for Soviet antireligious propaganda, but a film about the first Five-Year Plan could also fit the bill (Stepanov 1928, 23). This was the case with Cherniak's *Her Right* (Uzbekistan, 1931), which—though viewed as "not convincing enough"— could be of "significant use" once provided with "a complete political environment" (*Ee pravo* 1932, 3). By supplying political commentary, the orator played the role of an integrator, creating links in the social imaginary and building up a shared destiny. His words made it possible to include the spectators in a vast

Soviet reality and larger historical process, leading them to reassess their past and interpret it in a new light. Cinema was a way of linking and contextualizing the social and political transformations affecting a given place or social group (Pozner 2005, 170).

The various booklets for film lecturers suggested that projectionists, together with the political and administrative authorities, should study the social, economic, and political context to pinpoint their audience, especially in the countryside (the spectators in a permanent film theater varying but little), and consequently determine the appropriate film and means of communication (Bunegin 1922, 6–7). This also made it possible to prepare the "pictorial environment" for the screening, in the form of exhibitions (graphics, figures, photos, diagrams, press excerpts, and a "display poster") about the historical changes and political and economic advances since the beginning of Sovietization (Kefala 1932, 19).[133] It was recommended to hold a discussion a few days beforehand to promote the screening and prepare the audience, and then to give a talk on the day the film was screened. The screenings organized by the Iskra mobile unit started with a short prologue, translated into vernacular language when necessary, which described the subject of the film, the plot, and the main action. The Iskra team kept its interventions to a minimum during the screening of the film so as not to distract the audience's attention and disturb "the plenitude of unknown impressions," thus avoiding any digressions.

> However, at certain interesting stages in the film in terms of the new information provided or the heroism of the moment, the film was stopped (the apparatus was designed to be able to do this) for a brief explanation. For example, when the spectator could see on screen a wide shot taken from the top of a major railway station, a workshop in full swing, or else a shot of a factory bell ringing or of workers on a barricade.... Taken individually, all of this is new and interesting for a peasant, both in terms of the event and its details. In fact, the rule we followed was that all moments associated to production, the daily life of the worker, revolutionary struggle, and so on, were to be selected and emphasized. Our purpose was clear—these would later form the unconscious basis for fusing the town with the village. In brief, by the end of the screening we were facing an audience whose receptiveness and feelings had already been worked upon. The audience was already prepared, forming a malleable and receptive material.[134]

Oral accompaniment played a role in political education, but also in instructing audiences about film, because the "language" of cinema was rarely something a rural public in Uzbekistan or elsewhere in the Soviet Union was familiar with. Parallel editing and the use of cross-fading were problematic, with the viewer losing the link between the shots and thus unable to assimilate the content of the film (Bunegin 1933, 5). The discussion after the screening made it possible to assess the reception of the political message and to clarify any points in the story or in the cinematic technique that had not been properly understood. This discussion sometimes took the form of oratorical debates about political themes (*politboi*), particularly for historical films about revolution. The film lecturer briefly highlighted the key points of the film but needed to "display tact" so as not to hurt the feelings of any audience members who had not understood. He also had to assume his own mistakes to avoid losing face and to retain his authority: "Even if it is wrong, say it authoritatively! If you do not answer straight away you lose all credit" (Bunegin 1933, 28–30).

While oral commentary was essential, attention was also paid to the musical illustration of the films being screened. As Krinitskii remarked at the 1928 cinema conference, "musical illustration is an indissoluble part of the cinematic work, and must further the purpose of the cinematography, that is to say raise the cultural level of the masses" (1929b, 438). Silent films, and then talkies, sometimes had musical score specifically written by great composers. Dmitri Shostakovich started his career as a cinema pianist (Volkov 1980, 50) and composed the music for *The New Babylon* by Grigorii Kozintsev and Leonid Trauberg (1929), *The Donbass Symphony* by Dziga Vertov (1931), and *The Great Citizen* by Fridrikh Ermler (1937), while Sergei Prokofiev wrote the music for *Aleksandr Nevsky* (1938) and *Ivan the Terrible* (1944). In Uzbekistan, the ethnomusicologist Uspenskii composed the music for *The Jackals of Ravat* (1927) by Gertel' and *Jigit* (1936) by Ganiev. A small number of newsreels also benefited from this treatment (Yanov-Yanovskaia 1969, 28). The scores took their inspiration from traditional learned and popular music and songs and were a means of driving the diffusion of cultural norms and entrenching them. They encouraged closer identification with the filmic representation by cultivating the emotive aspect of propaganda, what Tchakhotin terms "senso-propaganda," unlike political education in the narrow meaning of discourse, which he calls "ratio-propaganda" (Tchakhotine 2006, 349).

For films for which no music had been specifically written, "the human passions projected on screen" (Volkov 1980, 50) could have an improvised musical accompaniment. While one pianist sufficed, the *Pravda Vostoka* reported in 1928 that each state cinema in Tashkent had a symphonic ensemble of eleven musicians.[135] And Uzbekkino endeavored to combine all these ensembles to form a symphony orchestra whenever war films were being screened. Musical accompaniment dated back to at least 1920. The musicians at the Apollo and Khiva cinemas in Tashkent were frequently called to order for being absent or late.[136] Booklets for propagandists also recommended using choirs and musical or vocal groups to perform the sung parts of films. This was the case in the brochure accompanying Frelikh's *The Covered Wagon* (1928), which includes the full text of the song and indicates that the accompaniment can be "replaced by a single guitar" (*Krytyi Furgon* 1932, 12–14). Equally, the manual for organizing anti-religious propaganda screenings has a list of songs and a musical repertoire, including Modest Mussorgsky's *Boris Godunov* and Nikolai Rimsky-Korsakov's *Christmas Eve* (Kefala 1931, 31–32).

The information found in the press and archives indicates that the most common form of accompaniment in town was provided by classical ensembles. There is no mention of accompaniment by traditional musicians, although certain "cinematic *mise en abîme*" indicate that this may have occurred. For instance, certain scenes in Cherniak's *Her Right* (1931) and Ganiev's *Upsurge* (1931) show cinema scenes accompanied by traditional musicians. The members of Iskra recognized that the use of local music needed to be envisaged, for using traditional instruments, which corresponded to public taste, made it easier to attract them to screenings.[137] Music could be played live or it could be recorded and played on a gramophone during the screening. For projectionists, diffusing songs was essential, as was diffusing the speeches of revolutionary leaders and "clearly recorded speeches in Turkic languages by famous agitators."[138]

### Soviet "Stratotegy," or the True Nature of Oratorical and Musical Performances

Although there are some convincing examples of political education conducted by projectionists, their task remained complicated over the course of the 1930s and was far from generating the expected effects. The work of the itinerant projectionists, who were sometimes exhausted by pushing their vocal cords to the limit due to the noise of the dynamo (Pozner 2005, 151), tended to be a matter of responding to urgent situations, leaving little room for preparation, and was conducted in difficult material and logistical conditions (transport problems, the absence of communication links, paper shortages, and so on). Although the population reacted favorably to cinema, Soviet organizations were less enthusiastic. Many projectionists reported encountering difficulties in their work. In the region of Kokand, for example, the cadre in charge of "propaganda and culture" informed the local Uzbekkino subsidiary that he did not want to be "bothered with cinema" because it was the "height of the seeding period."[139] The head of the Commissariat for Education was no more cooperative, and for the evening to inaugurate the Uighur red *choikhona* in Kokand refused to allow the projectionist to enter, considering the screenings to be "useless" and "a waste of time."[140] In addition to these difficulties in getting local authorities to accept screenings, projectionists' living conditions were particularly poor. They sometimes traveled around the kolkhozes for a month at a time without receiving any payment, carrying their equipment on their shoulders for over six kilometers if the directors of the kolkhoz refused to supply any means of transport.[141] They slept wherever they could, in the offices during winter and behind fences in summer, for there was not enough accommodation. In the Ferghana Valley, there was only one lodging, accommodating a maximum of eight people.[142] They were sometimes refused the food they felt they were entitled to, while the meager profits they made (the projectionists were financially independent) served primarily to cover expenses associated with organizing the screenings. This generated discontent and turnover among the personnel, with many abandoning their work.[143]

In 1933, the film institutions in the regions and national republics were said to be attaching insufficient importance to agitprop work (Bunegin 1933, 5). Oral accompaniment was what they dreaded most. The organization for providing minimal accompaniment (reading or translating the title cards plus the occasional commentary) was only in its early days.[144] Overall, the audiences, who had scant film culture, were rarely assured of receiving the most basic services of an oral translation and an explanation of the action. There were rarely any discussions after screenings.[145] The practice of "political lecturing" was rare in Uzbekistan in the 1930s. The situation became catastrophic in 1934, and Soviet Control remarked on "the total absence of cultural and political education work" with spectators in the countryside and on the "unsatisfactory work" in the towns.[146]

Although it has not been possible to determine whether there was any "resistance lecturing" against state institutions, the work of some lecturers with "an excessively low cultural level" and limited technical knowledge was nevertheless counterproductive.[147] The situation in towns was a bit better, but far from perfect. At 11:00 p.m. on March 11, 1936, "cultural instruction" was conducted at the Khiva cinema during a screening about the February Revolution: "The lecturer was a man of little culture. He mumbled and paused between his words. Instead of 'strategy' he said 'stratotegy.' . . . In their current form these 'lessons' and 'political hours' [*politchas*] are harmful."[148]

An article published in the *Pravda Vostoka* noted that the Komsomol cells were sometimes slow to set up discussions after the screening. For instance, many cells in factories and clubs had still not found the time to set up a discussion ten days after the screening of Ermler's *The Parisian Cobbler* (Russia, 1928).[149] The fault lay with those in charge, who did not devote enough time to youth education issues. And the situation was no better at the Komsomolets cinema, even though it was meant to set an example, since it belonged to the Communist Youth.

> There was grass growing in the film theater. At the entrance to the cinema you heard the same dubious and speculative jargon of the *papiros* smokers as you did outside other cinemas.150 And whilst in the neighboring film theaters there were enough benches and poor lanterns, there was none of that at all in the Komsomol cinema. Films were screened with insufficient light and it was not unusual to hear people swearing like troopers in the room. . . . Where is the mass work? Where are the kiosks with Komsomol literature? Where can screenings be organized for the masses, with discussions about the films seen?

Where is the reading room, where are the tables for playing chess and drafts and other activities? How could a Komsomol cinema be improved? In other words, why still call it the "Komsomol"![151]

In the 1930s, the operation of film theaters in Tashkent deteriorated markedly, as mentioned in several reports. The screenings themselves, poor management overview, and their inability to "liquidate disorder" were "justly condemned by the spectators."[152] Attendance dropped. For the town of Tashkent, attendance at two places (names not given) dropped from 444,000 spectators in the first quarter of 1931 to 245,000 spectators two years later, amounting to a drop of nearly 50 percent:[153] "Tashkent, the heart of Central Asia, should have model film theaters. But you will not find such dirty, disgusting, and dilapidated cinemas in any other Soviet capital as you do in Tashkent."[154] What buffets did exist were poorly supplied, while the "red corners" and "reading corners" in the lobby, the slogans, and the photo displays were nonexistent.[155] The absence of any explanatory charts of questions and answers to anticipate any questions from audience members was also noted with regret.[156] The situation worsened significantly between 1930 and 1934. The walls of the Iskra cinema were covered in a thick layer of dust, and dirty spider webs dangled from the ceiling, for instance. The "legal fifteen minutes" of cleaning after each screening were far from being respected: "Poor quality projection, frequent breakages, title cards the spectators were unable to read, incessant noise, and gibberish instead of the intelligible speeches of talking films were pretty much the norm."[157]

There was nothing to while away the time before the film was shown other than a few newspapers, which were far from being hot off the press. There were no exhibitions, no photographs, no presentations of "important contemporary moments," no political work or lessons. Musical accompaniment was virtually nonexistent, other than the orchestra of eleven musicians working at the Iskra cinema. Although there was a conductor, he refused to watch films before the public screening, preferring to improvise. The sound was particularly poor, and, instead of clear speeches, all the spectators could hear was "hissing and wheezing."[158]

Ideally, the screening would start at 7:00 p.m. with an introduction (five to ten minutes) and a brief presentation (twenty to thirty minutes), and then the film would be shown around 7:30 p.m. (lasting about an hour). The film would be followed by a discussion (thirty to forty-five minutes) (Kefala 1932, 32). But some screenings dragged on forever: "On June 7 [1932], in the Voinov workers' cinema, in Canteen no. 2, *The New Babylon* [by Kozintsev and Trauberg, 1929] was to be shown. By 9 in the evening nearly all the tickets had been sold and the seats were occupied, but the film still hadn't started. And for two hours, without any consideration for the wishes of the public, the film was not set in motion."[159] The cashier, ticket inspector, and employees responded with insults and mockery to the audience members who wanted to get their ticket reimbursed. And the reason for all this was that "the cinema manager was in a bar, drinking." The spectators had to wait until midnight to be reimbursed. In other instances, the projection became a drawn-out affair, such as a screening of *The Party Card* (1936) by Pyr'ev, which lasted four hours because the film kept breaking. But the most extreme case occurred in Behbudi: "Because of preposterous situation with the electricity, the screening lasted two consecutive evenings. The light went off and in the darkness the flat voice of the administrator intoned: 'come back tomorrow, tickets will be valid.'"[160]

In Jizzakh, the film theater equipped for sound had not projected any talking films for over six months. It was in a former infirmary, next to the morgue.[161] In Samarkand, the same film was shown after an interval, only under a different title. The Khiva cinema in Tashkent was criticized in the press for its dirtiness and its impolite staff. The management broadcast their final recommendations over loudspeakers just before films were shown: "Respect the cleanliness and tidiness! Don't push! Don't trample each other! Be civilized—spit into the spittoons!"[162] People were packed together in the cinema, there was pushing and shoving, and it was hard to breathe: "There was so much smoke that you wouldn't even have recognized your father five paces off. The smoke came into the room and hang there like a thick scum. Those sitting far from the screen saw the film as if through a fog."[163]

People queued outside, and the lobby was only opened to the public at the last moment, with nothing provided to pass the time while waiting. It was not easy to buy a ticket. The Society of Friends of Soviet Cinema, whose work was meant to extend across all Uzbekistan but who were only operating in Tashkent in January 1929, was accused of selling booklets of one hundred free tickets, primarily intended for "low-paid employees and workers." The Society of Friends of Soviet Cinema bought them for seven rubles apiece, then sold them for fifty rubles. And only 30 percent of the spectators at any given screening paid a reduced ticket price, leading to regular scandals: "Juicy curses floated in the air, subscriptions were thrown through the ticket office window at the cashier, accompanied by determined farewells, and some people even tried to throw punches through it."[164]

The only solution for subscription holders was to come an hour before the screening was due to begin, and even then they needed to be near the front of the queue. Otherwise there were always bootleggers. "He [a young man] called out in a loud voice to no one in particular: 'Do you want to see *Without a Dowry* [*Bezpridanitsa*]? I wouldn't queue if I were you! Come and buy tickets! . . . The second row is 3 rubles, and 7 for the front row.' And when the people waiting started to grow impatient, he called out again unperturbedly: 'You don't want them! It's as you wish!' Before adding: 'what skinflints! People don't even want to pay a little bit more!'"[165] Zakir Khanov was arrested for selling tickets in front of the Iskra and the Khiva cinemas to try to make a living after he had lost his job. An old razor blade was even found on him. Between 1930 and 1935 he had committed petty thefts, and he had taken the blade with him this time "just in case." He was sentenced to one year's hard labor for speculating on cinema tickets.

\* \* \*

The Uniformization of Hegemony

The period of the Cultural Revolution, examined in all its complexity, reveals the growing tensions that existed at just the moment the first national filmmakers were starting to produce films. Power relationships transpire on-screen in the realm of symbolism and representation, opposing concurrent pathways through modernity that were not yet completely mutually exclusive. The Red Army as a symbol of Soviet power (in *The Jackals of Ravat*) provided a means of national liberation, offering military backup and general support (literacy) to combat those (the Basmachi, Muslim clergy, and property-owning classes) presented as stifling a community aspiring toward a policy to emancipate women and promote secularization. But central Soviet power radicalized these tendencies, imposing a clean break with the past and with traditions. In destroying the old social structures and working to delegitimize the old religious and economic authorities, Soviet power created an "identity vacuum" that was partially filled by the new secular components of the emergent Soviet Uzbek identity (ethnogenesis, history, and national culture and folklore). This made ethnic and national referents even more important.

The great structural transformations in the world of cinema bring into focus the imperial nature of the Soviet Union, laying down solid bases for future indoctrination and for controlling any form of subjectivity. First, the restrictive economic framework introduced by the creation of Soiuzkino in 1930, though meeting with some resistance, was backed up by political control, given the increasingly important role played by the All-Union Communist Party in determining the theme of films. Second, the political purges obliged filmmakers to conform to official discourse, or at least appear to do so. Obviously, political injunctions and the reassertion of control in the field were not always enforced down to the last detail, and despite the Bolshevik leaders' wishes to see everything run smoothly, there were glitches that caused the machinery to seize up.

The political and institutional subordination of the periphery was structurally established, but it did not yet weigh down fully on cinematic discourse and was only partly taken up in the cinematic imaginary of the early Uzbek filmmakers, who still enjoyed some room for creativity. It was impossible to totally subordinate them, other than by imprisonment or death or by simply making it impossible for them to work.

# Part 3
# The Paradoxes of the Nationalities Policy: Nationalism versus Internationalism (1931–37)

# Part 3 Introduction

## *Working as an Uzbek Artist under Stalin: Ambivalence, Resistance, and Nationalism*

THE PERCEPTION OF imperial and Soviet Russia as a colonizing power has been a feature of intellectual discourse in Central Asia since the moment of its colonization until the present day. Despite this perception, Russia has always been a power that fascinates, exerting equal forces of attraction and repulsion. The relationship in this period between Central Asian intellectuals and Russia as a colonizing—and then Soviet—power was, in fact, ambivalent; the intellectuals admitted Russia's military superiority along with the technical and scientific backwardness of Central Asian Muslims, and hence recognized Russia's role as a necessary contact for stimulating the development of creative and intellectual potential and knowledge (Babajanov 2004, 79–80). For some, taking part in the Soviet government represented a means of development, and for as long as there was no prospect of independence on the horizon, it afforded a means of learning: "The colonial threat cannot be a threat to an enlightened nation. Everything must be learnt: the art of war, and that of running a government. It will be useful."[1]

The artist, like the politician, lies at the heart of these issues: "Soviet power behaves well toward the intelligentsia, providing it with work, and paying it well," Fitrat admitted,[2] surprised at the attitude of some writers, such as Chulpan (ca. 1897–1938), who positioned themselves as "true nationalists" and adopted a more radical position.[3] Yet Fitrat, by recommending dissimulation as the norm for writing, endeavored to pursue the same goals by other means: "You cannot say anything openly, and so have to hide behind the Soviet flag. . . . You have to give the idea of the oppressed and the oppressors, of the colony and the colonial yoke. There is no point in advancing openly," he observed about one of his plays.[4] Dissimulation is a strategy by which the artist accommodates power and the readership (or spectators) while ensuring that she or he maintains a place within the institution.

The idea of hiding behind the Soviet flag as evoked by Fitrat—considered by the political police as the most representative figure of Uzbek nationalism (uzbekism)—is a form of concealed resistance. Because this resistance is integrated within the bodies of state, it is possible to better defend national interests in accordance with the optic that prevailed prior to the great Stalinist transformations. The accommodation makes room for the tensions and conflicting ideological forces that still lent Soviet hegemony its heteroclite structure, thus enabling nationalism to survive. In 1928, the political police distinguished between two types of nationalism: one based on pan-Turkist tendencies, as represented by the Jadid reformists of the older generation, and one rooted in an Uzbekist or pan-Uzbekist tendency (uzbekist or panuzbekist in Russian, uzbekchi in Uzbek) based on the national political entity established in 1924.[5] But these differences between pan-Turkist nationalists, Uzbek nationalists, former Jadids, and communists were tending to disappear, as were the differences between those who were in favor of accommodation and those who excluded all forms of participation with Soviet power. The members of the Uzbek Communist Party acted as important backers, because their goals could be assimilated to those of nationalists who were not party members and who did not always enjoy the means for self-expression.

This Uzbek nationalism seeking to emancipate itself from the influence of Moscow was accompanied by a more localized form of chauvinism (*shovinizm*), which took the form of ignoring the interests of other national minorities.[6] Ethnic and national tensions rapidly became exacerbated after the ethnic and territorial delimitation of Central Asia, which brought an Uzbek hegemony decried by the nation's detractors as well as a chauvinism that rode roughshod over other minorities, and especially the Tajiks. While the Russians were accused of imperialism in Central Asia, so, too, were the Uzbeks, for "Russian imperial chauvinism and Uzbek imperial chauvinism overlap and are mutually supporting."[7] Violations of minority rights led to a situation of permanent conflict in which national minorities were assimilated, with Tajiks declaring themselves to be Uzbek during the 1926 census, for example (in Bukhara and Samarkand).[8]

The nationalist tendencies of the population are harder to assess, because certain archives are closed (in particular, those of the party and the political police). However, if we are to believe the same political police report and what Chulpan reportedly said, "an insignificant minority of the population support the government, the majority of those who understand and have national sentiment conceal their outrage."[9] This statement is backed up by a story in the press about an apparently trivial subject but which in fact indicates how deep-rooted the nationalist phenomenon was—the name of a cinema. Just as certain intellectuals were accused of "bourgeois nationalism" and were denounced or tracked down, a similar phenomenon occurred in relation to the Turan cinema, built in a public garden where the first film screening had been held in 1897. In an article published in 1933, a journalist railed against this name, which, by opposition to irân, refers directly to Turkic identity. For "the class enemy," *turân* is "the symbol of glory, and of the grandeur of the Muslim movement." It becomes synonymous with "religious obscurantism" and the "exacerbation of national hatred between the workers."[10] The fact that a cultural institute has been named Turan is "a great shame" in the journalist's opinion, for any enemy passing in front of the cinema is likely to rejoice: "Glory to God! May this holy name live forever!" But then in a culmination of nationalism—only this time Tajik nationalism—the journalist suggests renaming the cinema Lahuti in tribute to the famous Soviet Tajik poet who had recently been honored.[11]

"Will working together with Soviet power save our nation?" wondered one anti-Soviet schoolteacher of Turkish origin, living in Tashkent.[12] This is the question that the chapters in this final part examine. Chapter 5 looks at the first Uzbek national filmmakers, Nabi Ganiev and Suleyman Khojaev, seeking to understand their works and the gaps between the apparent discourse of their films and the more subtle discourse that remains concealed or dissimulated, whether consciously or not. While all their films were silent—despite the existence of musical scores for some of them—the film that was finally applauded by critics as "socialist realist" and "national in form, proletarian in content" was in fact a talking picture (studied in chap. 6). It dates from 1937, and analysis of it illuminates the "1937 moment" and the Stalinist purges.

# 5 The Nationalist Cinematographic Imaginary

*Subjugating Class to Nation*

> What a punishment it is not to be able to write the progress of one's own nation. Under such conditions there is no life in Uzbekistan. We are laboring under so many burdens. And nationalism is something we learn about from the Europeans.
>
> Attributed to Chulpan, political police report (1928)

THE HEART OF this chapter is formed by the 1930s work of the only two Uzbek filmmakers of the interwar period. First, Nabi Ganiev (1904–54), who—though never a member of the Communist Party—was regarded in the years after the Second World War as the founding father of Uzbek cinema. Second, Suleyman Khojaev (1892–1937) was close to Muslim reformist circles and only joined the Communist Party after the February 1917 revolution. Up until his imprisonment in 1934, Khojaev embodied revolutionary discourse, although he was ultimately shot for "bourgeois nationalism." Is this a case of life and honor for one and death and oblivion for the other? Although these two filmmakers might at first appear to be utterly opposed, they in fact had a point in common: the nationalist imaginary conveyed by their films.

Filmic discourse became more radical when the first Uzbek filmmakers started making their films under the impact of the ongoing institutional transformations examined in chapter 4 (in the form of economic centralization and political purges), Soviet policy in general, and their nationalities policy in particular. The national imaginary of 1928—based on promoting an ideal of community and citizenship (see the discussion of *The Jackals of Ravat* in chap. 3)—gave way to a far more exclusive and defensive image of the nation, and one that was particularly defiant of the Russians. According to Marxist-Leninist dogma, class discourse should normally have subjugated any idea of nation, but it was instead appropriated by the filmmakers to help underpin nationalism. Some of the themes explored in this chapter have been examined elsewhere in this book— for instance, it looks again at the antireligious propaganda in Ganiev's *Ramazan*

(1932) and the theme of the "1916 revolts" with Khojaev's *Before Dawn* (1934). But what matters here is not so much the theme as the way the filmmakers handle it—transposing, assimilating, selecting, or rejecting the main lines of the dominant ideology as they perceived it. Such a transposition was particularly tricky in the 1930s, when political and historiographical expectations were constantly shifting, offering further illustration of the course taken by the revolutionary dynamic.

There is also the issue of how to assess forms of resistance. As a partial answer, the work of the Uzbek filmmakers is best viewed as a tacit agreement to their position of subordination in a complex system of interdependence, and hence as a way of being seen to express their loyalty. They acknowledged the primacy of the revolutionary process for which they acted as the mouthpiece and recognized the hegemony of the policies embodying this process, because of which they had access to training and to the very considerable material and financial means at their disposal to make films. In exchange, the artist in them conceded to the political authorities the right to oversee how their works gave body to the revolution and the Soviet adventure. All outright resistance was impossible, so it took multiple forms instead (doublespeak, dissimulation, ambiguity, and ambivalence). These forms are examined in this chapter using, at least in part, the idea of a "public transcript" and a "hidden transcript" as formulated by James C. Scott (1990), adapted here to the context of film. Although it is not possible to know the hidden transcript (the personal opinions of the filmmakers about Soviet power) since certain sources are not accessible, it is possible to identify those elements that transpire in the public transcript (film) qua communicational performance. But it is necessary to go beyond the question of the author's initial intent and consider the work as a whole, for this transcends the author's conscious project.

The cinematographic performances of the two Uzbek filmmakers would appear to be diametrically opposed, and they will be treated separately, with the first part examining the apparently apolitical attitude and seeming conformism of Nabi Ganiev and the second part analyzing Suleyman Khojaev's revolutionary commitment to nationalist ends. But it is first necessary to look briefly at the policy of "indigenization" of the cultural sphere, thus enabling us to better situate the two filmmakers' individual trajectories.

## The Indigenization of Culture and the Studios

The fact that there were national filmmakers in Uzbekistan needs to be viewed in relation to the indigenization of the state institutions and the appointment of natives to administrative positions and other functions. This was one of the visible bases of the Soviet nationalities policy as formulated by Stalin, intended as "positive discrimination" (Martin 2001a; Cadiot 2007, 118). This was ostensibly the case for the most visible positions, primarily in regulatory authorities (for culture and teaching). The filmmakers were a case in point, although they were often assisted by nonnative head technicians, which sometimes caused conflict (see the section in chap. 4 titled "Personal Enmity: Nabi Ganiev and His Directors of Photography"). The indigenization of government bodies resulted at the local level in their Uzbekization, to the detriment of promoting other national minorities and their cultural development. But overall, the key posts (in coercive authorities, the political police, and the Central Asian Bureau) stayed in the hands of centrally appointed officials. This led some to claim: "Indigenization is a joke! When will the railways be 'indigenized'? . . . So far the only ones to have been 100 percent 'indigenized' are the stable hands!"[1]

Indeed, by July 1, 1931, out of the 11,500 people working in 118 state institutions in Central Asia, only 1,218 (10.5 percent) were of the nationality in question.[2] Out of the 9,626 Russians working in them, only 6 percent spoke the vernacular language, which—though supposedly used in the various decision-making authorities—in fact prevailed at only the district and village level in most government authorities.[3] Among Uzbek institutions taken as a whole, the Commissariat for Education acted as something of a role model, with the texts it drew up being produced in two languages (as of August 5, 1931)—the situation having improved since 1927 due to the political purges that had had a greater impact on staff of European origin than on others.[4] The numbers remained very low in other domains, and the situation did not improve over the following years, despite sixteen decrees to further indigenization being issued in Central Asia between 1923 and 1928.[5] In 1933, the central authorities were still far from satisfied with the number of Uzbek nationals promoted to positions of responsibility (in the party and in the cultural sphere).[6]

When the first Uzbek filmmakers started shooting their works in 1931, the results of the indigenization policy in the field of cinema had been mediocre at best. There were scriptwriting courses, for example, with the target of promoting 75 percent of the Uzbeks enrolled, though in fact the figure stood at 50 percent when the course was first set up and was only 20 percent by the end.[7] In addition, the course was plagued by lack of premises (classrooms), teacher absenteeism, and limited cooperation by national and European writers. Furthermore, only a small proportion of those taking the course were party members. A 1934 report about "the situation of cinema in Uzbekistan" states with regard to the training of filmmakers that hundreds of people were sent to Moscow between 1928 and 1932 to attend a course at the State Institute for Cinematography, without the course's actual usefulness or the conditions in which students were housed being taken into account. The institute finally selected thirty-six people, of whom just three completed the course, the others either returning home or completely changing their profession.[8] As for the technical personnel (projectionists and mechanics), the rural network was composed of 40 percent Uzbeks, and the urban network was made up of 32 percent Uzbeks (see table 9 in appendix).[9] A course created in Tashkent to train forty-seven projectionists produced mediocre results, and those selected included many married and pregnant women who were unable to leave Tashkent.[10] Even though there were few women technicians—and it was only in the 1960s that the first women filmmakers in the region appeared—all the personnel involved in postdistribution assembly and editing in 1934 were women, the majority of whom were Uzbek (nine women out of twelve in all).[11]

## Creating and Surviving under Stalin—Nabi Ganiev's Apparent Conformism

After attending a religious primary school (*maktab*), Nabi Ganiev (Ghanizoda in Uzbek) went on to study at the School of Fine Arts in Moscow (Vkhutemas), graduating in 1925 (Akbarov 2005, 13). Upon returning to Tashkent, he trained as an actor and filmmaker while working as a consultant on shoots in Central Asia.[12] He started making short documentary films, news reports, and newsreels before turning to full-length feature films, of which he made three in the 1930s: *The Upsurge* (1931), about the exploits of Uzbek Stakhanovites in a cotton factory; *Ramazan* (1932), a film of antireligious propaganda against fasting; and *Jigit* (1936), a remake of *Chapaev* by Sergei and Georgi Vasil'ev (1934), the first canonical Socialist Realist film. It was only with his subsequent work, and especially *Takhir and Zukhra* (1945), shot at the end of the Second World War with the help of the leading specialists of the period, that Ganiev came to be viewed as the "founding father of Uzbek cinema."[13] His 1930s films are characterized by a certain caution, for he was working under the permanent supervision of party cell members (see also Drieu 2010b).

### *The Upsurge* (1931): *The National Proletariat and Uzbek Supremacy*

*The Upsurge* is the first film produced in Uzbekistan to focus almost exclusively on the world of the factory. It includes positive stereotypes about production, such as the Stakhanovites and socialist emulation, output records, the atmosphere in the factory, the machines with their gleaming cogs, and the train and its whistle announcing imminent change. But the film also portrays negative aspects of the factory, such as sabotage, laziness, traitors (who are finally unmasked), and the theft of the cotton produced. The world of the cotton factory is presented as a symbol of Uzbekistan's modernity, with technical and mechanical progress enabling laborers and seasonal workers alike to free themselves from the injustice of hard manual labor. This rhetoric amounts to the film's public transcript, illustrating Ganiev's intention to situate his film in relation to the great topical themes of the moment and express a form of loyalty to the ideals of Soviet power that it embodies.

> *The Upsurge* (Rus. *Pod"em*) by Nabi Ganiev (Uzbekkino, 1931)
>
> Two seasonal workers are walking through the mountains toward cotton processing factory number 111 to look for stable employment. They encounter Karim (E. Khamraev), a seasonal worker who is mistreated by his boss and who decides to join them. Work is in full swing at the factory, with the machines running flat out to spin the cotton. The Komsomol orator Tulegan (Iu. Sabirov) is poring over communist literature, the mechanic Basyt (Iu. Agzamov) is carefully oiling machines, the former seasonal worker Iuldash (Irgash) is working for the Komsomol, the supervisor Shamsutdinnov (Akbashev) "is busy at his daily tasks," while the head of production and secretary to the party cell Kuchkarov is checking various quantities. Others are less industrious: The deputy secretary Pastukhov is getting ready to sabotage the work, and Petrukha (S. Bogdanov), an unqualified Russian worker who is permanently drunk, is rolling cigarettes. Work is frequently interrupted by the lack of raw materials, despite the efforts of the two brigades (that of Basyt and that of Pastukhov/Shamsutdinnov). To increase yields, Basyt's brigade goes to the mill that their factory supplies with cotton to learn about its production methods and improve coordination. Although the work carried out by the mill is perfect, its production is spoiled by the stained, poor-quality cotton sent to them by the factory. The brigade comes back, and Basyt draws up a system to mechanize the work, which produces excellent results. But there is still not enough cotton. Basyt's brigade decides to help with the harvest and discovers that some of the cotton is hidden. Meanwhile, back at the factory, the machines are damaged by saboteurs. Basyt is wrongly accused of the sabotage by Pastukhov's brigade. Basyt is put on trial by a factory tribunal, but the comrades on his brigade manage to prove his innocence. The real traitors, Pastukhov and Shamsutdinnov, are apprehended.

The public transcript of *The Upsurge* adopts all the filmic stereotypes of the period. But some aspects of the film stand out from the norm. First, the character of the political orator (Tulegan) embodies a distance from "Bolshevik speaking," which strikes the workers in the factory as foreign; as soon as Tulegan starts to talk, the workers quickly disappear and ridicule him, generating humor. Above all, the film constantly depicts the Uzbek workers and Stakhanovites as superior to Russians. This superiority transpires in their working "at Bolshevik rhythms," the Uzbeks being hardworking and careful about quality and yield. In contrast, the Russian worker Petrukha is "ready for anything other than work" and is constantly drunk, though largely inoffensive, and he balks at socialist emulation because it requires greater effort without any corresponding pay rise. The Uzbek workers also stand out for their spirit of initiative and their ability to come up with new working methods and put them into practice. Basyt embodies this spirit, progressing from being a lowly mechanic to "head engineer," when he presents his model for mechanizing cotton transportation in the factory. The Russian engineers agree with his plan, recognizing that it is clever, and help him to put it into action.

In representing the workers as mainly indigenized—the film, for that matter, worked with the very first generation of Uzbek actors—Nabi Ganiev insists on the hierarchy that largely subverts the stereotype of political guides being solely of Russian origin.[14] A fine illustration of this stereotype is afforded by the 1937 film *The Oath*, produced in Uzbekistan (see chap. 6). But for the time being, it was the Uzbeks who enjoyed exclusive, autonomous decision making and who held the most important political positions in the factory (heads of the party cells) and key production positions (such as heads of brigade and mechanics). Conversely, the overall representation of the Russians is negative. Pastukhov, the head of the other brigade, is a traitor. He sabotages and steals the cotton produced. He masterminds the wrongful actions carried out, even though he is assisted by subaltern (hence secondary) Uzbek personnel. Furthermore, there are no women in Pastukhov's brigade. In contrast, Basyt's brigade is an example of genuine gender equality, with numerous Uzbek women workers; it also displays a greater degree of internationalism because it includes a worker of Ukrainian origin (though no Russians).

The superiority of the Uzbek people, though never brought into doubt by the portrayal of relationships with the Russians, may also be presumed to hold with regard to the Tajiks, though to a lesser extent. Although the film never refers explicitly to national belonging, an indication is afforded by an article written when the film was being shot that mentions that the seasonal workers were of Tajik origin.[15] Acceding to the world of the Uzbek factory apparently enabled them to free themselves from the world of agriculture, perceived as inferior, unstable, and inegalitarian. Seasonal workers decided to go to the factory because they were looking for a permanent job and hoped to accede to an economically and socially superior form of labor organization and thus leave behind the particularly humiliating relationship of class domination that existed between *bais* and seasonal workers. That is the meaning of the first scene in the film. Karim, played by Ergash Khamraev, is risking his life to prevent his master's cargo of cotton disappearing into the ravine, and he is cruelly beaten before being saved by two other seasonal workers on their way to the factory.[16] The fact that the Uzbek factory assimilates Tajik seasonal farm hands depicts a community that transcends assigned ethnicities in a process of economic and social modernization.

In his new situation, Karim plays an important role, far removed from any form of degradation, because he is the one who unmasks the traitors Pastukhov and Shamsutdinnov.

Despite some reviews denouncing the improbable screenplay and poorly constructed plot, the film, which refuses to perpetuate the image of Uzbek subalternity to the Russians, was acclaimed upon its release in Uzbekistan for managing to portray the "national proletariat" without any exoticism.[17] *The Upsurge* assimilates stereotypes about production—both those that were firmly established and others that were becoming formally recognized with Socialist Realism—making it Ganiev's most openly committed film and the one that most fully embodies politics. It is also a film that nationalizes communist values (in which it is similar to the work of Suleyman Khojaev), here resumed to the modernity of labor, productivist exploits, a spirit of initiative, decisiveness, and gender equality. Ganiev's next two films, on the other hand, show a progressive distancing from expressing any kind of political opinion, which becomes more noticeably absent.

### Ramazan *(1932): The Ambiguity of Antireligious Discourse*

*The Upsurge* was not based on ambiguous discourse but, on the contrary, fully adopted communist ideals. This was not the case, however, for Ganiev's second feature film, *Ramazan*, which was intended to support the antireligious campaign of 1933. An analysis of the film reveals ambiguities in the storytelling as well as in the failure to apply cinematographic techniques in an exact manner, making making the film difficult to interpret at times.

---

*Ramazan* (Rus. and Uzb. *Ramazan*)
by Nabi Ganiev (Uzbekkino, 1932)

Timur (E. Khamraev) is an honest and religious man who works at the mosque and for the *bai*. He dreams of going on a pilgrimage to Mecca. The month of Ramadan arrives and the population is getting ready for it in various ways: Those working for Islam are preparing the mosque, while the head of the party cell and Najim (R. Akhmedov), the head of the kolkhoz, are organizing an antireligious demonstration in a teahouse (*choikhona*) and preparing for the cotton harvest. But Najim, working in alliance with the mullah and the *bai* (Ya. Azimov), is secretly working against Soviet power by trying to exploit Islam and fasting as a way to hamper work on the kolkhoz. They also sabotage the dike that controls the irrigation of the fields. When the head of the cell is trying to repair the dike, he falls into the water and starts drowning. Timur jumps in the water to save him, thus breaking his fast, since his body is immersed. After the head of the party cell has been saved, everyone crowds around both him and the head of the kolkhoz, who has always obtained Timur's support by luring him with the prospect that he will help him go to Mecca. The head of the kolkhoz is finally exposed.

### THE BIAS OF CLASS DISCOURSE

The filmic discourse is based on a series of simple oppositions between the world of the mosque and that of the red *choikhona*, as signified at the beginning of the film by the many parallel edits. The mosque is synonymous with technical backwardness since it has no electricity, only an oil lamp. The characters who go there are presented as simpleminded, credulous, and blinded by their faith. This is the case with Timur at the beginning of the film. They are also malevolent (the *bai*) or are smug and biased (the head of the kolkhoz, Najim, is a traitor). The mosque is also a place of individualism, selfishness, passivity, and immobility. The club, on the other hand, is the very embodiment of technical modernity (with electricity) and social modernity (with emancipated women), full of gaiety, tranquility, simplicity, honesty, and integrity (the head of the party cell); it is a place of unflagging dynamism and activity, where the values of the community are respected (sharing, solidarity, and respect). Only two characters link the relatively separate worlds of religion (the mosque) and the secularized modern world (the teahouse): Timur (and secondarily his wife), the positive hero who gradually starts moving away from religion, and the head of the kolkhoz, Najim, who is exposed at the end of the film.

Islam is never attacked head-on in this film despite its antireligious tenor; nor are its representatives and believers. So how are religious matters shorn of their legitimacy? In addition to the classic opening shots of ruined mosques indicating that Islam is a belief system from another era, the film's narrative, which should theoretically prioritize the denunciation of the great religious precepts, in fact concentrates only on the practices of sabotage and on the way in which former authority figures (the *bai*) and the "undercover agent" (the head of the kolkhoz) damage the cotton harvest and the work of the community by using the fast for their own ulterior purposes. The only religious authority portrayed in the film is a debonair mullah, in cahoots with the *bai* and head of the kolkhoz, who has a secondary and relatively discreet role. He does not foment any action against the work on the kolkhoz and is not particularly active in proselytizing.

The fast is primarily denounced as a form of sabotage. This is the meaning of the speech by the secretary of the party cell to the assembly of kolkhoz workers gathered at the red *choikhona*: "By respecting Ramadan, you are carrying out the wishes of the class enemy and sabotaging the cotton harvest." Fasting reduces output since the workers are physically weakened, doze off, and even have hallucinations, and the practice is criticized on the grounds that it generates antisocial behavior. The kolkhoz workers who observe the fast remain apart from the rest of the group; they are "ashamed to fast at the collective table" and become irritable and prone to fighting due to their lack of sustenance. Several shots emphasize how difficult it is to respect the fast (with close-ups on suffering faces), especially during the harvest, when it is very hot. In addition, the overly abrupt breaking of the fast at nightfall (and eating too rapidly) can result in death. This is what happens to Timur's father, who dies on the first evening. In fact, fasting is presented as a dangerous practice.

The film, however, presents no entrenched positions about Ramadan, and the invitation to respect the fast or to break it prematurely are presented as mere variables, both being used in turn for the ulterior motive of harming production. The inclusion of class discourse introduces a bias into the antireligious discourse and ends up replacing it, thereby undermining the initial propaganda objectives. So it is the *bai* rather than the mullah who is the character most closely associated with religious discourse. But what religious legitimacy may he lay claim to? The *bai* refers, for instance, to sharia in order to compel Timur to adopt exemplary religious behavior. On occasion he also uses roundabout ways to get others to fast and thereby damage the harvest (ordering the destruction of the kolkhoz's large cooking pot that is used to prepare the collective meal). But when the *bai* gives Timur some bread, suggesting that Timur eat it, the *bai* is obliging Timur to break his fast, thus losing his "religious credibility."

Religion is also used to denounce the relationship of class domination. The money spent for the *iftor*, the meal to break the fast each evening, is presented as unjust because it is far too much money for poorer families. Once again it is the *bai* who conveys the discourse, assuring the wealthy that they can redeem their sins financially should they break the fast—unlike Timur, who does not have the necessary financial wherewithal. But the *bai* is also a particularly vulgar character (he calls Timur a "son of a bitch") who drinks alcohol at the mosque, where he ends up completely drunk. The wine had been served by the mullah, who dipped a finger in it with a string of prayer beads around his wrist, though without drinking any. This scene is the only one in the film to represent the mosque in so crude a manner as a place of debauchery and drunkenness (fig. 5.1).

Ambivalence, Identification, and the Persistence of Values

The radical nature of this scene of drunkenness, as well as its extreme symbolic violence, raises the issue of whether the audience would adhere to what was being portrayed on-screen and the concomitant risk that the entire antireligious discourse might be discredited. There is scant information about how the local

 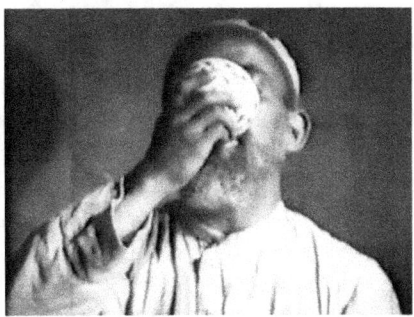

Figure 5.1, a-b. Drinking alcohol in a mosque. *Ramazan*. Screen stills.

population reacted to *Ramazan*. The fact that the film was not reviewed in the press suggests that it was not released commercially and that it was a work of agitation (*agitka*) intended for an exclusively Muslim population. If we are to believe a report by the head of Uzbek studios, the film met with the approval of "large masses of spectators."[18] However, observations by the Repertoire Committee of Soviet Russia mention that "the subject is complicated and confused," that "the representations in the screenplay are vulgar," and that cinematographic technique was not used properly to convey the message.[19]

Certain elements in the film support the skepticism of the Repertoire Committee. A first problem in interpretation arises from the failure to use elementary cinematographic techniques for silent films, such as dissolves and iris shots. These key transitional elements enable the viewer to establish the narrative link between two scenes by indicating a change in time frame or a shift from the main narrative to an embedded one. In *Ramazan*, these techniques are not used, forcing the audience to perform complex post hoc reinterpretation of some scenes—a task that is all the more difficult for a public considered to have little cinematographic culture. This is the case, for instance, in a scene in which an antireligious play is performed; the scene is inserted into the film without any transitional technique. The viewer understands that it is a play only when there is a shot of the audience members applauding, and then the viewer needs to recall the whole scene and reinterpret it accordingly.

Furthermore, the play contains ambiguous discourse about religion. When a young woman (Taksir) enters a room to bring an old man food to break the daily fast (*pit-ruza*), she finds him eating in the daytime during Ramadan. Although this means that the old man is a bad Muslim and hence a good Soviet kolkhozian, he tries to abuse her, invoking an argument referring to Islam: "Your age is of no importance . . . Mohammed married Aisha when she was only nine." The positive values (not fasting) are denied by the attempt at sexual abuse, justified by a comparison to the Prophet of Islam.

Given these ambiguities and the complex storytelling, how is the viewer meant to feel involved in the tale and identify with the positive heroes in the film? As Jacques Ellul has pointed out, the principle of modern propaganda is based on inciting people to act, where the purpose is not to generate a choice but rather to engender mimetic behavior and trigger reflexes (1990, 36–44). In fact, the only character the public can identify with is Timur—with the exception of the head of the party cell, who is less representative of the potential audience. This sort of positive hero—a slightly naive peasant—is characteristic of antireligious propaganda films such as *The Ishan's Fiancée* by Frelikh (Uzbekistan, 1931) and Sharifzade's *Bismillah* (Azerbaijan, 1925). Timur embodies positive values throughout the film. These are initially associated with a religious ethic (honesty, integrity, respecting the fast, dreaming of going on pilgrimage to Mecca) and throughout the film, though certain aspects are partially disconnected from the religious sphere as the film progresses. Once Timur understands that Najim is a traitor, he rejects the idea of going on pilgrimage to Mecca that the latter had dangled in front of him, but does he fundamentally reject pilgrimage? Equally, on jumping in the water to save the head of the party cell, Timur agrees to break his fast of his own free will (the fast is broken if more than half of the body is immersed). But does he reject the practice of fasting altogether, or is this simply a temporary way of saving a man's life?

It is difficult to assert that the values Timur conveys have been fully secularized on the basis of just these two examples. Although he differs from the old figures of authority (the *bai* and, indirectly, the mullah) and from the "internal enemies" of Soviet power (the head of the kolkhoz), Timur retains his moral rigor, shaped by his initial religious values. The scene of drunkenness in the mosque is a perfect illustration of this. By refusing to drink alcohol, Timur continues to behave with religious rigor. But he also acquires predominance by saving the head of the party cell from drowning; Timor affirms the superiority of the values he embodies over communist virtue and ensures that they survive. This idea of a transfer of values between religion and communism is also indicated at another moment in the film when the head of the cell, after destroying the kolkhoz cooking pot on Najim's orders, then suggests borrowing the mosque's pot, which they finally use. By using this object, the kolkhoz, together with its social and economic organization, symbolically reintegrate, at least in part, the values associated with Islam.

The film is far from a wholesale delegitimization of religious matters. Instead it is a way of thinking about how communist ideology, as locally perceived, feeds on ambivalence and combines values that can appear to be contradictory. This ambivalence within the antireligious discourse is illustrated by another sequence where Ganiev appears on-screen at prayer. Although he is making an antireligious propaganda film, Ganiev shows himself on-screen, on one sole occasion,

*The Nationalist Cinematographic Imaginary* | 175

Figure 5.2, a-b. Nabi Ganiev praying in his film, *Ramazan*. Screen stills.

appearing in the foreground of a crowd of the faithful, performing the first movements of the collective prayer (fig. 5.2).

## Jigit *(1936); or, Political Quietism as a Form of Commitment*

The last of Nabi Ganiev's films analyzed here is *Jigit*. The theme—the Basmachi movement—is one that was taken up very early on in Uzbek film production. *The Minaret of Death* by Viskovskii (1925) offered an exotic representation of this theme, inspired by the clichés of Arabian horsemen in the oriental films produced in Europe. *The Jackals of Ravat* by Gertel' (1928) also used the Basmachi uprising as its backdrop, as did *The Last Bek* by Sabinskii (1931), of which unfortunately no copies remain (Abul-Kasymova (1965, 73).[20] *The Last Bek* was criticized for being superficial and for its poor acting, and was remarked upon by the press "for its mediocrity." It sought to assimilate the Basmachi movement to a form of religious obscurantism (72). The unfinished film *Gharm* was also supposed to shed light on how the Soviet authorities fought the Basmachis. Finally, a screenplay held at the Tashkent Museum of Cinema displays numerous similarities with *Jigit*.[21] *Jigit* was shot in 1936, ten years after the height of the military confrontation between the Red Army and the Basmachis, and although it did not serve any immediate propaganda purposes, it did seek to provide a posteriori legitimacy to Soviet power by presenting those who partook in a common destiny and those who were excluded from it.

---

*Jigit* (Rus. *Dzhigit* and *Egit*, Uzb. *Iigit*) by Nabi Ganiev
(Uzbekkino, 1936)

Pulat (E. Khamraev), a seasonal worker in the service of Mumin Bai (G. Iunusov), lives in extreme poverty, as does his neighbor Karim-Ata with his daughter Ra'no (M. Mukhamedova), who live in a house in ruins.

> Bolta-Goi (R. Pirmukhamedov), Pulat's brother, loses everything he owns gambling, but his debts are bought up by the mullah, in exchange for which he must fight for Islam. Bolta-Goi leaves and joins the Basmachis. Their leader, Shaiki-bek (T. Turakhojaev), and Mumin Bai run an arms smuggling operation until Pulat witnesses what they are up to. Pulat is caught spying on them and is violently struck by Mumin Bai, but he manages to run away. He is saved by the guards of the Red Army, who make him a soldier and teach him how to use a machine gun. Later, Ra'no, who Pulat is in love with, is seized by the Basmachis. She is used as bait to attract Pulat back into their ranks, because he is now very much in demand thanks to his newly acquired military knowledge. Pulat plays along and places himself in the Basmachis' service while secretly working for the supporters of the Red Army. The final scene shows Pulat fighting the Basmachis from within as he turns his machine gun on them.

*Jigit* was shot within the hostile context of the 1931 purges and the sentencing to imprisonment or death of several members of the studio and crew working on *Gharm*, even though these sentences were not fully carried out. During the film shoot, an article in the *Pravda Vostoka* about the 1934 purges denounced several "acts of resistance" by Ganiev.[22] He was accused, first, of not having translated the screenplay into Russian, because he had declared that it was impossible to present a Russian version (a point on which he was supported by the head of studios). He was also accused of having lied to the Uzbek studio collective that the screenplay had been accepted by Moscow, when in fact nearly 100,000 rubles had already been spent before the "matter was cleared up." In 1934, the party's Purge Committee (*Komissiia po chistke partii*) initially decided to remove Ganiev from *Jigit* and fire him from the studios. But when this decision was about to be put into effect, the Bureau of the Uzbek Communist Party Central Committee held a screening of the takes; subsequently it was decided to let Ganiev continue with his work.[23] The musical score was written by the ethnomusicologist Uspenskii, who had produced the score for *The Jackals of Ravat*.[24] Finally, on December 22, 1935, the film was authorized for screening for all audiences for a period of three years.[25] Its total budget was an estimated 600,000 rubles, and 90,000 were assigned for adding sound in late 1935.[26]

Despite these acts of resistance and the tension in the studios at the period, *Jigit* is a conventional production with some exotic aspects, adopting numerous stereotypes from oriental films. The Basmachi leader Shaiki-bek, for example, is shown in his underground fief with panther skins decorating the walls, in a scene reminiscent of the harem of the emir of Bukhara in *The Minaret of Death*. He also sports an imposing fur hat and smokes a narghile. The screenplay employs other colonial-style representations with scenes in which the Basmachis are caricatured as violent men who behave like animals, "sniffing" at their food while others dribble, gnaw on bones, and fight over a scrap of meat. The plot also uses narrative elements taken from New Economic Policy films made in Central Asia in the 1920s, such as *From Under the Vaults of the Mosque* and *The Leper*, which had already been criticized. The revolutionary zeal of the hero Pulat is primarily motivated by his love for Ra'no, and he uses various ploys that the critics found improbable, such as when he puts on women's clothes to escape from the Basmachi guards and join the Red Army.[27] Echoing this device, Ra'no puts on Pulat's clothes to convince people that he is still present. Such outrageous exoticism led Hamid Sulaimon (the son of Suleyman Khojaev), who had trained as a director of photography, to leave the shoot early and abandon the film industry once and for all.[28]

The form of *Jigit* is inspired by earlier Uzbek films, and the scriptwriting and production are based on *Chapaev* by Sergei and Georgi Vasil'ev (Lenfilm, 1934), adapted from the eponymous novel published in 1923 by the writer Dmitri Furmanov (1891–1926), who had fought in the civil war. The film met with phenomenal success in the Soviet Union, where more than fifty million tickets were sold in the space of five years (Kenez 1972, 172). *Chapaev* was not only appreciated by the public, it was also praised by the authorities as the archetype of a Socialist Realist film. Ganiev adapted the plot to Central Asia and needed to show how the class consciousness of the Uzbek rural petite bourgeoisie evolved under the influence of the Red Army and the communists.[29] Ganiev retained a number of similarities between the characters in his film and those in its precursor: Pulat is Chapaev; Jura-Aka—like Furmanov in *Chapaev*—is a calm, benevolent, determined, and patient commissar who acts tactfully yet tenaciously in conducting Pulat's political education.

But the similarities between the two films go no further than the superficial character traits of the main characters, and the essence of the film is not in fact carried over. In *Chapaev*, Furmanov works for the party and helps reeducate the men, who go from being partisans to becoming real soldiers in the Red Army. The organizing role is thus carried out by the party (the commissar), who forms a bond with the masses to discipline and organize them, transforming the partisans into combatants for communism (Ferro 1993, 82; Kenez 1972, 172–76). But the party is wholly absent in *Jigit*. It is not through any conscious and rational decision that Pulat is led to the Bolshevik cause and to fight alongside the Red Army, but rather a matter of chance. In fact, it is not Pulat who joins the ranks of the partisans; they find him, take him back on a stretcher, and welcome him into their detachment after he has discovered the arms smuggling between the *bai* and the Basmachi leader who had struck him violently.

The critics writing in the Uzbek press were underwhelmed by the representation of the Red Army and of the poor peasants fighting in its ranks. The film does not explain how they enrolled, how they organized themselves, or how they fought the Basmachis.[30] For the State Repertoire Committee of Soviet Russia, the film failed to transcend its exotic content (consisting of chases). The social roots of the Basmachi movement were not described in detail, and the cinematographic treatment of the subject matter was deemed "superficial" and "clumsy" (Vel'tman 1936, 76). This criticism was leveled in particular against the negative characters (the *bai* and the mullah), who were criticized for being artificial, and against the Basmachis, presented as savage, rapacious, and brutal. The character of Ra'no was foreign to the daily reality of a village community, and her stubbornness failed to convince the critics. It was, however, noted that the positive secondary characters (Bolta-Goi, Karim-Ata, and the head of the partisans) were portrayed in a far more truthful manner. The character of Bolta-Goi, an "ordinary man with a simple heart," comparable to any young villager, was evidence of the film's "realism." He joins the Basmachi out of necessity and is one of the more successful characters in the film.[31] The seasonal worker Karim-Ata was also said to be "moving" due to his behavior and "his pure and simple heart." Last, the head of the partisans was singled out for his strong character and determination.

The reviews published in the Uzbek press considered *Jigit* to be a real step forward in Uzbekkino productions, for even if the Basmachi subject matter had already been treated, Ganiev's film provided a realist portrayal of it.[32] But it is difficult to overlook the fact that these reviews simply reproduce a political vocabulary used repeatedly in the central press and in the debates about Socialist Realism in literature since 1932 (Robin 1986, 72). As Régine Robin has observed, many reviews use the term "socialist realism" as a kind of conjuration; "using it amounts to summoning up its reality in fantasy" (79). In *Jigit*—just as in *Ramazan*—the inner evolution of the hero to a state of political awareness is not carried out under the aegis of the party at all, as implicitly required by Socialist Realism. "The word 'socialist' next to the word 'realism' is similar in meaning to the commissar acting as a military leader's double during the civil war"; this statement by the poet I. Sel'vinskii in February 1933 applies well to *Chapaev*, revealing just how contradictory a term it is.[33] Sel'vinskii continues: "The problem of Soviet dramaturgy is to reorganize the world, portraying the general tendencies of life."

It is precisely this reorganization of the world that Ganiev is endeavoring to bring about in all his works. First, the superiority of the party is not clearly asserted. Although the head of the cell is clearly present in *Ramazan*, he never really influences Timur. Their paths rarely cross, and they do not influence each other. Equally, in *Jigit*, Pulat actively fights against the Basmachis; he is trained by the guards of the Red Army, but his political trajectory is a result of a purely personal path, stemming from a change that is influenced solely by his own experience and by a fortuitous encounter with the partisans. Although Ganiev's films do not offer a clear illustration of the predominance of the party, *Jigit* seeks to represent Russian benevolence and superiority, unlike his earlier works. But here it is the outrageously positive representation of the Russian soldiers and the fact that this is diametrically opposed to how Russians were portrayed in *The Upsurge* that reveal the counterdiscourse and resistance to the canons of Socialist Realism.

Moreover, this reorganization of the world should theoretically lead to an insistence on class struggle and on how the Basmachis were essentially counter-revolutionary. But in *Jigit*, they are portrayed as issuing mainly from the peasantry (Bolta-Goi), not from the bourgeoisie (*bais*) or a religious milieu (mullahs and *ishans*).[34] In fact the truth about the Basmachi movement was not politically acceptable, because it was a relatively complex phenomenon lacking political uniformity. It was made up mainly of peasants and agricultural workers who had been ruined, at least in part, due to the collapse in cotton production during the civil war (Buttino 1997, 195). Its leaders had enjoyed extensive popular support ever since the Red Guards had annihilated the first autonomous Turkestani government in Kokand. Ganiev did not incorporate recent developments in the historiography of the Basmachi movement that were emerging in 1933, when it was progressively being assimilated to religious fanaticism and Muslim obscurantism in addition to being seen as exclusively bourgeois (Fraser 1987a, 1987b; Klimovich 1937, 34–35; Khalid 2006b, 873).

Ganiev's films have an ambiguous relationship to power and shifting political and historiographical norms. While giving rise to practices of open resistance, they also deploy political or filmic stereotypes and ultimately contribute to the constitution of a common Soviet destiny. *Jigit* was the last film Ganiev made during the interwar period, and none of his works of this time won him any fame. Ten or so years were to pass between *Jigit* and *Takhir and Zukhra* (1945), which led to his being anointed the founding father of Uzbek cinema. This period was marked by his time in prison from 1937 to 1939 (Akbarov 1993, 3), as well, of course, as the Second World War.[35]

## Creating and Perishing under Stalin: Suleyman Khojaev's Subversiveness

Whereas Nabi Ganiev's films addressed contemporary themes and took their inspiration from Soviet film production, *Before Dawn*—the only film that Suleyman Khojaev ever made—drew on recent history and is affiliated to the thought of reformist Muslim intellectuals, many of whom turned to literary fiction during the imperial period to spread their ideas (Dudoignon 2002).[36] Their works of fiction were the standard-bearers for a politicized discourse arguing that colonial domination needed to be questioned and calling for social modernization. In his choice of the theme of the 1916 uprisings, marking the tenth anniversary of the

Uzbek Soviet Socialist Republic, and by opting for a historical reconstitution, Khojaev sought to create for the screen the first founding national myth to legitimize the Soviet state. The 1916 uprisings, "an earthquake which took Turkestan from the seventeenth to the twentieth century,"[37] consumed the region in the wake of an imperial decree of July 8, 1916 (June 25 in the Julian calendar), ordering the formation of colonial military contingents and calling up Turkestan's Muslim populations for work away from the front line—something they had never been compelled to do before. The uprisings were a spontaneous, large-scale movement affecting both the nomadic and sedentary populations in Central Asia, and they were violently repressed by the Imperial Army (Brower 1994; Pianciola 2009, 87–152; Happel 2010). The colonial question and theme of the 1916 uprisings as the founding drama of collective resistance and a key moment in the history of Central Asia was already a prominent feature in literature, the press, and historical and cinematographic works.[38] And unlike the October Revolution, labeled a "colonial revolution," the 1916 uprisings were viewed by both the Bolsheviks and the vernacular elites as the basis on which to build the first founding myth. But interpretations of the event differed: Was it a struggle for national liberation or a struggle for popular liberation?

## *A Trajectory Typical of the First Communist Elite in Central Asia*

*Before Dawn* more fully expresses the vision of its filmmaker than do the other feature films analyzed so far; it allows for a more complex inquiry into its author's intentions. What meaning did Khojaev seek to give his film? To answer this question, we need first to examine his biography and understand the context in which the film was made.[39] It is important to bear in mind what the film-maker intended, but we need to factor in other considerations if we are to appreciate the scope of the work and better understand the multiple dimensions affecting its reception.

### SULEYMAN KHOJAEV'S RELIGIOUS AND POLITICAL EDUCATION

Suleyman Khojaev was born in Tashkent in 1892 and, like most intellectuals of the period, received a religious education at a traditional elementary school (*maktab*) before studying at the Kukaldosh madrasa until the age of eighteen (in 1910).[40] He then began moving in theatrical circles until the October Revolution, and in 1916 and 1917, he was part of the Turan amateur theatrical troupe set up in 1913 in the old town of Tashkent by Abdulla Avloni (1878–1934).[41] The purpose of this troupe was to develop local theater, and it was involved in performing contemporary national (*milii*) plays about issues of political education, instruction, and social modernization and performing them across Turkestan.[42] The troupe had many plays in its repertoire, including *The Wedding* by Nusrulla Qudratulla,

*The Patricide* by Mahmudhoja Behbudi (1874–1919), *The Unhappy Husband* by Abdulla Qodiri, and the musical *Leyla and Majnun* staged by Sidqi Ruhulla from Azerbaijan. Suleyman Khojaev, together with Mannon Uyghur (1897–1955) and the poet and playwright Ghulom Zafari (1899–1944), was one of the most active members of the Turan troupe, appearing in many roles.[43] The writer Qodiri was a childhood friend, and it is believed Khojaev also wrote a scenario with Fitrat.[44]

The Turan troupe lost many of its members in the wake of the February and October Revolutions of 1917.[45] Most of them were Communist Party members and were appointed to important positions in the new administration (T. Tursunov 1983, 10–11). Khojaev also took on new positions, first as local police chief for the district of Beshoghoch in Tashkent and then in the public school system, where he taught for several years in the reformed school of Mahmudhoja Behbudi (Karimov 1992a, 24).[46] He stayed in Moscow in 1922, before going back to Central Asia, and then to Pamir in 1923 as head writer for the Revolutionary Committee.[47] He also participated in various political organizations, such as the Turk Federalist Party and the National Independence Party (*Millii Isteqlol*).[48] Khojaev's membership in various parties at the time of the October Revolution is indicative of his quest for cultural and political autonomy within a federal state.

Khojaev finally started working for the film studios in 1926 and, like Ganiev, served as an ethnographic consultant on film shoots and as assistant director and actor.[49] In 1928 he attended a course on film directing at the Moscow State Institute for Cinematography but did not complete it, returning to Tashkent after one year.[50] Khojaev, who was also involved in the antireligious propaganda conducted by the League of Militant Atheists (*Soiuz bezbozhnikov*), would appear to have been sincerely grateful to the new Soviet authorities for this experience:[51] "I am perhaps the only one of the Uzbek nationals [*natsionaly*] . . . who, thanks to Soviet civilization, received such openness of mind and was able to become a film actor, scriptwriter, and author of artistic works in Uzbek and in Russian, as well as a playwright."[52] After shooting newsreels and a short film, *Machine and Cotton* (*Mashina i khlopok*), Khojaev went on to make *Before Dawn*, his only feature film. It was produced as part of the 1934 studio plan (accepted by the planning authority (*Gosplan*)) to make six fiction films. Some of these were to mark the tenth anniversary of Soviet Uzbekistan and others to celebrate "defense" and the "rural milieu."[53] But only two of the six planned films were ever made: Khojaev's *Before Dawn* and Klado's *The Well of Death*.[54]

## A Carefully Conceived Film of an Iniquitous, Corrupt, and Bourgeois Imperial Society

*Before Dawn* is a historical drama about the 1916 uprisings in the town of Jizzakh (near Samarkand), where the violence among the sedentary populations was at its most acute. There were cases in which the wealthier social classes bought exemptions from being conscripted (Kh. Tursunov 1962, 224–25), as was the case in other regions in Central Asia—a phase that naturally lent itself to a historical interpretation in terms of class struggle. Although this does not transpire in the film, the Jizzakh uprisings also gave rise to the proclamation of a local fiefdom (*begstvo* in Russian) whose ringleaders called for armed insurrection (*ghazavat*) and were not pardoned in the amnesty granted by the provisional government.[55]

To create his historical film, Khojaev started by conducting research, as indicated by the published screenplay, which explicitly refers to archival sources, and as confirmed by comparing the account provided in the film with prior publications about the uprisings. Little information is still available about this phase of preparatory work. The historian of Uzbek cinema, Khanjara Abul-Kasymova, writes of "lengthy, meticulous study of historical documents" about the 1916 uprisings. But there are few documents available, as is the case for other stages in the production of the film. Documents that do remain come primarily from the regulatory authorities, the authorities in charge of oversight (the Workers' and Peasants' Inspectorate), and the press.[56] Suleyman Khojaev had already pointed out in 1930 that it was difficult to find documents about him during the purges of that year, and the scarcity of documents is attributable to the fact that he was repressed in 1937.[57] However, precious information has been published in two articles written by historians in the 1990s, when the archives of the party and the political police were briefly opened.[58]

The 1916 uprisings had already provided the backdrop to Gertel''s *From Under the Vaults of the Mosque* (1927), though they did not form its principal subject matter. *Before Dawn* takes up some of the themes developed in Gertel''s film, such as the cotton industry, the exploitation of lowly people and their pauperization, the presence of a worker named Mikhail calling for subversion, and the choice of the locality of Jizzakh; the film even borrows some shots from the earlier work. But it differs in being a historical reconstitution. *Before Dawn* is a fuller expression of its filmmaker's vision than the other films discussed in this book, and—though a commission—it is a personal work that may be compared (anachronistically) to an auteur film. In addition to his involvement as a historian, Khojaev was the scriptwriter and the director. He even played an important role in the film—the character of the father.

> *Before Dawn* (Rus. *Pered rassvetom*, Uzb. *Tong oldidan*)
> by Suleyman Khojaev (Uzbekkino, 1934)
>
> Two peasants, Qadyr (Afandikhan) and his father Batyr (Suleyman Khojaev), sell their cotton to the factory owned by Nasyrbek (M. Akhmedov), a

> notorious bourgeois and head of the political organization Jadid-e Turan.[59] One day Batyr rebels when the person in charge of weighing the cotton and the commissar—the mullah Umar—try to cheat him over the value and weight of cotton delivered. Batyr is then thrown into prison. During the dispute, only one skilled worker, Vasilii Gorbunov (V. Baibakov), comes to his defense. Viewed as a dangerous element, Vasilii, too, is imprisoned on the intervention of Nasyrbek, who bribes the local police chief to this effect. Qadyr, Batyr's son, does everything he can to get his father released, selling his possessions and undertaking various administrative steps, but all to no avail. At this stage the imperial decree is issued conscripting the Muslim populations in Turkestan, triggering revolts that are violently quashed by the Imperial Army. The scale of the protests causes the decree to be modified, allowing notables to purchase exemption. Like many others, Qadyr becomes the ideal prey. The wealthier people are looking for someone poorer who is prepared to go to war in their stead in exchange for a sum of money. When he becomes the object in a transaction, Qadyr finally realizes that he is only "cattle." He rebels, takes command of a crowd of men and women, and leads them off into the mountains.

The plot in this film combines class discourse with the theme of anticolonialism.[60] The plot insists on how the indigenous (Sart) population is subjected to domination by, on the one hand, a local bourgeoisie (*bais*, Jadids) and its "agents" (mullahs, *aqsaqals*) and, on the other, Russian imperial power, which provides the historical framework for this dual domination. In the first take of the film, Russian imperial power is represented by the double-headed eagle, "the symbol of despotism and oppression" (Khojaev 1933, 7). The indigenous populations are plundered and exploited by local intermediaries, who are themselves dominated by the governor and implicitly by the tsar, who is at the pinnacle of this hierarchy of domination. The imperial administration is depicted as being easy to bribe, iniquitous, and unjust. The corruption of local administrative intermediaries (*mingboshi*s, scribes, and secretaries) and of representatives of the imperial military administration is a frequent subject of Jadid literature, and one that is abundantly represented here. Nasyrbek, for instance, manages to bribe the chief of police by slipping him a 100 ruble note bearing the image of Catherine II, who, thanks to special effects, smiles at him maliciously. Nasyrbek's weighing official tries to take advantage of Batyr's gullibility by lying about the amount of cotton.

This denunciation of Russian and indigenous colonial administration may be found in the discourse of Marxist historians denouncing the empire as well as in that of the Bolsheviks, who, since 1927–28, had been stigmatizing the former reformist elites of Central Asia.[61] The way the film represents the reformists combines these two aspects. In a scene depicting a political meeting (chaired by Nasyrbek) about how to react to the conscription decree and the revolts, Jadids refer to conscription as a way for the populations of Central Asia to become more fully part of the empire.[62] Given that they are the first to inform the Russian imperial authorities about the revolts, they thereby become "traitors." They also embody pan-Islamism and pan-Turkism in wondering how to send support to "their Turkish brothers" and raise funds for the caliphate. And they are, last, bourgeois in exploiting the people (Nasyrbek and his factory) and using them for their own purposes (the Jadid lawyer). Despite being members of the native population, they are not considered truly indigenous. The Jadid lawyer, who is a member of the Turan organization, has a peaceful garden in the colonial districts, where "no indigenous people, dogs, and soldiers [are] allowed."

Imperial society is depicted as one of inevitable pauperization and social degradation. From being a peasant with land, Qadyr becomes a seasonal worker forced to sell his labor, and then having to sell himself into selective military conscription. The living conditions of the peasantry, as exemplified by Batyr and Qadyr, grow irremediably worse. It is when Batyr is imprisoned that his son Qadyr starts his slow descent into the abyss. To provide for himself and try to get his father released, Qadyr first has to sell his horse and cart (the tools he uses to work) and then sell off his land to his neighbor Ivan Kravchenko, the kulak and settler, at a rock-bottom price. Then he spends the entire summer and winter wandering from one administration to another, paying out bribes (to the *mingboshi* Azam Khan and his servant) or bunging money to soothsayers, mullahs, and scribes. And when Qadyr starts looking for work, he inevitably meets with failure since nobody wants to employ the "son of a mutineer." Furthermore, like many of his fellow citizens, he does not have any qualifications. This point is not specifically referred to in the film with regard to Qadyr, though it is suggested in the script: "[Nasyrbek] writes the following lines in Arabic on a notepad: 'master—Russian; engineer—Russian; Chief of police—Russian; . . . !?!?!? . . .—Muslim,' without finding anything to put in the place of the exclamation and question marks" (Khojaev 1933, 11).

The remarks so far relate to only the first third of the film. The way it portrays imperial society fits official Soviet discourse of the 1920s and early 1930s, which demonized the empire while being historically fair on many points. The intellectual treatment of Turkestani society and the beginning of the 1916 revolts does not yet draw the audience into the tale. Rather, the viewer is assigned the position of external observer by the objective and indirect narrative, though the outcome for Qadyr becomes an increasingly emotive issue as he sinks into poverty beyond the point of no return. Dressed in an ever more ragged manner, with torn clothes and holes in his shoes, Qadyr meets with a final refusal from the imperial

Figure 5.3, a-b. Qadyr before the imperial decree. *Before Dawn*. Screen stills.

administration that he has unsuccessfully tried to bribe into releasing his father. At this stage, the film's narrative changes radically (fig. 5.3).

## Violence, Emotion, and Manipulation: A Film That Escapes Its Author's Intent?

The tipping point in the narrative comes with the publication of the decree, triggering revolts and their subsequent violent repression. The story shifts register, going from a work that builds up an intellectual reality toward a composition playing on affect and emotion.

### Toward Unbearable Reality: The Triggering of the Revolts

The decree is made public and is displayed to inform the population about conscription. A man reads it out loud in public, running his fingers along beneath the words: "On July 8, 1916, it was decided by the emperor and sovereign to order: for work to build the edifices required for the defense and military communication within the region occupied by the army, and, in general, for all other work necessary for the defense of the country, to call up for the duration of the current war the indigenous male populations of the empire aged between 19 and 43 and enumerated hereafter: the indigenous population of the regions of Syr Darya, Fergana, Samarkand, Semipalatinsk, Semirechie, Uralsk, Turgai, Caspian, etc."

Men and women listen as he reads out the decree. Then a mullah says: "Submit to God, to his Prophet, and to the man who rules over you." A woman reacts: "Let's not give our husbands, those who provide for us!" The list of those called up, the focal point of all the tension, is in the hands of the indigenous representative of the imperial administration (*ellikboshi*), who loses his patience: "Aren't you coming? I have your list in my hands," "I will denounce to the authorities anyone who does not submit to the order of the tsar!" A man calls out, "Hit him! Hit the *ellikboshi*," to which others echo: "Kill him!" The *ellikboshi* is killed by the crowd, and the mullah Umar hurries off to warn Nasyrbek, whom he finds busy reading the *Tarjuman* in agreeable female company.⁶³ Nasyrbek quickly writes notes to the district chief and station master to warn them: "Your Lordship! I am writing to warn you that the Muslim subjects have revolted against the Russians. Go into hiding quickly! There is danger. Your devoted servant." Men armed with staves cross the tracks. The note is also sent to the district chief, who, in a sweat, sends a message to the telegraph operator, who taps it out frantically. The insurgents come rapidly nearer and take up position in front of the district administrative headquarters. A woman in white—probably a symbol of national liberation—steps forward, showing her face. The district chief standing at the window raises his rifle, aims, and fires at the young woman, who falls to the ground. The cavalry prepare to face the insurgents, and the order is given to "open fire on the villages." Men and women run and barricade themselves inside their houses.

The repression starts. On several occasions the violence is exacerbated by various procedures. It is sometimes aestheticized by using low-angle and high-angle shots, which generate empathy among the audience. This empathy is directed toward the indigenous populations, and varying degrees of antipathy are trained against the indigenous elites and the military representatives of the imperial order. This violence is then concretely depicted using two military orders from archive documents.⁶⁴ These orders, which were not included in the copy of the film I studied, are used as captions in the published screenplay and are included in the list of title cards accompanying the film when it was sent to the Russian Repertoire Committee. The first order is dated July 20, 1916, and is about the appointment of Colonel Ivanov as head of the punitive brigade: "You are appointed head of the punitive brigade, be firm, determined, and pitiless, punitive actions are defined by the use of means against the indigenous populations, ranging as far as destroying zones peopled by the insurgent population. General Erofeev." The second order, dated July 30, 1916, was sent to the chief of staff, Colonel Mikhailov, and insists on the behavior to be adopted during punitive action: "I suggest you show the indigenous vermin [*tuzemnyi sbrod*] just how mad it is to revolt, and deprive them of all possibility of returning to their homes in the evening, leaving them without any means for survival, forcing them to die of hunger in the steppe and mountains. I require that the head of the brigade be calm and determined, and categorically order him to assert his self-confidence and make it clear that the old sole of a Russian soldier's boot is worth a thousand indigenous dogs [*tuzemnye svolochi*]. The head of the punitive expedition."⁶⁵ This title card alone symbolizes all the violence of the repression while also acting as an accusation, for it explicitly names the person responsible for the potential famine and asserts that the practice used by the Russian authorities to exterminate the rebellious population was in fact deliberate.

Figure 5.4, a-g. A mother is dying and her child survives. *Before Dawn*. Screen stills.

The audience's sensitivity is elicited once again in a scene in which a woman and the child she is breast-feeding both die in an explosion. The theme of the mother and child and of their premature death is taken up again elsewhere in the film. In a quiet house a woman is playing with her son, and on hearing explosions, she covers him with her arms to protect him. The house is entirely destroyed, and the mother dies, although the child survives (fig. 5.4).

The empathy of the audience, which until now had been elicited by the objective and indirect style, is now generated using other filmic techniques to draw them into the story, placing them in the position of victim, thus displacing them from their position as witness. By using subjective shots, the narration shifts from an indirect, objective mode to a direct, subjective one. This process encourages the viewer to identify not just with Qadyr but also with the young boy who is now an orphan. The complex position in which Suleyman Khojaev places the viewer is evident in a scene in which imperial soldiers (one of whom is the son of the settler Ivan Kravchenko) discover "an indigenous chicken that has not yet been killed" (bottom left of the second image). They take aim (subjective shot), but it is the child who falls down shot, to the disappointment of the soldiers who had been aiming at the chicken. And so the subjective shot of the imperial soldier preparing to fire assaults the spectator on three different levels: as a spectator sitting in the film theater (he is the target being fired at), but also as the "indigenous chicken" initially aimed at, and finally as the child who is shot dead by the soldiers (fig. 5.5). The final shot in this scene adds to this series of identifications. The audience has witnessed the scene through Qadyr's eyes, who sees the young orphan being killed by the imperial soldiers. So, at this stage in the film, the audience identifies once again with Qadyr. It is a strong scene, and one evoked by Ganiev in *Jigit* (fig. 5.6). All the scenes of violence, revolt, and repression close with the caption: "This is how tsarist power pacified the revolt which broke out spontaneously in Central Asia in 1916."

CREATING UNDER CONSTRAINT: DOUBLESPEAK AND
DOUBLE INTERPRETATION

Although it is not possible to provide a clear answer, the first question raised by the way violence is represented here is that of its potential impact on spectators in Central Asia. Even though the film was not widely screened, the question of reception is an essential and intrinsic part of filmmaking, since a film is created to be screened. The viewers, whether they had played a direct part in the revolts or witnessed them, all knew about this traumatic episode characterized by the violence and murderous events marking the period twenty or so years prior to the film's completion. Famines and conflicts (the First World War and civil war) had

Figure 5.5, a-f. The child is dying under Qadyr's eyes. *Before Dawn*. Screen stills.

Figure 5.6, a-b. Reference to *Before Dawn*, *Jigit*. Screen stills.

resulted in a sizable drop in population numbers and keen resentment against the recently arrived Russian population.⁶⁶ Central Soviet power was often perceived as the successor to imperial power.⁶⁷ By the 1930s, the former Russian settlers who had emigrated to Central Asia in the days of the tsar—pejoratively referred to as "Ivanovs"—were now members of committees, landowners, staff at the Central Asian State University, or officials dispatched by the center.⁶⁸ The anti-Soviet Basmachi movement, which had emerged in after the fall of the Autonomous Government of Turkestan (Kokand), together with the later process of collectivization and the attendant famines, had had dramatic consequences, resulting in the deaths of very many members of the nomadic and sedentary population or causing them to take flight. Certain zones of insurrection were a direct political legacy of the revolts that had broken out in 1916.⁶⁹ As noted in a report by the political police, national tensions ran so high that they could be sparked by the slightest incident, leading to riots.⁷⁰

The representation of violence and the exacerbation of virulent anti-Russian sentiment raise the question of whether *Before Dawn* was intended as an anti-Soviet film, which, within the context of the great Stalinist transformations of the 1930s, had recourse to doublespeak. *Before Dawn* carries on from the works of fiction about the colonial issue produced since the late 1910s (a strain that continued until just before the Second World War). This topic is particularly propitious semantic terrain for doublespeak and practices of dissimulation. Shawn Lyons (2001 and 2003) has shown that dissimulation—the possibility for authors to hide their true message without fundamentally altering their discourse—was used by the writer Fitrat. A comparison of Fitrat's "literary discourse" in two publications—one produced before the October Revolution and bloody repression of the Autonomous Government of Turkestan (Kokand, February 1918) and one produced after—enables Lyons to bring to light the process of dissimulation by showing the difference between what Fitrat says at these two periods.⁷¹

Despair, disillusionment, and fear of the Bolsheviks in *The Russians of Turkestan* (*Turkistonda Ruslar*), published in 1917, gives way in *Oriental Politics* (*Sharq Siyosati*), published in 1919, to a celebration of "Lenin's genius"—though this fooled no one. In his subsequent works, *True Love* (*Chin Sevish*) and *The Indian Revolutionaries* (*Hind Ikhtilolchilar*), both published in 1920, Fitrat denounces British imperialism in Muslim countries and the foreign policy they adopted toward oriental lands. He asserts the moral obligation to offer violent mass resistance to tyranny and oppression while considering anticolonial resistance to be the only true revolution, where self-sacrifice—"liberty or death"—is indicative of the refusal of all forms of capitulation. But this literal meaning needs to be decoded: The condemnation of British imperialism as one of the greatest perils to the Muslim world is in fact a condemnation of Russia's colonizing attitude in Central Asia.

The continuities between Russian and Soviet imperialism are, for that matter, suggested in the introduction to the second edition of *The Indian Revolutionaries*, which refers to Fitrat as an "eternal enemy of Marxism." This introduction invites readers to take the title *The Indian Revolutionaries* as meaning "the Turkestani revolutionaries." Here, therefore, doublespeak is no longer directly a matter of authorial intent but one of reception. Dissimulation and allegory, which are found in works by authors other than Fitrat, function via the association of ideas and make sense for a reader or spectator who may or may not be contemporary to the author.[72]

A 1928 political police document includes comments by Fitrat about how he intentionally used Aesopian language ("hiding behind the Soviet flag") as well as explains how the double meaning functions ("give the idea of the oppressed and oppressors, of the colony and the colonial yoke").[73] Such considerations make it possible to inquire into double meaning in terms other than those based solely on conscious authorial intent, which is impossible to determine with any degree of accuracy, especially in the Soviet case.[74] What they suggest is that what matters is to "give the idea," which, by transcending specific historical circumstances, touches on the universal theme of domination and hegemony, evoked in literature and in Khojaev's film through the prism of colonialism, a symbol of oppression, tyranny, subservience, and humiliation.[75] Hence the focal point shifts from the conditions in which "meaning is produced" in the work through an intrinsic process (authorial intent and "doublespeak") toward the conditions in which "meaning is projected" through an extrinsic process (public reception and "double interpretation").

### Revolts and Redemption: The Death of the Author

Suleyman Khojaev's film combines these two practices—doublespeak and double interpretation—in its representation of violence. The scenes of violence, which amount to about ten minutes, or one fifth of the film in all, are intensified by editing techniques Khojaev devised and selected (subjective shots, identifications) and that enjoy an ambiguous relationship with the norms of artistic creation and historiography. By exacerbating violent anti-Russian sentiment, Khojaev breaks with the tacit rules of literary production that held during the period. Allworth argues that, in general, artists of the period had to oppose the Soviet regime and Russian colonizers to satisfy the nationalists and the liberal critics, to avoid anti-Russian sentiment to satisfy the communists and save himself from destruction, and to glorify the new socialist era to encourage action along Marxist lines (1964, 62–63). But art does not follow the same norms of writing as history does. Although Khojaev does not respect these rules governing artistic creation, he does conform to the great political directives for writing the history of the Russian Empire, based on denouncing the imperial oppression of the colonized peoples and implicitly praising the Bolshevik's anticolonial and pro-national policy.

In this film in particular the audience is placed in a key interpreting role. The moving image and filmic techniques confront the audience with violence on a higher emotive plane than is found in writing (be it literature or history), where the latter is furthermore the preserve of a proportionately smaller, literate population. Visually confronting the audience members with this violence—of which they are sometimes the direct target—is an exhortation to experience a wide range of primarily negative emotions (fear, hatred, anger, aggression, pity, feelings of injustice, and humiliation) that transcend the historical reality and reach a universal and unanimously perceptible level. The universal is atemporal here by definition, and the representation of violence therefore acts as a "bridge back through time," because it touches on the very essence of despotic power of whatever nature. The denunciation of Russian imperial oppression therefore applies to other colonial situations or to the new Soviet and Russian hegemony in Central Asia. The emotion generated encourages the viewer to react, as indeed the etymology of the word indicates, coming from the Latin *emotio*, referring to movement and the action of moving. The audience members are unable to remain neutral, and they partake in a community of emotion binding them to the destiny of the characters in the film as well as to one another and, more distantly, to the destiny of those directly involved in the 1916 revolts.

The "no natives, dogs, or soldiers allowed" scene, where Qadyr briefly stops in the park after having left his father delivering cotton to the factory, is one of the colonial stereotypes of segregation, the basis of exclusion within colonial society. This segregation functions in tandem with feelings of humiliation, while another scene insists on the contempt directed against the indigenous population, whether they are at the bottom of the social ladder or intermediaries within imperial society. The scene in question is that in which the governor delivers a speech to the indigenous "pleb" to reassert his authority two weeks after the repression. The public space is divided into a lower area, where the indigenous people are sitting, and two raised areas—on one side are several gallows where the lifeless bodies of the leaders of the insurgency are still hanging, and on the other side is the tent for welcoming the governor and his guests. A reception committee comprising the upper echelons of indigenous society (the Jadid lawyer, Nasyrbek, the *bai*, and the mullah) and Russians (the kulak Ivan Kravchenko and an Orthodox priest) are awaiting the governor with gifts. He finally arrives—the indigenous public stands up—and casts his eye over the pleb (in a very low-angle shot)—the indigenous public kneels down, and some adopt a praying position with their foreheads touching the ground. The governor approaches the tent. He is greeted by the Turkestani notables, who kneel and lower their heads, while the Europeans, though greeting him with great deference, remain standing. A mullah comes forward bowing, followed by the *bai*, who, in a posture of adoration, takes the governor's hand, who rapidly pulls it away in disgust. This is followed by a long shot showing once again the indigenous pleb still in an attitude of extreme deference (below) and the governor's tent (above), with the guests in the middle; the governor starts speaking, with the Jadid lawyer translating: "His Excellency deigns to authorize you to raise your heads."

This scene depicting Turkestani society and the social positions of the various social and political classes (the governor and his "court," the intermediaries, and the people), with each clearly indicated by their spatial position, provides the audience with a far broader point of comparison. Several examples taken together indicate the intertext for this scene. The kneeling sequence of submission and humiliation stems directly from a photo symbolizing the pacification of the 1898 revolts. It is also evocative of a more recent experience described in a pamphlet signed Mustafa Chokay oglu [Chokaev] (1886–1941):[76] "On 21 January 1925, on the anniversary of Lenin's death, the Muslim population in old Tashkent, on the orders of the authorities, had to kneel down and remain in this degrading position of veritable colonial slavery for several minutes. This odious act by the Soviet authorities was long passed over in silence by the Soviet newspapers. It was only two and a half months later, on 9 April 1925, that the Tashkent newspaper *Qizil Uzbekiston* decided to publish an article by its Moscow correspondent" (Chokay 1928, 19).

Above and beyond these parallels evoking a set of possible reminiscences in the audience's mind, Khojaev's conscious discourse in fact lies elsewhere. One scene in particular provides a notable opening here, functioning in a way that is equivalent to the idea of the "*punctum*" Barthes put forward in his analysis of photography, where this corresponds to an element in the image that throws light upon the work, endowing it with its particular consistency.[77] In *Before Dawn* it is

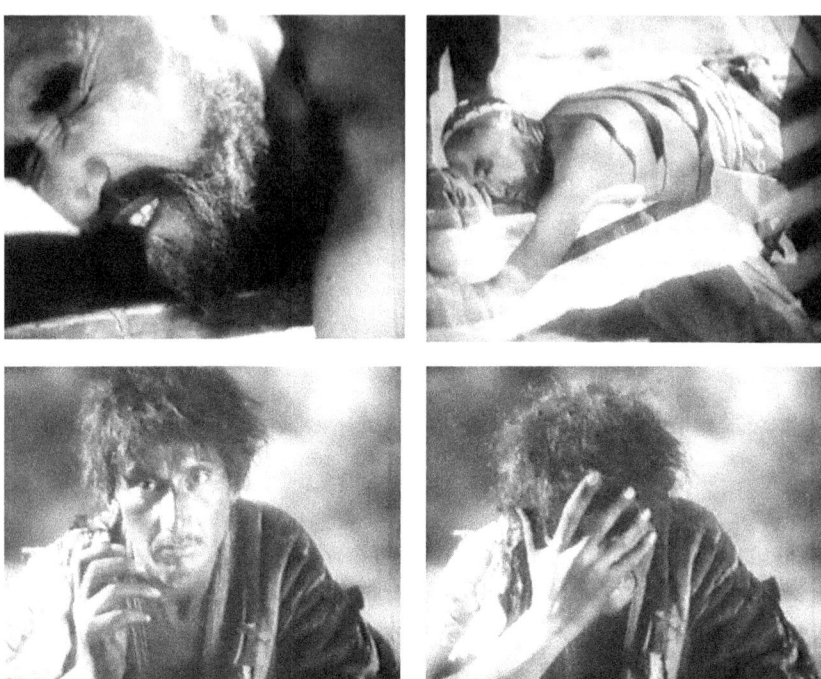

Figure 5.7, a-d. Batyr is dying. *Before Dawn*. Screen stills.

a scene, just after the title card: "Poor father! You have died beaten to death," in which Qadyr visualizes his father's death (fig. 5.7).

By "seeing" Qadyr's vision (and memory), the audience is again assimilated to this character, and more specifically to his mind. The audience, seeing Qadyr's father die, is once again included in the diegesis, and Qadyr's father thereby becomes the audience's father. The fact that Batyr is played by Suleyman Khojaev is of undeniable importance here, for it brings the historical tale into the present day. The fact that the director appears on-screen contradicts the historic time of the diegesis (1916) that the film is supposedly referring to, including it within the time when it was made (1933). The audience knows who Batyr really is thanks to a caption at the beginning of the film presenting the characters and the actors playing them: "Poor Batyr" is performed by "the artist Suleyman Khojaev." And so a symbolic line of descent is established linking the spectator to the director.

The impact of this scene is all the greater since Khojaev represents on-screen the death of the hero he is playing, thereby setting up a form of cinematographic martyrdom. What meaning can an artist attribute to the representation of his own death in his chosen medium? It is, in fact, premonitory: Khojaev was shot in

1937 after a period of imprisonment at the Malik camp near Tashkent (Akbarov 2005, 54). It was perhaps a conscious avowal of the risk he was taking, a faintly visible trace of its subversive dimension, the filmic equivalent of an artist's *pentimento*.[78]

Beyond the symbolism, the meaning of this scene relates primarily to the breakdown in proletarian solidarity between Russians and Uzbeks—an aspect of the film that came in for extensive criticism.[79] This solidarity transpires on only two occasions, with the silence on this matter being eloquent.[80] The first instance is when the skilled worker Vasili Gorbunov takes up Batyr's defense, and the second is when they are both in prison and start hatching a plan against "the *bai*s and officials working in cahoots [who] are the enemies of the destitute." This encounter leads inexorably to Batyr's death.

While this sequence insists on the deadly nature of "proletarian solidarity," the film's final scene ultimately denies all revolutionary paternity to either Russia or the Russians. This final scene completes my analysis of *Before Dawn* and enables us to apprehend Khojaev's conscious and unconscious thought mechanisms, for it reveals the full extent of the nationalist and revolutionary dimension to his film. Qadyr, the key character in the tale with whom the audience is associated on several occasions through a process of identification, symbolizes the social world and a form of atemporality. He remains outside history, not taking part in the revolts and not even attending the governor general's public speech, instead remaining in the middle of the road (of history) as a witness and, above all, as an inactive spectator. He points to a social reality made up of unemployment, spoliation, and pauperization, thereby facilitating the shift in meaning for the audience from the imperial period to the Soviet period due to the similarity of social outcomes. Qadyr is the figure of the nonhero, a run-of-the-mill, low-status seasonal worker doing a harsh job under miserable working conditions.[81]

Qadyr's social insignificance reaches its peak when the conscription decree is modified.[82] The wealthy can free themselves from their military obligations by buying a conscript to go in their stead. This is the beginning of a lengthy quest in which "everyone was looking for a tramp" and Qadyr becomes the ideal prey, to be haggled over by the manager of the public baths, who had "saved" him from poverty, and Nasyrbek, who looks on him as a member of his family. Nasyrbek wins the bidding in an auction reaching 1,000 rubles.[83] At this stage, Qadyr realizes that he is chattel and seizes an enormous stone with which he kills Nasyrbek. Qadyr only slowly becomes aware of this domination, and it is not until the last sequence in the film—the final images seen by the audience—that he realizes his position is literally that of a slave or chattel, and he revolts. Qadyr takes the knife his father had confiscated on the pretext that indigenous people are not allowed to carry bladed weapons, kills several police officers and imperial guards, tramples on the portraits of Nicolas II and the governor of Turkestan, and places himself at the head of a crowd of men and women that he leads toward the mountains (Khojaev 1933, 79). Qadyr embodies revolt against the established order without any Russian intercession, unlike his father who—like part of the first communist intellectual elite in Central Asia—had believed in proletarian solidarity, at the cost of his life. Qadyr embodies a new generation who went on to appropriate class discourse to place it at the service of national liberation.

### The 1916 Uprising and the Political Stakes: Praising "Turkestaniness"

*Before Dawn*—which finally cost 4 million rubles to make—was not released to the box office. It was, however, presented at two semipublic screenings for members of political and social organizations and studio collectives. Critics insisted on the lack of any "proletarian solidarity" and on the fact that national liberation relied solely on native forces. With the "dull" character of the qualified worker and revolutionary Gorbunov, Khojaev failed in the critics' opinion to show that "the only path for the liberation [of the laboring masses] is to struggle in close union with Russian workers under the direction of the proletariat."[84] Here once again, as in Ganiev's films, it was a matter of refusing to represent political subalternity. Khojaev's work is founded on an opposition between two "enemy camps," with the Russians being shown solely as dominating enemies. Criticism was directed primarily against the "nationalist" character of the film and the "bourgeois interpretation" of the 1916 revolts. The critics on the Repertoire Committee of Soviet Russia noted the tenor of the film's message, underlining Khojaev's "artistic incompetence," his "lack of cinematographic culture," and his inability to make the ideological transition between the movement of the 1916 revolts and the October Revolution. The committee deplored the fact that the conditions of the uprising, and the uprising itself, were represented "in a primitive," "naïve," "theatrical," "untrue," and "ridiculous" fashion, and that the "ideological desire to show the birth of class consciousness of the forgotten people during the period of the tsarist regime resulted in [illegible word] and an adventurous undertaking even."[85] As a consequence, the revolutionary movement in Central Asia was "trivialized by an author without any political or artistic talent." The film was banned by the Repertoire Committee of Soviet Russia.

These comments highlight the full extent of the political and historiographical tensions at the specific time when the film was completed. The 1916 revolts were a complex phenomenon and, especially as of 1926 (i.e., their tenth anniversary), were the subject of historical studies that initially adopted the anticolonial and nationalistic rhetoric that had been used by the Bolsheviks in the wake of the October Revolution. The 1916 revolts and their revolutionary potential made it possible to found a federating and legitimizing myth of Soviet power in Central Asia, unlike the

February and October Revolutions—described as a "colonial revolution" (Safarov [1921] 1985)—which in Turkestan were an exclusively Russian affair, in which the native populations had been denied any form of power sharing (Buttino 1991). For Marxist historians, the 1916 revolts were a failure, for they had not led to revolution.[86] They therefore needed to be seen as a revolutionary dawn, a transitory element leading the peoples of Central Asia toward awareness of class submission, pushing them to partake symbolically at least in the October Revolution.

But from the 1930s onward, with the rapid changes taking place in the historiography of the empire of the tsars, the Russian Revolution was first assimilated with this anticolonial uprising before then actually supplanting it. As of 1931, the glorious past of the Russian fatherland was progressively extolled, especially after the death of the historian Mikhail Pokrovskii (1868–1932).[87] Previously the Russian Empire had been demonized and defined as a "prison for the people" or as "absolute evil" (*absoliutnoe zlo*), as against the liberating and emancipating Soviet nationalities policy, but this now started to change. A decree dated May 16, 1934, on history teaching stipulated that it was necessary to go back to "concrete facts," patriotism, and the role of individuals, ordering that the history books be rewritten (Byrnes 1991, 307). The government authorized the exiled historians of the older generation to return to Moscow and Leningrad, providing them with the means to work; this was the case for the monarchist M. Liubavskii, who had described Russian colonization as a peaceful process (Byrnes 1991, 307). In Central Asia a decree dated May 23, 1934, issued by the Central Asian Bureau—which had disappeared before the year was out—recommended that the idea of imperial Russia as "bourgeois and colonizing" be eradicated from the historiography (Abdurakhimova and Rustamova 1994, 11). A bit later, imperial Russia became a "lesser evil" (*naimen'shee zlo*) (Tillet 1969, 45) before finally "saving" Central Asia from British domination. The pejorative term *conquest* was gradually replaced by *incorporation* or *integration*, and then by *voluntary union* (Fraser 1987a, 14). In 1955, for example, a person could read that "the historic act of accession of Central Asia was in the 'kinship interest' [*krovnii interes*] of the great popular masses in the region" and that the Russian people were "the faithful defenders of national freedom and independence" (Rajabov 1955, 13, 192).

Within this shifting context, the 1916 revolts were no longer treated in terms of their revolutionary potential. It was, on the contrary, the sending of Central Asian conscripts for military work in the rear—and implicitly the imperial policy—that was viewed as beneficial, because it had provided "political schooling for the workers of Central Asia": "The [colonial revolt] enabled the revolutionary situation to mature both in the mainlands and their colonies. And so, called upon for rear work, the inhabitants of Central Asia turned out to be effective carriers of the ideas of proletarian revolution, often initiating it in their homelands on returning on leave or after being demobilized in 1917. [They] conducted explanatory work to those they knew and to the population. Many of these rear soldiers, based in the large towns, receive a political education" (Shestakov 1936, 44).

Despite this shift, in 1934–35, this new historiography existed alongside works still denouncing Russia as a "barbarous, feudal, and semi-Asian gendarme" or railing against "the horrors of pillaging, murder, and violence against the Tatars, Bashkirs, and other national groups" (Shteinberg 1934, 51; Asfendiarov 1935, 110). The context of the Second World War and the evacuation of the great centers of learning (the Academy of Sciences) also provided fertile ground for this kind of writing, even though it remained a minority phenomenon (Manley 2009, 235).

While the Central Asian intellectuals and first Marxist historians had no doubt about the historical significance of this founding drama, especially within the context of creating a Soviet community progressively based on a common history, there were diverging interpretations about the very nature of these revolts. Some saw them as a "popular struggle for liberation" paving the way for the October Revolution; others saw them as a "struggle for national liberation," where this could be overlaid and invigorated with class discourse, as was the case in *Before Dawn*. But in this case class discourse was at the service of national liberation, to the detriment of any internationalism, which was reduced to representing the subordination of the historical destiny of Central Asia to that of revolutionary Russia.

Ultimately the film is a eulogy to Turkestan and "Turkestaniness"—subsequently inherited by "Uzbekness"—which, by assimilating the Marxist dogma of class struggle, somewhat contradicts the objective national elements in the Stalinist nationalities policy (state, territory, language, and ethnic criteria). The film indicates how persistent the idea of the nation, as previously formulated by the reformists, actually was. The anti-imperialist discourse used in *Before Dawn* for the purposes of nationalism does not support a strictly Uzbek form of nationalism stemming from territorial delineation, but rather a form of nationalism and Turkestaniness interpreted in far broader and more inclusive terms that include sedentary and nomadic populations (both shown in the film) as well as Turkic speakers and Persian speakers from Jizzakh. The film is an act of resistance to ideological assimilation by Soviet and Russian hegemony and ultimately insists on how unreal any imported national enterprise is while assimilating Russian revolutionary discourse. *Before Dawn* is an apologia for revolt (embodied by the character of Qadyr), making it a subversive act of agitprop that is characteristic of the revolutionary movement. But, as Jacques Ellul has observed: "The troops who made it possible to take power rapidly became elements of opposition, and continued to live under the hold of subversion propaganda" (1990, 91). This was the case for Suleyman Khojaev, who had been marked by the revolutionary ideal that was spawned of the 1916 revolts, but who was arrested and imprisoned in December 1934, a few months after making his film, after having been denounced for allegedly declaring he would have preferred to see Stalin assassinated instead of Kirov.[88]

# 6 The Empire of the Proletariat
## *Subjugating Nation to Class*

THE YEAR 1937 marked a break in the history of Uzbek cinema. It was both the year when talking films appeared and, more importantly, when the first national filmmakers lost their faculty of cinematic speech. Suleyman Khojaev was imprisoned, and although Nabi Ganiev continued to work in the studios, he did not direct again until after his prison sentence. Once again the studios called on management from outside Uzbekistan in a "new departure," as observed in the specialized journal *Iskusstvo Kino*: "Uzbekfilm lost all its managers for the rise of talking films, due to the activity of nationalist groups who had been in control. Production was entirely ruined. Over these years there was no longer a single qualified Uzbek director, a single actor, a single director of photography left in the studios. The new management had to start from scratch."[1]

But 1937 also flowed from the preceding periods in that it was the peak in the long process of political and symbolic violence resulting from the Soviet construction process that had been put in place during the 1920s and 1930s. This violence stemmed from the ceaseless interactions between center and periphery and the attendant adaptations, producing a vast mismatch between a paroxysm of violence (with the purges) and the "Bolshevik salvation" represented on film. *The Oath* was the first film to meet with genuine political success, consecrating both Socialist Realism and the dictum of "national by form, proletarian by content." It embodies all the violence of the Stalinist system and may be described as a totalitarian film. As of 1937, Soviet state structures, comparable to those of an empire (see chap. 4), were backed up by the imposition of ideological unity (as illustrated by *The Oath*) together with a Russian-Soviet hegemony that now acquired definitive shape and eliminated any form of dissent whatsoever.

Analysis of *The Oath* demonstrates that, despite its asserted atheism, religious elements (taken from Christianity and Islam) were deployed to lend Bolshevik political ideas legitimacy in the eyes of the Muslim population. The film insists on the idea of mission, salvation, and sacrifice and thus takes up the religious metaphor explored in previous productions and carries it through to its logical conclusion, though at the same time revealing rivalry between Islam and communist ideology over sacred status. Analysis of the production process, which was marked by numerous difficulties, also illuminates the possibilities for resistance exploited by the Uzbek managers and studio personnel. *The Oath* thus provides an opportunity to draw together the various strands of what Soviet "national" culture looked like in Uzbekistan in 1937.

## The Fable: The New Faith of Bolshevism

What references are made to the world of Islam and redeployed to legitimize communist ideals? Although frequently depicted as a world of superstition, stagnation, ruins, disease, sterility, servitude, and oppression, the world of Islam and certain religious aspects were still put to use to endorse a new conception of the world.

### Religious Elements in Silent Film and the Premises of the Bolshevik Mission

In Russia, the way the new Bolshevik power was represented and perceived was rapidly marked by the uptake of religious rhetoric in political discourse and propaganda. The Bolshevik project involved replacing religious beliefs and concepts with new secular values to fundamentally alter ways of thinking while drawing (whether deliberately or otherwise) on a mode of communication that was religious in style. Bolshevik political discourse and its iconography were influenced by Christian religious vocabulary and imagery, with Old Church Slavonic, for example, making a comeback in the terms used by the administration after the 1917 revolution (Ingerflom 1995, lx). Frontiers became holy (*sviashchennie*), and government decrees on cereal procurement were baptized "commandments" (*zapovedi*), for instance, while posters from the period took their inspiration from old Russian icons (Lewin 1982, 79; Tumarkin 1983, 69). From the outset, the October Revolution and the power of Soviets was partly conceived and articulated along religious lines, for the representatives of power were confronted with a deeply religious society, irrespective of denomination, with whom they were communicating. They also felt that they were invested with a mission; *The Ten Commandments of the Proletariat*, for example, was published in 1918 (Tumarkin 1983, 69).

When the Bolsheviks took power, some saw the event as the salvation of humanity and the liberation of the masses from obscurity; others viewed it as an apocalypse, and its main political representatives as the incarnation of the Antichrist. These two contradictory tendencies also transpired in cinema (Shlapentokh and Shlapentokh 1993, 40, 44–45). This counterrepresentation partly echoed the failure of the first antireligious campaigns in Soviet Russia in the early 1920s. The ostensible mockery young communists directed toward the great figures of holiness triggered particularly negative reactions among the population, leading the authorities to change their strategy and establish new substitute rituals, despite criticism by some who thought this constituted a betrayal of their initial ideals.[2]

Civic rituals and revolutionary counter-celebrations replaced the old popular pagan and religious feasts and were devised by the representatives of power, sometimes at the initiative of workers and citizens. The Feast of Saint Elias became Electricity Day, for example, while Industry Day replaced the Feast of the Transfiguration (Stites 1991, 297–98). Places of worship were transformed into "places of culture" (clubs, schools, museums, and cultural establishments) and especially into film theaters, which were set up in churches, synagogues (as in Perm), and mosques.[3] This was the case of the film studios in Uzbekistan, which were transferred in 1925 to the Ishankul mosque at the Shaykhantaur madrasa in Tashkent, where they remained for about forty years. The requisition of places of worship corresponded to the objectives of antireligious propaganda and furthered the project to replace religious belief with secular values, but it was also a response to the general shortage of infrastructure for transmitting the new ideology. As noted by Naum Kleiman, a historian of Soviet cinema, transferring profane art (cinema) to holy places engendered a dual process in which cinema acceded to a form of "sacredness" (ideology) because of where it was now sited, and religious space was desacralized by the profane.[4]

In Central Asia, the feeling of being invested with a revolutionary mission was perceptible in political discourse. Such was the case of Grigori Broido, Deputy Commissar of Nationalities, in his declaration of April 7, 1922, to the conference of the provisional government of the Khorezm People's Soviet Republic:[5] "We would not have fulfilled our obligations as representatives of the Russian [*rossisskaia*] Revolution and world revolution if we had simply left the workers of Khiva in peace. It is incumbent upon us to help all workers by all the means at our disposal, and in my capacity as a representative of the great Russian Revolution I do not stand here backed by a punitive expedition, but by teachers, doctors, engineers, manual workers, financial support, and so on."[6] For Broido, the revolutionary mission was a way of liberating the people from the government of the khans that had shackled them with heavy taxes, poisoned relations between the peoples, and "maintained them in obscurity." His speech insisted on the task facing the Russian revolutionaries, who needed to awaken this people who had lived in darkness and help them destroy once and for all the marks of the past, "enlightening the country and leading it along a better path."

References to Islam were sometimes used to support the legitimacy of Soviet power and facilitate its appropriation by its new Muslim "subjects." In the same speech, Broido quoted from the Koran and referred to Koranic law to emphasize that Russian revolutionary policy complied with the laws and behavioral norms governing Muslim life. The Khivan members of the provisional government pointed out that setting up a Soviet Republic of Khorezm would not meet any resistance from religious dignitaries given that the Koran prescribed government by "council" (*shura/sovet*). One of them noted that the Koran states that "the people are to be guided by a council, since it is the voice of the people," to the approval of his audience. The provisions of the People's Commissariat were thus acceptable, provided that they did not contradict Koranic law or religious teachings.[7] Broido also based his concluding remarks on the Koran, indicating that the order that "people should integrate Soviets for their affairs" and "consult" was right and fair.[8]

The use of religious rhetoric was not the sole preserve of Russian political representatives; it was also being deployed by Central Asian communists. Babajanov's study of articles published in the local Bolshevik press has highlighted several frequently used expressions associating communism and Islam, such as "God willing, under the banner of communism we . . . " and "The way of Lenin is followed by thousands of Muslims" (2007, 44–45). Such consecrated expressions and the choice of vocabulary were a way of transmitting new ideas using a rhetoric understood by much of the population. The religiosity of local communists, which was mocked in the satirical press of the period, sometimes transpired in the call to adulate the new authorities. It was not unusual for communist periodicals to use verses from the Koran and hadiths, something that was no longer possible from 1927 to 1928. These references were ideological in nature and are indicative of a calculation on the part of local Bolsheviks who were keen not to stir up anti-Soviet sentiment and wished to avoid open attacks on Islam.

But Bolshevism, as a "secular religion" and global vision of the world, inevitably came into direct conflict with the structures of action and thought legitimizing human existence and establishing a hierarchy of human purpose along different lines. The cult of Lenin started while he was still alive, during his illness (Tumarkin 1983, 119, 121), and the press promoted him to the status of "prophet of the East" and "real prophet." Mohammed's prophetic role was diminished accordingly, being henceforth (1924) relegated to the rank of "social prophet."[9] Human salvation on earth and the building of an earthly paradise were the end goals of Lenin's mission, the "prophet of true life." But this coexistence gradually disappeared, and Bolshevism and the representatives of the communist order entered into direct conflict with Islam on-screen. The opposition between religious order and secular order is particularly marked in the "exorcism" scene in *Chachvon*, which is brought to a close when the militia intervenes. Equally, in *The Ishan's Fiancée*, the men who are witnesses to Hakima's account of being raped decide to place the "holy" man on trial rather than take justice into their own hands. And the only way for Hakima's daughter to avoid marrying the "lascivious *ishan*" is for her to flee the world of religion to join the Komsomol in the factory, the new place of salvation. This is also the meaning when Taji swaps her traditional life and veil against the factory in *Her Right*.

Figure 6.1, a-d. The komsomol and the *ishan*. *The Ishan's Fiancée*. Screen stills.

Although the films stage a marked, frontal opposition between the representatives of order and the representatives of religion, the communists redeployed the symbolic capital of religion to demonstrate the existence of a legitimizing kinship, thereby seeking to sacralize the new state and its representatives. Thus, in *The Ishan's Fiancée*, Oiniso's religious kinship (she is the direct descendant of a religious dignitary, the *ishan* who raped her mother) sacralizes her initiation as a Bolshevik. This kinship and the parallel between the religious and the secular are signified in the film by parallel editing, opposing the emphatic, gesticulating speech of a young Komsomol woman urging people to build the kolkhoz to that of the *ishan*, where the two characters produce exactly the same gestures (fig. 6.1).

So although there was opposition, there was not yet complete rupture between the worlds of religion and communism, and the films insist on the transitional and symbolic aspects enabling the religious field to be reappropriated by the communist ideal. In *Ramazan*, the transition between these two worlds is symbolized by the cauldron at the mosque, which is used to feed the kolkhoz workers toiling in the fields. This was also the case with some political slogans—for example, the red head scarf of the Komsomol was to replace the veil (*chachvon*).[10] Above and beyond the idea of kinship, the films produced in Uzbekistan insist on the innate vocation of the communists and their virtues, for the characters do not become communist, they are communist by nature.

Religious practice was sometimes assimilated to sexual violence (with scenes portraying the rape of Halima crosscut with those showing the *dhikr*), a notion directly opposed to the world of the communists, who are devoid of any sexual desire or else have it fully under control. This is the case for the couple formed by Suleyman and Gulbibi in *The Jackals of Ravat*, and for that of Qumri and Umar in *The Second Wife*. The world viewed as backward (that of the *bai*s and religious dignitaries) is, on the contrary, portrayed as a world of temptation. It is also a world of vice, with homosexual relationships with young boys (*bacha*) who are prostitutes (Sadyq Bai and the young dancer Alloiar in *The Second Wife*). The communist activists become archetypes of ascetic commitment, assuming an arduous guiding function as a result of a long, slow initiation fraught with dangers.

### The Oath: *Destruction and Bolshevik Salvation*

The sacralization of Bolshevik ideology was used solely by filmmakers from outside the Uzbek Soviet Socialist Republic, mainly of Russian origin. Many films made before 1940 present Soviet power as a secular form of the divine and directly opposed to Islam. *The Oath* is a good illustration of this practice. Work on it had been under way since 1934, with a sizable provisional budget of 1.1 million rubles. The director, Aleksandr Usol'tsev-Garf (1901–70), wanted to create "a work of art such that it could help spectators assimilate Bolshevism."[11] He drew his inspiration from an initial scenario, called either *The Story of a Young Man* or *The Descendant of the Water Carrier*, by the journalist and short-story writer El' Registan.[12] Usol'tsev-Garf was not satisfied with this first draft, feeling it was too exotic and marked by stereotypes about the Orient, but he still used it as the basis for a new script. He wanted a resolutely "non-exotic" film and insisted on the fact that there was no love theme—which he considered to be essentially "oriental"— preferring instead to emphasize the "spirit of the people" (*narodnost'*) and social elements.[13] He wanted to portray the struggle between a medieval, feudal East and an East choosing to follow the path of modernity.

Two scriptwriters (Kudriavtsev and Ivanov) were entrusted with rewriting the script, and they drew on all the draft scripts in Uzbekfilm's possession, "keeping only the best" and emphasizing what the director viewed as essential, given that the film was to show the awakening of class consciousness.[14] The main modification requested was the intrusion of a Russian Bolshevik in the plot: Andrei Kravtsov is a central figure who does not appear in any earlier version.[15] Kravtsov, a modern-day apostle, has a dual mission to teach the people how Soviet power functions and to embed agrarian reform. The musical accompaniment was to be inspired by popular tunes in collaboration with the composer and ethnomusicologist Uspenskii, who had already written the music for *The Jackals of Ravat* (1927) and *Jigit* (1936).[16] But the soundtrack was finally written by the composer Kniazevskii. Filming was to start on April 1, 1936, and the two versions of the film (in Russian and Uzbek) were to be completed by December 31, though this date was pushed back to February 1937.[17] The only version I have found is the Russian one, so that is the one analyzed here.

---

*The Oath* (Rus. *Kliatva*, Uzb. *Qassam*) by Aleksandr Usol'tsev-Garf (Uzbekkino, 1937)

In 1926, Andrei Kravtsov (G. Liubimov), a young Bolshevik who has long been familiar with Central Asia, arrives in an Uzbek village to implement the agrarian reform policy and teach the people about how the new Soviet institutions function. On arriving, Kravtsov comes to the defense of Saodat (Sh. Rakhimova), the wife of Azim (A. Ismatov), who has been struck by the *bai* for having definitively refused to wear a veil. In his work on the Agricultural Council, Kravtsov has several loyal supporters, including Akhun Ata (N. Ishmukhamedov), Azim's father. However, their work is hindered by the head of the council, Hakim (Kh. Latipov), who tries to harm the Soviet authorities by falsifying the lists of landowners and the property in their possession. Azim, an agricultural worker for Qurban Bai (Ya. Babajanov), is initially in favor of the old order and refuses his wife's emancipation. But he progressively becomes the loyal defender of the new power and unmasks the traitors. It is his initiatory journey that forms the heart of the film.

---

Kravtsov embodies the defender of the oppressed who comes to establish a new order. On arriving, in the first scenes of the film, he physically confronts the *bai* on the town square to prevent him from hitting Saodat, who has dared to remove her veil. Saodat is pulled away from the blows of the *bai*, while men and women look on angrily before rapidly dispersing. Kravtsov has been invested by the Soviet authorities with the mission of embedding the agrarian reforms of 1924–26, but he also appears to have been entrusted with a divine mission. On several occasions the director refers to Islam to justify the action. The first is when the muezzin's call of the faithful to prayer coincides with Kravtsov taking up his position on the Agricultural Council. He listens to the call as if to emphasize how it coincides with his mission, and then says: "You see! Even Allah orders me to stay here!" (fig. 6.2).

On other occasions the filmmaker uses religious elements to legitimize Kravtsov's mission. The call to prayer may be heard once again when the land

Figure 6.2. Kravtsov, with arms outspread toward the sky: "You see! Even Allah orders me to stay here!" *The Oath*. Screen stills. Translation of text on image: "Allah himself gives me the order to stay here!"

decree is announced in the village (the voices of the two calls coincide), and in another sequence the militiaman announcing the decree seems to be reading it out in the manner of a muezzin.

Kravtsov is presented as a Christ-like and sacrificial figure who endures many sufferings for the earthly happiness of the Uzbek people. The first title card in the film draws on Christian religious vocabulary and announces the forthcoming miracle: "1926: this year the sacrosanct dream [*zavetnaia mechta*] of the Uzbek people is coming true. The government of the Uzbek Soviet Socialist Republic has decreed that earth and water are to be taken away from the landowners and *bai*s, and placed at the disposal of the poor and of agricultural workers." The fact that he is the only Russian in the film reinforces his singular and messianic character. Yet Kravtsov is not wholly foreign to the country. Several elements in the dialogues highlight his familiarity with local culture, for he has been serving in this region for twenty years and has the same ("hot") blood as the inhabitants, he explains. One shot shows him smoking a hookah, indicating that he is familiar with local customs.

From the outset, Kravtsov recognizes that his mission is a difficult one, and he is aware that it will require sacrifice and death. Not surprisingly, Kravtsov ends up being killed. Yet doubt remains as to the identity of his murderer until the final minutes of the film. Echoing the iconography of Lenin's lifeless body, Kravtsov is shown stretched out on a bed of flowers as he is carried to the middle of the village. The head of the agrarian committee pays a final tribute to him: "Our friend and helper has left us. Tomorrow you will be planting the first seeds in this earth that you have liberated. As you do so, remember Andrei Aka, the son of a great people—a people who will always stand by our side. Andrei Aka is dead because he helped us in our struggle towards a new, joyous, and radiant life. He loved this life. Even dead he still remembers us—the living."

Just before dying, Kravtsov writes the name of the culprit on a piece of paper, thus exculpating Azim, wrongly suspected by the villagers of having killed him. The head of the committee unfolds the piece of paper, naming Qurban Bai as the one who caused the fatal wound. "I am dying. It is Qurban Bai. Azim helped me to flee. He has understood his mistake. He must be forgiven!" Justice and pardon continue after Kravtsov's death, and, having been sacrificed to his duty—like Lenin, who "died a martyr" and was often compared to Christ and Saint George (Tumarkin 1983, 84)—Kravtsov is now resuscitated thanks to the voice-over while his face is shown in close-up. This effect makes it possible to dissociate the message from the body bearing it, thus making his work eternal and impersonal (Samson 1992, 56). Azim is the first to weep over the dead man. He won Kravtsov's recognition from the outset thanks to his discernment and clear-sightedness and his paternal affiliation. Azim's father, Akhun Ata, is an honest person and man of integrity, wholly devoted to building Soviet society. Kravtsov was always convinced of this, and when he was alive, he said on several occasions: "The son of such a father cannot be a traitor." Azim embodies the idea of the person who "becomes good" and the emergence of the new man—essential elements in Socialist Realism. As Maxim Gorky observed, it is a "projection of the future into the already-here" (quoted in Robin 1986, 90) (fig. 6.3).

Although the film conveys a Manichean vision of a world based on the messages of sacrifice and resurrection and seeks to transmit a message of salvation, it also retrospectively legitimizes Soviet power by basing its rhetoric on violence and threats. In an echo of the song "Glorious Sea, Sacred Baikal" (*Slavnoe more, sviashchennyi Baikal*), symbolizing the strength of the Russian people and their revolutionary aspirations (Ianov-Ianovskaia 1969, 19), Hakim warns Akhun Ata that he risks being deported to Siberia because he has hit his son. This song is used in the scene in which the peasants, directed by the Bolshevik, are organizing a self-defense militia to guard the newly collectivized land. The militia is formed to the words, "Hey, Barguzin [strong northwesterly wind on the Baikal], stir the billowing waves." Andrei Kravtsov joins in, "It is not too far to sail for a daring fellow?"[18] The song is not only addressed to the *bai* gathering up his goods to flee collectivization but also fills the extradiagetic space, potentially threatening

Figure 6.3. Akhun Ata and Azim. *Source:* AI, stills (no reference) given by the director.

audience members who might be tempted to follow his example. The following two lines accompany shots of Kravtsov: "Long have I worn noisy chains / Long have I wandered in the Akatui Mountains." Then several shots of peasants are shown as the song continues: "The old comrade has helped me to flee / I have returned to life, feeling the newly found freedom." Andrei Kravtsov resumes, further reinforcing his invincibility, "The camps of Shilka and Nerchinsk [imperial hard labor camps] frighten me no more / The mountain guards did not catch me." A militiaman is shown sleeping: "No wild beasts touched me in the thickets," but in his sleep his rifle accidentally discharges. The following line corresponds to the shot, though the words cannot be heard: "The bullet passed me by." The music is used as a warning to the audience and completing the meaning of the images.

Last, and perhaps the most important point about the way the film represents violence and threat, Azim is the only one to be endowed with authoritative and destructive speech, unlike Kravtsov, who is thereby "cleared" of any blame. Azim legitimizes the ideology that the Bolshevik represents for a non-Russian public, embodying hatred, a key component in the "socialist humanism" of the Stalinist period as described by Michel Heller (1985, 124). Azim's final speech, closing the film, is the oath that turns him into an activist. Azim approaches Kravtsov's body and strokes his cheek:

Figure 6.4, a-c. Azim, endowed with the voice of authority, solemnly promises and pledges to avenge Andrei's death. *The Oath*. Screen stills. Translations: "...dear Andrei Aka" (*top left*); "I shall find you" (*top right*); "I shall strangle your snakes' bodies with my own hands" (*bottom*).

The *bai* has killed our friend Kravtsov. . . . Touch my hands! They do not fatigue from work, and they will know no rest in the struggle against those who have spilt your blood, dear Andrei Aka. I shall make good my error. . . . May my mother's milk turns sour if I do not manage to avenge you. And you, Hakim Aka, you will be the first to answer for his blood. I know where, in which mountain hideouts, your friends are to be found, Qurban Bai! I will find you! I will find you! And I will strangle your snakes' bodies with my own hands to take you to your tomb.

Unlike the films studied earlier in this book, *The Oath* adopts the aesthetic of Socialist Realism, in which prolepsis (which may be defined as "knowing the future that is already there," or "anachronism by anticipation") plays an essential part (Robin 1986, 100). The film masterfully manipulates time. It returns to the origins of Soviet power, thereby thwarting any clear interpretation of the past; it anticipates the future; and finally produces its own closure. It illustrates the justice of the Bolshevik enterprise and a policy of terror against those who reject it. Socialist Realism stems from ideas developed in the late 1920s and "issued both from the depths of Soviet intellectual society, and from the summit of the Communist Party" which modified its meaning (Robin 1986, 76). Socialist

Realism—the expression emerged in 1929 and was officially adopted at the 1934 Writers' Congress—is not an objective form of realism. It represents life not as something "scholastic and dead" but, to use Zhdanov's expression, "in its revolutionary development" (Jdanov 1950, 8).[19]

The film thus partakes in the broader artistic production of the period that was mobilizing Soviet intellectuals, with an eye notably to the twentieth anniversary of the October Revolution. And it was part of a vast process, launched in the early 1930s, in which history was rewritten by art (Petrone 2000, 150). The new history that was being rewritten progressively denied the contribution made by the various Soviet nationalities, focusing instead on the role played by the Russian people, alone able to embody Marxism-Leninism (Brandenberger 2002, 34). Art had a didactic purpose, and its main objective was to transmit political ideas and provide a hyperbolic representation of reality that reflected the spirit of the party (*partiinost'*) (Pichon-Bonin 2004, 59). The flight away from reality and consequently the eviction of any "realist representation" may also be seen as an implicit condemnation of the world in which the populations and their leaders lived (Arendt 1979, 352). Film (and artistic creation in general) produced its own meaning via Socialist Realism. It did not express a preexisting meaning but was rather the material form of a unique ideology and discourse. "It is exactly as if the writer needed his theoretical framework to provide a protective shell against real history," Régine Robin observed about the debates on Socialist Realism at the 1934 Writers Congress (1986, 102). The strength of totalitarian propaganda, of course, "lies in its ability to shut the masses off from the real world" (Arendt 1979, 353). Now that we have examined the film that formed a "protective shell," it is time to look at the "real history."

### The Hell behind the Film: Creating a New World by Terror

In addition to *The Oath*, two full-length films featured in the 1936 plan. One, called *Near the Old Mill*, was initially accepted before finally being turned down, after nearly 15 percent of its budget had been spent, on the basis that its script was "ideologically defective."[20] The scenario for a second film, which was never made, was for a "historical documentary" called *Gulistan*, addressing the issue of cotton in the pre-Revolutionary period with an eye to the celebration of the twentieth anniversary of the October Revolution. But like *Before Dawn*, the script failed to sufficiently integrate the historiographical changes of the mid-1930s.[21] The plan was accepted locally, and filming started prior to receiving definitive approval from the Directorate of Cinematography in Moscow, which finally decided against the documentary genre, leading all work on the film to stop.[22] *The Oath* was the only Uzbek studio production to be released in 1937.

## The Context of Production for The Oath

Despite the message of salvation and liberation borne aloft by *The Oath*, production did not run smoothly. On several occasions the director, Usol'tsev-Garf, detailed the obstacles he encountered in letters he sent to political and administrative figures and in press articles he published in *Pravda Vostoka* and *Komsomolets Uzbekistana*.

### A Script Accepted at Bayonet Point

The first frictions concerned the reworking of the script, which was particularly irksome, with the director admitting that he had got it accepted "at bayonet point."[23] It was criticized on two points: First, and mainly with regard to content, a Russian Bolshevik intruded into the plot; and, second, in financial terms, the director apparently profited from his position to obtain additional payment. Usol'tsev-Garf denounced the "nationalists" who were trying to hinder the shoot, and he accused by name the studio directors and the head of the Directorate of Uzbek Cinematography as well as filmmakers such as Ganiev. According to Usol'tsev-Garf, they wanted to remove the character of the Russian Bolshevik, Kravtsov, from the new script on the grounds that he was a "vulgar calumny" against Uzbek spectators. Usol'tsev-Garf argued on the contrary that Uzbek audience members would feel "genuine love" for Kravtsov.

Usol'tsev-Garf attacked the overwhelming majority of the representatives of national cinema, accusing them of nationalism and resistance. Only one article written in response has been found. Its author denounces the mercantile interests of the director, accusing him of making a handsome profit from his activities with the Uzbek studios and sarcastically comparing Usol'tsev-Garf to a "metamorphosing insect:"[24] "If you open volume 5 of the *Small Soviet Encyclopedia* at page 165, you will find the following explanation of the Greek word 'metamorphosis': the passing from one form of external appearance to another. In zoology, this phenomenon is widespread amongst amphibians, spiders, and worms, as well as being frequent and typical of insects in particular. The editors of the *Encyclopedia* have failed to take into account one of the varieties of the animal kingdom: the director Usol'tsev. But maybe he belongs to one of the above-mentioned categories?"

The author then proposes to draw up a "diagnosis" for the reader, mentioning the results obtained after "clinical observation" of Usol'tsev-Garf's metamorphosis. He denounces the advantageous treatment received by Usol'tsev-Garf when he first appeared in the Uzbek studios in December 1933 (when he was granted a salary, accommodation, and total creative freedom). The article states that it was at this moment that the director was infected by a "harmful bacillus"; biological metaphors were a standard trope of Soviet discourse. Usol'tsev-Garf also got his wife employed as an assistant sound engineer, even though it was not possible to make a talking film due to lack of equipment. The author of the article explains that Usol'tsev-Garf asked to be paid 10,000 rubles for rewriting the script, a figure that increased to 25,000 once work had been completed while arbitrarily getting rid of the original scriptwriter, El' Registan, for his "vulgar" work. The article concludes with the following lines: "From a zoological point of view, the metamorphosis of Usol'tsev may be classified under the category of insects in the family of worst parasites. As for the legal diagnosis, we invite the prosecutor, investigating judge, or other supervisory bodies to pronounce."[25] There was an exchange of criticisms and accusations, and this article was the last to publicly blame Usol'tsev-Garf. Despite the noxious climate, the director was pleased once filming started with the shots of landscapes showing the apricot trees in full flower and a "lively and joyful" natural world.[26]

### The Choice of Actors

The choice of actors was another area of resistance. Filming started in Isfara (a locality frequently chosen) before the director and team knew who would be playing the main roles of Azim, Saodat, and even that of the Bolshevik, Kravtsov. The director considered this choice to be up to the Uzbek studios, which had only one official actor—Pirmukhamedov (the militiaman). The studios thus approached the Hamza Theater, headed by Ziia Saidov, who, according to Usol'tsev-Garf, "kept on using as a pretext tours" for which it needed actors. The director complained directly about this to Fayzulla Khojaev, the chairman of the Council of the People's Commissars, subsequently congratulating himself when the "red terror" had started for having "unmasked" Saidov.[27] Usol'tsev-Garf asked Khojaev to intervene directly to obtain the best theater actors: Uigur, Khidoiatov, Ishanturaev, and Babajanov, who went on to number among the great actors of post-1945 Uzbek cinema. This request was backed up by a letter to Khojaev from the former head of planning at the Directorate of Uzbek Cinematography, cosigned by Usol'tsev-Garf.[28] The Central Directorate of Cinematography also sent a letter to the first secretary of the Uzbek Communist Party, Akmal Ikramov, and to the chairman of the Sovnarkom, Fayzulla Khojaev, pointing out that the production of the first talking film in Uzbekistan was of significance not only locally but across the Soviet world and the entire world even. Heavyweight actors were thus essential.[29]

Finally, only two actors from the Hamza Theater took part in the film: Babajanov (Qurban Bai) and Latipov (the traitor Hakim). The search continued for the

Figure 6.5, a-b. The actor Rakhimova in the role of Saodat in *The Oath*. *Source:* AI, stills (no reference) given by the director.

other roles among actors from the regional theaters, especially Andijan, where Ismatov (Azim) and Rakhimova (Saodat) were selected (fig. 6.5). There was also an actor from the theater in Kokand, Ishmukhamedov (Akhun Ata, Azim's father). Preparatory work was planned for these actors, for whom it was their first time on film, focusing on bearing, gaze, and bodily comportment, to homogenize their acting style and bring them up to the level of Soviet cinema.[30]

PASSIVE RESISTANCE AND TECHNICAL SABOTAGE

The next phase of filming presented difficulties, too. The film was shot mainly outside, requiring numerous scouting expeditions, which took their toll on the budget. Although the filming remained highly localized, the main problem was the lack of transport. Not a single one of the five vehicles planned had been given to the studios by March 1936.[31] In addition, sound recording suffered from the inexperience of the poorly qualified team, despite the presence of Russian trainers and specialists. The equipment (recording material and sound-editing console) was slow to arrive, bearing in mind that the length of production for full-length talking fictions was limited to ten months (as of 1936). An extension of two and a half months was granted for the national language version, which was allocated an additional 75,000 rubles on top of the total average budget decided by the Soviet Union Central Directorate of Cinematography of 800,000 to 900,000 rubles.[32] The Uzbek authorities viewed this modest sum as indicative of chauvinism and thought it needed to be doubled, as was the case for films made in Georgia and Armenia.

To organize work on the film, a storyboard (*graficheskii stsenarii*) was prepared that was accepted by the Uzbek management, then partially approved by Moscow. All the artistic and technical elements of production were consigned in detail on graph paper and illustrated with diagrams, plotted lines, and drawings. The storyboard was attached to a large panel measuring 2.60 meters long on which each millimeter corresponded to 1.0 meters of film, the total length of the film being based on 2,600 meters. And contrary to prior accounting practice, "scene budgets" were drawn up, with each scene being allocated a specific budget covering all the standard expenses (props, actors, blank film, transport, costumes, and makeup), allowing for greater precision and making it possible to instantly pinpoint any savings made or cost overruns.[33]

Last, the postproduction was also affected by difficult working conditions, with Usol'tsev-Garf once again denouncing "acts of resistance" by management and personnel and the technical weakness of the studios. Given that the Central Directorate of Cinematography only authorized sound equipment (a *kinap* editing console made in Leningrad) on the condition that there was a script for a talking film, the material was fairly slow to arrive and was only complete in February 1935.[34] Then the workshops and equipment were destroyed overnight by a fire on March 10–11, 1936.[35] The total loss was initially estimated at about 100,000 rubles, before being reassessed in June 1936. Reequipping the workshops cost 216,900 rubles, and a request of this scale obliged the Commissariat for Finance to draw up a new financial plan for the studios.[36]

A brief press insert mentioned that the inquiry concluded the fire had been accidental and caused by the catastrophic state of the electrical wiring. Despite studio management having been warned about this on several occasions, the necessary repair work had never been carried out.[37] It was hazardous to attribute the fire to an act of sabotage—the warehouses were generally highly flammable due to the presence of nitrate film—and the press did not mention this hypothesis even though the coincidence was worrying. It was surprising that the fire was not classified as sabotage, which was a very common accusation at the time. Usol'tsev-Garf accused the former head of the studios of slowing down work on the sound by "deliberate hindrances" and of delaying the reequipping of the workshops. When the new equipment did arrive, it was late, incomplete, and unchecked, leading to a lengthy interruption of work. Finally, the sound quality was unsatisfactory, as was the development of the film in the laboratories, leading to 75 percent of the imported negatives being lost.[38]

Figure 6.6. Filming on *The Oath*. Source: AI K (F) I-90 no. 21.

The filmmaker and director accused studio management of not having bothered to come to see the takes or to have informed team members about the viewing.[39] And with the stock of negative film running out, the rest of the shoot was under threat. The final hindrance by the "nationalists" was circumvented thanks to the intervention of the first secretary of the Uzbek Communist Party, Akmal Ikramov. The so-called nationalists had sought to get the film directly transferred to the archives to block work on it.[40] Recording of the Russian and the Uzbek versions of the dialogues for *The Oath* was finally completed on April 1.[41] The Russian version was recorded by actors from the Gorki Russian Drama Theater, which was founded in Tashkent in 1934.[42]

Although it is clear that some of these acts may be attributed to resistance, other obstacles Usol'tsev-Garf attributed to "nationalist acts" were often due to organizational problems, which had been chronic since the studios had first been set up; to differences in the standards and working conditions prevalent in Moscow and in Tashkent; and to the slow and difficult process of adapting to management methods implemented on a pan-Soviet scale. The remoteness, difficulty purchasing and transporting equipment, and disorganized working conditions were perceived as acts of resistance, whereas they were, in fact, structural problems inherent to living conditions in the Uzbek capital.

## Film Release in Russia and in Uzbekistan and the Beginnings of the Great Terror

*The Oath* was part of the celebration of Soviet Uzbek arts and was programmed as part of the first Uzbek Art Decade held in Moscow on May 21–30, 1937. For this event center stage was given to playwrights, composers, and musicians, with writers, literature, and cinema playing a slightly less prominent role (Allworth 1964b, 153).

### THE MOSCOW TEN DAYS OF UZBEK ART (MAY 1937)

The elation in the press at the presence of Stalin, party members, and representatives from the other Soviet republics knew no bounds. Six hundred and fifty people came from Uzbekistan to attend the festivities, including Uigur (a theater actor and director), Babajanov (the theater actor who played in *The Oath*), the playwright Saidov (from the Hamza Theater), who was arrested a few months later, and the Uzbek dancer of Armenian origin Tamara Khanum.[43] The celebrations opened with the opera *Gulsari*, staged by Yashen and Mukhamedov to music written by the composer Glière, who was involved in the process of Europeanizing the traditional music of national operas (Frolova-Walker 1998, 331–71). The performance was followed by the musical drama *Farhâd and Shirin* based on a play by Mir Ali Shir Nawa'i to music composed by Uspenskii. The entire Uzbek delegation was received on June 1, 1937, at the Kremlin, where they were welcomed by Stalin, Molotov, Kaganovich, Kalinin, Yezhov, Ikramov, and other dignitaries.[44] The high point of the Ten Days (*dekada*) was the performance of Uzbek folk dances, which "spread life and joyous chirruping everywhere."[45] The dancer Tamara Khanum added: "It is not we who sing but our souls. Life is so marvelous that we cannot do other than sing and dance," echoing Stalin's famous pronouncement of November 1935: "Life has improved, comrades. Life has become more joyous" (fig. 6.7).

The Ten Days of Uzbek Art provided an artistic overview of the Soviet nationalities policy in the field of art, and it followed on from several other Ten Day programs devoted to other Soviet republics.[46] It was partly via art, the visible face of power, that the nationality policies acquired full force, giving concrete form to Stalin's famous pronouncement of fifteen years earlier, which subsequently went on to guide policy: "Proletarian culture, which is socialist in content, assumes different forms and modes of expression among the different peoples who are drawn into the building of socialism. . . . Proletarian in content,

Figure 6.7. Uzbek Art "Dekada," cover of the June 2, 1907, issue of *Pravda Vostoka*.

national in form—such is the universal culture towards which socialism is proceeding. . . . The 'imperialist chauvinists' are still today prepared to treat Uzbek Art disdainfully as 'primitive' art."[47]

Thanks to this policy, the "miraculous and hidden talents" of the Uzbek people were revealed—especially those of women, who had been "stooped and silent" for centuries, covered by "their somber *paranji*, and not daring to lift their eyes towards the sun." Now they were coming out of the shadows, like Tamara Khanum or the actor Halima Nasyrova, "to shine brightly throughout the country by their marvelous art." They were now the "pride" of Uzbek art and entered the constellation of artists drawn from the peoples of the Soviet socialist republics. These events were described in press reviews emphasizing the support given by "the artists of the great Russian people." While necessarily admitting that modern artistic forms such as opera, drama, and ballet had appeared before the October Revolution, the chairman of the Council of People's Commissars, Fayzulla Khojaev, in one of his last public declarations, timidly let slip the titles of a few plays written by the old Jadids—now deemed to be "bourgeois nationalists"—while of course denigrating them in what was, after all, an official declaration: "In the final years before the Revolution, amateur groups tried to stage plays in Bukhara, but the Emir did not authorize this. Some prerevolutionary plays were famous, such as *The Parricide*. *Bekzhan* and other plays were written on local themes by nationalist bourgeois playwrights. But they cannot be taken seriously. They were of very mediocre quality, and unpopular because of their content. And the artistic means to perform them were not available."[48]

## Reception in Moscow

*The Oath* was presented at the Ten Day program and saluted by critics after a public screening described in the press as a great success, with the acting of Ismatov (Azim) being greeted with particular enthusiasm.[49] The Moscow newspaper *Vecherniaia Moskva* noted the cinematic mastery of the filmmaker in the scenes depicting the popular celebration at the redistribution of land and in those showing "the strong and unalterable friendship between the peasants and the Russian Bolshevik."⁵⁰ It was this representation of the friendship of peoples that made the film a major event in the development of Soviet nationalities cinema. "These scenes display the national character [*narodnost'*] of the film, making it one of the liveliest events in national Soviet cinematography."

One hundred and fifty copies were made of the film to start (subsequently reaching three hundred copies in all), and it was released on July 21, 1937, in thirteen Moscow cinemas.⁵¹ It was only some time later that it received a distribution permit for the entire Soviet territory issued by the Central Directorate of Cinematography, which requested that a silent version of the film also be made.⁵² Uzbekistan initially received ten copies (five in Russian and five in Uzbek) but went on to receive thirty in all.⁵³ The bureau for exporting Soviet films abroad sent it to France and received purchase requests from Iran, Turkey, and countries in Latin America.⁵⁴

The press articles unanimously applauded the numerous episodes in the film that were "poignant and remain engraved in your memory. Also praised was the skillful acting—particularly by Babajanov, who played the role of Qurban Bai in "simple, authentic, living, and expressive manner," and that of Ismatov (Azim), who was convincing in his role.⁵⁵ The performance of the Uzbek actors was also appreciated by the filmmaker Klado, who had worked on several occasions in Uzbekistan. He nevertheless pointed out that the character of Kravtsov, played by Liubimov, was weak and inexpressive, with a stony face, embarrassed gestures, and monotonous voice, thus diminishing the impact of the central character.⁵⁶ Liubimov's performance marred what was otherwise uniformly good acting. This was the sole negative criticism leveled against the film.

Uzbekistan thus emerged as a leading cinematic force. The formation of an Uzbek *national* cinema was now complete in the eyes of the critics. Klado, writing in the specialized review *Iskusstvo Kino*, pointed out that film production had been reduced to nil with the loss of the main professionals (filmmakers, technicians, and actors) due to "nationalist activities" and had had to start again from scratch. The film was an even greater success for the critics, given that it was highly professional and its production qualities were worthy of the great Soviet studios. For *Pravda*, *The Oath* proved that cinema was of use for artistic propaganda and educating the masses, in an atmosphere of international fraternity.⁵⁷

Reception in Uzbekistan in the Context of the 1937 Purges

How was *The Oath* received in Uzbekistan? The film came out on the screens in Tashkent on July 10, 1937, with distribution lasting through the month of August. Two cinemas in Tashkent presented the Uzbek version, while the Russian version was shown in the film theaters in the new town districts.⁵⁸ It was then shown at

Termez, where it met with "enormous success"—to such an extent that at each screening many people were unable to acquire a ticket.[59] At Urgench, the audience arrived from the surrounding kolkhozes, coming to town to see the film, and the Uzbek cinema organization received several demands from districts and kolkhozes wanting to show it. Mobile units equipped for sound were used to screen the film in the countryside.

It is hard to ascertain how the film was received locally, even in political terms. The Council of Commissars of the Uzbek People passed a decree officially recognizing the merit of those involved, and the Central Directorate for Artistic Affairs gave a bonus of 25,000 rubles to those involved in making it (the director, scriptwriters, and film crew).[60] There were, however, virtually no reviews published in the national press, other than lengthy quotations from the central press, with two articles in particular used as a basis: one written by Klado[61] and one by Snegov.[62] This "national disenfranchisement" of Uzbek critics for the "first national talking film" reached its peak with the article in *Qizil Uzbekiston*, which was a full translation of Snegov's article.[63] Equally, the *Komsomolets Uzbekistana* did not publish an article about the film but, like its Uzbek-language counterpart, reprinted the *Pravda* article.[64] The May 22, 1937, issue of *Pravda Vostoka* ran an article cowritten by Hafiz—who had reported extensively on cinema throughout the 1920s and 1930s—and a person named Pint. In this instance it was not a central press article that was reprinted, but the precredit sequence: "Soviet Uzbek cinematography dedicates its first talking film to the best sons of the great Russian people who were of unforgettable help and support in the struggle to free our remarkable and prosperous Uzbekistan from the servitude of feudalism and capitalism."

The mismatch between the representation of sovereign power (in *The Oath*) and its reality (the purges) was inordinate in scale. The Bolshevik Kravtsov sacrificed himself for the good of the Uzbek people and, by his patience and compassion, trained precious national disciples. In fact, the main architects of Soviet power in Uzbekistan and much of its intellectual elite, along with several thousand anonymous people, were arrested and then shot. The first screening of the film on July 10, 1937, symbolizes this paradoxical key moment. It took place the day before the arrest of the chairman of the Council of the People's Commissars, Fayzulla Khojaev—who had been involved in getting the film made—and one week after the July 2, 1937, decision signed by Stalin, which marks the beginning of the purges against "anti-Soviet elements" (Karimov 2005, 255). Ernest Gellner's observation about Nazi Germany applies perfectly to the Soviet case: "Its [the regime's] self-image and its true nature are inversely related, with an ironic neatness seldom equaled even by other successful ideologies" ([1983] 1997, 125). At the same time, these antagonisms combined symbolically in the yoking together of hegemony and terror, with the creation of a new world being rooted in eliminating the old world. The film is an example of a virtually instantaneous realization of the "prophecy of extinction" that Hannah Arendt sees as characteristic of totalitarian regimes (1979, 349). Like the Moscow trials and their parody of justice, cinema here is a "formidable screen-event," masking mass repressive actions (Werth 2006, 3).

It is difficult to apprehend the scale of the purges in Uzbekistan since the sources are either not available or difficult to exploit, being composed of fabricated files and "testimonials," false confessions, and falsified transcripts of interrogations conducted using violence (Khlevniuk 1998, 201). The process of repression started with the replacement of leading figures at the Ministry of the Interior and in party organizations. In Uzbekistan the people concerned were not of Uzbek origin but Russian, Armenian, and Georgian (Karimov 2005, 20–25). For the period from 1937 to 1939, forty-one thousand people were apparently arrested in Uzbekistan, of whom thirty-seven thousand were put on trial and about seven thousand executed (Karimov 2005, 8).[65] The 1937–38 purges may be seen as the culmination of the process of managing society through violence, which had been inherent to the system from the outset but had been scaled up over the course of the 1930s with dekulakization, the deportation of the peasants, and enforced sedentarization to eradicate "all socially and ethnically harmful elements from the new Soviet society" (Werth 2007, 267). Authoritarianism, terror, and repression took on particular scale. After having been weakened by the First World War, the civil war, and the great Soviet transformations (of collectivization and industrialization), which worked in tandem with the rural exodus and the resulting process of deculturation, society was "becoming primitive," to use Moshe Lewin's expression (1982, 81), providing fertile ground for the increasing role of the state and authoritarianism.

Among those repressed in Uzbekistan, many political figures, such as Fayzulla Khojaev and Akmal Ikramov (the first secretary of the Communist Party) and many intellectuals, such as the writers Chulpan, Abdulla Qodiri, and Fitrat, were arrested and shot. For those involved in Uzbek cinema, repression rarely took the form of execution—unlike in Moscow (Miller 2006, 17; 2010, 71–90). Instead, it usually involved prison sentences (Nabi Ganiev) or dismissal from work. Exceptions include Suleyman Khojaev and probably Kudoibergen Devanov. No information is available about the fate of the Russian and Uzbek actors who performed in the films, other than for the Russian actor Messerer, who played many female Uzbek characters (*The Second Wife*, *The Leper*) and who died in the purges.[66] As for the rest of the personnel, the director of the children's film *Klych*, Agzamov, lost his position at the Uzbek studios.[67] Within one year, nearly 120 of the 180 people working at the studios had been dismissed.[68] This partly explains the difficulties encountered in producing films and drawing up plans. The director Nabi Ganiev, the scriptwriter and actor Ergash Khamraev, and actors including Pirmukhamedov and Turakhojaev were accused of belonging to a nationalist group and being supporters of Fayzulla Khojaev.

## "National in Form, Proletarian in Content": An Obscure Theoretical Aspect of the National Question

Cultural Stalinism, defined as a "cultural monologism" based on a unique, unitary, vertical, hierarchical practice (Robin 1986, 20) and dominated by Russian elements in various guises, ultimately triumphed in Uzbek cinema from *The Oath* onward—a state of affairs lasting at least until the Second World War. The shoot and the film itself mark the end of the period of transaction and interplay between center and periphery, and which Uzbek nationalism embodied. The example of *The Oath* and the way it was officially received highlight the polysemy and ambiguity of the word *national* as used in Soviet discourse during the late 1930s, especially with regard to culture. The example of *The Oath* also shows that Soviet ideological hegemony could only be totally unified and homogeneous if accompanied by extreme mass violence crushing all forms of dissent.

### Internationalist National Culture Is Not an "Idiotic Contradiction"

An analysis of *The Oath* will complete the argument developed in this book and show in concrete terms how, after multiple delays and much procrastination, a temporary solution was finally provided to the awkward equation of "national in form" plus "proletarian in content." As the official review of *The Oath* points out, the film's principal merit resides in "its truly national form, incorporating revolutionary content, the spirit of the people, and artistic simplicity."[69] The film was feted as a positive event in Soviet cinema and as the consecration of the "national in form, proletarian in content" slogan that had been approved in the resolutions of the Sixteenth Congress of the All-Union Communist Party (June 27, 1930) but first pronounced by Stalin on May 18, 1925, in a speech delivered at a student meeting at the Communist University of the Toilers of the East (*Kommunisticheskii Universitet Trudiashchikhsia Vostoka*):

> I will speak later about the idea of national culture in the Soviet republics of the East. But what is national culture? How is it to be reconciled with proletarian culture? Did not Lenin say before the war already that there are two cultures—bourgeois and socialist; that the slogan of national culture is a reactionary slogan of the bourgeoisie, who try to poison the minds of the working people with the venom of nationalism? How is the building of national culture, the development of schools and courses in the native languages, and the training of cadres from the local people, to be reconciled with the building of socialism, with the building of proletarian culture? Is there not an idiotic contradiction here? Of course not! We are building proletarian culture. That

is absolutely true. But it is also true that proletarian culture, which is socialist in content, assumes different forms and modes of expression among the different peoples who are drawn into the building of socialism, depending upon differences in language, culture, and so on. *Proletarian in content, national in form*—such is the universal culture [*obshchechelovecheskaia kul'tura*] toward which socialism is proceeding. Proletarian culture does not replace national culture, it gives it content. And equally, national culture does not abolish proletarian culture, it gives it form. The slogan of national culture was a bourgeois slogan for as long as the bourgeoisie was in power and the consolidation of nations proceeded under the aegis of the bourgeois order. The slogan of national culture became a proletarian slogan when the proletariat came to power, and when the consolidation of nations began to proceed under the aegis of Soviet power. Whoever fails to understand the fundamental difference between these two situations will never understand either Leninism or the essence of the national question.[70]

First, it needs to be observed that this speech proceeds directly from what Lenin had said in 1913, emphasizing that national culture (*natsional'naia kul'tura*) was a "watchword of capital importance" for Marxists but that in promoting it, one ran the risk of "implementing the most refined and absolute form of nationalism."[71] Marxism, working within the multinational Soviet sphere and being theoretically irreconcilable with nationalism, needed to channel the progressive forces within national movements—that Lenin initially viewed as legitimate—in order to develop an internationalism that would enable nations to fuse together in "a supreme unity." The slogans of "national culture" were thus primordial. Second, this speech coincides with a perspective encouraged by Stalin in which national cultures initially underwent a period of excessive flourishing and development before then disappearing of their own accord. Ultimately, the development of "national" cultures was to be dissociated both from vernacular nationalisms, viewed as a "poison" proceeding from a reactionary bourgeois ideology, and from Russian ethnonationalism, which would necessarily lead to a call for assimilation (Russification) identified with the policies of the defunct tsarist empire. "Culture" and "nation" needed to be kept distinct, and the new Soviet *national* cultures were to successfully combine national elements (the form or particularizing signifier) with proletarian and internationalist elements (the content or universal signified) without there being any contradiction between the two.

Up to 1937, however—and particularly with the cinema produced in Uzbekistan—the coproduction of Soviet cultural hegemony was based on contradictory goals and conflicting rationales, which, among other failings, were unable to make the national form coincide with the proletarian ideology without one thereby subjugating the other. But these tensions and internal ideological struggles, which are probably inherent to all hegemonic structures, far from being an obstacle to establishing common destinies, were in fact an essential aspect in the conquest and expansion of power. Furthermore, and anecdotally, even Stalin himself fell afoul of contradiction in a letter responding to a student named Kasatkin, who had written to him about a paradoxical aspect of the national question: the excessive development of the state in tandem with national languages and cultures prior to their total disappearance. "Is it contradictory?" Stalin wrote. "Yes, it is contradictory. But contradiction is vital, and all Marxist dialectic reflects this fact."[72]

In fact, the main blind spot in the functioning of the Soviet hegemonic system was that it was based on a universal ideology but carried forward solely by the Russian people. The development of "national" cultures was to be conducted on the Russian model (*rossiiskii* as an enveloping identity) deemed to be superior and "more advanced"; at the same time, these cultures were meant to be protected from Greater Russian chauvinism (*russkii* as an ethnic identity), viewed by Stalin as the most dangerous form of nationalism.[73] Taking the example of Caucasia—here extended to include Central Asia—Stalin affirmed in 1913 that the national question "can be solved only by drawing the belated nations and nationalities into the common stream of a higher culture" (Stalin 1913). This idea was reformulated at the Twentieth Congress of the All-Union Communist Party (March 8–16, 1921): "Within the federal Soviet government there are no longer oppressed nations or dominant nations, national oppression is destroyed. Yet due to the *de facto* cultural, economic, and political inequality between more cultivated and less cultivated nations, a legacy of the old bourgeois order, the national question acquires a form necessitating measures to facilitate the economic, political, and cultural progress of the peoples and working masses of backward nations, allowing them to catch up with Russia, which is more advanced, central, and proletarian."[74] Stalin, being "'Russian' in behavior and profession if not in national origin"—as the historian Yuri Slezkine has put it (1994a, 425)—became the main promoter of "Russianness" (*rossiiskii*), single-handedly embodying the contradiction of the Soviet system and lending it credibility. The new proletarian Russian identity became the common factor of the multinational Soviet state as of 1933, invoked both for interpreting the Soviet past and for its political organization. The multiethnic character of the history of the Soviet Union was rejected to instead focus on the role played by the Russian people (Martin 2001a, 393; Slezkine 1994, 443; Brandenberger 2002, 34), with the metaphor of the family being deployed to establish hierarchical ties between the peoples.[75] But at the end of the day, it was Russian ethnonationalism that dominated on-screen.

Resolving These Contradictions; Or, the Nation as Fiction

It was only after *The Oath* that this homogeneous, unified conception of Soviet hegemony based around Russian elements triumphed in Uzbek cinema, at least until the Second World War. While being a tribute—and a self-glorifying one given the conditions under which it was made—to the "finest sons of the Great

Russian people" (*velikii russkii narod*), enabling the Uzbeks to realize "their sacrosanct dream" (of agrarian reform), the film was viewed by the critics as resolutely antinationalist. Usol'tsev-Garf, who centered the plot on the "unshakeable friendship" between the Soviet peoples, included the intrusion of the Russian Bolshevik, the "universal signified," in the screenplay in the hope of "counteracting" the tendency to assimilate "colonizing Russia" with the Soviet Russian people: "For the Uzbek people it was legitimate to feel hatred against the Russian colonizer. In the years following the Revolution, counter-revolutionary *bai*s, mullahs, *ishan*s, and nationalists did all they could to redirect this hatred against the Russian people, even though it was they who were teaching the Uzbek people how to fight against age-old forms of oppression."[76]

To reach a state of "univocal" hegemony and resolve the contradictions in the system, the transactional interplay that had built up between the center and the periphery—thereby instituting Uzbek cultural nationalism as an alternative ideology—needed first to be brought to an end. And for this to occur, the vernacular discourse of Uzbek filmmakers needed to be violently silenced (via imprisonment or death sentences). Soviet Russian hegemony was only fully asserted through violence and coercion. Adherence was thus no longer a matter of consent and assent but one of constraint—a ritual rooted in domination and expressions of loyalty, embodied by the "oath" in the film. The violence of the Stalinist purges brought the Cultural Revolution to its conclusion, but this state of affairs could only be maintained for a short period.

Proletarian universalism was embodied within Russian ethnonationalism, but this in itself does not explain how the national took on material form. The difficulty for cultural production was to draw on traditions and unearth symbolic cultural markers ("particularizing signifiers") to anchor the representation, make it recognizable, and even bring about a form of identification while opposing the edification of a culture based solely on these national components, which in Uzbekistan involved traditional and Muslim elements. Nor should these elements be presented as exotic, archaic, or primitive—a stance that was now viewed as characteristically "chauvinistic," "imperialistic," and "nationalistic." Within this mind-set, exoticism fed into nationalist expectations regarding cultural creation: "The 'nationalists' required a slowness and fluidity said to be highly characteristic of the Orient. They were supported by the imperialistic chauvinists who demanded that this 'exotic' slowness be preserved. Slowness characterizes prayer, the bazaar, the approach adopted by the khans, but peasants work at a completely impetuous pace. Usol'stev managed to get around this mendacious tradition by showing the rapid, lively rhythms of the life of an Uzbek worker."[77]

The advent of a Soviet Uzbek *national* culture was ultimately a victory over Islam and the "lifeless Islamic mediaeval aesthetic" forbidding the representation of living beings. The October Revolution was thus said to have given birth to artists issuing from the people and to have offered them the right to a figurative art form—namely, cinema.[78] By enabling women—and in particular dancers and actors—to perform onstage, the authorities freed them from their dull *paranji* and the *ichkari*. As they performed beneath the spotlights, they were the "pride of Soviet Uzbekistan."[79] From this point on, filmic representation was dispossessed of its national essence, with traditional elements being valued uniquely for their "ornamental capacity." Most of the time they were reduced to folklore, even though this, together with the many heritagization policies, continued to provide a sure and inalienable basis for cultural nationalisms in the peripheries.

## Fiction and Cinema as Sociopolitical Condensers

The filmmakers and their works, as the visible face of the nationalities policy and a cog within the machine of Soviet hegemony, provide a way of analyzing the relationship between art and politics and the mechanisms of nationalism within the context of severe political and economic constraints. Standing at the intersection between, on the one hand, a cultural legacy endowed with its own specific resilience and, on the other, a particularly aggressive process to politicize people's mind-sets, the films studied here are endowed with a system of values and intermediary cohesion that sought to trigger mass mobilization and loyalty among the nameless, uprooted populations. Without being radically opposed to the fundamentals of Bolshevik ideology, both Ganiev and Khojaev rejected any representation of subalternity or submission to Russia or the Russians. In their films, class is at the service of the nation, and is subjugated to it.

Their work has many points in common, and so one may legitimately wonder why Ganiev did not perish in the Stalinist purges too. Given that there were only two national filmmakers, did the authorities calculate that they should keep at least one of the two? The example of the Belarusian poet Yanka Kupala might shed some light on this question. Kupala was arrested for nationalism in 1930 and then rapidly released, going on in the late 1930s to be lionized throughout the Soviet Union (Martin 2001a, 444). Arts and fiction were important to the authorities given their capacity to mobilize communities and bind them together. And then, in Uzbekistan, the Soviet authorities needed to silence the national filmmakers to effect the delicate transition from a propaganda of agitation and subversion toward a propaganda of integration in order to stabilize, unify, and reinforce the social body as well as to alienate it (Ellul 1990, 89). This transition coincided with the shift to talkies, which was not without its difficulties, in a process that was taking place in Uzbekistan in 1937.

It was also at this time that Uzbekistan acquired a temple to cinema where ideology was made stone (Golomshtok 1994, 240). The Rodina cinema, like other cultural establishments, acted as a "new social condenser" (Kopp 1967, 37) within

Figure 6.8. The Rodina/Vatan cinema (1938). UzRMDA 2343/1/16, 4.

which social mutations were to take place, thus ultimately making it comparable to the "Palace of Edification" (*dar al-ibrat*) that had been mooted in 1913.[80] The Rodina cinema was a grandiose building that was emblematic of Soviet architecture, both reflecting social changes and acting as a place for transforming society. It was built for the twentieth anniversary of the October Revolution, and the Rodina or Vatan cinema ("homeland" in Russian and Uzbek, respectively) symbolized Sovietization and the motto of "national in form, proletarian in content."[81] Outside, great, broad ornamental columns evoked the wooden pillars of traditional Central Asian sedentary architecture. The building also incorporated Russian neoclassicism, which was used as the lingua franca for Stalinist architecture and held aloft as an example by Socialist Realism (Castillo 1995, 739). The film theater had seating for seven hundred people (with five hundred in the stalls and two hundred on the balcony) and a total floor area of 18,200 square meters.[82] The lobby and cloakrooms were capacious, and people would remove their coats, hats, and rubber galoshes on entering the building.[83] "Whilst awaiting the film, the spectator may descend to the lower floor to have a shower, smoke in a special room, shoot, or play billiards, or have their photo taken in a workshop." Audience members could also eat in a vast buffet room or brush up their learning in a spacious library on the second floor. The cinema opened on December 15, 1938, after lengthy building works plagued by difficulties due to the lack of building materials (wood, electrical material, cables, and equipment), recurrent transport problems, and fuel shortages[84] (fig. 6.8).

The Rodina cinema, though stylistically very different, was just as majestic as the Shir Dor madrasa on Registan Square, where thirty years earlier a magic lantern show had been staged. The Rodina was destroyed in the 1966 earthquake; in its place stands the Hamza Theater, still standing today

# Conclusion

> "You did say 'the empire,' didn't you?" she said, trying to strike up conversation. "In the town where I lived there was a hotel called the 'empire.' It was on the hill, a mountain really, with a river flowing at the bottom. There was a garden in front of the hotel, in front of the garden there was a drop, a precipice."
>
> Chulpan, *Nuit,* 2010

Sometime before the First World War, in a Turkestani brothel, a prostitute made these observations about the empire in a brief discussion with a representative of the indigenous administration (*mingboshi*), who wondered what the empire of the tsars was like. With hindsight, and after the initial devastating years of the Soviet "precipice," the Russian Empire and its colonies in Central Asia may in many ways have looked like a bucolic landscape, to which the Great War and, in its wake, the October Revolution had set fire. The Bolshevik regime, the first objective of which was to propagate the initial revolutionary movement, rapidly reduced the scale of its geographical ambitions in order to firmly establish "socialism in one country"—the objective launched in December 1924 when the ethnic and territorial delimitation of the Uzbek Soviet Socialist Republic took place. The dynamic of expansion and conquest turned inward from that point on. By the late 1930s, the initial centralist objectives of the Bolshevik leaders with regard to the economy (planning, institutional subordination), ideology and politics (political domestication and purges), and the arts (the development of the aesthetic norm of Socialist Realism) had been attained. The empire had arisen from its ashes.

## The Chaos Structuring the Interwar Period

The confusion and the reorganization of states and communities that characterize this period amounted to an imperial interstice that forms the heart of this study. The decision to focus primarily on the period from 1924 to 1937 has made it possible to understand how the Soviet state was created in Central Asia and, more specifically, in Uzbekistan; to appreciate the relationship of autonomy and dependency that grew between the center and the periphery; and to see how a Soviet Uzbek national culture emerged in a particularly dynamic process. Despite the increasing atomization of society in the totalitarian regime, characteristic of the nature of power, in the late 1930s and over the course of those dark years of violence, the Soviet system generated spaces of creativity where national imaginaries acted as "ideological mediators" during the interwar period, giving rise to a system of intermediary and, on occasion, subversive cohesion.

The construction of the Soviet Empire as a spatial, territorial, and institutional structure took place in tandem with the development of a hegemonic relationship throughout the 1920s and until the late 1930s. Using the prism of film to analyze the nationalities policy as an imperial transaction brings into focus the tensions, struggles, and interplay of consent and constraints that progressively emerged, revealing the nature of the relationship between the (local national) structure and the (Soviet) superstructure. Indeed, the vernacular dimension to the formation of the Soviet ideological system and the *métissage* (melting pot) of the Soviet imperial undertaking corresponds to the hypothesis of a "joint invention of knowledge, power, and techniques of government" (Bertrand 2008, 34). The terms of exchange between those involved in this coinvention were, of course, far from equal. Hegemony is necessarily a contradictory process, except when it is accompanied by a moment of extreme physical violence (the 1937–38 purges), compounded in the case of Uzbekistan by symbolic violence and the denial of national cinematographic expression (*The Oath*).

The new period that began in 1937–38 returned to a conception of the exercise of political authority over the governed. This was based on a vertical power hierarchy and a unilateral relationship between elites, societies, and the state, which had characterized the Russian Empire at least until the First World War. The Great Patriotic War (1941–45) and the communal effort it required crystallized a feeling of belonging to the Soviet homeland and increased patriotic sentiment. Soviet identity, no longer understood in the ideological sense of "communist" but rather as a matter of shared citizenship, was reinforced. The war provided fertile ground for the reemergence of identification with the national cultural realm and its reappropriation. The internal regime of terror was temporarily attenuated, with artistic and scientific centers (film studios) becoming less structured and then scattering; many went on to regroup in Central Asia, where they integrated the local populations. The state of war resulted in artistic production being organized in a different way, based on working across the divide between local and Russian elites and, above all, on the renewed involvement of local elites and the persisting lack of reciprocity in power relations. The Great Patriotic War sealed a communal destiny—now a Soviet one—and played a primordial role in the imaginaries of the 1960s and 1970s, acting as the common founding drama of the Soviet populations drawn from diverse denominations, ethnic groups, and nationalities.

## The Great Seal of the Nation

Shortly after the purges, which formed but a moment, those national elites who had survived returned to the discursive realm of cinema. The extreme degree of violence was not tenable in the long run, and the application of the "national in form, proletarian in content" motto became impossible. This had been briefly mentioned in relation to *The Oath* when a critic observed that dramatic conflicts and tensions were only appropriate for "national material" (*natsional'nyi material*)—the "particularizing signifier"—and in numerous cases stood in contrast to it, "not fusing into an organic whole" (*ne slivaias' s nim v organicheskom edinstve*).[1] It was precisely the character of Andrei Kravtsov, the revolutionary Bolshevik—"the Socialist and universalist signified"—who struck a discordant note in the film. In fact, the "organic fusion" would take place once the character tasked with embodying Bolshevism could also be a national hero. Even though the roots of this change are in the 1930s, the process only crystallized after the Second World War, in the 1950s, commonly referred to as "film anemia" (*malokartin'e*). Although few films were made, this period is still worthy of interest, for nearly all the films produced in Uzbekistan portrayed the great historical figures of premodern history: Avicenna, Al-Biruni, Mir Ali Shir Nawa'i, Ulugh Beg, and others. In these hagiographic films, the *communist* word was now embodied in a distant *national* herald. The organic fusion could now take place thanks to the national appropriation of a national and proletarian culture.

In Uzbekistan, the great "Uzbek" poet Mir Ali Shir Nawa'i as portrayed in the film about him is emblematic of this new national cultural expression. Ali Shir Nawa'i (1441–1501) was born into a cultivated Turkic family in Herat and is universally regarded as the greatest representative of Chaghatay literature (Subtelny 1993, 91–92; Allworth 1990, 230), assimilated from 1938 to ancient Uzbek by the Soviet school. In the mid-1920s, when Fitrat drew attention to Nawa'i's influence on Uzbek literature, the critics had bristled at such a comparison between the Timurid past and the Soviet Uzbek present. But ten or so years later, Nawa'i was definitively recognized as an "Uzbek poet" (Semenov 1940), thereby causing a few problems of historical concordance since the Uzbeks had not at that time invaded the region (Bregel 1996, 11). But as the first line of Yakubovsky's pamphlet on the ethnogenesis of the Uzbek people observes: "It is necessary to distinguish between the conditions in which one people or another are formed, and their name" (1941, 1). And it was the Nawa'i committee, set up in 1938 to organize the jubilee of the five hundredth anniversary of the poet's birth, who had commissioned Yakubovsky's founding publication.[2] By acting as a seal for Uzbek ethnogenesis and indigenousness, he participated in creating a primordialism (Suny 2001a) that graced Uzbekistan with a distant yet continuous history (Yakubovsky 1941, 18).

The committee also planned to produce a film, initially scheduled for 1941. However, the film was delayed by the outbreak of war and the resulting necessity to produce patriotic films. It was finally made in 1947 by Kamil Yarmatov. *Alisher Navo'i* won critical acclaim along with many prestigious awards. Yarmatov was awarded the Stalin prize, as were the two main actors, Razzak Khamraev and Assat Ismatov (Drieu 2005). The film traces the Uzbek nation back to ancestral times while preaching the communist word with such fluency that, in a discussion after the reading of the screenplay at the Union of Uzbek Writers, one poet observed wryly that "all he [Nawa'i] now had to do was apply to join the Communist Party."[3] Yarmatov's biopic, while steering clear of evoking reality (a potentially fatal undertaking during this period of early Stalinism), offers a series of retrospective proofs of the ancestral character of the nation and the continuous lineage from which it is said to be descended.

The intellectual and political elites who survived the 1937–38 purges took part in creating this cultural heritage and constructing these national historical narratives. As Yuri Bregel observes, national historians played a particularly active role in the process of rewriting history, going much further than their Russian counterparts—to such an extent that at a conference held in 1988 on the ethnogenesis and ethnic history of Central Asia, historians from Leningrad and Moscow complained about the tendency in certain republics to trace the history of their people back to the earliest possible origins, and without sufficient proof (1996, 7–8, 17).

In the equally revealing case of the film *Alisher Navo'i*, Yarmatov claimed to have successfully won over Zhdanov at a cinema summit. Zhdanov had initially refused to allow the film to be made on the grounds that the Soviet people did not need historical films but rather films that "tend[ed] to the wounds of war." Yarmatov addressed him in the following exchange:

> Excuse me Andrei Aleksandrovich [Zhdanov] . . . , I am from Tashkent. And I am not only the maker of a film which has been suspended by your committee, I am also the artistic director of the Uzbek studios. It is very difficult for me to have a clear idea of the line we are henceforth meant to take. May I ask you some questions?
>
> Go ahead.
>
> I believe that the Ministry for Cinematography has taken a decision and suspended all historical films. But there are "films" and then there are "films." Is it wrong to make a film about Tolstoy, Mendeleev, or Glinka?
>
> Whoever said that?
>
> But that is what is happening, Andrei Aleksandrovich. You see, I wanted to make a film about Ali Shir Nawa'i. Have you read it?
>
> Who? Who did you say?

Nawa'i is the founder of Uzbek literature, a great poet, philosopher, a political actor on a grand scale. He is the pride of the Uzbek people. In 1941 we started making a film about Nawa'i in preparation for his 500th anniversary. And then we were stopped by the war. We are now coming back to this film. And a little while ago I read that a certain Mr Bethem, a Conservative MP in the British Parliament, on speaking to the House of Commons, declared that there were still "half savage nomadic tribes" [*poludikie kochuiushchie plemena*] in Soviet Central Asia. I find that hurtful. I would really like to show in my film what this Central Asian Renaissance is all about, giving birth to such great figures as Rudaki, Ferdowsi, Omar Khayyám, Hafez, Nawa'i, Avicenna, Al-Khorezmi, and Al-Biruni. . . . The warriors from all the nations of our country, even the Uzbeks, the Tajiks, the Kazakhs, the Kirghizs, and the Turkmens, had the title of "hero" bestowed on them—and this Bethem has never even heard of these nations. These heroes are the heirs to our great ancestors, and our culture is built on a great culture created by these ancestors. And so our film would actively serve modernity!

. . .

And what does Comrade Yusupov [first secretary of the Uzbek Communist Party] think about all this?

Comrade Yusupov supports the initiative to make this film.

Fine, in that case I ask you to give the screenplay to Comrade Aleksandrov [in charge of Soviet cinematography].

In his account of this meeting, Yarmatov goes on to congratulate himself, observing that "my arguments really hit the bullseye" (1987, 161–62).

From then on it was no longer a matter of "ornamental culture" in accordance with the "national in form, proletarian in content" slogan of which *The Oath* was so characteristic but a renewed mobilization to appropriate the cultural sphere for the nation—and perhaps to slightly alter the meaning along the way. For in his film Yarmatov intended to "go back over the pages of Ali Shir Nawa'i's life and show millions of people around the world that in the center of Asia in the fifteenth century, humanist ideas (*gumanisticheskie idei*) sprang forth that were just as significant as any in Europe." He thus hoped to meditate on Ali Shir Nawa'i's "great mission of citizenship" (*vysokaia grazhdanskaia missiia*), his influence on social life, and on the destiny of his homeland and its people (Yarmatov 1987, 163–64).

# Appendix

Table 1. Film theaters in the Republic of Turkestan in 1920

| Town | No. of theaters |
|---|---|
| Tashkent (new town) | 7 |
| Tashkent (old town) | 2 |
| Arys' (station) | 1 |
| Petrovsk | 1 |
| Turkestan | 1 |
| Chiily | 1 |
| Kazalinsk | 1 |
| Aral'skoe more | 2 |
| Tishkar | 1 |
| Ursat'evskaia | 1 |
| Charjui | 2 |
| Samarkand (new town) | 4 |
| Merv | 2 |
| Polteratsk | 2 |
| Qizil-Arvat | 1 |
| Krasnovodsk | 2 |
| Katta-Kurgan | 1 |
| Bukhara (new town) | 1 |
| Kushka | 1 |
| Takhta-Bazar | 1 |
| Cheryialevo | 1 |
| Aulia-Ata | 1 |
| Pishpek (Bishkek) | 1 |
| Tekmak | 1 |
| Vernyi | 2 |
| Kokand | 2 |
| Andijan | 1 |
| Namangan | 1 |
| Khojent | 1 |
| Chimion | 1 |
| Qizil-Kiia | 1 |
| Khylkovo | 1 |

(*Continued*)

Table 1. (continued)

| Town | No. of theaters |
|---|---|
| Draremirevo | 1 |
| Sulokta | 1 |
| Osh | 1 |
| Skobelev (Ferghana) | 1 |
| Termez | 1 |
| Koki | 1 |
| Pere-Aleksandrovsk | 1 |
| Total number of permanent theaters | 56 |
| Mobile units | 10 |
| Total | 66 |

*Source:* UzRMDA 34/1/600, 60.

Table 2. Release dates of films produced by Uzbekkino, 1925–28

| Year | Film title | Release date in Moscow | Release date in Tashkent |
|---|---|---|---|
| 1925 | *The Minaret of Death* | December 8, 1925 | February 10, 1926 |
| 1925 | *The Muslim Woman* | September 29, 1925 | Unknown |
| 1927 | *The Second Wife* | April 10, 1927 | April 1, 1927 |
| 1927 | *From Under the Vaults of the Mosque* | January 10, 1928 | February 19, 1928 |
| 1928 | *The Covered Wagon* | January 31, 1928 | May 18, 1928 |
| 1928 | *The Leper* | April 10, 1928 | July 24, 1928 |

*Sources: Sovetskie khudozhestvennye fil'my: annotirovannyi katalog,* 4 vols. Moscow, 1961–68; various articles in *Pravda Vostoka.*

Table 3. Sales of films produced by Uzbekkino, 1927–28

| Film title | No. of copies sold | Sales revenue (rubles) |
|---|---|---|
| *The Second Wife* | 46 | 23,000 plus 7,000 (promotional material) |
| *The Jackals of Ravat* | Rights sold | |
| *From Under the Vaults of the Mosque* | 60 | 40,000 |
| *Chachvon* | 45 | 30,000 |
| *The Covered Wagon* | 60 | 40,000 |
| *The Leper* | 50 | 47,920 |
| Total | | 175,000 |

*Source:* UzRMDA 93/3/122, 42.

Table 4. Estimated costs and real costs of films produced by Uzbekkino, 1927–28

| Film title | Initial budget (rubles) | Real cost (rubles) | Overspend (rubles) | Overspend (%) |
|---|---|---|---|---|
| The Second Wife | 28,981 | 46,046 | 17,065 | 58.8 |
| The Jackals of Ravat | 26,936 | 51,035 | 24,099 | 89.5 |
| From Under the Vaults of the Mosque | 34,619 | 81,084 | 46,465 | 134.2 |
| Chachvon | 35,000 | 35,692 | 692 | 2 |
| The Covered Wagon | 35,724 | 44,815 | 9,091 | 25.4 |
| The Leper | 30,865 | 47,920 | 17,055 | 55.3 |
| Total | 192,125 | 306,592 | 114,467 | 59.6 |

*Source:* UzRMDA 93/3/122, 126.

Table 5. Attendance at screenings organized by the projectionist Tarynin (Uzbekbrliash)

| Region | Town/Village | No. of screenings | Attendance per screening | % of women per screening | Observations |
|---|---|---|---|---|---|
| Tashkent | Chinaz | 1 | 1,500 | 5% Uzbek | |
| | Old town Tashkent | 1 | 500 | 2% Uzbek 4% European | |
| | Piskent | 1 | 600 | 0.5% Uzbek 10% European | |
| | Trotskoe | 1 | 400 | 12% European | Exclusively European population |
| | Lunacharskoe | 1 | 700 | No women | Majority European population 20% Uzbek |
| | Zangiata | 1 | 500 | 5% Uzbek | |
| | Kauchin | 1 | 700 | 3% Uzbek 3% European | |
| Qashka-Daria | Kasan | 1 | 800 | 7% Uzbek | |
| | Behbudi (Qarshi) | 2 | 3,000 | No women | |
| | Shahrizabz | 1 | 1,500 | 8% Uzbek | |

(*Continued*)

Table 5. (continued)

| Region | Town/Village | No. of screenings | Attendance per screening | % of women per screening | Observations |
|---|---|---|---|---|---|
| Middle Zeravshan Valley | Bukhara | 2 | Unknown | | One screening solely for women: 400 persons |
| | Kagan | 1 | Unknown | | |
| | | 1 | 900 | 70% Uzbek | Screening for women |
| | Bogautdin | 1 | 1,300 | 16% Uzbek | |
| | Zerabat | 1 | 1,000 | 12% Uzbek | |

Source: UzRMDA 34/1/2559, 21–22.

Table 6. Soviet and foreign films as a proportion of Uzbekkino's programs, 1924–35

| Period | No. of programs | No. Soviet | % Soviet | No. Foreign | % Foreign |
|---|---|---|---|---|---|
| 1924/1925 | 254 | 40 | 16 | 214 | 84 |
| 1925/1926 | 397 | 129 | 32 | 268 | 68 |
| 1926/1927 | 451 | 207 | 46 | 244 | 54 |
| 1927/1928 (November 1) | 378 | 200 | 53 | 178 | 47 |
| On January 1, 1934 | 443 | 411 | 93 | 32 | 7 |
| 1935 | 668 | 636 (including 518 silent) | 95 | 32 (including 6 silent) | 5 |

Sources: UzRMDA 93/3/122, 75; UzRMDA 2343/1/7, 11; UzRMDA 2343/1/8, 84.

Table 7. Network of film theaters during the first two Five-Year Plans, 1928–37

| | First Five-Year Plan (built) | | | | Second Five-Year Plan (planned) | | | |
|---|---|---|---|---|---|---|---|---|
| Year | 1927/1928 | 1928/1929 | 1929/1930 | 1931 | 1932 | 1933 | 1934 | 1935 | 1936 | 1937 |
| No. of theaters | 80 | 106 | 160 | 255 | 577 | 1,024 | 1,679 | 2,565 | 3,757 | 5,402 |

Source: UzRMDA 88/3/1361, 12.

Table 8. Film theaters equipped for sound in Uzbekistan on January 1, 1937

| Town | In operation | Observation |
|---|---|---|
| Karakul | Yes | |
| Pap | No | |
| Piskent | Out of order | No electricity |
| Toi-Tiube | Yes | |
| Bagdat | Yes | |
| Stalinsk | Yes | |
| Khakul-Abad | Yes | |
| Koganovicha | Out of order | No electricity since February 1937 |
| Kirovskii | Yes | |
| Voroshilovskii | Yes | |
| Ikramovskii | Yes | |
| Khatyrchinskii | Yes | |
| Babkent | Yes | |
| Jar-Qurgan | Yes | |
| Boysun | Yes | |
| Denau | Out of order | No electricity since October 1937. No permanent theater |
| Mirabad | Out of order | No electricity since July 1937 |
| Kermene | Yes | |
| Akmal Abad | Yes | |
| Jizzakh | Yes | |
| Leninsk | Yes | |
| Shahrisabz | Yes | |
| Khiva | Yes | |
| Khanki | Yes | |
| Selektsionnai Stantsiia | Yes | |
| Zaamin | Yes | |
| Molotovskii | Out of order | Equipment used for work in the villages |

*Source:* UzRMDA 837/32/58, 4.

Table 9. Number of Uzbek and European projectionists on August 10, 1934

| | Samarkand | Termez | Andijan | Kokand | Novo-Urgench | Behbudi | Tashkent | Bukhara | Total |
|---|---|---|---|---|---|---|---|---|---|
| Native | 3 | 0 | 6 | 17 | 11 | 0 | 2 | 5 | 44 |
| European | 19 | 6 | 18 | 7 | 1 | 3 | 16 | 5 | 75 |
| Total | 21 | 6 | 24 | 24 | 13 | 3 | 18 | 10 | 119 |

*Source:* UzRMDA 81/1/44, 70.

# Glossary

**Aqsaqal**  Literally "white" (*aq* or *oq*) "beard" (*saqal*), thus men of authority, elders.

**Arba/araba/arava**  A two-wheeled cart common in Central Asia, Caucasia, and southern Russia. The word has been taken up in Russian as *arba*.

**ARK (Assosiatsiia Rabotnikov Kinematografii)**  Association of Cinema Workers. In 1929 it became the Association of Revolutionary Cinema Workers (*ARRK—Assosiatsiia Rabotnikov Revolutsionnoi Kinematografii*).

**Aryk**  Diversion canal.

**Bai**  Wealthy peasants and merchants and owners of land or cattle who employed laborers. They were particularly stigmatized from the late 1920s and were the hardest hit by collectivization, at a time when the Soviet authorities were seeking to eliminate them (via "dekulakization" or "debaization"). The term rapidly became synonymous with "bourgeois."

**Basmachi (or Bosmochi)**  The term *Basmachi* ("bandit" in Russian political discourse) comes from the Turkish word *bosmoq* (to crush or press). It has been taken up in Western academic literature and designates the insurgency movement structured around warlords or *qorbashi* (who were clerics, tribal leaders, and notables). The movement had no real political unity, despite an attempt to unify it by the former Ottoman minister of war, Enver Pasha, who was assassinated in 1922. Some authors trace the origins of the Basmachi movement back to armed resistance against Russian colonization. The movement was virulent during the first half of the 1920s, subsided, and then became active again in the early 1930s in response to the collectivization of agriculture. Many Basmachis took refuge in Afghanistan.

**BNSR (Bukharskaia Narodnaia Sovetskaia Respublika)**  Bukharan People's Soviet Republic, which existed from 1920 to 1924, with the old town of Bukhara as its capital. It had a surface area of 182,000 square kilometers and more than 2.2 million inhabitants. It was renamed the Bukharan Soviet Socialist Republic on September 19, 1924, at the Fifth Congress (*kurultai*) of the Soviets. It became part of the Uzbek Soviet Socialist Republic when this was created by the ethnic and territorial delimitation on October 27, 1924.

**Boz-kashi (or kokburi)**  A widespread game in Central Asia and Afghanistan in which two teams of horsemen compete using a sheepskin filled with grain or stones.

**Central Asian Bureau (or SredAzBuro)**  The Central Asian Bureau was the plenipotentiary of the Central Committee of the All-Russian Communist Party (*VKP(b)*; see separate entry) in Central Asia. It was set up on the basis of the Turkestan Bureau (*Turkbiuro*) on May 19, 1922, with the purpose of strengthening local Soviet power, and ceased operating on October 2, 1934, once central power had been solidly established. In early 1920, there were eight bureaus, one per broad geographical area.

**Chachvon** A horsehair fabric used in Central Asia to cover women's faces (for Jews and Muslims). This fabric was covered by the *paranji* (see separate entry). These garments were viewed by the Soviet authorities as symbols of enslavement and "religious obscurantism." They were particularly stigmatized by the policy to emancipate women (the *hujum*) and were burned in public at great collective events.

**Chapon/chapan** A thick padded garment normally made from cotton and worn by men.

**Choikhona** Teahouse.

**Dehkân/dehqon** Peasant. Taken up in Russian as *dekhkan*.

**FKO (Foto-kino otdel)** Photo-Cinematographic Department.

**GARF (Gosurdastvennyi Arkhiv Rossiiskoi Federatsii)** State Archives of the Russian Federation.

**GFF or Gosfilmofond (Gosudarstvennyi Fond Kinofil'mov Rossiiskoi Federatsii)** State Film Archive of the Russian Federation.

**Glaviskusstvo** Principal Directorate for Literary and Artistic Affairs.

**Glavpolitprosvet (Glavnii politiko-prosvetitel'nii komitet)** Principal Committee for Political Education.

**Glavrepertkom** Repertoire Committee (or censorship committee).

**Goskino (Tsentral'noe gosudarstvennoe kinopredpriiatie)** Central State Cinematographic Enterprise, created in late 1922, when the Soviet Union was formed; it was superseded by Sovkino in 1925.

**Gosplan (Gosudarstvennaia planovaia komissiia)** State Planning Committee, in charge of planning.

**GPU (Gosudarstvennoe politicheskoe upravlenie)** State Political Directorate, or political police. The GPU was replaced in December 1922 by the *OGPU* (*Ob''edinennoe gosudarstvennoe politicheskoe upravlenie*), the Unified State Political Directorate, which was replaced in turn in 1934 by the *NKVD* (*Narodnyi kommissariat vnutrenykh del*; see separate entry).

**GUKF (Glavnoe upravlenie kino-foto promyshlennosti)** Principal Directorate for the Photo and Film Industry.

**GUTZ (Glavnoe upravlenie teatrami i zrelishnymi predpriiatiiami)** Principal Directorate of Theaters and Spectacle Enterprises.

**Ichkari** Women's lodgings.

**Ishan or ishon** A spiritual leader (equivalent to a sheikh).

**Isirik** Plant with antiseptic and magical properties (against the evil eye).

**Kalym** "Bride price"—material compensation a future husband paid to the parents of his betrothed.

**Karnai** Long metal trumpet used in many ceremonies.

**Khalat** Tunic generally worn by women.

**Kokburi** See *boz-kashi*.

**Kulak** See *bai*.

**KUTV (Kommunisticheskii Universitet Trudiashchikhsia Vostoka)** Communist University of the Toilers of the East, founded in 1921; trained party cadres destined to work in the national Soviet republics or other countries in the East.

**Mingboshi (or mingbashi, and pristav in Russian)** Literally, "head of one thousand." The term designates the head of indigenous administration until 1917. Beneath him was the *iuzboshi* ("head of one hundred") and the *ellikboshi* ("head of fifty").

**MOPR (Mezhdunarodnaia organizatsiia pomoshchi bortsam revoliutsii)** International Organization for Aid to Revolutionary Fighters, known in the West as International Red Aid.

**MTS (Mashino-traktornaia stantsiia)** machine and tractor station; an organization that supplied and distributed agricultural machinery to the kolkhozes as well as exerting oversight.

**Narkompros (Narodnyi kommissariat prosveshcheniia)** People's Commissariat for Education.

**Narkomzem (Narodnyi kommissariat zemledelia)** People's Commissariat for Agriculture.

**NKVT (narodnii kommissariat vneshnei torgovli)** People's Commissariat for External Trade.

**ODSK (Obshchestvo druzei sovetskogo kino)** Society of Friends of Soviet Cinema.

**OGPU** See *GPU*.

**Paranji** Placed over the head and *chachvon* (see separate entry), the *paranji* (or *paranja* in the Russified term) was a large tunic worn by women that completely covered the body.

**Plov** Traditional dish made with rice, carrots, onions, mutton, and cotton oil.

**PUR (Politicheskoe upravlenie revvoensovet)** Political Directorate of the Red Army.

**Qishloq (kishlak)** Term used by sedentary populations to designate the village. It also refers to winter encampments (from the word *qish*, meaning winter).

**Qo'rboshi** See *basmachi*.

**Revvoensovet (Revoliutsionnyi voennyi sovet)** Military Revolutionary Council.

**RGALI (Rossiiskii gosudarstvennyi arkhiv literatury i iskusstva)** Russian State Archives of Art and Literature.

**RGASPI (Rossiiskii gosudarstvennyi arkhiv sotsial'no-politichesoi istorii)** Russian State Archives of Political and Social History.

**RGVIA (Rossiisskii gosudarstvennyi voenno-istoricheskii arkhiv)** Russian State Archives of Military History.

**RKP(b) (Rossiisskaia Kommunistichestkaia Partiia [Bol'shevikov])** Russian Communist Party (of Bolsheviks).

**RSFSR (Rossiiskaia sovetskaia federativnaia sotsialisticheskaia respublika)** Russian Soviet Federative Socialist Republic, referred to in the text as the Russian Soviet Federation.

**SAGU (Sredne-aziatskii gosudarstvennyi universitet)** Central Asian State University.

**Sart** In the early twentieth century, the term designated sedentary populations in Central Asia without any tribal tradition. It was rapidly replaced in the early 1920s by the term *Uzbek* (see introduction). In certain cases, it may also be translated as "indigenous."

**SAVO (Sredne-aziatskii voennyi okrug)** Central Asian Military Department of the Red Army.

**Sovnarkom (Sovet narodnykh kommissarov) or SNK** Council of People's Commissars (the equivalent of a government cabinet).

**Surnai** A sort of oboe.

**Suzane** Traditional embroidery (in Uzbekistan and Tajikistan).

**TASSR (Turkestanskaia Avtonomnaia Sovetskaia Sotsialisticheskaia Respublika)** Turkestan Autonomous Soviet Socialist Republic. This was founded as part of the RSFSR (see separate entry) on April 30, 1918, at the Fifth Congress of Turkestan Soviets, and it disappeared with the ethnic and territorial delimitation on October 27, 1924.

**Toi** Festival or ceremony (wedding, circumcision, etc.).

**Topi** Traditional cap worn by sedentary populations in Central Asia.

**TsIK (Tsentral'nyi ispolnitel'nyi komitet)** Executive Central Committee.

**TsSDF (Tsentral'naia studiia dokumental'nykh fil'mov)** Central Documentary Film Studios.

**Turkbiuro (Turkestanskii biuro Ts KRKP(b))** Turkestan Bureau of the Central Committee of the All-Russian Communist Party (Bolshevik). See *Central Asian Bureau*.

**Turkkommissiia (Turkestanskaia kommissia)** The Turkestan Commission, or Commission for Turkestan Affairs (*Kommissiia po delam Turkestana*) was established on October 8, 1919, by a decree issued by the *VTsIK* and the *SNK* of the *RSFSR* (see separate entries). It had six members (G. Bokii, F. Goloshchëkin, V. Kuibyshev, Ya. Rudzutak, M. Frunze, and Sh. Eliava). It was a state and party organization that made all the important decisions about the Turkestan Autonomous Socialist Soviet Republic before it was replaced by the Turkestan Bureau in the summer of 1920.

**Uzbekkino or Uzbekgoskino** Uzbek State film body in charge of cinematographic policy in the country. It was also called *Uzbebgoskinprom* (*Uzbekskii gosudarstvennyi trest kinopromyshlennosti*), or Uzbek State Trust for the Cinematographic Industry.

**Uzbekfilm** Uzbek film studios.

**VKP(b) (Vsesoiuznaia Kommunistichestkaia Partiia (Bol'shevikov))** All-Russian Communist Party (Bolsheviks), the forerunner of the Communist Party of the Soviet Union.

**Vkhumtemas (Vysshie gosudarstvennye khudozhestvenno-tekhnicheskie masterskie)** Higher Applied Arts Workshops (Moscow, 1920–26).

**VTsIK (Vsesoiuznyi tsentral'nyi ispolnitel'nyi komitet)** Federal Executive Central Committee.

**VUFKU (Vseukrainskoe Foto-kino-upravlenie)** Pan-Ukrainian Photo-Film Directorate.

# Notes

## Prologue

1. The Sacrifice Feast is when Muslims commemorate Abraham's act of submission to God in accepting to sacrifice his son Ishmael. Shir Dir is one of the two madrasas on Registan Square in Samarkand.
2. That is, Turki (the equivalent of Old Uzbek). As the *Russkii Turkestan* journalist mentions, it was N. Ostroumov in person who did the translation.
3. The text mentions four hundred square *sazhens*. The *sazhen* is an obsolete Russian unit of measurement equivalent to 2.133 meters
4. The Karelin workshops were created by Andrei Karelin (1837–1906). He started taking an interest in photography in the mid-nineteenth century while following classical training at the Saint Petersburg Academy of Arts. In 1869 he set up a photography and painting workshop, which in 1898 started making magic lantern slides to illustrate public talks and readings. Nikolia Ge (1831–94) was a Russian painter and portraitist who knew Tolstoy.
5. The text quoted from Ostroumov's *The Sarts* comes from the *Russkii Turkestan* newspaper and has been cut in places. The original, published in 1901 (issue no. 38), has thus been used to complete this quotation. Nikolai P. Ostroumov (1846–1930) studied under the orientalist Nikolai Il'minskii and went to Tashkent in 1877 to run all the schools in the province. He was a specialist in Turkic languages and in Islam and had ties to the imperial authorities as well as being editor of the official Turki-language newspaper *Turkiston Viloiatining Gazeti*.

## Introduction

1. Yarmatov was one of the great Tajik filmmakers, though most of his career was in fact spent in Uzbekistan, where he was a studio head. His first film, *The Émigré* (1934), produced at the Stalinabad studios (Dushanbe), was followed by more than twenty films, all made after the Second World War. *Alisher Navo'i* (1947) is one of his great films and part of the Uzbek national pantheon.
2. Alan Crosland's *The Jazz Singer* (1927) is often considered the first talking film in the United States, a role filled by Nikolai Ekk's *Road to Life* (*Putevka v zhizn'*) (Mezhrabpomfilm, 1931) in the Soviet Union.
3. This expression of Nicolas Werth insists that repressive policies converged at this precise moment (2009, 67–74).
4. There are currently three detailed catalogs covering this period in Central Asia, which were produced for the festivals hosted by the Georges Pompidou Center in Paris (Radvanyi 1988, 1992, 1993). In English, see Rouland, Abikeyeva, and Beumers (2013). For discussion of early Ukrainian cinema, see Hosejko (2001).

5. For an overview of these currents within the Soviet Union, see, for instance, Werth (1993, 2001) and Dreyfus and Lew (2001). For a general view of how the concept of totalitarianism has evolved in history, see Enzo Traverso's extensive introduction to Traverso (2001, 9–110).

6. This is a point of difference between this work and the position set out by Alain Besançon ([1977] 1996, 345–60).

7. For works in Western languages of a fairly liberal and conservative bent with parts about Central Asia, see Caroe (1953), Kolarz (1952), Carrère d'Encausse (1978), Conquest (1986), Gretton (1964), and Pipes (1954). Using the expression "Soviet empire" is also a way of implying that it was soon to collapse (Beissinger 1995). Note, however, that Alain Besançon (1980) rejects the comparison of the Soviet Union to an empire.

8. This is, for instance, the position adopted by Olivier Roy (1997) in his analysis of the interwar period, chap. 4, "La soviétisation de l'Asie centrale" (93–137), as well as by Alexandre Bennigsen (1975; 1986, 142–47). For a more accurate view, see the excellent article by Yuri Bregel (1996).

9. To cite recent publications, see the works by Stéphane A. Dudoignon, Adeeb Khalid, and Paolo Sartori for discussion of Islam and Muslim reformism and those by Marianne Kamp, Shoshana Keller, Isabelle Ohayon (2006), and Douglas Northrop (2004) on authoritarian modernization policies. For a more general discussion of the history of Central Asia, see the works by Marco Buttino and Nicolo Pianciola, and Juliette Cadiot (2007), Adrienne Edgar (2006), Arne Haugen (2003), Francine Hirsch (2005), and Terry Martin (2001a) on nation building. For a critical bibliography on Central Asia, see Dudoignon (2008, 2010).

10. Analysis of empire in English-language works tends to take two books (Doyle 1986; Motyl 2001) as the starting point for defining concepts. For Ronald G. Suny, empire is "a particular form of domination or control between two units set apart in a hierarchical, inequitable relationship, more precisely a composite state in which a metropole dominates a periphery to the disadvantage of the periphery" (2001b, 25). Mark Beissinger (1995, 155) and Terry Martin (2002, 105), rather than focusing on objective power structures, insist on the advantages of a subjective approach (based on how state policies are perceived). Last, Peter Blitstein (2006b) suggests that we think of empire in terms of a conservative and inclusive political sphere favoring differentiation between its constituent groups, in which it differs from the functioning of a nation-state, which is exclusive and imposes transformation on societies with a view to their unification.

11. Slezkine (2000) criticizes the absence of theoretical underpinnings to the three principal theses presenting the Soviet Union as a colonial power (Hirsch 2005; Northrop 2004; Michaels 2003). Marc Ferro, contrary to what the title of his article implies, argues that the idea of colonialism applies to the Russian Empire, though not to the Soviet Union (1995, 75–80).

12. The text is available in English at Stalin (1913).

13. Muslim reformism, or Jadidism, was a social and cultural movement that first emerged at the turn of the twentieth century, springing up in the Muslim regions of Russia—notably, in Crimea with Ismail Bey Gasprinskii. It called for the modernization of society, a new phonetic method for teaching the Arabic alphabet (*usul-i jadid*), the acquisition of modern knowledge, the setting up of new civic institutions, and improvements to the position of women in society. Jadid thought formed against the backdrop of Russian colonization and conquest and initially spread among the Tatar populations in Crimea and

Idel-Ural before reaching Central Asia, via the *Terjuman* and *Vaqt* newspapers and the new merchant middle class, where this Tatar influence was not the sole trigger of reformism. The first generation of Jadid intellectuals in Central Asia came predominantly from traditional milieus, and the movement subsequently acquired scale in the 1910s with the arrival of a second generation conveying its ideas. The main channels used by Jadids to disseminate their ideas were the press, theater, literature, and poetry in addition to places for socializing, such as reform schools, discussion circles (known as *gaps*), and associations. For discussions of the origin, development, and historiography of Jadidism, see Dudoignon (1996a, 1996b) and Khalid (1998).

14. The term *Chaghatay* provided a counterpoint to Turkic identity in the Ottoman Empire and was used primarily in the south and east of Central Asia. Historically, it is synonymous with *Sart* and *Tajik* and designated an urban Turkish-speaking population without tribal ties, and was largely a self-assigned identity. It disappeared in 1922, when the Chaghatay Gurungi—a nationalist cultural circle that was seeking to constitute a Turkic literary heritage in Turkestan—was banned.

The term *Turk* designated populations that were indigenous to the region, without having any pan-Turkist connotations. It was not used in Soviet discussion of nationalities. Few ethnographic studies have looked at this term, which did not refer solely to Turkish-speaking populations but also, for instance, included non-Turkic populations in Turkmenistan (the Tajiks, Iranians, Persians, and Kalmyks); Russian State Archive of Economy (hereafter RGAE) 1562/336/41, 154, quoted in Cadiot (2007, 126). According to studies carried out by ethnologists M. Andreev and I. Zarubin, people who viewed themselves as Turk during this period did so in contrast to the Uzbek group. The term was viewed as largely corresponding to the first tribes to have peopled the region before the Turkic invasions and said to have retained their tribal traditions (see works by ethnologist B. Karmysheva). Though initially reluctant to view themselves as Uzbek, Turks apparently ended up doing so in an opportunistic response to the Uzbek nationalist stirrings stemming from the territorial delimitation. Furthermore, the terms *Turk* and *Tajik* did not necessarily coincide with the language, and some groups identified as Uzbek despite speaking Persian—as in Bukhara, for instance (Khalid 2010, 1998, 188–89, Baldauf 1991, 84–85; Schoeberlein-Engel 1994, 392).

The etymology of the word *Sart* has not been clearly established. According to Vassilii Barthold, it is a Sanskrit term for "merchant," but others view it as a contraction of *sary it* ("yellow dog") used by Kazakh and Kyrgyz nomads to refer to sedentary populations. From 1893 onward, the term was criticized by Muslim reformists, who viewed it as insulting and did not see it as relating to the idea of nation (Khalid 1998, 201, 203, 205–7).

15. The military authorities of Turkestan started studying the dominated populations in military and scientific expeditions (de Meaux 2010, 46–48; Brower 2003, 45).

16. The 1920 census was incomplete, with the region of Ferghana being wholly excluded from the count due to a major insurrectional movement, for instance. The 1926 census is more reliable (Buttino 1990, 66).

17. Turkestanism may be defined as a feeling of belonging to a community united by a common historical territory (Turkestan) and a common religion (Islam), but the term *Uzbek* partially redeploys these ideas (Khalid 2004, 141–42).

18. National and ethnic self-definition in the 1920s census was approximate, with the name of the town, government of origin, or religion serving as the point of reference. Censors conducting the 1926 census were allowed to make corrections by recording the "evident

nationality." Finally, nationality was attributed as of 1938 on the basis of the origin of the father, thus no longer being a matter of self-declaration. It could be checked, resulting in arbitrary bureaucratic decisions and stigmatization based on family name and language, even though this was contrary to the 1936 constitution (Cadiot 2007, 123, 125–26, 179–80).

19. See Stalin (1913); see also Blitstein (2006a) and Slezkine (1994).

20. Analysis of the 1918, 1924, and 1936 constitutions shows that the right to self-determination was not backed up by any provisions for its implementation, thereby annulling any real impact (Lirou 2009, 144–70; also see Isoart 1981).

21. Russian State Archive of Sociopolitical History (hereafter RGASPI) 558/11/132, 36–42 (in Gatagova, Kosheleva, and Rogovaia 2005, 614). References to archives are indicated using the format: ARCHIVES record group/calendar/file.

22. Leo Trotsky, "Vodka, tserkov' i kinematograf," *Pravda*, July 12, 1923; Krylov (1928).

23. This term is based on the Russian *kinefikatsiia*.

24. A total of ninety-one films were made in Uzbekistan between 1924 and 1935 and distributed in the Soviet republics, including sixteen full-length feature films.

25. RGASPI 5/2/28, 19–21 (in Gatagova et al. 2005, 78).

26. For Ellul, it is precisely the action that makes the propaganda effective and irreversible (1990, 37). For a discussion of propaganda, see also Tchakhotine (2006).

27. Interviews conducted in Tashkent on June 5, 2004, and September 1, 2009.

28. Interview conducted in Tashkent on February 7, 2006.

29. Interview conducted in Moscow on July 12, 2006.

30. A second interview conducted in Nantes in November 2010 was far more informative because he was starting work on a documentary about his father.

## Part 1

1. In the colonial period, the province of Turkestan was a military governorate comprising five administrative regions (*oblast*): Transcaspia, Samarkand, Syr Darya, Ferghana, and Semirechie. The Emirate of Bukhara and the Khanate of Khiva were Russian protectorates, and there was also a Governorate of the Steppes corresponding to regions in present-day Kazakhstan. In the wake of the 1917 Russian Revolutions and until 1924, the region went through several political regimes; the Turkestan Socialist Federative Republic was followed by the Turkestan Autonomous Soviet Socialist Republic, both of which were part of the Russian Soviet Federative Socialist Republic.

2. The conquest of Central Asia, which was easier to overrun than Caucasia, served to restore Russia's "imperial reputation" (de Meaux 2010, 44–74).

3. Safarov was a member of the Turkestan Commission (*Turkkommissia*) sent by the central Bolshevik government to assess the political situation in Turkestan. He took a very critical view of the "revolutionary" situation there but remained a fervent supporter of Soviet power (Khalid 2006b, 866; Sahadeo 2007, 214–20).

4. The word *Basmachi* comes from the Turkish *bosmoq* (to crush or to press) and was the equivalent of "bandit" in Russian political discourse. This insurrectional movement was based on warlords (tribal chiefs, sheikhs, ulemas, bandits, etc.) known as *qo'rbashi*. It did not have any real unity or political program, despite an attempt by the former Ottoman minister of war, Enver Pasha, who was assassinated in 1922. The movement, which was virulent during the first half of the 1920s, subsequently subsided before reawakening in the early 1930s with

the collectivization of agriculture. Many Basmachis took refuge in Afghanistan. See Fraser (1987a, 1987b), Ritter (1985, 1990), and Penati (2007).

5. Mikhail V. Frunze (1885–1925) was a military commander and politician and had been a member of the Communist Party since 1904. In 1920, he was a commander on the Turkestan front and took part in the collapse of the regimes in Bukhara and Khiva.

6. "The Russians do not trust the Uzbeks. There is not a single Uzbek in the GPU [the political police]. There is not a single Uzbek in the highest authorities"; RGASPI 81/3/127, 206–33 (in Gatagova, Kosheleva, and Rogovaia 2005, 575). Between 1935 and 1941, the Uzbek Soviet Socialist Republic Ministry of the Interior was run by Zagvozdin (a Russian), Apresian (an Armenian from Tiflis), and Sadzhaia (a Georgian). This was also the case for the heads of regional departments (Karimov 2005, 20–24).

7. *Nasha Gazeta*, July 14, 1918 (quoted in Sahadeo 2007, 212).

## Chapter 1

1. See also *Haqiqat Leninobod*, May 20, 1960.

2. Mesguich was taken on as one of the Lumière brothers' first operators in January 1896, to work around the world. He started in North America before going to Russia in November 1897, where he met Nicholas II. In July 1898, Mesguich took part in the Nizhnii-Novgorod fair before setting off for Caucasia and Central Asia (Mesguich 1933).

Devanov came from a family connected with the khan of Khiva and was taught photography by Wilhelm Penner, a German from the Mennonite community living near Khiva. Devanov took advantage of a diplomatic mission to visit Saint Petersburg, where he bought a Pathé camera. He was a member of the Young Khivans Party and finance minister during the Khorezm People's Soviet Republic. In the 1920s, he produced numerous news reports as a correspondent for the Central Documentary Film Studios. He then worked for the Uzbek Documentary and News Studios before being arrested and executed on October 4, 1938 (Golender 2009; Malik Kaiumov, "Nachalo xx veka, Turkestan, Uzbekistan: pervye shagi natsional'nogo kinematografa." *Narodnoe Slovo*, October 11, 1995).

3. UzRMDA 34/1/594, 70.
4. Ibid., 29.
5. UzRMDA 34/1/600, 56.
6. UzRMDA 34/1/1037, 77–78.
7. There was also talk about exchanging films abroad against Astrakhan fur, UzRMDA 34/1/1035, 104.
8. UzRMDA 34/1/594, 77.
9. UzRMDA 34/1/735, 411–12.
10. UzRMDA 34/1/600, 56.
11. UzRMDA 34/1/594, 58–60.
12. UzRMDA 34/1/1037, 16.
13. UzRMDA 34/1/600, 60.
14. UzRMDA 34/1/603, 320.
15. Activists on the trains targeted representatives of Bolshevik power who abused their authority over local populations. Safarov wrote *The Colonial Revolution* on the strength of his experience aboard the Red East.
16. UzRMDA 34/1/41, 229–30.

17. UzRMDA 34/1/1035, 89.
18. UzRMDA 34/1/1044, 2; UzRMDA 34/1/1059, 29–30; UzRMDA 34/1/2087, 33.
19. UzRMDA 34/1/1037, 359.
20. UzRMDA 34/1/1566, 3; UzRMDA 34/1/755, 11–12.
21. UzRMDA 34/1/1533, 81.
22. UzRMDA 34/1/2087, 15; UzRMDA 34/1/1533, 81.
23. UzRMDA 34/1/1533, 206–10.
24. Ibid.
25. Ibid., 209.
26. UzRMDA 34/1/1562, 86.
27. Goskino was set up by a decree issued by the RSFSR Sovnarkom on December 19, 1922 (Gak 1962, 131).
28. State Archives of the Russian Federation (Gosurdastvennyi Arkhiv Rossiiskoi Federatsii, or (GARF; formerly TsGAOR) 5446/31/9, 94 (quoted in Gak 1962, 133).
29. GARF (TsGAOR) 5446/31/10, 86 (quoted in Gak 1962, 136).
30. UzRMDA 34/1/1785, 50.
31. UzRMDA 34/1/2171, 100.
32. UzRMDA 34/1/1785, 50.
33. UzRMDA 34/1/2087, 150–51.
34. "Organizatsiia novykh otdelenii," *Proletkino*, no. 6–7 (1924).
35. UzRMDA 34/1/2171, p. 11.
36. UzRMDA 736/1/83, 5.
37. Ibid., 17.
38. This republic existed from 1920 to 1924, with Bukhara as its capital. It was renamed the Bukharan Soviet Socialist Republic in September 1924, when it was incorporated into the Uzbek Soviet Socialist Republic, founded on October 27, 1924, by the territorial delimitation (Khalid 2010).
39. UzRMDA 34/1/2171, 100.
40. UzRMDA 20/1/547, 23–24.
41. Ibid., 17.
42. National Archives of the Region of Saint Petersburg and the Russian Federation (TsGASPb, formerly GAORSS LO) 3296/2/21, 81 (quoted in Abul'khanov 1962, 58).
43. Ibid., 17 (quoted in Abul'khanov 1962, 56).
44. Khojaev was the son of a rich merchant from Bukhara and spent most of his childhood in Russia. When his father died in 1912, he returned to Bukhara, where he was influenced by reformist intellectuals. He took part in the Young Bukharan revolutionary movement that opposed the emir. After the October Revolution, Khojaev was a member of the government of the Bukharan Republic and then of the Uzbek Soviet Socialist Republic (as chairman of the Sovnarkom). He was arrested on July 9, 1937, and executed on March 13, 1938, in the region of Moscow.
45. Haugen argues in particular against the view put forward by Roy (1997) and the Western historiography of the 1960s and 1970s, which is based on fairly scant resources and championed primarily by Alexandre Bennigsen, Hélène Carrère d'Encausse, and Richard Pipes.
46. RGASPI 5/2/28, 19–21 (in Gatagova et al. 2005, 78).
47. RGASPI 17/112/566, 16–28 (in Gatagova et al. 2005, 207). Turar Ryskulov was born into a family of livestock farmers from the region of present-day Almaty. He took part in the 1916

revolts and was arrested before being released on the collapse of the Russian Empire. He joined the Communist Party in September 1917. In 1919 and 1920, he held various positions within the TASSR. In 1921–22, he worked for the RSFSR Commissariat of Nationalities, before becoming a member of the Turkestan Republic Sovnarkom in 1922 (and its chairman in 1924) and a member of the Central Asian Bureau of the Central Committee of the All-Russian Communist Party.

48. RGASPI 17/112/566, 16–28 (in Gatagova et al. 2005, 207).
49. Ibid.
50. RGASPI 17/86/24, 17 (in Karasar 2002, 207).
51. RGASPI 62/1/6, 53 (quoted in Obiya 2001, 108).
52. RGASPI 17/86/24, 16 (in Karasar 2002, 206).
53. Tashkent was the capital of the TASSR, and remained a cultural and economic center in the 1924–29 interlude, when Samarkand became the capital.
54. RGASPI 62/1/20, 72 (quoted in Eisener 1994, 114).
55. There was also talk of a Central Asian Soviet Socialist Republic; RGASPI 17/112/566, 31–39 (in Gatagova et al. 2005, 216–17).
56. RGASPI 17/112/566, 16–28 (in Gatagova et al. 2005, 212).
57. RGASPI 17/3/443, 3–4 (in Gatagova et al. 2005, 227).
58. UzRMDA 20/1/547, 3.
59. Ibid., 5–10.
60. Ibid.
61. Ibid., 28.
62. UzRMDA 87/1/5, 42.
63. UzRMDA 94/1/17, 92.
64. UzRMDA 94/1/94, 56.
65. UzRMDA 94/1/215, 114; UzRMDA 94/1/51, 57; UzRMDA 86/1/2328, 449.
66. UzRMDA 94/1/54, 30–31.
67. UzRMDA 94/1/220, 212–14.
68. UzRMDA 20/1/547, 60; UzRMDA 20/1/547, 64.
69. UzRMDA 94/1/220, 212–14.
70. Ibid., 214.
71. "Teatr i Kino. Uzbekkino sokhraniaet samostoiatel'nost,'" *Pravda Vostoka*, July 12, 1926.
72. UzRMDA 94/1/215, 114.
73. UzRMDA 94/1/51, 57–64.
74. Ibid.
75. UzRMDA 86/1/2932, 112.
76. Interview with Malik Kaiumov, Tashkent, September 1, 2009.
77. UzRMDA 86/1/2762, 347.
78. UzRMDA 94/1/220, 204–6.
79. RGALI 2494/1/54, 1; RGALI 2494/1/106, 5.
80. V. Dobrzhanskii, "Kak my rabotali," *Vtoraia Zhena*, 1928: 3.
81. Mahmudhoja Behbudi, "Teatr nadur?" *Oiina*, May 10, 1914 (in Norqulov and Rabbimov 2001, 62–64). See also Khalid 2005, 204.
82. Mirmuhsin, "Bizlar ham 'ibrat alailuk," *Turkiston Vilayatining Gazetasi*, July 27, 1914. I thank Dilbar Rashidova for having brought my attention to this reference, and Adeeb Khalid for helping translate it.

83. "Qishlâqdâ kina," *Yer Yuzi*, May 30, 1928.
84. "Uzbekistândâ kinâkartinkachilik bâshlanghichi," *Yer Yuzi*, March 5, 1926.
85. Ibid.

## Chapter 2

1. "Kino v Uzbekistane," *Sovetskii Ekran*, no. 8 (1927).
2. "Shakaly Ravata," *Pravda Vostoka*, December 13, 1926.
3. "Kak my rabotali nad 'Musul'mankoi,'" *Sovetskii Ekran*, no. 24 (1925).
4. "Kak stavilas kartina *Shakaly Ravata*," *Pravda Vostoka*, December 22, 1926.
5. "Iki dunia," *Yer Yuzi*, November 30, 1926; G. Levkoev, "Kino ekspeditsiia na Vostok," *ARK*, no. 6–7 (1925): 28.
6. "Kak my rabotali nad 'Musul'mankoi,'" *Sovetskii Ekran*, no. 24 (1925).
7. Nearly 80 percent of foreign films distributed in the Soviet in 1924 were German, but these were rapidly displaced by American films (Kenez 1972, 72).
8. "Tret'ia zhena mully," *Kino*, no. 31 (1928).
9. *Pravda Vostoka*, February 13, 1925; "Minaret Smerty," *ARK*, no. 2 (1926).
10. RGALI 2410/1/21, 1; GFF 1/2/1/522.
11. UzRDMA 20/1/547, 7.
12. RGALI 2410/1/21, 1.
13. UzRMDA 25/1/1819, 78, 76.
14. RGASPI 62/2/431, 12–38.
15. Ibid., 19.
16. Bassalygo studied law at the University of Moscow before starting a theatrical career in 1910 and then going on to work for the Khanjonkov company in 1915. He served in the Red Army during the civil war but was demobilized in 1920. He joined Proletkino in 1923 and ran it until 1926. In 1938 he joined the Tretiakov Gallery, where he stayed until the Second World War. In 1944, he worked at the Higher Institute for Diplomacy (Foreign Affairs Commissariat). "Nashi kino-rabotniki," *ARK*, no. 8 (1925).
17. "Kak my rabotali nad 'Musul'mankoi,'" *Sovetskii Ekran*, no. 24 (1925).
18. RGALI 2733/1/1121, 42.
19. RGALI 2494/1/59.
20. Bartenev, "Kino v Srednei Azii," *ARK*, no. 10 (1925); *Pravda Vostoka*, September 14, 1925.
21. UzRMDA 95/1/625, 13.
22. A. Qodiry, "Râvât qâshqirlâri," *Qizil Uzbekiston*, April 28, 1927.
23. *Vecherniaia Moskva*, June 2, 1925; *Vechernaia Moskva*, July 2, 1925.
24. Qodiry came from a family of writers. After studying at an elementary religious school (*maktab*) from 1904 to 1906, he became a shopkeeper and scribe and attended a Russian-indigenous school from 1908 to 1912. He also studied religion at the madrasa (1916–17). Qodiry started his career as a writer and novelist before the 1917 February revolution and played a major role in the birth of modern Uzbek literature. He was inspired by classical literature (in Persian and Chaghatay Turkish) as well as by Russian literature, and his writings (sometimes signed using the pseudonym "Julqunboy") explore the political and social context in which he lived. He was also the correspondent for the Jadid newspapers

*Sada-yi Turkistan*, *Samarqand*, and *Ayina*, the latter two founded by Mahmudhoja Behbudi. Qodiry wrote plays and poems promoting reformist ideas. He had links to the world of film through his friendship with the Uzbek filmmaker Suleyman Khojaev (see chap. 5). His famous novel *Days Gone By* (*Otkan kunlar*) was published in the *Inqelab* newspaper of 1923 and adapted as a film in 1969 by Agzamov. Qodiry was executed in 1938 for nationalism and counterrevolutionary activities (Khalid 1998, 99; Allworth 1964b, 252; Murphy 1992).

25. Qodiry, "Râvât qâshqirlâri."
26. Smith makes a similar remark, observing that spectators left the room when the film premiered in Bukhara (1997, 652).
27. "Musul'manka," *Pravda Vostoka*, July 1, 1926.
28. E. Kaufman, "Sovietskaia kartina na vneshnem rynke," *Kino-front*, no. 6 (April 15, 1927).
29. E. Kaufman, "Nashi kino-fil'my za granitsei," *Vecherniaia Moskva*, June 1, 1928.
30. Such as T. Dixon Jr.'s *The Fall of a Nation* (United States, 1916), which leaves "a general impression of unpleasantness" given its "tawdry patriotism," *Pravda Vostoka*, May 23, 1923; *Robin Hood* by A. Dwan (United States, 1922) with a "leaping Fairbanks" is a "trashy film" (*khaltura*), which did not prevent it from being shown at the Red International of Labor Unions (*profintern*) club, *Pravda Vostoka*, April 12, 1926, and *Pravda Vostoka*, August 15, 1926. But Bek-Nazarov's *Namus* (Armenia, 1925), Cooper and Schoedsack's *Chang* (United States, 1927), and Chaplin's *Modern Times* were all appreciated, *Komsomolets Vostoka*, May 16, 1929; *Pravda Vostoka*, August 6, 1936; *Yer Yuzi*, September 7, 1927; *Proletkino*, no. 3 (1924).
31. RGALI 2494/1/185, 8; Vel'tman (1927, 1).
32. "Minaret Smerty," *Pravda Vostoka*, September 17, 1925.
33. "Minaret Smerty," *Sovetskoe Kino*, no. 1 (1926); "Kino i sovetskii vostok," *Kommunisticheskaia Revoliutsiia*, nos. 21–22 (1925); *Kino* (Leningrad), no. 1 (1926); *Sovetskii Ekran*, no. 1 (1926).
34. V. Korolevich, "Litso natsional'nogo kino-proizvodstva," *Sovetskii Ekran*, no. 7 (1927).
35. *Vecherniaia Moskva*, December 11, 1925.
36. A. Fevral'skii, "Novye fil'my," *Pravda*, August 12, 1924 (quoted in Abul'khanov 1962, 64).
37. "Minaret Smerty," *ARK*, no. 2 (February 1926); *Sovetskoe Kino*, no. 1 (1926).
38. RGALI 2494/1/185, 8. However, the *Online Encyclopaedia of National Cinema* gives 1933 as his year of death, http://www.russiancinema.ru/names/name2202.
39. A. Skachko, "Kino dlia Vostoka," *ARK*, no. 10 (October 1925).
40. "Musul'manka," *Vecherniaia Moskva*, September 21, 1925.
41. *Vecherniaia Moskva*, October 8, 1924.
42. "Minaret Smerty, *ARK*, no. 2 (February 1926); "Vostochnyi ekran," *Sovetskii Ekran*, no. 21 (1926).
43. "Minaret Smerty," *ARK*, no. 2 (February 1926); RGALI 2494/1/185, 8.
44. He was an architect by training and worked in the cinema in Uzbekistan and Belarus in the 1920s. In 1927 he directed *From Under the Vaults of the Mosque* and *The Jackals of Ravat*, and then *I Want to Be a Woman Pilot* in 1928. He was accused of spying and arrested on November 5, 1937, before being sentenced and executed on January 8, 1938.
45. "Iz-pod svodov mecheti," *Kino*, no. 3 (1928).
46. See *Turksib* by Viktor Turin (1929). Russians, generally engineers and doctors, are presented as far superior to nomadic Kazakhs (Payne 2001b, 37–62). The same type of

representation may also be found in French colonial cinema, in which modernity equates to French (Western) supremacy (Slavin 1997, 24).

47. GFF 1/2/1/360, 13.
48. "Iz-pod svodov mecheti," *Kino*, no. 3 (1928).
49. GFF 1/2/1/360, 13.
50. "Iz-pod svodov mecheti," *Kino*, no. 3 (1928).
51. "Prokazhennaia," *Pravda Vostoka*, July 26, 1927.
52. Rakhil' Messerer-Plisetskaia (1902–93) was a popular actor of Polish origin. She graduated from the Film Institute in 1925 (GIK), where she had been taught by Kuleshov, and appeared in several Uzbek films. She was a victim of political repression and in March 1939 was sentenced to eight years in the Gulag. She was then exiled to Kazakhstan, where she gave dance lessons. In 1941 she returned to Moscow, shortly before the Soviet Union entered the Second World War. Her daughter Maya Plisetskaya (born in 1925) was a great solo dancer with the Bolshoi theater in Moscow.
53. Hafiz, "Na s''emkakh v Uzbekistane," *Sovetskii Ekran*, no. 46 (1927):10.
54. "Prokazhennaia," *Kino*, no. 16, 1928.
55. "Vtoraia zhena," *Trud*, 1927 [exact date illegible], in GFF 1/2/1/144.
56. "Vtoraia zhena," *Pravda Vostoka*, April 21, 1927; "Vtoraia zhena," *Nasha Gazeta*, May 24, 1927, in GFF 1/2/1/144.
57. "Vtoraia zhena," *Sovetskii Ekran*, no. 5 (1927).
58. M. Khojaev, "'Ikinchi khatun' kartinkasi tughrisida," *Qizil Uzbekiston*, January 18, 1927.
59. "Vtoraia zhena," *Nasha Gazeta*, May 24, 1927, in GFF 1/2/1/144.
60. "Iz-pod svodov mecheti," *Kino*, no. 3 (1928).
61. "Prokazhennaia," *Pravda Vostoka*, July 26, 1927.
62. "Prokazhennaia," *Vecherniaia Moskva*, April 28, 1928; "Prokazhennaia," *Kino*, no. 16 (1928).
63. Kh. Khersonskii, "Vtoraia Zhen," *Pravda*, June 4, 1927.
64. "Iz-pod svodov mecheti," *Kino*, no. 3 (1928); "Prokazhennaia," *Vecherniaia Moskva*, April 28, 1928.
65. "Iz-pod svodov mecheti," *Pravda Vostoka*, April 11, 1928; GFF 1/2/1/360, 13; Vel'tman (1927, 8).
66. "Chto tvoristsia v Uzbekkino?" *Kino*, no. 18 (1928).

## Chapter 3

1. "Shakaly Ravata," *Kino* no. 27 (1927).
2. "Shakaly Ravata," *Pravda Vostoka*, July 31, 1927.
3. UzRMDA 1745/1/2, 12–13.
4. Hafiz, "*Shakaly Ravata* na otsenku massovogo zritelia," *Pravda Vostoka*, March 22, 1927.
5. Said Ziia, "'Râvât qâshqirlâri' uzbikning tungghach kartinkkasi," *Qizil Uzbekiston*, April 20, 1927.
6. Hafiz, "*Shakaly Ravata*; "Shakaly Ravata, prodolzhaem obsuzhdenie," *Pravda Vostoka*, March 28, 1928.
7. "Shakaly Ravata," *Rabis*, July 12, 1927.
8. A. Qodiri, "Râvât qâshqirlâri," *Qizil Uzbekiston*, April 28, 1927.

9. Ibid.
10. "Shakaly Ravata" *Sovetskii Ekran*, no. 6 (1927).
11. Ibid.
12. Ziia, "Râvât qâshqirlâri."
13. Uspenskii was a musician, ethnographer, composer, and People's Artist of the Turkmen Soviet Socialist Republic in 1929 and of the Uzbek Soviet Socialist Republic in 1937. After classical music training at Leningrad, he set up the first People's Conservatory in Tashkent, where he taught. He went on several ethnographic expeditions in Central Asia, wrote several works about popular and traditional classical music (*shashmaqâm*), and composed musical dramas such as *Farhad and Shirin*, which was based on a work by the poet Mir Ali Shir Nawa'i (1936).
14. Viktor Uspenskii, "Muzyka k Shakalam Ravata," *Pravda Vostoka*, January 11, 1927.
15. Fitrat came from Bukhara and was one of the first generation of prolific influential Muslim reformists. He followed religious training before traveling (in Iran, India, and Chinese Turkestan) and residing for several years in the Ottoman Empire (1909–13). On returning to Turkestan, he helped set up reform schools and became a member of the Young Bukharan Party after the February 1917 revolution. He went on to hold important political positions in the Bukharan People's Soviet Republic. After the Uzbek Soviet Socialist Republic was founded, Fitrat became increasingly disillusioned with Soviet power and started writing allegorical works. He was arrested in 1937 and executed in 1938, before being posthumously rehabilitated in 1956.
16. The texts in Tajik were written down by the musicologist Viktor Beliaev in 1940 (Jumaev 1993, 46–48).
17. GFF 1/2/1/1050 (*The Jackals of Ravat*).
18. "Shakaly Ravata," *Komsomolets Vostoka*, March 28, 1927.
19. Hafiz, "Shakaly Ravata."
20. GFF 1/2/1/1050 (*The Jackals of Ravat*).
21. This observation is based on comparing the list of title cards adjoined to the minutes of the committee (for the 1927 copy of the film) with the film found in the archives and the official documents detailing the film's technical characteristics, GFF 1/2/1/1050 (*The Jackals of Ravat*): Montazhnyi list na kartinu Shakaly Ravata 1939.
22. "Shakaly Ravata," *Pravda Vostoka*, July 31, 1927.
23. Mikhail Averbakh studied under Lev Kuleshov from 1923 to 1925, before ending up in 1927 at the Central Institute of Theatrical Art. He cut his teeth as a director on *Chachvon*. He was made a Merited Artist of the Russian Soviet Federation in 1968, and continued making films until 1973.
24. The first term to be used for the emancipation campaign was *tajjovoz* (rape). It appeared in the translation of the speech by Zelenskii (a member of the Central Asian Bureau) that was published in *Qizil Uzbekiston* on October 15, 1926 (quoted in Kamp 2006, 164). The emancipation campaign also drew inspiration from what was happening in Turkey with Ataturk and in Afghanistan under Amanullah Khan (Northrop 2004, 71, 80; Edgar 2006).
25. Jewish women also wore the *paranji*.
26. There was also resistance from Soviet institutions (delegations, neighborhood commissions, letters and petitions, and so on) and non-Soviet ones (mullahs, sheikhs, etc.) (Northrop 2004, 91–101).

27. The International Organization for Aid to Revolutionary Fighters (*Mezhdunarodnaia organizatsiia pomoshchi bortsam revoliutsii*, or *MOPR*), known as International Red Aid in the West, was established in late 1922 to protect victims of the "white terror." It provided various forms of aid—including material and legal assistance and moral support. Its headquarters were based in Moscow until 1937, then in Paris until 1939; it was suspended during the war, though a section continued to exist in the Soviet Union until 1947.

28. UzRMDA 34/1/2559.
29. Ibid., 7–8.
30. Ibid., 8–9.
31. Ibid., 9.
32. Ibid., 11.
33. *Pravda Vostoka*, news in brief, September 1926.
34. "Kak stavilas' kartina *Shakaly Ravata*," *Pravda Vostoka*, December 22, 1926.
35. Davlat, "Qishlâqda kino," *Yer Yuzi*, May 30, 1928.
36. Amo Bek-Nazarov was an actor, scriptwriter, and director of Armenian origin who started his career before the revolutions of 1917 and went on to work for all the Caucasian studios (in Armenia, Georgia, and Azerbaijan).
37. M. Insarov-Vaks, "Moskva-Tashkent, Na s"emkakh v Uzbekistane," *Sovetskii Ekran*, no. 4 (1927); UzRMDA 1745/1/3, 3.
38. Barkov was a Soviet filmmaker and Artist of the People in the Turkmen Soviet Socialist Republic. From 1918 to 1924, he was director and then production manager with Sovkino, and in 1925 started making films on revolutionary and antireligious themes. He worked for Turkmenfilm from 1938 to 1958. Petrov-Bytov was a filmmaker and scriptwriter who was active from 1924 to the 1960s. "Kino, k 10-i godovshchine Oktiabria," *Pravda Vostoka*, August 10, 1927.
39. RGALI 2494/1/41, 28.
40. RGALI 2494/1/42, 12.
41. RGALI 2494/1/106, 7.
42. *Chernaia iazva* in Russian: anthrax, an infectious disease affecting certain herbivores and transmissible to humans which leaves black lesions on the infected person.
43. "Châchvân," *Yer Yuzi*, October 27, 1927.
44. "Ob otvetrabotnikakh, divane, kartine 'Chachvan' i kinoprokate," *Pravda Vostoka*, December 14, 1927.
45. Ibid.
46. Shirbek, "Châchvân kartinkasi toghrisidâ," *Qizil Uzbekiston*, October 31, 1927.
47. Ibid.
48. Skniga, "Chadra," *Komsomolets Vostoka*, August 21, 1928.
49. The film was in made forty days (nineteen days for the shoot, fifteen for the rough cut, and twelve for the final cut), RGALI 2494/1/106, 3.
50. Ibid., 28.
51. Ibid., 7–21.
52. GFF 1/2/1/1005 (*Chachvon*).
53. RGALI 2494/1/106, 7.
54. Ibid.
55. Ibid., 21, 30.

56. This was the official supranational body charged with overseeing and regulating Central Asian Islam (Ro'i 2000, 100–180). For discussion of the re-Islamization of Central Asia after the Second World War, see Dudoignon (2011).

57. The religious schools were shorn of government funding from 1926 onward (Khalid 2007b, 72).

58. Yemelian Yaroslavskii, whose real name was Miney Gubel'man, was a politician and historian. He joined the Communist Party in 1898 and in 1922 founded the antireligious journal *Bezbozhnik*, which was published until 1941 (Bryan 1986).

59. RGASPI 17/113/612, 23–24 (in Gatagova et al. 2005, 538). The antireligious calendar of events in Kemalist Turkey is very similar to that of Central Asia (Luizard 2008, 112–13; Khalid 2007b, 108).

60. UzRMDA 94/1/492, 119–20.

61. For a list of the titles of articles about Islam in the newspaper's pages, see Bryan (1986, 40–47).

62. Mannan Ramiz was a politician, writer, and playwright. He was a member of the Uzbek Communist Party and worked for the Public Instruction.

63. Sultan-Galiev was a Muslim intellectual of Tatar origin who sought to adopt the principles of Marxism-Leninism to the specific conditions of his people and of Muslims in the former Russian Empire. He held various positions within Soviet governing bodies (including the Commissariat of Nationalities) before being expelled from the Communist Party and arrested and then released in 1924. He was arrested again in 1928 for "nationalism" and the following year was sent to a camp, where he died (Bennigsen and Lemercier-Quelquejay 1960, 1986).

64. Especially in the pages of the widely distributed satirical newspaper *Molla Nasreddine*, which was published from 1906 to 1914 in Tiflis (Tbilisi) (Bennigsen 1962, 505–20; Sartori 2007, 171).

65. UzRMDA 94/1/492, 118–20.

66. He was a Buddhist monk who advocated Buryat and Kalmyk pan-Mongolism and called for a Buddhist state to be created as a Russian protectorate (de Meaux 2010, 325).

67. This was the case at Marghilan, for example; RGASPI 17/67/202, 220–24 (in Gatagova et al. 2005, 102).

68. Sultan Galiev reports that in Soviet Russia each church served between ten thousand and twelve thousand people on average, compared with seven hundred to one thousand people per mosque (Sultan-Galiev 1921, 50).

69. The brotherhoods were active in the regions of Andijan and Kokand and increased their influence by holding *dhikr*, which enabled them to recruit new disciples; UzRMDA 94/1/492, 118–19.

70. RGASPI 17/113/315, 19–23 (in Gatagova et al. 2005, 502).

71. Antireligious propaganda in this film coincides with denunciation of the bourgeois economic order. The Aga Khan, considered by Ismaili believers to be the incarnation of the divine on earth, is at the head of an economic empire (the system of religious taxation [*zakat*] came under particular fire from the Soviet authorities), and he symbolizes a dual form of imperialism (being close to the tsarist empire and Orthodox Church and attacked for being an Anglophile). Furthermore, the principle in the Ismaili tradition of dissimulating belief (*taqiyya*) was perceived as a threat. The Aga Khan represents a sanctified and sacralized form of capitalism (Klimovich 1937).

72. Abbas Mirza Sharifzade started his career playing theater and film roles before going on to become one of the first Azeri filmmakers. Stalin denounced the ceremony as a "national particularity" to be suppressed.

73. M. Insarov-Vaks, "Moskva-Tashkent, Na s"emkakh v Uzbekistane," *Sovetskii Ekran*, no. 4 (1928).

74. Enver Pasha was a former minister of war under the Ottoman Empire who sought to unify the Basmachi movement in Central Asia. He was assassinated in 1922 in present-day Tajikistan.

75. M. Rudman, "Poslednii bek," *Sem' dnei*, August 1929, with a translation into Uzbek in *Yuzi*, August 30, 1929.

76. The *dhikr* of the *naqshbandiyya najriyya* has the particularity of being recited aloud and accompanied by dances (Zarcone 2003–2004).

## Chapter 4

1. RGASPI 5/2/28: Stalin, letter to Lenin, September 22, 1922 (in Gatagova et al. 2005, 78).

2. The Workers' and Peasants' Inspectorate (NK RKI or RKI) was an important institution of power used by Stalin to control administrators (Blum and Mespoulet 2003, 106). The work of the Uzbek film organization was assessed by the inspectorate over a period of one month (May 21 to June 20, 1928); UzRMDA 93/3/122, 5–10.

3. UzRMDA 94/1/730, 34.

4. UzRMDA 93/3/122, 42.

5. Financial statement, UzRMDA 93/3/122, 42. Rights were transferred in exchange for thirty-three films, UzRMDA 93/3/122, 34–35.

6. UzRMDA 2343/1/1, 87, 90–92; UzRMDA 2343/1/7, 137.

7. UzRMDA 94/5/334, 66; UzRMDA 93/3/122, 30.

8. UzRMDA 93/3/122, 129.

9. Ibid., 127.

10. It was difficult to purchase film stock, which was expensive, came from far away (Baku), and was an object of commercial speculation; UzRMDA 95/7/4, 131.

11. The director Doronin (*The Second Wife*) requested additional payment for rewriting the script. In addition to his salary as director, he was paid for his work as an actor and invoiced his accommodation at the House of the Soviets for using it as an editing workshop. The directors Gertel' (*The Jackals of Ravat*) and Frelikh (*The Leper, The Covered Wagon*) also asked to be paid for rewriting the scripts; UzRMDA 93/3/122, 127–33.

12. UzRMDA 89/1/285, 224.

13. UzRMDA 93/3/122, 123; UzRMDA 94/5/101, 42.

14. For criticism of scriptwriters, see UzRMDA 93/3/122, 128–29; "Chto tvoritsia v Uzbekgoskino?" *Kino*, no. 18 (1928): 4. For criticism of Sobberey's film *From Under the Vaults of the Mosque*, see UzRMDA 95/7/4, 135. Information on Chulpan communicated during an interview with the Uzbek historian Naim Karimov, Tashkent, August 18, 2009.

15. UzRMDA 837/11/819, 181; UzRMDA 88/9/2692, 23.

16. UzRMDA 93/3/122, 31–33, 134; UzRMDA 95/7/4, 54; UzRMDA 93/3/122, 7; UzRMDA 95/7/4, 1; UzRMDA 94/5/334, 66–67.

17. "Opiat' ob Uzbekgoskino," *Vecherniaia Moskva*, July 5, 1928.

18. UzRMDA 94/5/334, 67, 73.

19. RGASPI 62/2/1983, 93.
20. UzRMDA 89/1/285, 222.
21. UzRMDA 89/1/182, 1.
22. "Chto tvoritsia v Uzbekkino," *Kino*, May 1, 1928; UzRMDA 95/1/1064, 165.
23. On the founding of Soiuzkino, see also UzRMDA 837/9/695, 51, 54: Soiuzkino statutes accepted by the Supreme Economic Council representative (May 21, 1930).
24. Shumiatskii was part of the Bolshevik old guard and profoundly transformed Soviet cinema in the 1930s (Laurent 2000, 35–37).
25. UzRMDA 837/9/695, 56.
26. UzRMDA 95/7/950, 81.
27. Film stock was produced by the factories in Shostka and Pereiaslavl (Lebedev 1939, 388) and was of poor quality (Miller 2010, 30–31).
28. UzRMDA 95/7/950, 107.
29. UzRMDA 89/1/285, 77–78.
30. Ibid., 37.
31. UzRMDA 837/9/695, 58.
32. Sovnarkom decision taken August 4, 1930, UzRMDA 837/16/109, 130.
33. UzRMDA 89/1/285, 108.
34. Ibid., 37.
35. UzRMDA 837/9/695, 54–55.
36. UzRMDA 837/16/109, 104.
37. UzRMDA 837/9/695, 59.
38. UzRMDA 837/11/819, 101; UzRMDA 837/11/824, 41.
39. UzRMDA 95/7/950, 31.
40. UzRMDA 95/7/949, 7.
41. UzRMDA 95/7/948, 85.
42. UzRMDA 95/7/1111, 16.
43. UzRMDA 95/7/948, 85–88.
44. Ibid., 88.
45. UzRMDA 95/7/949, 15–20.
46. UzRMDA 95/7/948, 108.
47. UzRMDA 95/7/1404, 10.
48. UzRMDA 95/7/1111, 1–2.
49. Ibid., 5.
50. Ibid., 42–45.
51. UzRMDA 95/7/948, 80.
52. UzRMDA 95/7/1401, 1.
53. UzRMDA 95/7/1404, 4–5.
54. UzRMDA 95/7/949, 19.
55. UzRMDA 95/7/1111, 22.
56. Ibid., 20.
57. E. Reizvikh, "Chistka partii, bol'shoi urok," *Pravda Vostoka*, October 17, 1934.
58. UzRMDA 88/9/2692, 25.
59. Decision of the Seventeenth Congress of the All-Union Communist Party (January–February 1934). This commission became the People's Commissariat in December 1940, UzRMDA 81/1, 1–6.
60. UzRMDA 88/1/44, 46; UzRMDA 837/12/633, 137.

61. RGASPI 62/2/3372, 47–48.
62. UzRMDA 837/10/450, 1.
63. UzRMDA 95/7/950, 59–60.
64. UzRMDA 837/10/901, 91.
65. UzRMDA 95/7/291, 7.
66. UzRMDA 837/11/824, 7; RGASPI 62/2/3372, 59.
67. UzRMDA 837/10/901, 91.
68. These audits were carried out for *Gharm* by Vasil'chikov as well as for Ganiev's *The Upsurge* and Klado's *The American from Baghdad*.
69. UzRMDA 95/7/950, 82.
70. "*Garm* na ekrane," *Pravda Vostoka*, July 4, 1929.
71. UzRMDA 95/7/948, 69.
72. UzRMDA 95/7/950, 75–76.
73. UzRMDA 95/7/948, 70.
74. UzRMDA 95/7/950, 76.
75. The name given to the capital of Tajikistan, Dushanbe, between 1929 and 1961.
76. UzRMDA 95/7/950, 79–82.
77. UzRMDA 95/7/948, 59, 73.
78. UzRMDA 95/7/950, 80; UzRMDA 95/7/948, 59, 63.
79. UzRMDA 95/7/948, 62.
80. "Prigovor nad rabotnikami Uzbekkino," *Pravda Vostoka*, April 2, 1932.
81. E. Negrov, "Batrak, radio i kino," *Pravda Vostoka*, September 29, 1929.
82. UzRMDA 34/1/2559, 3–13.
83. UzRMDA 217/1/106, 10.
84. UzRMDA 34/1/2559, 3.
85. Ibid., 20.
86. Ibid., 12.
87. D. Yashin, "Shaitan, Shaitan," *Sem' Dnei*, June 8, 1928.
88. Davlat, "Qishlâqda kino," *Yer Yuzi*, May 30, 1928; D. Yashin, "Shaitan, Shaitan." The word *anasha* now designates hashish, UzRMDA 94/1/417, 12.
89. "Kino v aule," *Pravda Vostoka*, September 13, 1925.
90. UzRMDA 34/1/2559, 6.
91. E. Reizvikh, "Agitator," *Pravda Vostoka*, September 17, 1936, 4.
92. UzRMDA 34/1/2559, 10.
93. Davlat, "Qishlâqda kino."
94. D. Yashin, "Shaitan, Shaitan."
95. UzRMDA 34/1/2559, 5.
96. Ibid.
97. UzRMDA 94/1/215, 164.
98. UzRMDA 34/1/2559, 9.
99. Ibid.
100. Ibid., 7.
101. UzRMDA 217/1/106, 10–11.
102. "Qishlâqdâ kina," *Yer Yuzi*, May 30, 1928.
103. UzRMDA 93/3/122, 121.
104. For the lack of interest, see RGASPI 62/2/2967, 61. The dubious nature of the content is mentioned in UzRMDA 1745/1/3, 32.

105. UzRMDA 95/7/950, 63.
106. UzRMDA 1745/1/5, 1–6.
107. Ibid.
108. UzRMDA 94/5/305, 126.
109. RGASPI 62/2/1983, 132–33.
110. RGASPI 62/2/3219, 6.
111. UzRMDA 93/3/122, 122.
112. Ibid., 51.
113. Data established on the basis of table 6 and table 7 in the appendix; RGASPI 62/2/3372, 54.
114. UzRMDA 88/9/2697, 9.
115. UzRMDA 89/1/179, 19.
116. UzRMDA 89/1/285, 120.
117. RGASPI 62/2/2967, 61.
118. RGASPI 62/2/3372, 56.
119. D. Yashin, "Shaitan, Shaitan." It has not been possible to check these figures against other sources.
120. UzRMDA 89/1/285, 83.
121. UzRMDA 837/11/819, 45.
122. UzRMDA 2343/1/6, 12.
123. This shift was accompanied by lesser forms of progress (such as a change in the width of film) which hampered distribution. About one hundred of the sets of screening apparatus received by Uzbekkino could not be used because they did not match the format of the films, UzRMDA 837/12/633, 100.
124. UzRMDA 88/3/1361, 12.
125. UzRMDA 95/1/905, 1.
126. UzRMDA 837/10/901, 84.
127. RGASPI 62/2/3372, 47; UzRMDA 88/9/1339, 29.
128. UzRMDA 95/1/905, 3.
129. "25 ozvuchennykh kinozal," *Komsomolets Uzbekistana*, June 22, 1934.
130. "Po Sovetskomy Soiuzu," *Revoliutsiia i Natsional'nosti*, no. 3 (1937).
131. Dmitri Shostakovich, "Eshche raz o kinomuzyke," *Iskusstvo Kino*, no. 1 (1954): 87.
132. Various terms were used in Uzbekistan, including agitator (Rus. *agitator*, Uzb. *tashviqotchi*), organizer (Rus. *massovik*), orator (Rus. *orator*, Uzb. *notiq* or *suhbatchi*), lecturer (Rus. *lektor*, Uzb. *dokladchi*), and explainer (Rus. *ob'iasnitel'*).
133. Or *viktorina-plakat* in Russian, a sort of poster based on an entertaining series of questions and answers.
134. UzRMDA 34/1/2559, 8.
135. "Kino letom," *Pravda Vostoka*, May 15, 1928.
136. UzRMDA 34/1/602, 8.
137. UzRMDA 34/1/2559, 11.
138. Ibid., 12.
139. RGASPI 62/2/2967, 61.
140. Ibid.
141. UzRMDA 837/11/819, 264.
142. RGASPI 62/2/2967, 61.
143. UzRMDA 837/11/819, 265; UzRMDA 837/11/819, 112.
144. UzRMDA 34/1/2559, 12.

145. RGASPI 62/2/3372, 58.
146. UzRMDA 81/1/44, 44.
147. UzRMDA 837/12/633, 37.
148. "Tesno i griazno v kino 'Khiva,'" *Pravda Vostoka*, March 23, 1936.
149. *Komsomolets Vostoka*, August 30, 1928.
150. *Papiros* are cheap cigarettes recognizable by their long cardboard filter.
151. "Nazyvaetsia teatr komsomol'skim . . . ," *Komsomolets Uzbekistana*, July 14, 1933.
152. UzRMDA 837/11/819, 99
153. Ibid., 45.
154. UzRMDA 837/12/633, 53.
155. UzRMDA 88/9/2692, 26.
156. "Nuzhda v kul'turnost,'" *Komsomolets Uzbekistana*, March 22, 1934.
157. UzRMDA 837/12/633, 53.
158. "Nuzhda v kul'turnost.'"
159. "Khuliganstvo v kino," *Pravda Vostoka*, July 6, 1932.
160. "Seans kotoryi dlit'sia dva dnia," *Pravda Vostoka*, June 13, 1936.
161. Ibid.
162. "Tesno i griazno," 4.
163. Ibid.
164. "U vkhoda v kino," *Pravda Vostoka*," April 15, 1929, 4.
165. "Spekuliant kinobiletami," *Pravda Vostoka*, March 14, 1937, 4.

## Part 3

1. Quoted in Munavar Qori, RGASPI 81/3/127, 206–33 (in Gatagova et al. 2005, 584).
2. RGASPI 81/3/127, 206–33 (in Gatagova et al. 2005, 586). Dmitri Shostakovich's highly ironic portrait of the Kazakh bard Jambul Jabaev, the national singer of Stalinist ideology, echoes this declaration. The only Russian word Jambul knew was *fee* (*gonorar*) (Volkov 1980, 252–54).
3. Chulpan's (or Tchulpân's) real name was Abd al-Hamid Sulaimon. He was a poet and playwright from Andijan and part of the first group of Central Asian intellectuals who were influenced by debates on Muslim reformism and inspired by colonial and national issues. He attended a Koranic school and several madrasas (in Andijan and Tashkent) and then a native Russian school, studying classical subjects (Arabic, Persian, and Chaghatay) and theology as well as modern European disciplines and Russian. He started writing in the press in 1908, and his first short stories were published just before the Great War. The hopes awakened by the February 1917 Revolution were short-lived, and in the wake of the first political purges, Chulpan went into exile in Moscow. It was there that he met the poets Vladimir Mayakovsky and Sergei Yesenin, who exerted a great influence on him. Chulpan was particularly popular and subject to virulent political criticism for his "anti-Russian nationalism." He was sentenced to death in October 1938. For further details, see the afterword by Dudoignon in his translation of Chulpan's novel *Night* (Tchulpân 2010, 417–34).
4. The play in question is *The Revolutionaries of India* (*Hind ikhtilolchilari*), first published in Tashkent in 1920.
5. Pan-Turkism, which may be assimilated to pan-Islamism, is based on the unity of Muslims, and not exclusively on Islam. As a product of the late nineteenth and early

twentieth centuries, it draws on the ideas of progress, nation, and ethnicity and corresponds to a transnational public sphere in which elites and their works circulate (Khalid 2005). For pan-Uzbekist tendency, see RGASPI 81/3/127, 206-33 (in Gatagova et al. 2005, 586).

6. RGASPI 81/3/127, 206-33 (in Gatagova et al. 2005, 574).
7. RGASPI 17/113/725, 109-11 (in Gatagova et al. 2005, 621).
8. Of the 800,000 Tajiks at the moment of the territorial delimitation in 1924, only 350,000 officially declared themselves as such, RGASPI 17/113/725, 109-11 (in Gatagova et al. 2005, 620).
9. RGASPI 81/3/127, 206-33 (in Gatagova et al. 2005, 587).
10. "Na radost' klassovomu vragu," *Komsomolets Uzbekistana*, July 11, 1933.
11. Abdul'qasim Ahmedzade Lahuti (1887–1957) was born in Kermanshah in Iran and became the bard of the *irân* and the Russian revolution. After his arrival in the Soviet Union, he became one of the most important Tajik poets.
12. RGASPI 81/3/127, 206-33 (in Gatagova et al. 2005, 587).

## Chapter 5

1. RGASPI 81/3/127, 206-33 (in Gatagova et al. 2005, 575).
2. A. K-P, "Bez reshitel'noi korenizatsii apparata ne mozhet byt' podlinnoi bor'by za Leninskuiu natsional'snuiu politiku," *Pravda Vostoka*, August 11, 1931.
3. GARF 374/27s/1707, 110-12, quoted in Martin (2001a, 134).
4. The Commissariat for Education was indigenized by evicting its former heads, viewed by members of the Central Asian Bureau as "counterrevolutionary bourgeois nationalists"; UzRMDA 94/5/101, 63. This had an effect on the languages the authorities used. Prior to 1927, Russian had predominated due to a shortage of bilingual secretaries, translators, and Uzbek typewriters. Yet Uzbek was the language used for 70 percent to 80 percent of communication at the district level, or both languages were used in the regions of Tashkent and Ferghana (where 50 percent of the population were of European origin). All in all, 31 percent of the staff at the Commissariat for Education were Uzbek on January 1, 1928, when only one person of European origin could speak Uzbek.
5. A. K-P, "Bez reshitel'noi."
6. RGASPI 62/2/3193, 78.
7. UzRMDA 95/7/1111, 16.
8. RGASPI 62/2/3372, 48.
9. UzRMDA 88/9/2692, 25.
10. RGASPI 62/2/3372, 48.
11. The first women filmmakers included Margarita Kassymova in Tajikistan and Kamara Kamalova in Uzbekistan but in the late 1970s only. The figure of nine out of twelve is from UzRMDA 2343/1/7, 138.
12. RGASPI 62/2/1983, 89.
13. The Russian and Ukrainian studios had relocated to Central Asia due to the war and the advancing German troops. Ganiev worked with Speshnev on the script for *Takhir and Zukhra* as well as with the director of photography Demutskii, who had worked for Dovzhenko on *Arsenal* (1929) and *Earth* (1930). Demutskii continued working on the production of other Uzbek films, including *Alisher Navo'i* by Yarmatov (Uzbekistan, 1947).
14. For details of actors, see B. Mar, "Pod"em," *Komsomolets Vostoka*, August 24, 1930.

15. Ibid.
16. Ergash Khamraev—the father of Ali Khamraev, one of the great Uzbek filmmakers of the 1970s—was of Tajik origin and the main actor in Nabi Ganiev's films. He also wrote several scripts after training at the Mosfilm studios; "Kliatva," *Komsomolets Uzbekistana*, March 3, 1937.
17. For criticism, see N. Kar, "Fal'shivaia nezhiznennaia fil'ma kino," *Komsomolets Uzbekistana*, November 18, 1931. For a more positive view, see L. Lench and V. Levich, "Pod"em," *Pravda Vostoka*, December 24, 1930.
18. UzRMDA 837/11/823, 60.
19. GFF 1/2/1786.
20. AI no. 25, 12.
21. The script for *Vatan* (about Ibrohim-Bek) was written by Ergash Khamraev and read out to the members of the studios and the Central Asian political command and military general staff. The script needed to be altered with the help of a commander and a lieutenant who were appointed as consultants, but the film was never made; "Liubov's k rodine," *Pravda Vostoka*, April 20, 1936.
22. E. Reizvikh, "Chistka Partii, Bol'shoi Urok," *Pravda Vostoka*, October 17, 1934.
23. UzRMDA 81/1/108, 5.
24. "Egit, novyi fil'm rezhissera N. Ganieva," *Pravda Vostoka*, May 4, 1935.
25. GFF 1/2/1/244.
26. UzRMDA 837/13/54, 5.
27. "Realizm iolida," *Qizil Uzbekistan*, September 30, 1935.
28. Interview with Malik Kaiumov in Tashkent, September 1, 2009; Sulaimon (1966).
29. "Egit, novyi fil'm rezhissera N. Ganieva."
30. "Realizm iolida."
31. Ibid.
32. Ibid.
33. *International Literature* 3 (1933), 136–37 (quoted in Robin 1986, 70).
34. Reizvikh, "Chistka partii."
35. Hamidulla Akbarov, "Davr fozhiiasini keltirgan tufon," *Toshkent Oqshomi*, April 13, 1993.
36. Suleyman Khojaev is not to be confused with Fayzulla Khojaev, chairman of the Uzbek Soviet Socialist Republic Council of People's Commissars.
37. *Vaqt*, August 30, 1916 (quoted in Qosimov 1996, 118). *Vaqt* was a Jadid literary and political newspaper published in the Tatar language in Orenburg (from 1905 to 1918).
38. The revolts act as the backdrop to the historical novel *Night* (Tchulpân 2010). They were also the theme of the planned film *The 1916 Revolts*, which was never made; UzRMDA 89/1/179, 7. But a film was made by M. Levin about Kazakh territory, *Amangeldy* (1938), produced by Lenfilm and based on a script by Ivanov, Mailin, and Musrepov. In the film, Amangeldy Imanov (who really did lead revolts in the steppes region) is introduced to Bolshevik ideas by a Russian soldier. Amangeldy then becomes a revolutionary and plays an active part in the combat against nationalists and counterrevolutionaries from the Alash Orda party, in conformity with the historiography of the late 1930s (Siranov 1966, 343).
39. For a discussion of the issues of authorship, intervention, and the meaning of literary works, see Compagnon (1998, 51–110).

40. He also came from a religious family, and his maternal grandfather and uncle were reciters of the Koran at the madrasa (*qori*).

41. Avloni was a journalist, poet, writer, stage director, and actor from Tashkent. He was part of the reformist current and subsequently joined the Communist Party, going on to become a diplomat for the Turkestan Autonomous Soviet Socialist Republic. He wrote for various newspapers, including *Sadâ-i Turkistan*.

42. Expressing the idea of a "common destiny" and without any ethnic dimension, in which they differed from the dominant tendency after the 1924 territorial delimitation.

43. Mannon Uyghur, whose real name is Abdulmannon Mazhidov, was a stage director, actor, and playwright. He started working for the Turan troupe in 1916 as an actor and in 1918 began to work as a director (of plays by Avloni, Fitrat, Qodiri, etc.). He was also involved in writing the script for *Alisher Navo'i* (1947), which Yarmatov directed in Uzbekistan.

44. Little is known about his private life. His first marriage was against the will of his grandfather, and he separated from his wife in 1919, officially divorcing her in 1929. Meanwhile he remarried an "educated Tatar" who was adulterous, then lived with a young woman of German nationality as his common-law spouse. He was married a third and final time in 1929, to a Muscovite; UzRMDA 95/7/950, 57; see also Hamidulla Akbarov, "Bevaqt sundirilgan iste'dod," *Toshkent Oqshomi*, February 3, 1992.

45. Two new companies were formed from the remnants of Turan: a troupe headed by M. Uyghur, which kept the name Turan, and the Karl Marx Dramatic Company (*Karl Marks Namida Dram Truppasi*), which was more progressive but not entirely pro-Russian despite appearances. This latter troupe was criticized for staging nationalist and patriotic works, particularly plays by Fitrat and Chulpan. In 1920, it became the Uzbek National Dramatic Theater (*Uzbek Davlat Dram Teatri*) (Allworth 1990, 215–16).

46. See also UzRMDA 95/7/950, 53; UzRMDA 95/7/1404, 14.

47. UzRMDA 95/7/950, 50.

48. The Turk Federalist Party (*Turk Adam-i Markaziiat Firkasi* in Uzbek, and *Obshchestvo tiurskikh federalistov* in Russian), in a manifesto adopted on August 23, 1917, considered that the new Russian state needed to be organized on the principle of a federation in which Turkestan would enjoy greater national and territorial autonomy than "small nations" (Volga and Crimean Tatars), which would only have cultural autonomy (Komatsu 1992, 44–50). This federal state was to take into account the specific features of the Muslim population's social life, based on Koranic law (*sharia*) and customary right (*adat*) (Agzamkhojaev 2006, 159–65). The political police is said to have been involved in creating the National Independence Party to identify supporters of independence; interview with Naim Karimov in Tashkent, January 17, 2006 (see also Turdiev, 1996, 2005).

49. For *The Leper*, *The Jackals of Ravat*, and *The Ishan's Fiancée*.

50. UzRMDA 95/7/1404, 14.

51. UzRMDA 95/7/950, 56. He also wrote a collection of short stories (Khojaev 1931).

52. UzRMDA 95/7/950, 55.

53. UzRMDA 88/9/2692, 18, 15; UzRMDA 1803/2/7, 41.

54. This film has not been included in the corpus under study here because it portrays Turkmen populations.

55. The term used was *ghazavat*, not *jihad*. *Ghazavat* denotes a one-off armed insurrection that is not sanctioned by any religious legal decision (*fetwa*), unlike *jihad*.

56. I have not been able to consult any oral source: Suleyman Khojaev's son had died several years earlier. He did, however, leave an account: Hamid Sulaymon (Khamid Suleymanov in Russian), "Otam haqida," *Kino*, no. 11 (1966). As for the filmmaker's grandson, he either did not know or chose not to talk about his grandfather's life.

57. The studio's archives were transferred to the Uzbek Communist Party Central Committee; UzRMDA 95/7/950, 57.

58. Akbarov, "Bevaqt sundirilgan iste'dod"; Karimov (1992a, 1992b, 1992c, 1993).

59. In the film this political body stigmatizes Muslim reformists and their pan-Turkist political views. An eponymous organization was headed by Avloni (Agzamkhojaev 2006, 128).

60. The first difficulty for analyzing this film sixty years after it was made resides in identifying the copy obtained in Uzbekistan. It has been authenticated by comparing a shot-by-shot analysis of the film to two reports from 1934 found in the Film Archives (Gosfilmofond). The list of title cards included with these reports acts as a means of authentication, because they provide the narrative framework of the copy as originally edited that was sent to the censorship authorities. They correspond to the film found in Uzbekistan; GFF 1/2/1/933, 5, 8.

61. Jadid and nationalist literature did not yet come in for criticism during the period 1917 to 1927. But as of 1927, official opinion about the Jadid movement shifted, and reformists went from being categorized as "progressive" to "reactionary." Jadidism became officially undesirable (Allworth 1964, 62–63; Fedtke 1998, 483–512).

62. Some Jadids viewed this conscription as a way for Central Asian populations to become more fully integrated in the empire (Khalid 1998, 241).

63. This newspaper, founded in 1883 by Ismail Gasprinskii (Gaspiraly), played a key role in spreading Muslim reformist ideas.

64. The published script indicates that these orders came from "central archives" (Khojaev 1933, 61).

65. The image of the "boot of the Russian soldier" was referred to in the account published by *Yer Yuzi* (quoted in Qosimov 1996, 119) and taken up by Levin in *Amangeldy* (Kazakhstan, 1938) about the 1916 revolts on the steppes.

66. The indigenous Turkestan population dropped by 30.5 percent between 1915 and 1920 as a result of famines, the First World War, and the civil war (Buttino 1990, 65).

67. The Soviet authorities were perceived by the final Jadid generation, after the repression of the Kokand Autonomy, "as the continuation of the process of territorial expropriation, economic ruin, and cultural regression of native Muslim communities" (Dudoignon 2002, 159). "The revolution brought us nothing, everything is as it was before, under tsarism, all that has changed is the flag!" attributed to Munavar Qori (1878–1931), RGASPI 81/3/127, 206-33 (in Gatagova et al. 2005, 574–75). See also Khalid (2001, 146).

68. RGASPI 81/3/127, 206-33 (in Gatagova et al. 2005, 574).

69. Particularly the region of Turgai (Ohayon 2006, 182–88) and the collection of archives about numerous uprisings (Alimova 2006).

70. RGASPI 62/2/1808, 1, 5, 20 (quoted in Martin 2001a, 153–54). Martin takes the example of a riot that took place in Margilan in April 1931 when three hundred Uzbeks wrecked a silkworks while chanting slogans against "Russian oppression."

71. After this repression, the Jadids, who had held out hope that the new Soviet ideology would modernize education, admitted that they had been mistaken, but they were nevertheless obliged to accommodate the wishes of the new authorities (Qosimov 1996, 109).

72. When in 1946 Sadriddin Aini described Bukhara as having once been dominated by "social injustice, bloody arbitrary decisions, and contempt for the law of feudal society," he awakened a far more contemporary view of reality in his public's mind (Dudoignon 1993, 97). Dudoignon (1993), writing about Fitrat, notes that power of expression also makes sense to readers who are not the author's contemporaries: "Even Fitrat's *The Last Judgment* [*Qiyamat*], an antireligious satire written at the very beginning of the 1920s and regularly republished for schoolchildren, was read as denouncing the flaws of the youthful Soviet State." Allworth sums it up another way: "In Bukhara and its environs, the past is the present" (2002, xvi).

73. Aesop was a Greek writer (seventh and sixth centuries BC) regarded as the father of the fable genre. Soviet artists often used the expression "Aesopian language" in definitions of doublespeak. Observations made about the play *The Revolutionaries of India* (1920), RGASPI 81/3/127, 206–33 (in Gatagova et al. 2005, 586).

74. Erwin Panofsky points out that intention can never be absolutely determined, being fashioned by the norms of the epoch and milieu, while our apprehension of it is influenced by our attitude, which depends in turn upon our personal experiences and historical context (1969, 41). Furthermore, the context of Soviet surveillance and the closure of numerous archive groups mean that fewer documents are available to gauge the filmmaker's intentions. Last, for *Before Dawn*, it is not possible to base analysis on changing pronouncements by Khojaev, since he only made one film. For a discussion of the topic of intention and how it is eclipsed by the subjective nature of reception, see Compagnon (1998, 51–110, 163–94).

75. My observations about the universal nature of oppression and tyranny (*zolm*) owe much to the late Altan Gökalp.

76. Mustafa Chokay oglu was one of the great figures in Turkestan's struggle for independence. He was born into an aristocratic family from the region of Qizil Orda (in present-day Kazakhstan), studied law at Saint Petersburg, and played an active part in the political life of Turkestan. He was one of the leaders in the short-lived Autonomous Government of Turkestan, based in Kokand (from December 1917 to February 1918). He went into exile in France, England, and then Germany, where he died.

77. For the person looking at a photo, the *punctum*, in opposition to the stadium (an average affect relating to a photo), is a "sting, speck, cut, little hole—and also a cast of the dice. A photograph's *punctum* is that accident which pricks me (but also bruises me, is poignant to me)" (Barthes 1980, 26–27).

78. Analysis of how the literature addresses the theme of the death of the hero and exemplary self-sacrifice as a literary code of the period would no doubt be revealing. Lyons provides one or two examples (2003, 308).

79. *Pravda Vostoka*, September 11, 1933, and February 28, 1934.

80. In his discussion of the significance of silences, Lyons notes that Fitrat makes no reference to either the October Revolution or socialism (2003, 311).

81. All of which are characteristic of seasonal workers; *Vaqt*, August 30, 1916 (quoted in Qosimov 1996, 118).

82. Low-level representatives of the local administration were exempted, including imams, mullahs, teachers from Koranic schools, and those with noble privileges.

83. Rich Turkestanis could pay between 1,000 and 1,500 to be exempted; *Vaqt*, August 30, 1916 (quoted in Qosimov 1996, 118).

84. O. Or, "Tong Oldidan, Pered rassvetom," *Pravda Vostoka*, September 11, 1933.

85. GFF 1/2/1/933.

86. Or, "Tong Oldidan."
87. The point of departure for this revision is Stalin's letter "*O nekotorykh voprosakh istorii bol'shevizma. Pis'mo v redaktsiiu zhurnala 'Proletarskaia Revoltutsiia'*" and the resolution passed by Central Committee of the All-Union Communist Party on July 31, 1931, pertaining to the publication of works about the civil war. These directives related primarily to the history of the party and of the civil war (Germanov 1998).
88. Akbarov, "Bevaqt sundirilgan iste'dod"; Akbarov (2005, 54). Sergei Kirov (1886–1934) was an old-guard Bolshevik. His assassination marked the beginning of the Great Purges and was used as a pretext for numerous arrests, including in Uzbekistan (for discussion of his assassination, see Conquest 1970, 52–69).

## Chapter 6

1. N. Klado, "Kliatva," *Iskusstvo Kino*, no. 7 (1937), 33.
2. The most representative example of this was the building of Lenin's mausoleum despite his widow's protests and official disapproval of the veneration of relics (Lewin 1982, 79).
3. *Kino*, no. 25 (1930); UzRMDA 86/1/2932, 112.
4. Paper given at the "Cinéma soviétique: le dégel de l'histoire" conference, Pompidou Center (Paris), February 1, 2003.
5. Broido (1885–1956) was born in Vil'no (Vilnius) and, before the February Revolution, studied at the Vernii gymnasium (nowadays Almaty), where he became acquainted with Frunze. After his higher education, Broido became an attorney in Pishkek (Bishkek). He joined the party in 1903 and was editor of *The Soldier's Gazette* (*Soldatskaia Gazeta*) and head of the Tashkent Soviet during the February Revolution. He condemned the policy of the tsar and the violent repression meted out to the Kyrgyz and Kazakhs after the 1916 uprisings. Broido's position became untenable and he was dispatched to the army. From 1921 to 1923, he was deputy commissar for nationalities (Russian Soviet Federation) alongside Stalin and in 1923 was appointed rector of the University of the Toilers of the East, a position he held until 1926. He was a member of the Central Committee of the Tajik Communist Party (1926–33) and became its first secretary in 1933, going on to become a member of the Central Committee of the All-Union Communist Party from 1934 to 1939. In 1941, he was expelled and sentenced to twenty years in a camp. He was granted amnesty in 1953.
6. RGASPI 17/84/87, 3–5 (in Gatagova et al. 2005, 32).
7. Ibid., 34–35.
8. He erroneously referred to Sura 36, verse 4, probably instead of Sura 42 (Consultation), verse 38: "whose affair is [determined by] consultation among themselves," Koran, Sahih International translation.
9. Abuziam, "Lenin i Vostok," *Pravda*, February 6, 1924. Abuziam was a member of the Central Committee of the Palestinian Communist Party. Mustafa Chokay quotes from an article titled "Lenin, Is He a Prophet or Not?" published in the *Qizil Uzbekiston* newspaper but without providing an exact reference. The article uses sura from the Koran to demonstrate that "Lenin was a prophet" and that he "had a gift of prophetic foresight" (1928, 41).
10. "May the red head scarf of the *komsomols* replace the *chachvon* everywhere!" UzRMDA 94/1/262, 487.

11. Usol'tsev-Garf, "Kak sozdavalas' 'Kliatva'," *Pravda Vostoka*, July 15, 1937. Usol'tsev-Garf was an actor, scriptwriter, and director who studied drama at Barnaul (1914–17) before joining the Red Army and then moving to the Moscow State Institute of Cinematography as an actor from 1923 to 1926. He made films for Proletkino and Sovkino and then for the Tashkent Studios (from 1934 to 1942). He was the head of the cinema team on the first Belarusian front during the Second World War and worked on the filming of the documentary *Berlin* by Iulii Raizman. In 1945–46, he worked for Mosfilm and then for Sovexportfilm in the German Democratic Republic.
12. "Istoriia molodogo cheloveka," *Komsomolets Uzbekistana*, November 12, 1934.
13. Usol'tsev-Garf, "Kak sozdavalas' 'Kliatva'."
14. "Potomok vodonosa," *Komsomolets Uzbekistana*, December 10, 1934; A. Usol'tsev-Garf, "Pervyi uzbekskii zvukovoi fil'm," *Pravda Vostoka*, August 16, 1936.
15. Usol'tsev-Garf, "Kak sozdavalas' 'Kliatva'."
16. "Istoriia molodogo cheloveka"; Usol'tsev-Garf, "Pervyi uzbekskii zvukovoi fil'm."
17. "Chetyre fil'ma," *Pravda Vostoka*, January 11, 1936.
18. The song is available at http://sovmusic.ru/download.php?fname=baikal.
19. The statutes of the Writers' Union provide the following definition: "Socialist Realism, the basic method of Soviet literature and literary criticism, requires the sincere writer to provide a historically concrete presentation of reality in its revolutionary development. Hence veracity and the historically concrete aspect of the artistic representation of reality need to be tied to the task of effecting ideological change and educating workers in the spirit of socialism" (Robin 1986, 40).
20. UzRMDA 93/11/450, 3.
21. UzRMDA 837/11/821, 4–7; UzRMDA 837/14/73, 170–72.
22. UzRMDA 837/14/120, 33, 38; UzRMDA 81/1/108, 2–6.
23. Usol'tsev-Garf, "Kak sozdavalas' 'Kliatva'."
24. M. Mai, "Metamorfoza," *Komsomolets Uzbekistana*, July 12, 1935.
25. Ibid.
26. A. Usol'tsev-Garf, "Gulistan," *Pravda Vostoka*, June 8, 1936.
27. UzRMDA 837/14/623, 36; Usol'tsev-Garf, "Kak sozdavalas's 'Kliatva'."
28. UzRMDA 837/14/623, 25.
29. Ibid., 73.
30. Usol'tsev-Garf, "Kak sozdavalas' 'Kliatva'"; UzRMDA 837/14/623, 36.
31. UzRMDA 837/14/623, 25.
32. Ibid., 24–26.
33. Ibid.
34. "Fabrika, liudi, rabota," *Komsomolets Uzbekistana*, July 12, 1935; Usol'tsev-Garf, "Pervyi uzbekskii zvukovoi fil'm"; "Potomok vodonosa," *Komsomolets Uzbekistana*, December 10, 1934.
35. "Proisshestviia, pozhar na kinofabrike," *Pravda Vostoka*, March 27, 1936.
36. UzRMDA 837/14/624, 4.
37. "Proisshestviia, pozhar na kinofabrike."
38. Usol'tsev-Garf, "Kak sozdavalas' 'Kliatva'."
39. Usol'tsev-Garf, "Gulistan."
40. Usol'tsev-Garf, "Kak sozdavalas' 'Kliatva'."
41. "Ozvuchenie 'Kliatvy'," *Pravda Vostoka*, March 21, 1937.

42. "Kliatva," *Komsomolets Uzbekistana*, March 3, 1937.
43. "Tvorcheskii otchet uzbekskogo iskusstva," *Pravda Vostoka*, May 10, 1937.
44. "Priem v Kremle uchastnikov dekady uzbekskogo iskusstva," *Pravda Vostoka*, June 2, 1937.
45. I. Iras', "Vozrozhdenie narodnogo tvorchestva," *Pravda Vostoka*, May 10, 1937.
46. In chronological order: Ukraine (March 11–21, 1936), Kazakhstan (May 17–25, 1936), Georgia (January 5–15, 1937), Azerbaijan (April 5–15, 1938), Kyrgyzstan (May 26–June 4, 1939), Armenia (October 20–29, 1939), Belarus (June 5–15, 1940), Buryat-Mongolia (October 20–27, 1940), and Tajikistan (April 12–20, 1941).
47. "Torzhestvo leninsko-stalinskoi natsional'noi politiki," *Pravda Vostoka*, June 2, 1937.
48. Faizulla Khodzhaev, "Dekada Uzbekskogo iskusstva," *Pravda Vostoka*, May 22, 1937.
49. "Obshchestvennyi prosmotr '*Kliatvy*'" *Pravda Vostoka*, May 30, 1937.
50. L. Vaks, "Kliatva," *Vecherniaia Moskva*, May 27, 1937.
51. "Ogromnyi uspekh 'Kliatva'," *Pravda Vostoka*, July 15, 1937; "'Kliatva' na ekranakh Moskvy i Tashkenta," *Pravda Vostoka*, July 29, 1937.
52. The permit ran until June 1, 1941, GFF /1/3/1/1002, 1, 3.
53. "'Kliatva' na ekranakh Moskvy i Tashkenta."
54. "Fil'm 'Kliatva' idet na ekrany Frantsii," *Komsomolets Uzbekistana*, September 1, 1937.
55. Vaks, "Kliatva," 3; GFF/1/3/1/1002.
56. Klado, "Kliatva," 37.
57. A. Snegov, "Kliatva," *Pravda*, August 7, 1937.
58. *Pravda Vostoka*, July 10, 1937.
59. "Kliatva na ekranakh respubliki," *Komsomolets Uzbekistana*, August 22, 1937.
60. "Uspekh 'Kliatvy'," *Pravda Vostoka*, September 20, 1937.
61. Klado, "Kliatva."
62. Snegov, "Kliatva."
63. A. Snegov, "Qasam," *Qizil Uzbekiston*, August 3, 1937.
64. A. Snegov, "Kliatva," *Komsomolets Uzbekistana*, August 10, 1937.
65. The figures provided by Oleg Mozukhin are slightly lower, with a little over 36,000 arrests in the Uzbek Soviet Socialist Republic between 1937 and 1939 (Mozukhin 2006, 332–43). Across the Soviet Union as a whole, nearly 1,400,000 people were sentenced for political reasons, of whom 682,000 were executed (Khlevniuk 1998, 205). Nicolas Werth gives broadly similar figures: In 1937–38, 1,500,000 people were arrested, of whom 1,350,000 were sentenced by special tribunal; 680,000 were shot, with the others receiving sentences of eight to ten years in prison camps, with a margin of error of between 10 percent and 25 percent (2007, 267-268). The "Great Terror" came to an end when the Politburo passed a secret resolution on November 17, 1938 (31).
66. Interview with Khanjara Abul-Kasimova, Tashkent, October 20, 2005.
67. UzRMDA 81/1/108, 8. This film has disappeared.
68. Ibid., 2–6.
69. Snegov, "Kliatva."
70. J. Stalin, "O politicheskikh zadachakh Universiteta Narodov Vostoka," *Pravda*, May 22, 1925.
71. V. Lenin, "Kriticheskie zametki po natsional'nomu voprosu," and point number 4 in particular: "Kul'turno-natsional'naia avtonomiia," some of which is available (in French) at

www.marxists.org/francais/lenin/works/1913/10/vil19131000e.htm and in Russian in a version of the complete works at http://vilenin.eu/t24/p131 (vol. 24, p. 131).

72. RGASPI 558/11/132, 36–42 (in Gatagova et al. 2005, 614).

73. Ibid., 613, 614. See the thesis of "positive discrimination" affirmative action (Martin, 2001a).

74. For extracts from Stalin's speech to the Tenth Congress of the All-Russian Communist Party (March 8–16, 1921), see www.magister.msk.ru/library/stalin/5-1.htm.

75. The metaphor of the family was not a new one. It provided a way to promote the unity and cohesion of multiethnic populations, especially in the army, and had been used during the days of empire as well as in the years immediately after the October Revolution (Sanborn 2001, 96).

76. Usol'tsev-Garf, "Kak sozdavalas' 'Kliatva'."

77. Klado, "Kliatva," 38.

78. Iras', "Vozrozhdenie narodnogo tvorchestva."

79. "Torzhestvo leninsko-stalinskoi natsional'noi politiki." For illustration of this idea in a different context, witness the murder of the actor Nurkhon and the media campaign that was exploited by Soviet propaganda to symbolize fanaticism about images. Nurkhon was killed by her brother (on the orders of her father and under the influence of clerics) when she had fled the family home to join the theater troupe in Samarkand. Interview with S. Akhmedov in Tashkent, February 11, 2006. Her brother and father were sentenced to death (Kamp 2006, 205–206).

80. Mirmuhsin, "Bizlar ham 'ibrat alailuk," *Turkiston Vilayatining Gazetasi*, July 27, 1914.

81. "Novye kinoteatry v Uzbekistane," *Revoliutsiia i Natsional'nosti*, no. 3 (1937).

82. UzRMDA 2343/1/16, 4–26.

83. "Luchshii kinoteatr v Tashkente," *Pravda Vostoka*, October 11, 1936, 4.

84. UzRMDA 2343/1/16, 13–18. The overall cost, estimated at 1.8 million rubles in 1936, finally rose to 2.5 million rubles.

## Conclusion

1. Klado, "Kliatva."

2. This process had thus started before the war but had not found full expression. A modest celebration was, however, held at the Hermitage (in Leningrad) in 1941.

3. UzRMDA 1803/3/9, 10.

# Sources and Selected Bibliography

Primary Sources

*Unpublished Archives: Uzbekistan*

Central State Archives of the Republic of Uzbekistan—*Uzbekiston Respublikasi Markazii Davlat Arkhivi* (UZRMDA)

### High-Ranking Political Bodies
F (fond). 3: Turkestan Autonomous Soviet Socialist Republic People's Commissariat for Education (1917–24)—*Narkompros TASSR*
F. 94: Uzbek Soviet Socialist Republic People's Commissariat for Education (1925–29)—*Narkompros UZSSR*
F. 837: Council of People's Commissars and then Government Cabinet of the Uzbek Soviet Socialist Republic (early 1924)—*Sovnarkom UZSSR*, then *Sovmin UZSSR*
F. 25: Turkestan Autonomous Soviet Socialist Republic Council of People's Commissars (1917–24)—*Sovnarkom TASSR*
F. 17: Executive Central Committee of the Councils of the Turkestan Autonomous Soviet Socialist Republic (1917–24)—*TurkTsIK*
F. 86: Executive Central Committee of the Councils of Peasants and Workers Delegates and of the Red Army (1925–28)—*UzTsIK*

### Cinematographic and Artistic Activity
F. 1803: Sharq Iulduzi Studio, then *Uzbekfilm* (1926–1970)
F. 1745: Uzbek Government Trust for the Cinematographic Industry—*Uzbekkino* (1923–25)
F. 2343: Uzbek Soviet Socialist Republic Ministry of Culture's Principal Directorate for Cinefication and Distribution (1928–63)
F. 2530: Uzbek Bureau for Film Distribution for the Uzbek Soviet Socialist Republic Government Cabinet (1937–67)
F. 2087: Directorate for Artistic Affairs for the Uzbek Soviet Socialist Republic Government Cabinet (early 1936)

### High-Ranking Economic Bodies
F. 89: Uzbek Soviet Socialist Republic Supreme Economic Council (1924–32)—*VSNKH UzSSR*
F. 88: Uzbek Soviet Socialist Republic State Planning Committee (early 1924)—*UzGosPlan*
F. 93: Uzbek Soviet Socialist Republic People's Commissariat for Finances (1925–30)
F. 217: Uzbek Union for Consumer Companies for the Union of Soviet Socialist Republics Central Union of Consumer Companies Union (1925–53)
F. 10: Central Asian State Committee for the Central Asian Economic Council (1925–34)—*SredAzGosPlan*

## Supervisory Bodies

F. 6: Directorate of the Plenipotentiary People's Commissariat of the Union of Soviet Socialist Republics Workers' and Peasants' Inspectorate in Central Asia (1923-31)—*Upolnarkom RKI v Srednei Azii*

F. 41: People's Commissariat of the Turkestan Autonomous Soviet Socialist Republic Workers' and Peasants' Inspectorate (1918-24)

F. 81: Directorate of the Plenipotentiary Committee for Soviet Control of *Sovnarkom* for Uzbekistan (1934-37)

F. 95: People's Commissariat of the Uzbek Soviet Socialist Republic Workers' and Peasants' Inspectorate (1924-32)—*NK RKI*

## Professional Activities

F. 790: Turkestan Region Bureau of the All-Russian Union of Art Workers (1920-21)

F. 791: Plenipotentiary of the Central Committee of the Professional Trade Union of Art Workers of the Union in Turkestan (1924)

F. 792: Republican Committee of the Trade Union of Art Workers (1927-53)

### REPUBLIC OF UZBEKISTAN CENTRAL STATE ARCHIVES FOR CINEMATOGRAPHIC, PHOTOGRAPHIC AND PHONOGRAPHIC DOCUMENTS—*UZBEKISTON RESPUBLIKASI KINO, SURAT VA OVOZLI KHUJJATLAR DAVLAT ARKHIVI* (UzRKSOKh)

### ARCHIVES OF THE BUKHARA REGION

Certain documents were consulted, but they do not correspond to the period under study.

F. 690: Arts Department of the Council of People's Delegates of the Bukhara *Oblast* Executive Committee

F. 898: Department for Cinefication of the Bukhara *Oblast*

### ARCHIVES OF THE REPUBLIC OF UZBEKISTAN ART ACADEMY— *AKADEMIIA ISKUSSTVOZNANIE* (AI)

### Archives of the Republic of Tajikistan

Certain documents were consulted, but they do not correspond to the period under study.

## *Unpublished Archives: Russia (Moscow)*

### RUSSIAN STATE ARCHIVES OF ART AND LITERATURE—*ROSSIISKII GOSUDARSTVENNYI ARKHIV LITERATURY I ISKUSSTVA* (RGALI)

F. 2494: ARK/ARRK – Association of Revolutionary Cinema /Association of Revolutionary Cinema Workers (1923-32)

F. 2680: V. Bassalygo (1903-67)

### Catalogs Consulted

F. 631: Record Group of the Writers' Union

F. 985 and 989: Goskino (1918-25)

F. 2450: Ministry for Cinema (1932-53)

F. 2489: Vostokfil'm
F. 2495: Soviet Cinematography Society of Friends –*Obschestvo Druzei Sovetskogo Kino* ODSK (1926–29)
F. 2497: Sovkino

Russian State Archives of Political and Social History—*Rossiiskii Gosudarstvennyi Arkhiv Sotsial'no-politichesoi Istorii* (RGASPI)

The main record groups consulted were those of the Turkestan Bureau (*Turkbiuro*—F. 61) and the Central Asian Bureau (*Sredazbiuro*—F. 62).

State Archives of the Russian Federation— *Gosurdastvennyi Arkhiv Rossiiskoi Federatsii* (GARF)

F. 8326: Film Production and Distribution Corporation
F. 7816: *Sovnarkom* Union of Soviet Socialist Republics Cinematographic Affairs Committee

Russian State Film Archives—*Gosudarstvennyi Fond Kinofil'mov Rossiiskoi Federatsii* (GFF or Gosfilmofond)

The paper archives (*fil'movye dela*) contain many documents about censorship of films produced in Uzbekistan and numerous documents produced by the Committee for Repertoire Oversight and opinions about Uzbek films in the corpus.

## Published Archives

Alimova, D. A., ed. 2006. *Tragediia sredneasiatskogo kishlaka*. 3 vols. Tashkent, Uzbekistan: Sharq.
Gatagova, L. C., L. P. Kosheleva, and L. A. Rogovaia, eds. 2005. *TsK RKP (b)-VKP (b) i natsional'nyi vopros (1918–1933)*. Moscow: Rosspen.
Karimov, Naim, ed. 2005. *Repressiia 1937–1938, dokumenty i materialy*. Tashkent, Uzbekistan: Sharq.
Vinogradov, V. K. 2001. "Ob osobennostiakh informatsionnykh materialov OGPU kak istochnika po istorii sovetskogo obshchestva." In *"Sovershenno sekretno": Lubianka-Stalinu o polozhenii v strane (1922–1934)*, edited by Iu. L. D'iakov, vol. 1, 31–73. Moscow: IRI RAN.

## Published Primary Sources

Bratoliubov, Sergei. 1976. *Na zare sovetskoi kinematografii*. Moscow: Iskusstvo.
Bunegin, M. 1933. *Massovaia kino-rabota v natsional'nykh raionakh*. Moscow: Roskino.
Chokay [Tchokaieff], Mustafa [Moustapha]. 1928. *Chez les soviets en Asie central: réponse aux communistes français*. Paris: Messageries Hachette.
———. 2001. *Otryvki iz vospominanii o 1917 g*. Moscow: RAN.
Duchène, Ferdinand. 1926. *Kamir, roman d'une femme arabe*. Paris: Albin Michel.
*Ee pravo*. 1932. Moscow: Upravlenie Kinefikatsii SSSR.

Fillipov, I. 1926. *Islam v svete istoricheskogo materializma*. Rostov-on-Don, Russia: Sevkavkniga.
Fitrat, abd al-Ra'uf. 1993. *O'zbek klassik musiqasi tarixi*. Tashkent, Uzbekistan: Fan.
Gaidovskii, G. 1930. "Uzbekistan na plenke," *Kino i Zhizn'* 15:18.
Goldobin, A. 1924. *Kino na territorii SSSR*. Moscow: Gosudarstvennoe izdatel'stvo.
Jdanov, Andreï. 1950. *Sur la littérature, la philosophie et la musique*. Paris: Éditions de la nouvelle critique.
Kefala, M. 1931. "Antireligioznyi kinodoklad 'doch' sviatogo.'" *Antireligioznik* no. 6: 92–96.
———. 1932. *Kak organizovat' anti-religioznyi kino-vecher*. Moscow: Roskino.
Khojaev, Suleiman. 1931. *Khudosizlar qishloqi (kino roman)*. Tashkent, Uzbekistan: Ozneshr.
———. 1933. *Tong Oldidan (Pered rassvetom)*. Moscow: Soagiz.
Klimovich, L. 1937. "Ismailizm i ego reaktsionnaia rol.'" *Antireligioznik* 8: 34–40.
Kosior, Stanislav. 1928. "K itogam obsuzhdeniia voprosov kino." *Revoliutsiia i kul'tura* 6: 5–7.
———. 1929. "Otkrytoe soveshchaniia: vstupitel'noe slovo." In *Puti kino, pervoe vsesoiuznoe partiinoe soveshchanie po kinematografii*, edited by V. S. Ol'khov, 9–13. Moscow: Teakinopechat'.
Kotiev, B. 1931. "Kino sredi natsional'nostei." *Revoliutsiia i natsional'nosti* 5: 68–73.
Krinitskii, A. I. 1929a. "Itog stroitel'stva kino v SSSR i zadachi sovetskoi kinematografii (1)." In *Puti kino, pervoe vsesoiuznoe partiinoe soveshchanie po kinematografii*, edited by V. S. Ol'khov, 15–48. Moscow: Teakinopechat'.
———. 1929b. "Itog stroitel'stva kino v SSSR i zadachi sovetskoi kinematografii (2)." In *Puti kino, pervoe vsesoiuznoe partiinoe soveshchanie po kinematografii*, edited by V. S. Ol'khov, 429–44. Moscow: Teakinopechat'.
Krylov, S. 1928. *Kino vmesto vodki, k vsesoiuznomu partsoveshchaniiu po voprosam kino*. Moscow: Moskovskii Rabochii.
*Krytyi Furgon*. 1932. Moscow: Roskino.
Kurbanbaev, S. 1930. "Zadachi kul'turnoi revoliutsii na sovetskom vostoke." *Revoliutsiia i natsional'nosti* 1:72–75.
Lebedev, N. A. 1939. *Partiia o kino*. Moscow: Goskinoizdat.
Liubimova, Serafima. 1928a. *Rabota partii sredi zhenshchin*. Tashkent, Uzbekistan: Turkpechat'.
———. 1928b. "Uroki 'nastupleniia.'" *Antireligioznik* 2: 20–26.
Lukashevskii, A. 1930. "Voprosy antireligioznoi propagandy." *Revoliutisiia i kul'tura* 19–20: 112–16.
Mesguich, Félix. 1933. *Tours de manivelle: souvenirs d'un chasseur d'images*. Paris: Bernard Grasset.
*Montazhnyi list na kartinu Shakaly ravata*. 1939. Tashkent, Uzbekistan: Komitet po delam iskusstv pri SNK UZSSR.
Norqulov, Naim, and Kamoliddin Rabbimov. 2001. *Oiina (1914–1915)*. Tashkent, Uzbekistan: 'Akademiia' Nashrioti.
Ol'khov, V. S. (ed.). 1929. *Puti Kino, Pervoe vsesoiuznoe partiinoe soveshchanie po kinematografii*. Moscow: Teakinopechat'.
Ostroumov, N. P. 1908. *Sarty, etnograficheskie materialy (obshchii ocherk)*. Tashkent, Uzbekistan.
Pis'mennyi, S. 1928. "O nekotorykh osnovnykh momentakh kul'turnoi revoliutsii v natsrespublikakh Srednei Azii." *Revoliutsiia i kul'tura* 10: 11–20.

Safarov, Grigorii. 1985. *Kolonial'naia revoliutsiia (opyt Turkestana)*. Oxford: Society for Central Asian Studies, Reprint Series 4. First published 1921 by Gosudarstvennoe Izdatel'stvo.
Said-Galiev, S. 1929. "Antireligioznaia rabota sredi musul'man." *Antireligioznik* no. 4: 62–67.
Shestakov, A. V. 1936. "20-letie vosstaniia v Srednei Azii." *Revoliutsiia i natsional'nosti* 9: 41–44.
Shteinberg, E. 1934. *Ocherki istorii Turkmenii*. Moscow.
Shvedchikov. 1929. "Organizatsionnye i khoziaistvennye voprosy sovetskoi kinematografii." In *Puti kino, pervoe vsesoiuznoe partiinoe soveshchanie po kinematografii*, edited by V. S. Ol'khov, 233–54. Moscow: Teakinopechat'.
Stalin, Joseph. 1913. *Marxism and the National Question*. Accessed May 1, 2018. https://www.marxists.org/reference/archive/stalin/works/1913/03a.htm#s1 (accessed July 1, 2018)
———. 1925. "O Politicheskikh zadachakh Universiteta Narodov Vostoka." *Pravda*, May 22.
Stepanov, V. 1928. "Kino i antireligioznaia propaganda." *Antireligioznik* no. 5: 19–23.
Sulaymon [Suleimanov], Hamid [Khamid]. 1966. "Otam haqida." *Kino* (Tashkent) 11: 6–10.
Sultan-Galiev, M. 1921. "Metody antireligioznoi propagandy sredi musul'man." *Zhizn' natsional'nostei* 29.
Trotsky, Leo. "Vodka, tserkov' i kinematograf," *Pravda*, 12 July, 1932, p. 2.
Uspenskii, L. 1927. "K voprosu ob izychenii musul'manstva." *Antireligioznik* 7: 29–31.
Vainshtok, V., and D. Yakobzon. 1926. *Kino i molodezh'*. Moscow: Gosudarstvennoe izdatel'stvo.
Vel'tman, S. 1927. *Zadachi kino na vostoke (pravda i nepravda o vostoke)*. Moscow: Nauchnaia Assotsiatsiia Vostokovedeniia pri Prezidiume TsIK SSSR.
———. 1936. "Ob otstavanii kino v natsrespublikakh." *Revoliutsiia i natsional'nosti* 10: 75–77.
Yakubovskii [Iakubovskii], A. 1941. Iu. *K voprosu ob etnogeneze uzbekskogo naroda*. Tashkent, Uzbekistan: Uzfan.
Yaroslavskii [Iaroslavskii], Emelian. 1928. "Antireligioznaia propaganda i kul'turnaia revoliutsiia." *Revoliutsiia i kul'tura* 5: 31–38.
———. 1929. "Iskusstvo na sluzhbe u religii i iskusstvo bezbozhe." *Antireligioznik* 2: 7–13.

## Full-Length Feature Films

*The Minaret of Death* [Rus. *Minaret smerty*, Uzb. *azhal minareti*] by V. Viskovskii (Bukhkino, 1925).
*The Muslim Woman* [Rus. *Musul'manka*, Uzb. *musulman qyzy*] by D. Bassalygo (Proletkino, 1925).
*Chachvon* [Rus. *Chadra* or *Chachvan*, Uzb. *chachvon*] by M. Averbakh (Uzbekgoskino, 1927).
*The Jackals of Ravat* [Rus. *Shakaly ravata*, Uzb. *ravot qashqirlari*] by K. Gertel' (Uzbekgoskino, 1927).
*The Second Wife* [Rus. *Vtoraia zhena*, Uzb. *ikichi khanum*] by M. Doronin (Uzbekgoskino, 1927).
*From Under the Vaults of the Mosque* [Rus. *Iz-pod svodov mecheti*] by K. Gertel' (Uzbekgoskino, 1928).
*The Leper* [Rus. *Prokazhennaia*] by O. Frelikh (Uzbekgoskino, 1928).
*Her Right* [Rus. *ee pravo*] by G. Cherniak (Uzbekgoskino, 1931).
*The Ishan's Fiancée* [Rus. *Doch' sviatogo*, Uzb. *avliia qizi*] by O. Frelikh (Uzbekgoskino, 1931).

*Upsurge* [Rus. *Pod″em*] by N. Ganiev (Uzbekgoskino, 1931).
*Ramazan* [Rus. and Uzb. *Ramazan*] by N. Ganiev (Uzbekgoskino, 1932).
*Before Dawn* [Rus. *Pered rassvetom*, Uzb. *tong oldidan*] by S. Khojaev (Uzbekgoskino, 1933).
*Jigit* [Rus. *Dzhigit* or *egit*, Uzb. *iigit*] by N. Ganiev (Uzbekgoskino, 1935).
*The Oath* [Rus. *Kliatva*, Uzb. *qasam*] by A. Usol'tsev-Garf (Uzbekgoskino, 1937).

## Periodicals

### Cinema Journals and Newspapers

Cinema journals and newspapers were only published in Moscow and Leningrad. There was no Uzbek cinema newspaper until 1965, when the first issue of *Kino* was published by the Uzbek Soviet Socialist Republic Ministry for Culture. The dates in parentheses correspond to those examined.

*Iskusstvo Kino* (1936–40)
*Kino* published in Moscow (1922–23)
*Kino* published in Leningrad (1926–31)
*Kino i Zhizn'* (1929–30)
*Kinovedcheskie Zapiski* (1988 onward)
*Proletarskoe Kino* (1925–35)
*Proletkino* (1924–25)
*Sovetskii Ekran* (1925–29)
*Sovetskii Kino-Ekran* (1939–40)
*Sovetskoe Kino* (1926–27)

### Technical and Professional Cinema Journals

*Kinofotopromyshlennost'* (1932–34)
*Kinofotokhimpromyshlennost'* (1937)
*Kinomekhanik* (1937–41)
*Rabis* (1929–34)
*Vestnik rabotnikov iskusstva* (1921–26)

### Literary and Cultural Journals

These journals were published monthly in Uzbekistan (Tashkent).
*Er Iuzi* (1925–31)
*Literaturnyi Uzbekistan* published in Russian by the Uzbek Soviet Socialist Republic Writer's Union only as of 1935

### Journals about the Nationalities Policy and Cultural Policy

*Revolutsiia i kul'tura* (1927–30)
*Revolutsiia i natsional'nosti* (1930–37)
*Revolutsiia i pis'mennost'* (1932)

### Journals of Antireligious Propaganda

*Antireligioznik* (1926–41)
*Bezbozhnik* (1925–28)

## Newspapers

### In Russian

*Komsomolets Vostoka* (1927–32), the name of this paper changed in 1932 to *Komsomolets Uzbekistana* (1933–39)
*Pravda* (1924–38)
*Turkestanskaia Pravda* (1922–24); the name of this paper changed in 1925 to *Pravda Vostoka* (1925–38); I also consulted its weekly cultural supplement *Sem' Dnei* (1926–28)
*Vecherniaia Moskva* (1924–37)

### In Uzbek

*Qizil Uzbekiston* (1925–38)

## Secondary Sources

Abdurakhimova, N., and G. Rustamova. 1994. *Kolonial'naia sistema vlasti v Turkestane vo vtoroi polovine XIX-pervoi chetverti XX v.v.* Tashkent, Uzbekistan: Avtoreferat.
Abul-Kasymova, Khanzhara. 1965. *Rozhdenie uzbekskogo kino*. Tashkent, Uzbekistan: Nauka.
———. 1968. *Nabi Ganiev*. Tashkent, Uzbekistan: Ghafur Ghulam.
Abul'khanov, R. 1962. "Bukharo-russkoe kinotovarishchestvo." In *Iz istorii kino* (5th ed.), 53–70. Moscow: Akademiia nauk SSSR.
Agzamkhojaev, Saidakbar. 2006. *Istoriia turkestanskoi avtonomii (turkeston mukhtoriiati)*. Tashkent, Uzbekistan: Toshkent islom universiteti.
Akbarov, Hamidulla. 1993. "Davr fozhiiasini keltirgan tufon," *Toshkent Oqshomi*, 13 April.
———. 2005. *Kino san'ati tarikhi*. Tashkent, Uzbekistan: Toshkent islom universiteti.
Akhrorov, Ato, 1971. *Tadzhikskoe kino*. Dushanbe, Tajikistan: Donish.
———, ed. 1980. *Tadzhikskii ekrani*. Dushanbe, Tajikistan: Irfon.
Alimova, D. A., ed. 2000. *Turkestan v nachale XX veka: k istorii istokov natsional'noi nezavisimosti*, Tashkent, Uzbekistan: Sharq.
Allworth, Edward. 1964. *Uzbek Literary Politics*. London: Mouton.
———. 1990. *The Modern Uzbeks: From the Fourteenth Century to the Present: A Cultural History*. Stanford, CA: Hoover Institution Press.
———. 2002. *Evading Reality: The Devices of Abdalrauf Fitrat, Modern Central Asian Reformist*. Leiden, Netherlands: Brill.
Aminjonov, R. N. 2006. "K istorii pervoi zapisi shashmakoma." *Izvestiia akademii nauk respubliki Tadzhikistan* 2:161–65.
Anderson, Benedict. 1983. *Imagined Communities*. London: Verso.
Arendt, Hannah. 1979. *The Origins of Totalitarianism*. San Diego: Harcourt Brace.
Argenbright, Robert. 2011. "Vanguard of 'Socialist Colonization'? The *Krasnyi Vostok* expedition of 1920." *Central Asian Survey* 30 (3–4): 437–54.
Asfendiarov, S. D. 1935. *Istoriia kazakhskoi SSR (s drevneshikh vremen)*. Alma-Ata, Kazakh Soviet Socialist Republic: Kazakhstanskoe kraevoe izdatel'stvo.
Babajanov, Bakhtiiar. 2004. "Russian Colonial Power in Central Asia as Seen by Local Muslim Intellectuals." In *Looking at the Colonizer: Cross-Cultural Perceptions in Central Asia and the Caucasus, Bengal, and Related Areas*, edited by Beate Beschment and Hans Harder, 75–90. Würzburg, Germany: Ergon.

———. 2007. *Zhurnal 'haqiqat' kar zerkalo religioznogo aspekta v ideologii jadidov*. Tokyo: Nihu Program Islamic Area Studies.
Baldauf, Ingeborg. 1991. "Some Thoughts on the Making of the Uzbek Nation." *Cahiers du monde* 32 (1): 79–96.
Barthes, Roland. 1980. *La Chambre claire: note sur la photographie*. Paris: Gallimard, Seuil, Cahiers du Cinéma.
Barthold, W. 2008. "Abu'l Khayr." In *Encyclopaedia of Islam*, edited by P. Bearman, Th. Bianquis, C. E. Bosworth, E. Van Donzel, and W. P. Heinrichs, vol. 1, 135. Leiden, Netherlands: Brill.
Bayart, Jean-François. 1996. *L'Illusion identitaire*. Paris: Fayard.
———. 2008. "Hégémonie et coercition en Afrique subsaharienne: la 'politique de la chicotte.'" *Politique Africaine* 110: 123–52.
Bayart, Jean-François, and Romain Bertrand. 2006. "De quel 'legs colonial' parle-t-on?" *Esprit* 12: 134–60.
Becker, Howard. 1982. *Art Worlds*. Berkeley: University of California Press.
Becker, Seymour. 2004. *Russia's Protectorates in Central Asia, Bukhara and Khiva (1865–1924)*. London: Routledge Curzon.
Beissinger, Mark R. 1995. "The Persisting Ambiguity of Empire." *Post-Soviet Affairs* 11 (2): 149–84.
———. 2006. "Soviet Empire as 'Family Resemblance.'" *Slavic Review* 65 (2): 294–303.
Benali, Aabdelkader. 1998. *Le Cinéma colonial du Maghreb*. Paris: Cerf.
Benammar Benmansour, Leïla. 2000. "'L'Algérianité.' Ses expressions dans l'édition française (1919–1939): 'Et le livre devient média.'" PhD diss., University of Paris.
Benjamin, Walter. 2010. "The Work of Art in the Age of Its Technological Reproducibility [First version]." *Grey Room* 39: 11–38.
Bennigsen, Alexandre. 1962. "*Mollah Nasreddin* et la presse satrique musulmane de Russie avant 1917." *Cahiers du monde russe* 3 (3): 20.
———. 1975. "The Crisis of the Turkic National Epics (1951–1952): Local Nationalism or Internationalism?" *Canadian Slavonic Papers* 17 (2–3): 463–74.
———. 1986. "Soviet Minority Nationalism in Historical Perspective." In *The Last Empire: Nationality and the Soviet Future*, edited by R. Conquest, 142–47. Stanford, CA: Hoover Institution Press.
Bennigsen, Alexandre, and Chantal Lemercier-Quelquejay. 1960. *Les Mouvements nationaux chez les musulmans de Russie: le "sultangalievisme" au Tatarstan*. Paris: Mouton.
———. 1986. *Sultan Galiev, le père de la révolution tiers-mondiste*. Paris: Fayard.
Bergne, Paul. 2007. *The Birth of Tajikistan: National Identity and the Origins of the Republic*. London: I. B. Tauris.
Bertrand, Romain. 2008. "Politique du moment colonial. Historicités indigènes et rapports vernaculaires au politique en 'situation coloniale.'" *Questions de recherche* 26: 1–49.
Besançon, Alain. (1977) 1996. *Les Origines intellectuelles du léninisme*. Paris: Gallimard.
———. 1980. "L'Empire russe et la domination soviétique." In *Le Concept d'empire*, edited by Maurice Duverger, 365–73. Paris: Presses Universitaires de France.
Bhabha, Homi K. 1997. "L'autre question: stéréotype, discrimination et discours du colonialism." *Les Lieux de la culture*. Paris: Payot: 121–46.
Blitstein, Peter. 2006a. "Cultural Diversity and the Interwar Conjuncture: Soviet Nationality Policy in Its Comparative Context." *Slavic Review* 65 (2): 273–93.

———. 2006b. "Nation and Empire in Soviet History." *Ab Imperio* 1:197–219.
Blum, Alain, and Martine Mespoulet. 2003. *L'Anarchie bureaucratique: statistique et pouvoir sous Staline.* Paris: la Découverte.
Blum, Alain, and Yuri Shapoval. 2012. *Faux coupables: surveillances, aveux et procès en Ukraine soviétique (1924–1934).* Paris: CNRS.
Boulanger, Pierre. 1975. *Le Cinéma colonial: de l'"Atlantide" à "Laurence d'Arabie."* Paris: Seghers.
Brandenberger, David. 2002. *National Bolshevism: Stalinist Mass Culture and the Formation of Modern Russian National Identity (1931–1959).* Cambridge, MA: Harvard University Press.
Bregel, Yuri. 1996. "Notes on the Study of Central Asia." *Papers on Inner Asia* 28: 1–61.
Brower, Daniel. 1994. "Kyrgyz Nomads and Russian Pioneers: Colonization and Ethnic Conflict in the Turkestan Revolt of 1916." *Jahrbücher für die Geschichte Osteuropas* 44 (1): 41–53.
———. 2003. *Turkestan and the Fate of the Russian Empire.* London: Routledge Curzon.
Bryan, Fanny. 1986. "Anti-Islamic Propaganda: *Bezbozhnik* 1925-35." *Central Asian Survey* 5 (1): 29–47.
Buttino, Marco. 1990. "Economic Crisis and Depopulation in Turkestan, 1917–1920." *Central Asian Survey* 9 (4): 59–74.
———. 1991. "Turkestan 1917: la révolution des Russes." *Cahiers du monde russe* 32 (1): 61–78.
———. 1997. "Éthnicité et politique dans la guerre civile: à propos du *basmachestvo* au Fergana." *Cahiers du monde russe* 38 (1–2): 195–222.
Byrnes, Robert. 1991. "Creating the Soviet Historical Profession (1917–1934)." *Slavic Review* 50 (2): 297–308.
Cadiot, Juliette. 2007. *Le Laboratoire impérial: Russie-URSS 1860–1940.* Paris: CNRS.
Cardinal, Serge. 1997. "La mélancolie du nom. Cinéma et identité nationale." *Cinémas* 8 (1–2): 13–33.
Carlisle, Donald S. 1994. "Soviet Uzbekistan: State and Nation in Historical Perspective." In *Central Asia in Historical Perspective*, edited by Beatrice Manz, 91–132. Boulder, CO: Westview.
Caroe, Sir Olaf. 1953. *Soviet Empire: The Turks on Central Asia and Stalinism.* London: Macmillan.
Carrère d'Encausse, Hélène. 1978. *L'Empire éclaté.* Paris: Flammarion.
Castillo, Greg. 1995. "Peoples at an Exhibition: Soviet Architecture and the National Question." *South Atlantic Quarterly* 94 (3): 715–46.
Castro, Teresa. 2008. "Les Archives de la planète d'Albert Kahn." *1895* 54: 57–81.
Chivallon, Christine. 2007. "Retour sur la 'communauté imaginée' d'Anderson. Essai de clarification théorique d'une notion restée floue." *Raisons Politiques* 27:131–72.
Chomentowski, Gabrielle. 2009. "L'Amitié des peuples à travers l'objectif de la caméra soviétique. Politique des nationalités et cinéma en URSS de 1928 à 1941." PhD diss., University of Paris.
Chulpan [Tchulpân], 'Abd al-Hamid Sulaymân. 2010. *Nuit.* Translated by Stéphane A. Dudoignon. Paris: Bleu Autour.
Compagnon, Antoine. 1998. *Le Démon de la théorie: littérature et sens commun.* Paris: Seuil.
Conquest, Robert. 1970. *La Grande terreur.* Paris: Stock.
———, ed. 1986. *The Last Empire: Nationality and the Soviet Future.* Stanford, CA: Hoover Institution Press.

Corriou, Morgan. 2012. "Tunis et les 'Temps modernes': les débuts du cinématographe dans la Régence (1896–1908)." *Cahiers du CERES* 5:95–133.
Dallet, Sylvie. 2003. "Filmer les colonies, filtrer le colonialisme." In *Le Livre noir du colonialisme: de l'extermination à la repentance (XVIE–XXIE siècles)*, edited by Marc Ferro, 939–69. Paris: Hachette.
David-Fox, Michael. 1999. "What Is Cultural Revolution?" *Russian Review* 58 (2): 181–201.
De Meaux, Lorraine. 2010. *La Russie et la tentation de l'Orient*. Paris: Fayard.
Doyle, Michael W. 1986. *Empires*. Ithaca, NY: Cornell University Press.
Dreyfus, Michel, and Roland Lew. 2001. "Communisme et violence." In *Le Siècle des communismes*, edited by M. Dreyfus, Bruno Groppo, Claudio Ingerflom, R. Lew, Claude Pennetier, Bernard Pudal, and Serge Wolikow, 715–37. Paris: Éditions de l'atelier/Éditions ouvrière.
Drieu, Cloé. 2005. "Alisher Navoi: prix Staline 1948. Cinéma et politique des nationalités." *Théorème* 8:119–27.
———. 2010a. "Cinema, Local Power and the Central State: Agencies in Early Anti-Religious Propaganda in Uzbekistan." *Die Welt des Islams* 50:532–63.
———. 2010b. "Nabi Ganiev, cinéaste ouzbek sous Staline: l'idéologie à l'épreuve de la diffraction nationale." *Dissidences* 9. Accessed October 14, 2003. http://dissidences.net/complements_vol9.htm.
———. 2012. "De la pratique en 'situation colonial' aux usages totalitaires: le film et son environnement sonore et visuel en Asie centrale (1908–1937)." *Cahiers du CERES* 5:231–60.
———. 2015. "Grande Guerre Patriotique et propagande cinématographique en Ouzbékistan: les motifs du renouveau nationaliste (1937–1945)." In *Écrans d'Orient: Propagande, innovation et résistance dans les cinémas de Turquie, d'Iran et d'Asie centrale (1897–1945)*, edited by Cloé Drieu, 219–66. Paris: Karthala.
Dudoignon, Stéphane A. 1993. "Changements politiques et historiographie en Asie centrale (Tadjikistan et Ouzbékistan, 1987–1993)." *Cemoti* 16:85–134.
———. 1996a. "Djadidisme, mirasisme, islamisme." *Cahiers du monde russe* 37 (1–2): 13–40.
———. 1996b. "La question scolaire à Boukhara et au Turkestan russe, du 'premier renouveau' à la soviétisation (fin du XVIIIe siècle–1937)." *Cahiers du monde russe* 37 (1–2): 133–210.
———. 2002. "Islam et nationalisme en Asie centrale au début de la période soviétique (1924–1937). L'exemple de l'Ouzbékistan à travers quelques sources littéraires." *Revue des mondes musulmans et de la méditerranée* 95–98:127–65.
———, ed. 2008. *Central Eurasian Reader*. Vol. 1. Berlin: Klaus Schwarz.
———, ed. 2010. *Central Eurasian Reader*. Vol. 2. Berlin: Klaus Schwarz.
———. 2011. "From Revival to Mutation: The Religious Personnel of Islam in the Tajik SSR from the Opening of the Gulag to the Dissolution of the Soviet Union (1955–1991)." *Central Asian Survey* 30 (1): 53–80.
Duverger, Maurice, ed. 1980. *Le Concept d'empire*. Paris: Presses Universitaires de France.
Edgar, Adrienne. 2006. "Bolshevism, Patriarchy, and the Nation: The Soviet 'Emancipation' of Muslim Women in Pan-Islamic Perspective." *Slavic Review* 65 (2): 252–72.
Eisele, John. 2002. "The Wild East: Deconstructing the Language of Genre in the Hollywood Eastern." *Cinema Journal* 41 (4): 68–94.
Eisener, Reinhard. 1994. "Some Problems of Research Concerning the National Delimitation of Soviet Central Asia in 1924." In *Bamberger Mittelasienstudien*, edited by Bert Fragner, 109–17. Berlin: Klaus Schwarz.

Ellul, Jacques. 1990. *Propagandes*. Paris: Economica.
Ernazarov T. E., and Akbarov A. I. 1977. *Istoriira pechati Uzbekistana*. Tashkent: Uqituvchi.
Fedtke, Gero. 1998. "Jadids, Young Bukharans, Communists and the Bukharan Revolution: From an Ideological Debate in the Early Soviet Union." In *Muslim Culture in Russia and Central Asia from the 18th to the Early 20th Centuries*, edited by Anke Von kügelgen, Michael Kemper, and Allan Frank, 483–512. Berlin: Klaus Schwarz.
———. 2007. "How Bukharans Turned into Uzbeks and Tadjiks: Soviet Nationalities Policy in the Light of Personal Rivalry." In *Patterns of Transformation in and around Uzbekistan*, edited by Paolo Sartori and Tommaso Trevisani, 19–50. Reggio Emilia, Italy: Edizioni Diabasis.
Ferro, Marc. (1977) 1993. *Cinéma et histoire*. Paris: Gallimard.
———. 1995. "Colonialisme russe-soviétique et colonialisme occidentaux : une brève comparaison." *Revue d'études comparatives Est-Ouest* 26 (4): 75–80.
———. 2003. "Le colonialisme, envers de la colonisation." In *Le Livre noir du colonialisme. xvie–xxie: de l'extermination à la repentance*, edited by Marc Ferro, 9–49. Paris: Robert Laffont.
Fitzpatrick, Sheila. 1978. "Cultural Revolution as Class War." In *Cultural Revolution in Russia (1928–1931)*, edited by Sheila Fitzpatrick, 8–40. Bloomington: Indiana University Press.
Fraser, Glenda. 1987a. "Basmachi-I." *Central Asian Survey* 6 (1): 1–73.
———. 1987b. "Basmachi-II." *Central Asian Survey* 6 (2): 7–42.
Frodon, Jean-Michel. 1998. *La Projection nationale: cinéma et nation*. Paris: Odile Jacob.
Frolova-Walker, Marina. 1998. "'Nation in Form, Socialist in Content': Musical Nation-Building in the Soviet Republic," *Journal of the American Musicological Society* 51 (2): 331–71.
Gak, A. 1962. "K istorii sozdaniia sovkino." In *Iz istorii kino* (5th ed.), 131–44. Moscow: Akademiia Nauk SSSR.
Gellner, Ernest. (1983) 1997. *Nations and Nationalism*. Oxford: Basil Blackwell.
Germanov, Valerii. 1998. "Expansion of the Marxist Historiographic Mentality in Central Asia, or Specialties of International 'Witch-Hunt' in the 1930s." *Izhtimoii fikr-obshchestvennoe mnenie* 1: 54–63.
Golender, Boris. 2009. "The First Uzbek Photographer." *San'at*, no. 2. http://www.sanat.orexca.com/eng/4-09/boris_golender.shtml.
Golomshtok, Igor'. 1994. *Totalitarnoe iskusstvo*. Moscow: Galart.
Gretton, George, ed. 1964. *Communism and Colonialism: Essays*. London: Macmillan.
Günther, Olaf. 2008. *Die Dorboz im Ferghanatal: Erkundungen im Alltag und der Geschichte einer Gauklerkultur*. Frankfurt: Peter Lang.
Happel, Jörn. 2010. *Nomadische Lebenswelten und zarische Politik: der Aufstand in Zentralasien 1916*. Stuttgart: Franz Steiner.
Haugen, Arne. 2003. *The Establishment of National Republics in Soviet Central Asia*. Basingstoke, UK: Palgrave Macmillan.
Heller, Michel. 1985. *La Machine et les rouages: la formation de l'homme soviétique*. Paris: Calmann-Lévy.
Hirsch, Francine. 2000. "Toward an Empire of Nations: Border-Making and the Formation of Soviet National Identities." *Russian Review* 59 (2): 201–26.
———. 2005. *Empire of Nations*. Ithaca, NY: Cornell University Press.
Hjort, Mette, and Scott Mackenzie, eds. 2000. *Cinema and Nation*. London: Routledge.

Hobsbawm, Eric. 1990. *Nations and Nationalism since 1780: Programme, Myth, Reality.* Cambridge: Cambridge University Press.

Hodgson, Katharine. 1998. "The Poetry of Rudyard Kipling in Soviet Russia." *Modern Language Review* 93 (4): 1058–71.

Honarpisheh, Farbod. 2004. "The Oriental 'Other' in Soviet Cinema, 1929–34." *Critique: Critical Middle Eastern Studies* 13 (2): 185–201.

Hosejko, Lubomir. 2001. *Histoire du cinéma ukrainien.* Die, France: Éditions à Die.

Husband, William. 1998. "Soviet Atheism and Russian Orthodox Strategies of Resistance, 1917–1932." *Journal of Modern History* 70 (1): 74–107.

Ingerflom, Claudio Sergio. 1995. "Communistes contre castrats (1929–1930). Les enjeux d'un conflit." In *La Secte russe des castrats*, edited by V. Volkov, xi–lxii, Paris: Les Belles Lettres.

Isoart, Paul. 1981. "Approche constitutionnelle du problème des nationalités en URSS (1920–1940)." In *L'Expérience soviétique et le problème national dans le monde (1920–1939). Actes du colloque organisé par l'Institut national des langues et civilisations orientales,* 159–99. Paris: INALCO.

Jumaev, Alexandr. 1993. "Power Structures, Cultural Policy and Traditional Music in Soviet Central Asia." *Yearbook for Traditional Music* 25: 43–50.

Kaiumov, Malik. 1982. *Zhizn' moia—kinematograf.* Tashkent, Uzbekistan: Ghafur Ghulam.

Kamp, Marianne. 2001a. "Remembering the Hujum: Uzbek Women's Words." *Central Asia Monitor* 1: 1–12.

———. 2001b. "Three Lives of Saodat: Communist, Uzbek, Survivor." *Oral History Review* 28 (2): 21–58.

———. 2006. *The New Woman in Uzbekistan: Islam, Modernity and Unveiling under Communism.* Seattle: University of Washington Press.

Karasar, Hasan Ali. 2002. "Chicherin on the Delimitation of Turkestan: Native Bolsheviks versus Soviet Foreign Policy. Seven Letters from the Russian Archives on razmezhevanie." *Central Asian Survey* 21 (2): 199–209.

Karimov, Naim. 1992a. "Uzbek kinosining qaldirghochi." *Nafosat*, no. 1: 24–26.

———. 1992b. "Uzbek kinosining qaldirghochi." *Nafosat*, no. 2: 25–27.

———. 1992c. "Uzbek kinosining qaldirghochi." *Nafosat*, no. 3: 14–15.

———. 1993. "Uzbek kinosining qaldirghochi." *Nafosat*, no. 4: 18–19.

———. 2005. *Repressia.* Tashkent, Uzbekistan: Sharq.

Keller, Shoshanna. 1992. "Islam in Soviet Central Asia, 1917–1930: Soviet Policy and the Struggle for Control." *Central Asian Survey* 11 (1): 25–50.

———. 2001a. "Conversion to the New Faith: Marxism-Leninism and Muslims in the Soviet Empire." In *Of Religion and Empire, Missions, Conversions and Tolerance in Tsarist Russia*, edited by Robert Geraci and Michail Khodarkovsky, 311–34. Ithaca, NY: Cornell University Press.

———. 2001b. *To Moscow, Not Mecca: The Soviet Campaign against Islam in Central Asia 1917–1941.* Westport, CT: Praeger.

———. 2003. "The Central Asian Bureau, an Essential Tool in Governing Soviet Turkestan." *Central Asian Survey* 22 (2–3): 281–97.

Kenez, Peter. 1992. *Cinema and Soviet Society 1917–1953.* Cambridge: Cambridge University Press.

Kepley, Vance. 1996. "The First Perestroika: Soviet Cinema under the First Five-Year lan." *Cinema Journal* 35 (4): 31–53.

Khalid, Adeeb. 1998. *The Politics of Muslim Cultural Reform*. Berkeley: University of California Press.

———. 2000. "Russian History and the Debate over Orientalism." *Kritika: Explorations in Russian and Eurasian History* 1 (4): 691–99.

———. 2001. "Nationalizing the Revolution in Central Asia: The Transformation of Jadidism (1917–1920)." In *A State of Nations: Empire and Nation-Making in the Age of Lenin and Stalin*, edited by Ronald Suny and Terry Martin, 145–62. Oxford: Oxford University Press.

———. 2004. "Nation into History: The Origins of National Historiography in Central Asia." In *Devout Societies vs Impious States? Transmitting Islamic Learning in Russia, Central Asia, and China through the Twentieth Century*, edited by S. A. Dudoignon, 127–45. Berlin: Klaus Schwarz.

———. 2005. "Pan-Islamism in Practice: The Rhetoric of Muslim Unity and Its Uses." In *Late Ottoman Society: The Intellectual Legacy*, edited by Elisabeth Özdalga, 201–24. London: Routledge Curzon.

———. 2006a. "Backwardness and the Quest for Civilization: Early Soviet Central Asia in Comparative Perspective." *Slavic Review* 65 (2): 231–51.

———. 2006b. "Between Empire and Revolution. New Work on Soviet Central Asia." *Kritika: Explorations in Russian and Eurasian History* 7 (4): 865–84.

———. 2007a. "The Fascination of Revolution: Central Asian Intellectuals (1917–1927)." In *Empire, Islam, and Politics in Central Eurasia*, edited by Tomohiko Uyama, 137–52. Sapporo, Japan: SRC.

———. 2007b. *Islam after Communism: Religion and Politics in Central Asia*. Berkeley: University of California Press.

———. 2010. "The Bukharan People's Soviet Republic in the Light of Muslim Sources." *Die Welt des Islams* 50 (3–4): 335–61.

Khamraeva, Asal. 2006. "La Construction des frontières en Asie centrale soviétique: limites nationales et logiques économiques." DEA thesis, École des hautes études en sciences sociales.

Khlevniuk, Oleg. 1998. "Les Mécanismes de la grande terreur des années 1937–1938 au Turkménistan." *Cahiers du monde russe* 39 (1–2): 197–208.

Khojaev, Faizulla. 1970. *Izbrannye trudy v trekh tomakh*. Tashkent, Uzbekistan: Fan. Accessed October 2003. http://uz-left.narod.ru/txt/hodzhaev/39.html.

Kolarz, Walter. 1952. *Russia and Her Colonies*. London: G. Philipp.

Komatsu, Hisao. 1992. "The Turkic Federalist Party in Turkistan: A Preliminary Analysis." *Bulletin of the Association for the Advancement of Central Asian Research* 5 (1): 44–50. http://vlib.iue.it/carrie/texts/carrie_books/paksoy-4/5-1.html.

Kopp, Anatole. 1967. *Ville et revolution*. Paris: Anthropos.

Lacasse, Germain. 2000. *Le Bonimenteur de vues animées*. Québec: Nota Bene.

Laruelle, Marlène. 2008. "Stalinisme et nationalisme. L'introduction du concept d'ethnogénèse dans les historiographies d'Asie centrale." In *D'Une édification l'autre: socialisme et national dans l'espace (post-)communiste*, edited by M. Laruelle and Catherine Servant, 201–34. Paris: Petra.

Laurent, Natacha. 2000. *L'Œil du Kremlin: cinéma et censure en URSS sous Staline (1928–1953)*. Paris: Privat.

Lewin, Moshe. 1982. "Aux prises avec le stalinisme: quelques réflexions historiques." *Actes de la recherche en sciences sociales* 43 (1): 71–82.

———. 1985. *La Formation du système soviétique*. Paris: Gallimard.
Leyda, Jay. 1976. *Kino: histoire du cinéma russe et soviétique*. Lausanne, Switzerland: l'Âge d'homme.
Lirou, Raphaëlle. 2009. *La Russie entre fédération et empire. Contribution à la définition constitutionnelle de l'État russe*. Clermont-Ferrand, France: Fondation Varenne.
Listov, Viktor. 1991. "Early Soviet Cinema: The Spontaneous and the Planned, 1917–1924." *Historical Journal of Film, Radio and Television* 11 (2): 124–25.
Luizard, Pierre-Jean. 2008. *Laïcités autoritaire en terres d'islam*. Paris: Fayard.
Lyons, Shawn. 2001. "Resisting Colonialism in the Uzbek Historical Novel *Kecha va Kunduz* (Night and Day), 1936." *Inner Asia* 3 (2): 175–92.
———. 2003. "Chase Away This Pig from the Mosque: Eastern Politics in the Indian Dramas of Abdurauf Fitrat." *Central Asian Survey* 22 (2–3): 299–313.
Mac Chesney, R. D. 2008. "Özbeg." In *Encyclopaedia of Islam*, edited by P. Bearman, Th. Bianquis, C. E. Bosworth, E. Van Donzel, and W. P. Heinrichs, vol. 8, 132–33. Leiden, Netherlands: Brill.
Manley, Rebecca. 2009. *To the Tashkent Station: Evacuation and Survival in the Soviet Union at War*. Ithaca, NY: Cornell University Press.
Martin, Terry. 2001. *The Affirmation Action Empire: Nations and Nationalism in the Soviet Union (1923–1939)*. Ithaca, NY: Cornell University Press.
———. 2002. "The Soviet Union as Empire: Salvaging a Dubious Analytical Category." *Ab Imperio* 2: 91–105.
Massel, Gregory. 1947. *The Surrogate Proletariat*. Princeton, NJ: Princeton University Press.
Mauss, Marcel. 2004. *Sociologie et Anthropologie*. Paris: Presses Universitaires de France.
Memmi, Albert. 1985. *Portrait du colonisé, portrait du colonisateur*. Paris: Gallimard/folio.
Metz, Christian. (1977) 2002. *Le Signifiant imaginaire*. Paris: Christian Bourgeois.
Mezhenina, E. 1962. *Agitpoezd 'Krasnyi vostok'*. Tashkent, Uzbekistan: Gosizdatel'stvo UzSSR.
Michaels, Paula. 2003. *Curative Powers: Medicine and Empire in Stalin's Soviet Central Asia*. Pittsburgh, PA: University of Pittsburgh Press.
Miller, Jamie. 2006. "The Purges of Soviet Cinema." *Studies in Russian and Soviet Cinema* 1 (1): 5–26.
———. 2010. *Soviet Cinema: Politics and Persuasion under Stalin*. London: I. B. Tauris.
Motyl, Alexander J. 2001. *Imperial Ends. The Decay, Collapse, and Revival of Empires*. New York: Columbia University Press.
Mozukhin, O. 2006. *Pravo na repressii*. Moscow: Kuchkovo Pole.
Murphy, Christopher. 1992. "Abdullah Qadiriy and the Bolsheviks. From Reform to Revolution." In *Muslims in Central Asia*, edited by Jo-Ann Gross, 190–201. Durham, NC: Duke University Press.
Nattiez, Jean-Jacques. 1974. "Sur les relations entre sociologie et sémiologie musicales." *International Review of the Aesthetics and Sociology of Music* 5 (1): 61–75.
Northrop, Douglas. 2004. *Veiled Empire: Gender and Power in Stalinist Central Asia*. Ithaca, NY: Cornell University Press.
Obiya, Chika. 2001. "When Faizullah Khojaev Decided to Be an Uzbek." In *Islam and Politics in Russia and Central Asia*, edited by S. A. Dudoignon and H. Komatsu, 99–118. London: Kegan Paul.

O'Brien, Charles. 1997. "The 'Cinéma Colonial' of 1930s France: Film Narration as Spatial Practice." In *Visions of the East: Orientalism in Film*, edited by Matthew Bernstein and Gaylyn Studlar, 99–129. London: I. B. Tauris.
Ohayon, Isabelle. 2006. *La Sédentarisation des Kazakhs dans l'URSS de Staline: collectivisation et changement social (1928–1945)*. Paris: IFEAC/Maisonneuve et Larose.
Panofsky, E. 1969. *L'Œuvre d'art et ses significations*. Paris: Gallimard.
Payne, Matthew J. 2001a. *Stalin's Railroad: Turksib and the Building of Socialism*. Pittsburgh, PA: University of Pittsburgh Press.
———. 2001b. "Viktor Turin's *Turksib* (1929) and Soviet Orientalism." *Historical Journal of Film, Radio and Television* 21 (1): 37–62.
Penati, Beatrice. 2007. "The Reconquest of Eastern Bukhara: The Struggle against the Basmachi as a Prelude to Sovietization." *Central Asian Survey* 26 (4): 521–38.
Petrone, Karen. 2000. *Life Has Become More Joyous, Comrades: Celebrations in the Time of Stalin*. Bloomington: Indiana University Press.
Pianciola, Niccolo. 2008. "Décoloniser l'Asie Centrale? Bolchéviks et colons au Semirechie (1920–1922)." *Cahiers du monde russe* 49 (1): 101–43.
———. 2009. *Stalinismo di Frontiera, Colonizzazione Agricola, Sterminio dei Nomadi e Costruzione Statale in Asia Centrale (1905–1936)*. Rome: Viella.
Pichon-Bonin, Cécile. 2004. "Entre engagement politique et expression picturale: éléments d'analyse pour un tableau de Serafima Rjangina." *Cahiers d'études slaves* 8: 59–76.
Pipes, Richard. 1954. *The Formation of the Soviet Union: Communism and Nationalism 1917–1923*. Cambridge, MA: Harvard University Press.
Pomian, Krzystof. 1995. "Totalitarisme." *Vingtième Siècle. Revue d'histoire* 47: 4–23.
Pozner, Valérie. 2005. "Le bonimenteur 'rouge': Retour sur la question de l'oralité à propos du cas soviétique." *Cinémas* 14 (2–3): 143–78.
Pruner, Ludmila Zebrina. 1992. "The New Zemlianukhin Wave in Kazakh Cinema." *Slavic Review* 51 (4): 791–801.
Qosimov, Begali. 1996. "Sources littéraires et principaux traits distinctifs du djadidisme turkestanais (début du XXe siècle)." *Cahiers du monde russe* 37 (1–2): 107–32.
Radvanyi, Jean, ed. 1988. *Le Cinéma géorgien*. Paris: Centre Georges Pompidou.
———, ed. 1992. *Le Cinéma d'Asie centrale soviétique*. Paris: Centre Georges Pompidou.
———, ed. 1993. *Le Cinéma arménien*. Paris: Centre Georges Pompidou.
Rajabov, Sali Ashurovich. 1955. *Rol' velikogo russkogo naroda v istoricheskikh sud'bakh narodov Srednei Azii*. Tashkent, Uzbekistan: Gosizdatel'stvo UZSSR.
Ritter, William S. 1985. "The Final Phase in the Liquidation of Anti-Soviet Resistance in Tadzhikistan: Ibrahim Bek and the Basmachi, 1924–1931." *Soviet Studies* 37 (4): 484–93.
———. 1990. "Revolt in the Mountains: Fuzail Maksum and the Occupation of Garm, Spring 1929." *Journal of Contemporary History* 25 (4): 547–80.
Robin, Régine. 1986. *Le Réalisme socialiste, une esthétique impossible*. Paris: Payot.
Ro'i, Yacov. 2000. *Islam in the Soviet Union: From World War I to Perestroika*. London: Hurst.
Rosenberg, William G. 1991. "Introduction: NEP Russia as a 'Transitional' Society." In *Russia in the Era of NEP*, edited by Sheila Fitzpatrick, Alexander Rabinowitch, and Richard Stites, 1–11. Bloomington: Indiana University Press.
Rouland, Michael. 2005, "Creating a Cultural Nation: Alexander Zataevich in Kazakstan." *Comparative Studies of South Asia, Africa and the Middle East* 3: 533–53.

Rouland, Michael, Gulnara Abikeyeva, and Birgit Beumers, eds. 2013. *Cinema in Central Asia: Rewriting Cultural History*. London: I. B. Tauris.
Roy, Olivier. 1997. *La Nouvelle asie centrale ou la fabrication des nations*. Paris: Seuil.
Rubailo, A. I. 1976. *Partiinoe rukovodstvo razvitiem kinoiskusstva (1928–1937)*. Moscow: Izdatel'stvo Moskovskogo Universiteta.
Sahadeo, Jeff. 2007. *Russian Colonial Society in Tashkent: 1865–1923*. Bloomington: Indiana University Press.
Said, Edward. 1979. *Orientalism*. New York: Vintage Books.
Salys, Rymgaila. 2009. *The Musical Comedy Films of Grigorii Aleksandrov: Laughing Matters*. Bristol, UK: Intellect.
Samson, Pierre. 1992. "Marc Ferro, de Braudel à Histoire parallèle", *CinémAction* 65: 53–60.
Sanborn, Joshua. 2001. "Family, Fraternity, and Nation-Building in Russia (1905–1925)." In *A State of Nations: Empire and Nation-Making in the Age of Lenin and Stalin*, edited by Ronald G. Suny and Terry Martin, 93–110. Oxford: Oxford University Press.
Sartori, Paolo. 2007. "The Tashkent 'Ulamâ' and the Soviet State (1920–1938): A Preliminary Research Note Based on NKVD Documents." In *Patterns of Transformation in and around Uzbekistan*, edited by P. Sartori and Tommasso Trevisani, 161–84. Reggio Emilia, Italy: Diabasis.
———. 2010. "What Went Wrong? The Failure of Soviet Policy on *Shar'ia* Courts in Turkestan (1917–1923)." *Die Welt Des Islams* 50: 397–434.
Schimmelpenninck van der Oye, David. 2009. "Vassilij V. Vereshchagin's Canvases of Central Asian Conquest." *Cahiers d'Asie centrale* 17–18: 179–209.
———. 2010. *Russian Orientalism: Asia in the Russian Mind from Peter the Great to the Emigration*. New Haven, CT: Yale University Press.
Schmulevitch, Éric. 1997. *Une décennie de cinéma soviétique en textes (1919–1930): le système derrière la fable*. Paris: L'Harmattan.
Schoeberlein-Engel, John. 1994. "Identity in Central Asia: Construction and Contention in the Conception of 'Özbek,' 'Tâjik,' 'Muslim,' 'Samarqandi' and Other Groups." PhD thesis, Harvard University.
Scott, James C. 1990. *Domination and the Arts of Resistance: Hidden Transcripts*. New Haven, CT: Yale University Press.
Semenov, A. 1940. *Portrety epokhi Navoi*. Tashkent: Gostekhizdat UzSSR.
Shlapentokh, Dmitry, and Vladimir Shlapentokh. 1993. *Soviet Cinematography (1918–1991), Ideological Conflict and Social Reality*. New York: Aldine de Gruyer.
Siranov, K. 1966. *Kino Iskusstvo sovetskogo Kazakhstana*. Alma-Ata: Kazakhstan.
Slavin, David H. 1997. "French Cinema's Other First Wave: Political and Racial Economies of 'Cinema Colonial' (1918–1934)." *Cinema Journal* 37 (1): 23–46.
Slezkine, Yuri. 1994. "The USSR as a Communal Apartment, or How a Socialist State Promoted Ethnic Particularism." *Slavic Review* 53 (2): 414–52.
———. 2000. "Commentary: Imperialism as the Highest Stage of Socialism." *Russian Review* 59 (2): 227–34.
Smith, Michael G. 1997. "Cinema for the 'Soviet East': National Fact and Revolutionary Fiction in Early Azerbaijani Film." *Slavic Review* 56 (4): 645–78.
Sorlin, Pierre. 2008. "Comment aborder le problème de la réception? L'exemple de la guerre civile espagnole." Paper presented at the Réception des objets médiatiques conference, Université Paris I and Université Paris III, Centre Michelet, January.

Stites, Richard. 1991. "Bolshevik Ritual Building in the 1920s." In *Russia in the Era of NEP*, edited by Sheila Fitzpatrick, Alexander Rabinowitch, and R. Stites, 295–309. Bloomington: Indiana University Press.

———. 1992. *Russian Popular Culture: Entertainment and Society since 1900*. Cambridge: Cambridge University Press.

Subtelny, Maria Eva. 1993. "Mir 'Ali Shir Nawa'i," *Encyclopédie de l'Islam*, vol. 7: 91–92

Studlar, Gaylyn. "'Out Salomeing Salome': Dance, The New Woman, and Fan Magazine," *Michigan Quaterly Review* 34 (4): 487–510.

Suny, Ronald G. 2001a. "Constructing Primordialism: Old Histories for New Nations." *Journal of Modern History* 73: 871–78.

———. 2001b. "The Empire Strikes Out: Imperial Russia, 'National' Identity, and Theory of Empire." In *A State of Nations: Empire and Nation-Making in the Age of Lenin and Stalin*, edited by R. G. Suny and Terry Martin, 23–66. Oxford: Oxford University Press.

Taylor, Richard. 1979. *The Politics of the Soviet Cinema (1917–1929)*. Cambridge: Cambridge University Press.

Tchakhotine, Serge. (1939) 2006. *Le Viol des foules par la propagande politique*. Paris: Gallimard.

Tillet, Lowell. 1969. *The Great Friendship: Soviet Historians on the Non-Russian Nationalities*. Chapel Hill: University of North Carolina Press.

Traverso, Enzo, ed. 2001. *Le Totalitarisme: le xxe siècle en débat*. Paris: Seuil.

Tsikounas, Myriam. 1992. *Les Origines du cinéma soviétique: un regard neuf*. Paris: Cerf.

Tumarkin, Nina. 1983. *Lenin Lives!* Cambridge, MA: Harvard University Press.

Turdiev, Sherali. 1996. "Rol' Rossii v podavlenii jadidskogo dvizheniia." *Tsentral'naia Aziia* 1. http://www.ca-c.org/journal/13-1998/st_15_turdiev.shtml.

———. 2005. "Khojaev Suleiman." In *Uzbek Millii Ensiklopediasi*, vol. 9, 550. Tashkent, Uzbekistan.

Tursunov, Kh. 1962. *Vosstanie 1916 goda v Srednei Azii i kazakhstane*. Tashkent, Uzbekistan: Gozizdatel'stvo UZSSR.

Tursunov, T. 1983. *Oktiabr'skaia revoliutsiia i uzbekskii teatr*. Tashkent, Uzbekistan: Fan.

Vichnevski, Anatoli. 1995. "L'Asie centrale post-soviétique: entre le colonialisme et la modernité." *Revue d'études comparatives Est-Ouest* 26 (4): 101–23.

Volkov, Solomon. 1980. *Témoignages: les mémoires de Dimitri Chostakovitch*. Paris: Albin Michel.

Werth, Nicolas. 1993. "De la soviétologie en général et des archives russes en particulier." *Le Débat* 77:126–44.

———. (1996) 2001. "Totalitarisme ou révisionnisme? L'histoire soviétique, une histoire en chantier." In *Le Totalitarisme: le xxe siècle en débat*, edited by Enzo Traverso, 878–96. Paris: Seuil.

———. 2006. "Les opérations de masses de la 'grande terreur' en URSS, 1937-38." *Bulletin de l'IHTP* 86:1–167.

———. 2007. *La Terreur et le désarroi: Staline et son système*. Paris: Perrin.

———. 2009. *L'Ivrogne et la marchande de fleurs: autopsie d'un meurtre de masse (1937–1938)*. Paris: Tallandier.

Werth, Nicolas, and Alain Blum. 2010. "La grande terreur des années 1937–38: un profond renouveau historiographique." *Vingtième Siècle, revue d'histoire* 107:3–19.

Widdis, Emma. 2003a. "Les représentations des frontières dans le cinéma soviétique des années 1930: une esthétique de la conquête." In *Le Cinéma "stalinien": questions d'histoire*, edited by Natacha Laurent, 111–21. Toulouse, France: Presses Universitaires du Mirail/La Cinémathèque de Toulouse.

———. 2003b. *Visions of a New Land: Soviet Film from the Revolution to the Second World War*. New Haven, CT: Yale University Press.

Yanov-Yanovskaia, N. 1969. *Muzyka uzbekskogo kino*. Tashkent, Uzbekistan: Fan.

Yarmatov, Kamil, 1987. *Vozvrashchenie*. Tashkent, Uzbekistan: Ghafur Ghulam.

Youngblood, Denise. 1991a. "The Fate of Soviet Popular Cinema during the Stalin Revolution." *Russian Review* 50 (2): 148–62.

———. 1991b. *Soviet Cinema in the Silent Era (1918–1935)*. Austin: University of Texas Press.

Zarcone, Thierry. 2003–4. "Les danses *naqshbandî* en Asie centrale et au Xinjiang: histoire et actualité." *Journal of the History of Sufism*, no. 4: 181–98.

Zemlianukhin, Sergei. 1994. *Fil'my Rossii: Katalog*. Moscow: Progress.

Ziiaev, K. 1991. "Natsional'no-osvoboditel'noe vosstanie 1916 goda v Turkestane." *Obshchestvennye nauki v uzbekistane* 7: 27–36.

# Index

*adat*, 92
agency, 5, 7
*agitka*, 108, 173
*Alisher Navo'i* (film), xiv, 231
Alma-Ata, 3
Andijan, 29, 33, 95, 144, 148, 213, 233, 237
anticolonial, 8, 57, 71, 72, 75, 191–193, 197
anticolonialism, 8, 183
antireligious, 111–115, 117, 120, 142, 149, 164, 167, 170–174, 181, 200, 201
Armenian, xii, 101, 216, 220
Association of Cinema Workers, 63, 65, 96, 101, 109, 239
authority: 14, 15, 16, 17, 29, 36, 54, 65, 73, 86, 89, 115, 123, 126, 127, 135, 137, 138, 139, 142, 151, 166, 171, 174, 177, 193, 200, 202, 209, 225, 229, 239; administrative, 150; Bolshevik, 11, 27, 111, 112; central, 20, 26, 27, 41, 42, 86, 96, 127, 166; cinema, 36; coercive, 166; cultural, 86; economic, 156; education, 32, 38, 48, 49, 146; film, 36; government, 166; imperial, 184; judicial, 33; Karatag, 138; literary, 126; local, 137, 138, 140, 141, 144, 152; military, 26; planning, 181; political, 56, 65, 95, 165; regional, 147; regulatory, 165, 182; religious, 9; Russian, 10, 69, 78, 186; Soviet, 28, 35, 43, 85, 90, 98, 111, 114, 129, 136, 148, 175, 181, 193, 205, 225, 239, 240; Turkestan, 31; Uzbek, 48, 127, 128, 130, 214
autonomy: 2, 5, 7, 12, 14, 16, 27, 50, 127, 128, 181, 228; cultural, 12, 16, 19, 20, 28, 40, 41, 49, 54, 123, 128; national, 47, 48,
Averbakh, Mikhail, 89, 96, 101, 102, 109, 110
Avloni, Abdulla, 180
Azerbaijan, 115, 174, 181

*bai*, 67, 68, 71, 78, 90, 92, 94, 96, 102, 120, 121, 131, 169, 170–172, 174, 177–179, 183, 193, 195, 204–207, 209, 224, 239

Baku, 31, 32, 51, 56
Basmachi: 33, 40, 56, 58–62, 90–92, 94–96, 136, 156, 176–179, 239; movement, 5, 31, 90, 95, 175, 190; rebellion, 61; resistance, 26, 44, 95
Bassalygo, Dmitrii, 56, 57, 62
*Before Dawn* (film), 72, 165, 179–182, 190, 193, 195, 196, 198, 210
Behbudi, Mahmudhoja, 155, 181
Bek-Nazarov, 101
*Bezbozhnik*, 112, 120, 181
*Bismillah* (film), 115, 118, 174
Bolshevik: 12, 14, 26, 31, 33, 43, 44, 61, 85, 86, 94, 111, 114, 123, 129, 156, 177, 180, 183, 191, 192, 196, 199, 202–205, 207–209, 211, 212, 218, 219, 224, 230, 241, 242; discourse, 27, 55, 95, 96, 200; government, 111; hegemony, 81; ideology, 204, 225; mission, 200; party, 25; power, 12, 26, 200; press, 202; project, 29, 200; regime, 8, 228; rhetoric, 95; revolution, 114; revolutionary strategy, 9; salvation, 199, 204; speak, 135, 168; *see also* authority
bourgeois: 11, 65, 81, 131, 132, 177, 179, 181, 184, 196, 197, 217, 221–223; nationalism, 162, 164; nationalist, 86, 217
bourgeoisie, 44, 71, 73, 78, 82, 86, 179, 183, 221,
Broido, Grigori, 201, 202
Bukhara, 107, 144, 148, 162, 176, 217, 233, 236, 237
Bukharan: intellectuals, 93; People's Soviet Republic, 93
Bukhkino, 38–40, 48, 49, 54, 56, 59, 65

censor, 16, 20, 71, 72, 81
censorship, 4, 19, 38, 90, 129
Central Asian Bureau, 26, 27, 43, 44, 47, 48, 56, 60, 62, 166, 197

Central Executive Committee, 26, 33, 111
centralization, 4, 20, 87, 123–125, 127–129, 139, 164
centralized: administration, 7; state, 12, 21
*Chachvon* (film), 89, 96, 101, 102, 105, 107–110, 116, 126, 202
*chachvon* (veil), 79, 92, 97, 102, 107, 108, 117, 203
*Chapaev* (film), 197, 177, 178
Cherniak, G., 120, 121, 149, 152
*choikhona*, 71, 141, 152, 170, 171
Chokay, Mustafa, 193
Chulpan, Abdl Al Hamid Sulayman, 126, 161, 162, 164, 220, 228
*Cinefication*, 14, 138, 146–148
citizenship, 8, 164, 229, 232
civil war: 5, 19, 25, 27, 29, 31, 33, 111, 138, 177–179, 188, 220; legal, 6; Russian, 34
coercion, 8, 26, 224
Cold War, 5
collectivization, 20, 112, 117, 120, 190, 207, 220
colonial: 13, 25, 27, 28, 29, 32, 41, 44, 54, 58, 60, 65, 71–76, 81, 82, 94, 96, 161, 177, 179, 180, 183, 184, 190, 191, 193; cinema, 55, 66; film, 20, 55, 57, 64, 66–68, 70, 78; revolution, 25, 197, situation, 192; *see also* domination, empire
colonialism, 7, 66, 191
colonization, 9, 10, 26, 28, 41, 80, 161, 197
Committee for Cinematography, 17, 36, 66
Constitution, 12
constitutional, 6, 123
Council of People's Commissars, 31, 32, 48, 124, 128, 135, 148, 217 see also *Sovnarkom*

decolonization, 13, 27
Devonov, Khudoibergan, 29
*dhikr*, 115, 118, 204
domination: 5, 6, 8, 16, 20, 41, 60, 61, 81, 82, 183, 191, 195, 224; bourgeois, 72; British, 197; class, 91, 169, 172; colonial, 72, 179; discourse of, 66; imperial, 58, 73, 123; Soviet, 21; structure of, 19, 75
Doronin, Mikhail, 66, 79
Duchène, Ferdinand, 74, 75, 76, 80
Dushanbe, 17

emancipation: 20, 33, 60, 75, 78, 94, 98, 102, 105, 108, 121, 205; campaign, 101, 105, 107; of people, 12; of women, 14, 64, 85, 86, 89, 91, 96, 97, 112; national, 47; policy, 61, 62, 98
empire: 10, 12, 21, 25, 44, 55, 75, 83, 86, 124, 183–185, 199, 228, 228; British, 75; colonial, 82; concept of, 123; European, 20, 27, 54; of the proletariat, 199; of the tsar, 197; Ottoman, 29, 96; Russian, 1, 12, 13, 19, 20, 33, 42, 54, 55, 71, 72, 96, 192, 197, 228, 229; Soviet, 123, 229; tsarist, 72, 222
Enver Pasha, 116, 239
Europe, 53, 55, 58, 61, 175, 232

*fait national*, 8
First World War, 5, 8, 25, 34, 52, 188, 220, 228, 229
Fitrat (Abdurauf), 93, 161, 181, 190, 191, 220, 230
folklore, 21, 93, 156, 225
Frelikh (Oleg), 58, 59, 66, 73, 74, 80, 117, 151, 174
*From Under the Vaults of the Mosque* (film), 66–68, 70–72, 77, 78, 101, 126, 177, 182, 234, 235
Frunze, Mikhail, 26, 43

Ganiev, Nabi, 3, 19, 21, 125, 130–132, 134, 151, 152, 163–170, 174–179, 181, 188, 196, 199, 211, 220, 225
Germany, 35, 58, 64, 219
Gertel', Kazimir, 20, 66, 68, 89, 90, 151, 175, 182
Goskino, 36, 37, 38, 48, 49, 66
Great Patriotic War, 6, 21, 229

hadith, 202
Hamza Theater, 212, 216, 227
hegemony, 5, 8, 27, 45, 54, 81, 82, 124, 156, 162, 165, 191, 192, 198, 199, 219, 221, 222, 223, 224, 225, 229
*hujum*, 77, 97, 102

identity: 10, 13, 69, 156, 207, 223; ethnic, 10, 223; national, 16; proletarian, 6; Russian, 223; Soviet, 229; Tajik, 93; Turkestan, 46; Turkic, 43, 162; Uzbek, 41, 46, 93, 156

ideology, 5, 13, 21, 56, 75, 85, 96, 109, 123, 125, 145, 165, 174, 199, 201, 204, 208, 210, 222–225, 228
Ikramov, Akmal, 11, 212, 215, 216, 220
imperialism, 12, 27, 42, 44, 82, 162, 191
indigenization, 76, 86, 126, 129, 132, 135, 165, 166
indigenized, 169
indigenizing, 86
Iran, xiii, 29, 169, 218
*Ishan*, xii, 115, 116, 117, 118, 120, 179, 202, 224
Ishankul, 51, 201
*Ishan's Fiancée, The*, (film) 89, 117, 119, 120, 145, 147, 174, 202, 203
*isirik*, 91
Islam, 9, 10, 42, 44, 75, 112, 113, 114, 115, 117, 118, 120, 121, 170, 171, 173, 174, 176, 199, 200, 201, 202, 204, 205, 224
Islamism, 11; *see also* pan-islamism; pan-islamist

*Jackals of Ravat, The* (film), 20, 89, 90, 92, 93, 96, 100, 103, 125, 126, 147, 151, 156, 164, 175, 176, 204, 205, 234, 235
Jadid, 9, 10, 85, 96, 162, 183, 184, 193, 217
Jadidism, 45, 86
*jigit*, 59, 74
*Jigit* (film), 151, 167, 175–179, 188, 205
Jizzakh, 68, 155, 181, 182, 198, 237

Kaiumov, Malik, 18, 51, 58, 63, 65, 149
*kalym*, 61
Kazakh, 2, 3, 41, 46, 48, 141, 232
Kazakhstan, 2, 10, 49, 50, 93, 111
Khamraev, Ali, 19
Kharmraev, Ergash, 19, 168, 169, 170, 175, 220
Khamraev, Razzak, 231
Khiva (cinema), 29, 34, 35, 148, 151, 153, 155, 156
Khiva (city and Khanat), 3, 26, 29, 46, 59, 63, 201, 237
Khojaev, Fayzulla, 40, 43, 44, 45, 46, 48, 127, 212, 217, 219, 220, 221
Khojaev, Mu'min, 79

Khojaev, Suleyman, 3, 19, 21, 72, 90, 94, 102, 117, 131, 163–165, 170, 177, 179–182, 188, 191–196, 198–220, 225
Kirghiz, 3, 46, 232,
Klado, 138, 181, 218, 219
Kokand: 26, 32, 33, 46, 144, 147, 148, 152, 179, 190, 213; autonomy, 26
Komsomol, 73, 103, 107, 110, 114, 117, 121, 131, 141, 144, 153, 154, 168, 202, 203
Koran, 113, 114, 116–118, 201, 202
Koranic, 68, 71, 202

Lenin, Vladimir Ilich, 9, 12, 31, 33, 42, 43, 85, 107, 113, 114, 123, 129, 141, 144, 191, 193, 202, 207, 221, 222
Leningrad, 38, 40, 58, 59, 137, 197, 214, 231
Leninism, 34, 210, 222
Leninist, 164
*Leper, The* (film), 66, 67, 69, 71, 73–76, 78–80, 82, 89, 101, 126, 177, 220, 234, 235

Marxism, 9, 191, 210, 222
Mesguich, Felix, 29, 57
Messerer, Rakhil', 66, 74, 76, 79, 81, 220
*Minaret of Death, The* (film), 3, 31, 40, 48, 56, 58–60, 63–65, 73, 81, 89, 91, 175, 176, 234
*mingboshi*, 183, 184, 228
Mirmuhsin, 52
modernity, 14, 20, 28, 68, 76, 83, 102, 108, 139, 156, 167, 170, 171, 204, 232
Moscow, 18, 19, 26, 32, 33, 36, 39, 43, 45, 49, 58, 61–63, 65, 68, 72, 85, 93, 101, 102, 105, 108–110, 114, 116, 126, 128, 136, 137, 162, 166, 167, 176, 181, 193, 197, 210, 214–218, 220, 231, 234
Muslim: 9–11, 25, 28, 31, 32, 36, 37, 56, 62, 69, 75, 77, 78, 85, 97, 103, 107, 111–116, 140, 156, 161, 162, 173, 179, 180, 183, 184, 186, 193, 199, 201, 202, 224; Bureau, 42; community, 46; countries 4, 191; reformism, 52, 113; reformist, 114, 164; world, 8, 44, 191
*Muslim Woman, The* (film), 36, 56, 57, 60, 62–64, 66, 74, 81, 89, 91, 103, 234

Namangan, 33, 148, 233
*Narkompros*, 31

nation: 2, 10, 13; building, 13, 21, 42, 56, 95, 125
national: 2, 7–9, 11–16, 20, 21, 39, 42, 54, 86, 90–93, 98, 102, 109, 123–125, 128, 129, 132, 161–163, 166, 169, 180, 181, 198, 213, 218, 221, 223, 224, 229, 230; appropriation, 90, 230; body, 4, 128; cadre, 8, 86, 137; cinema, 4, 211, 218; construction, 10, 13, 19; culture, 4, 9, 11–13, 86, 89, 156, 200, 221–224, 228; demarcation, 41, 44; differentiation, 7, 8; elite, 3, 86, 230; emancipation, 47; essence, 225; film, 82, 89, 125, 127, 128; filmmaker, 15, 20, 156, 163, 165, 199, 225; identity, 13, 16, 41; in form, 21, 86, 163, 217, 221, 222, 226, 230, 232; liberation, 8, 21, 25, 156, 180, 186, 196, 198; movement, 27, 222; minority, 49, 162, 166; origin, 130, 132, 223; press, 91, 105, 219, proletariat, 167, 170; question, 9, 41, 86, 192, 120–223; republics, 45, 64, 127, 128, 132, 153; state, 48; *see also* Uzbek
nationalism, 4, 8, 10–13, 16, 21, 42, 85, 86, 132, 159, 161–164, 198, 211, 222–225
nationalist, 1, 7–9, 12, 13, 16, 21, 42, 86, 89, 161, 162, 164, 165, 192, 195–199, 211, 215, 217, 218, 221, 224
nationality: 7, 10, 11, 44, 90, 132, 166, 216; Commissar of, 9, 201; Commissariat of, 26, 49; Soviet policy, 7–10, 12, 27, 47, 159, 164, 165, 197, 198, 225, 229
New Economic Policy (NEP), 31, 34, 36, 62, 85, 123, 124

*Oath, The* (film), 3, 21, 169, 199, 200, 204, 205, 209–211, 215–219, 221, 223, 229, 230, 232
Orient: 54, 56–58, 64–66, 74, 80–82, 91, 102, 111, 204, 224; Soviet, 55, 121,
Oriental: films, 54–56, 58, 63–66, 82, 90, 91, 125, 126; exoticism, 62; studies, 9; women, 108, 121
orientalism, 54, 64
orientalist, 82
Ostroumov, Nikolai, 1

pan-Islamism, 8, 184
pan-Islamist, 42
Pan-Turkist, 42, 162
*paranji* (or *paranja*), 81, 97, 100, 102, 105, 107, 118, 121, 217, 225

*Qawm*, 46
Qodiri, Abdulla, 92, 181, 220

*Ramazan* (film), 164, 167, 170, 173, 178, 203
Red Army, 25, 26, 32, 33, 35, 90, 91, 94, 95, 112, 114, 136, 142, 147, 156, 175–178
Repertoire Committee, 17, 71, 72, 81, 94, 95, 109, 173, 178, 186, 196
revolution: 25, 45, 55, 66, 85, 111, 191, 200, 217, 224; Bolshevik, 114; cultural, 20, 81–85, 86, 121, 122, 156, 224; February, 27, 34, 153, 164, 181, 197; French, 144; October, 8, 9, 34, 50, 71, 101, 110, 113, 123, 136, 180, 181, 190, 196–198, 200, 210, 217, 225, 226, 228; proletarian, 72, 197; *See also* revolution
revolutionary: 12, 43, 58, 60, 68, 69, 71–73, 82, 94, 143, 150–152, 164, 165, 177, 179, 195, 196, 198, 201, 207, 210, 221, 230; Committee, 48, 60, 65, 181; exoticism, 54; rationale, 3; strategy, 9
*Right, Her* (film), 120, 121, 149, 152, 202
Russian, 197, 198, 201
Ryskulov, Turar, 42, 43, 64

Safarov, Giorgi, 25, 33, 197
salvation, 6, 21, 78, 79, 199, 200, 202, 207, 211; *see also* Bolshevik
Samarkand, xi, 29, 32, 45, 49, 62, 117, 126, 144, 148, 155, 162, 181, 185, 233, 237
Sart, xi, xii, 10, 11, 46, 66, 67, 78, 79, 89, 101, 147, 183
Scientific Association for Oriental Studies, 49
*Second Wife, The* (film) 204, 220, 234, 235
secularization, 14, 20, 85, 86, 89, 111, 112, 156
Seifullina, Lola Khan, 66, 80, 126
self-determination, 11, 12
settlement, 140
settlers: 184, 188; Russian, 25, 190
Shaykhantaur, 201
socialist realism, 110, 129, 135, 163, 167, 170, 177–179, 199, 207, 209, 210, 226, 228
Sovkino, 49, 59, 125
*Sovnarkom*, 31, 128, 135, 212
Stalin, 198, 216, 219, 221–223
Stalinism, 221, 231
Stalinist, 198, 199, 208, 224–226, 231

## Index

subjective camera, 68, 101, 103
Sufi, 115, 117

Tajik: 10, 45, 47, 93, 136–138, 145, 146, 162, 163, 169, 232; Communist Party, 137
Tajikistan: 3, 17, 44, 47, 115, 120, 136, 137, 138, 146; Autonomous Republic, 48
Tamara Khanum, 216, 217
Tashkent, 45, 47–49, 51, 52, 60–64, 93, 98, 100, 102, 105, 112, 136–141, 144, 145, 147–149, 151, 154, 155, 163, 167, 175, 180, 181, 193, 195, 201, 218, 231, 233–235, 237
Tatar, 9, 10, 49, 59, 96, 110, 114, 139, 198
Tatarstan, 114
*Thief of Bagdad, The* (film), 54, 58, 64
totalitarian, 4, 5, 199, 210, 220, 229
totalitarianism, 4–6, 8, 13, 21
Trotsky, Leo, 14, 129
Turkestan: 10, 27, 29, 31–33, 35–38, 44, 45, 47, 54, 68, 72, 74, 75, 78, 110–112, 180, 183, 190, 191, 196, 197, 198, 233; Autonomous Soviet Socialist Republic, 3, 26, 29, 31, 34, 42, 43; commission, 43, 112; Communist Party, 112; Bureau, 26; Republic, 33, 37, 38; *see also* authority; identity
Turkestani: elite, 43; brothel, 228; intellectual, 12, 25, 26; notable, 193; society, 184, 193; revolutionary, 191
Turkestaniness, 196, 198
Turkestanism, 11
Turan, 162, 163, 180, 181, 183, 184
Turkkino, 35, 37, 18, 48, 49, 54, 142, 143, 147

Turkmen: 3, 46, 61, 73, 120, 232; Soviet Socialist Republic, 48
Turkmenistan, 43, 50, 73, 146
*Turksib* (film), 67

Ukraine, 89, 114
*Upsurge* (film), 131, 152, 167, 168, 170, 179
Usoltsev-Garf, Aleksandr, 21, 204, 205, 211, 212, 214, 215, 224
Uspenskii, Viktor, 93, 151, 176, 205, 216
Uzbek: nation, 13, 21, 47, 95, 231; nationalist, 162; nationalism, 161, 162, 221; nationals, 166, 181; national cinema, 218; *see also* national cultural
Uzbekfilm, 128, 199, 204,
Uzbekkino, 49, 50, 51, 56, 66, 68, 74, 79–81, 90, 92–94, 101, 102, 108, 109, 110, 117, 119, 121, 125–133, 135, 137, 138, 145–148, 151, 152, 168, 170, 175, 178, 182, 205, 234–236

Vel'tman, Mikhail, 49, 50, 64, 66
Viskovskii, Viacheslav, 3, 40, 56, 58, 59, 65, 175

Whites, the, 31

*Yangi Yol*, 61
Yarmatov, Kamil, 3, 68, 70, 92, 231, 232
Yaroslavskii, Yemelian, 112, 113
*Yer Yuzi*, 53, 100, 105

Ziia, Said, 92

CLOÉ DRIEU is Research Fellow at Centre National de la Recherche Scientifique (National Center of Scientific Research, Paris) in the Centre d'études turques, ottomanes, balkaniques et centrasiatiques (CETOBAC). She is a specialist of late imperial history, the First World War, and the early Stalinist period in Central Asia.

ADRIAN MORFEE is Senior Lecturer in English Translation and Literature at University of Rennes, France.

www.ingramcontent.com/pod-product-compliance
Lightning Source LLC
Chambersburg PA
CBHW052013290426
44112CB00014B/2225